# Sacred Sacrifice

Rick Franklin Talbott

# Sacred Sacrifice

## Ritual Paradigms in Vedic Religion and Early Christianity

PUBLISHERS
*Eugene, Oregon*

Wipf and Stock Publishers
199 W 8th Ave, Suite 3
Eugene, OR 97401

Sacred Sacrifice
Ritual Paradigms in Vedic Religion and Early Christianity
By Talbott, Rick Franklin
Copyright©1995 by Talbott, Rick Franklin
ISBN: 1-59752-340-2
Previously published by Peter Lang, 1995

# CONTENTS

| | |
|---|---|
| Acknowledgments | vii |
| Introduction | 1 |
| **1 The Historical Background of Vedic Fire Sacrifice** | 7 |
|   1:1 Vedic Literature | 9 |
|   1:2 Vedic Mythology | 15 |
| **2 Interpreting Sacrifice** | 39 |
|   2:1 Violence and the Quests for Origins: Burkert, Girard, and Heesterman | 52 |
|   2:2 Transcendence and Immanence | 56 |
|   2:3 The Sacrificial Solution | 77 |
|   2:4 Sacrificial Leftovers | 83 |
| **3 The Example of the Ashvamedha** | 107 |
|   3:1 A Description of the Ashvamedha | 111 |
|   3:2 The History of New Testament Interpretation | 126 |
|   3:3 The Ashvamedha: A Summary | 134 |
| **4 The Sacrificial Background of the Eucharist** | 167 |
|   4:1 The History of Interpretation | 168 |
|   4:2 First Century Eucharists | 183 |
|   4:3 Israel's Sacrifices | 188 |
|   4:4 Hellenism, Judaism, and Jesus' Open Table Fellowship | 196 |
|   4:5 Greek Philosophy and Sacrifice | 204 |
| **5 Transcendence and Immanence in the Eucharist** | 259 |
|   5:1 Sacrificial Developments | 259 |
|   5:2 The Eucharistic Link between the East and West | 269 |
|   5:3 The Church Fathers | 275 |
|   5:4 The Reformers and "Real Presence" | 279 |
|   5:5 Prayer of Hippolytus | 283 |
|   5:6 Prayer of Sarapion | 284 |
|   5:7 Prayer of James | 285 |
| **Epilogue** | 315 |
| **Bibliography** | 325 |
| **Index** | 347 |

# Acknowledgments

The following names represent only a few deserving recognition for the inspiration and completion of this book.

I wish to thank Dr. Robert O. Fife, cofounder of the Westwood Christian Foundation, for establishing academic ties to the University of California, at Los Angeles. It was under his auspices that I became aware of the vital relationship between theology and history. While at U.C.L.A. Professor Kees W. Bolle brought to life the value of comparative studies for interpreting religious texts and the importance of the subject of religion to understand history. He made several helpful suggestions to me from Read College in Portland having taken valuable time away from his own teaching and writing projects. Professor S. Scott Bartchy provided essential guidelines for the material dealing with early Christian history. He made himself available to me when students inundated the halls of the History Department at U.C.L.A. waiting to see him. Professor Michael Kurze from Occidental College in Los Angeles has given me sound advise and warm encouragement on several occasions which included the title of this book. Professor Randal Cummings offered insights from his comprehensive scholarship and the type of motivation that one can only receive from a life long friend. I am grateful to Professor James Goss, chair of the Department of Religious Studies at California State University, Northridge. Dr. Goss has gone out of his way to accommodate a teaching schedule that also allows me to offer courses at U.C.L.A. Dr. Goss maintains an "open door" policy to his office from which I continue to learn helpful strategies in the challenging task of teaching religion. A word of thanks to my friend Timothy N. Kuns who introduced me to a higher level of computer technology with all the skill, good will and humor of a Bodhisattva.

# INTRODUCTION

This book examines the problem of God's transcendence and immanence in the context of Vedic fire sacrifice and the early historical development of the Christian Eucharist. Both religious traditions insist on sharp contrasts between the transcendent world of the sacred and the world of human beings. But at the same time both Vedic religion and Christianity require a vital link between these two worlds. Religious human's fundamental orientation around the sacred also requires that the sacred be present for the profane world. No where does this paradox appear more profoundly than in the sacrificial ritual that mysteriously unites the sacred and human beings.

The experience of transcendence becomes a problem in the ritual by virtue of the mythological separation of the two worlds. Humans use ritual to solve this problem by transforming their profane surroundings so that contact with the sacred can become possible. But while such religious rituals made the sacred accessible to humans they also created another problem. Immanence likewise causes a problem of distance in which case the space between human beings and God is not too far but rather too near. Transcendence maintains an indisputable distinction between God and humans. Immanence threatens this distinction between the sacred and profane, holiness and sinfulness, real and unreal, eternal and transient, creator and creatures.

In general terms, the sacrificial ritual contrasts human sin and God's holiness while also transforming the human condition. Ritual consecration and purification temporarily provided a way to come into contact with the untouchable. Vedic sacrifices required elaborate rituals that took the sacrificer through many steps of gradual preparation rites until the actual moment of encounter accomplished through the sacrificial victim. But having removed all sin and impurities, the consecrated sacrificer still faced danger from improper ritual action. The Indian *Shatapatha Brâhmana* text reads, "sacrificing on an incorrectly built altar is not only unsuccessful, it can be dangerous."[1] The Eucharist developed its own preparation rites and elaborate liturgies to make union possible between sinful humans and a holy God in the ritual act. Already in the first Christian generation the apostle Paul warned the congregation at Corinth by saying, "many of you are weak and sick, and a number of you have fallen asleep," all because they partook of the "Lord's table" in an "unworthy manner."[2]

The delicate balance between God's transcendence and immanence in the sacrificial ritual stands as an intriguing and ominous signpost for all who participate. The problem of ritual distance, or divine transcendence and immanence, dramatizes this ambivalent nature of religious ritual. Sacrificial ritual does not merge the worlds together so that God's transcendence becomes something comprehensible for human's reason or commonly accessible to humans apart from the sacrifice. The Indian worshipper having attained the world of the gods in the sacrifice nonetheless had to return to human world where sacrifice would be required all over again. The Christian who has received redemption through Jesus Christ's sacrificial death still requires the on going priestly mediation of Christ before approaching God the "consuming fire."[3] Christian theology explains that Jesus Christ was not only human and therefore like us, but also God and different from us. The great protestant theologian Karl Barth said of this contrast:

> ...when we make this comparison between Jesus and ourselves and the presupposition of our whole enquiry is that we have to see and understand man in this comparison - the antithesis between Jesus and ourselves points not merely to the contrast between man and God, creature and Creator, eternity and time, but to God's judgement upon man; not merely to the nature and order of God and man, but to God's indictment against man, to His sentence and punishment, and to man's existence under His wrath. What we have been describing is sinful man in time.[4]

The ritual encounter between God and humans did not palliate God's transcendence but rather affirmed it by returning everything back to the profane realm afterwards. For this reason Vedic sacrifice and the Eucharist took care to properly exit from the ritual. Ritual leftovers that had come into contact with the sacred fire and the holy remains of the sacramental bread and wine on the altar were disposed of in proper ritual fashion. This act redefined the distinction between the sacred and profane by the separation of what had become holy through the ritual. The consecrated bread remains could not be left undifferentiated in a profane setting outside of the ritual's protection anymore than Agni's ashes, leftover from the sacred fire, could merely be thrown aside on profane soil.

The specific historical differences between Vedic religion and Christianity abound. The dates, places, languages, texts, cultural backgrounds and developments multiply the differences between the two. The fact that Vedic religion and ultimately Hinduism do not have a founder such as Jesus Christ in Christianity sets the two significantly apart. But even more significantly, Vedic religion emphasized a different aspect of their religious symbolization than Christianity. Vedic religion stressed the symbolic act or ritual over their symbolic words or myths. On the other hand Christianity emphasized the importance of the Gospel of Jesus Christ and faith. But despite of the basic historical and theological differences our comparison remains tenable along the lines of the religious symbolism each used to address the problem of transcendence and immanence in the fire sacrifice and the Eucharist respectively. We may even speak of a similar symbolic structure for each ritual based on the preparation rites, the actual moment of encounter or union with the transcendent realm, and the exit rites. The question of whether or not the Eucharist should be characterized as a sacrifice does not prevent us from examining its sacrificial symbolism and its symbolic structure. As we shall see, at certain junctures in the Eucharist's historical development some Christian writers did consider it as a sacrifice that offered Christ again and the participants consumed his flesh and blood. But the Eucharist's sacrificial symbolism remains the core of this comparative study with the symbolism used in the Indian sacrifice.

I recognize the immensity of information as well as the historical and theological problems surrounding these two rituals. Therefore the above mentioned basic structure built around the problem of transcendence and immanence in the ritual act shall provide the specific focus of this study. I am also aware that the transcendence - immanence dichotomy does not provide the only way to investigate sacrifice nor the best way. I offer this scheme because of the importance that religious symbolism plays in ritual and also as one method of examining the phenomena.

Works dealing with ritual and sacrifice continue to conjure a variety of different theories and methodological issues. Because this book employs a multidisciplinary approach I found it necessary to address some of the central presuppositions about ritual and sacrifice. No one school of thought has solved all of the problems and cooperation between fields is not the exception to the rule. However, some of the most helpful authors seem to have wallowed in their own success to the point that they have become impervious to even friendly criticism. I do have some affable criticism for some of the great scholarly vessels used to advance my own research and understanding of ritual in general and sacrifice in particular. For this reason I briefly examine E.B. Tylor, William Robertson Smith, Hubert and Mauss, some of the Durkheimiam functionalists; as well as René Girard, Walter Burkert, Frits Staal, and a few others.

The present comparison between Vedic fire sacrifices and the sacrificial developments in the early Christian eucharists recognizes that their respective historical conditions helped shape each tradition's rituals. But the evidence also shows that the mythic dimension involving the idea and experience of the presence of the sacred during the ritual act also contributed to the discernable structure of sacrificial rituals. Not everything in a sacrifice can or should be reduced to economic and political forces. In fact, our examples will suggest that during the ritual act the mythological elements often take precedence over the prevailing social conventions, conscious or unconscious, personal or collective. This ultimately emerges in the texts that govern sacrifice in India and the liturgical protocol in Christianity.

## ENDNOTES TO THE INTRODUCTION

[1] Copied from, Naama Drury, *The Sacrificial Ritual in the Shatapatha Brâhmana*, Shri Jainendra Press, Delhi, 1981, p. 112.

[2] I Corinthians 11:30, N.I.V.

[3] Cf. Hebrews 12:29.

[4] Barth, *Church Dogmatics*, translated by Harold Knight et al; edited by G. W. Bromiley. Edinburgh, T.& T. Clark, vol. III, part two, p. 517.

CHAPTER ONE

# THE HISTORICAL BACKGROUND OF VEDIC FIRE SACRIFICE

Excavations of the two cities, at present-day Harappa and Mohenjo-daro, have revealed that a highly developed civilization already existed in the Indus valley around 2500 B.C.E. Before 1921 scholars thought that the Indo-Europeans had established this high culture when they invaded the Indus Valley.[1] Today we know that this sophisticated ancient society was in decline prior to the first wave of Indo-European conquerors that began to arrive perhaps as early as 1800 B.C.E. By around 1200 B.C.E. these warriors, who called themselves Arya ("Noble"), had successfully used the horse drawn chariot and the sword to enter the Ganges plain.

The Aryan military conquest paved the way for a new civilization. This new civilization was gradually formed from the indigenous inhabitants living together with the Indo-Europeans.[2] Vedic religion emerged as one aspect of this symbiosis. We know comparatively little of the religion of peoples who lived in the basin of the Upper Indus Valley before the Aryan migration began.[3] From the urban Harappan civilization we know of a great goddess and a sitting male divinity who is surrounded by animals in a depiction similar to the Hindu god Shiva.[4] Only a few other characteristics of pre-Aryan religious symbolism are known, and since the only written sources are brief seal inscriptions, not as yet deciphered, we are left with religious texts for residual traces of this enigmatic religion.

The Arya's first texts give evidence of an early symbiosis with the autochthons. The Vedic texts speak of campaigns against the Dasa, a dark skinned people with a strange language, phallus cult and who "are rich in herds and live in fortified settlements (Pur)."[5] Eliade said that the Vedas contain certain myths of an "autochthonous origin."[6] Even with the ambiguity that shrouds pre-Aryan religion in the Indus valley the ancient archeological sites of Harappa and Mohenjo-daro convey an important symbolic structure. Ancient cites were built around a sacred center where earth could be linked with heaven. If these two cities, of which we do not know their original names, deviated from this archaic paradigm, a most unlikely, indeed unique phenomenon would have been established in the ancient world according to Eliade. Homo-religiosus has always sought to orient life around the sacred and there fix "the center of the world."[7] The Vedic emphasis on linking up with the world of heaven through sacrifice could not have been altogether different from the autochthons' understanding of their place in the cosmos.

The Aryans brought a host of cultural elements that were eventually assimilated and revalorized in the development that led to Vedic religion. The most important instrument used in the Aryanization of India was an Indo-European language, Sanskrit.[8] The Aryans exhibited an extraordinary exactness in the way their language was spoken. This strict phonetic precision centered on the ritual act, and insured remarkable reliability in a long oral tradition that eventually led to their earliest written texts.[9]

The earliest text, the *Rig Veda*, also provides the names of the Indo-European gods who made the track to India with the Aryans via the language of Sanskrit. The oldest Indo-European idea of god clearly signifies the notion of "celestial sacrality, that is, with light and transcendence."[10] The Sanskrit word for "god", Deva, belongs to the Indo-European root for "sky." This Indo-European heritage manifests itself in the old, if not oldest, Aryan god Dyauspitar. This Sanskrit word translates to "Sky Father" and corresponds to the Greek god Zeus-Pater, and Latin god Jupiter.

Another important item that helped fashion early Vedic religion can also be traced back to its Indo-european origins. The sacred fires had already served as an important part of Indo-European religious thought.[11] The sacred fire played a role in the home hearth. Here offerings of food were given to a personal deity through the fire. The Indo-Iranians honored the particular god who was invited to their house. This ceremony took place around a special altar built for such an occasion. The Aryans brought the sacred fire with them and its significance soon spread to rites connected with the preservation, restoration and enhancement of life. As in the case of the Iranians, the Aryans also developed these early home fire sacrifices into a cult that was administered by priests. We shall see that the use of the fire sacrifice in Vedic religion became increasingly vital as the vehicle to address what we may call the problem of transcendence.

**1:1 Vedic Literature**

The texts that usually fall under this category are the *Samhitâs, Brâhmanas, Aranyakas* and *Upanishads*, and ritual *Sûtras*. In order to understand the formation and development of the Vedic texts we must first recognize the intensive religious enterprise of those ancient seers who compiled the texts. At the heart of all Vedic literature lies the matter of ritual thought. In the early texts everything religious is a matter of acting. This emphasis upon sacred act in Vedic religion shows up in the Sanskrit word Karman which early on denoted ritual activity. When used in the context of gaining immortality (Amrtam) Karman is "identified with Agni, the fire ritual."[12] The centrality of ritual thought remained even in the later speculative texts of the *Upanishads* that shifted from the outer ritual act to its inner spiritual meaning. In other words, Vedic literature did not evolve from "nothing more than the naive superstitious fantasies of untaught and materialistic barbarians", as Sri Aurobindo has also rejected.[13] Instead of fools awed by nature, Early Hindu society revolved around a religious insight that recognized this world's relationship with the transcendent world. This insight or knowledge came by way of revelation (Shruti) which presupposed a ritual context. The ancient Indians received sacred wisdom from the ritual or more specifically from the first sacrifice performed by the gods. This knowledge served primarily as a paradigm for early Hindu society. The primordial sacrifice revealed that humans' foremost responsibility was to sacrifice as the gods did in the beginning. The development of Vedic literature preserves for us the persistence of a civilization bent on proper religious conduct.

The collection or *Samhita* consists of four different types of *Samhitâs*: the *Rig Veda*, hymns of praise to the gods; the *Yajur Veda*, sacrificial formulas; the *Sama Veda*, ritual chants; and the *Athavar Veda*, esoteric texts. Before these four Vedas were codified into their respective group they were preserved orally (Amnaya) in families of highly skilled poet-priests. The special skills of these priestly families entailed not only the creation and preservation of the texts but also later involved complicated commentaries and ritual formulas based on the

*Samhitâs* (see *Brâhmanas*). The texts of the *Samhitâs* contain hymns that, for the most part, deal with ritual.

Except for the ritual *Sûtras,* the entire corpus of Vedic literature participates in divine authority and eternity of Shruti, "that which is heard." The poets of the Vedas were considered seers or Rishi who communicated the sacred Shruti. All other later texts were only Smriti, "that which is remembered."

The *Rig Veda* is the most ancient collection of Vedic texts offering some 1,028 hymns in ten books or Mandalas ("cycles"). Mandalas II through VII make up the fulcrum of this entire collection and was separated from the rest of the mandalas which are "less ritually oriented."[14] One family of seers had arranged and codified mandalas II through VII probably before 600 B.C.E. with a great deal of authenticity.[15] Unlike the other four mandalas, II through VII were arranged with hymns addressed to the god Agni followed secondly by hymns to Indra and then other deities. Within this general framework these hymns (Suktas) were arranged according to decreasing numbers of verses.

The fact that Agni stands at the head of this list most likely reveals part of his mythological role as mediator between the gods and humans in Vedic religion. As the domestic priest (Purohita) Agni carried out several priestly functions that included the warding off of evil.[16] As the god of fire and the sacred fire himself Agni carried the sacrifice to the gods.

Inculcated within the *Rig Veda* we find a division of three types of gods representing the three different realms of Vedic cosmology; celestial deities such as Dyaus, Varuna, and Vishnu; atmospheric deities such as Indra and Rudra; and terrestrial deities such as Agni, Soma, and Brihaspati to name only a few of these three types. This arrangement and division in the *Rig Veda* shows the increasing importance that sacrifice held in the development of Vedic religion. Terrestrial deities, and especially Agni, played a vital role in aiding humans and the gods in the sacrifice.

To say that the celestial deities "declined in interest"[17] because a decreasing number of hymns were attributed to them can become somewhat problematic. This should not be construed to indicate that the *Rig Veda* in general and Vedic religion in particular grew less interested in the notion of transcendence and concerned themselves primarily with merely manipulating the mundane world through magic.[18] Nothing could be further from the truth when reading the texts. The growing importance of the so called terrestrial deities correlates directly to their role in the sacrificial ritual. Here again the division of deities into a terrestrial group does not obfuscate the importance of transcendence in Vedic religion.

An utilitarian classification of the gods can miss the essential feature of Vedic religion by stressing the evolution of the its literature while ignoring its religious claims. Sacrificial ritual meant linking humans up with the sacred and all of the subsequent results this act had for both worlds. Kees Bolle has taken note of the fact that "traditional Western philologists were not very capable of seeing meaning in Vedic ritualism; hence they did not inquire into texts such as these with articulate questions concerning meanings."[19]

The *Brâhmanas* represent an extensive body of literature that owes its existence to ritualistic speculation on the texts of the Vedic Samhitâs. The priestly tradition that had created and preserved the early Vedas also expanded Vedic literature through explanations and commentaries. This tradition distinguished two types of Brâhmanas according to L. Renou : "les prescriptions (Vidhi)," and "les explications (Arthavada)."[20]

The texts of the *Brâhmanas* were composed from around 800 B.C.E. to 1200 C.E. These mostly prose texts were divided according to particular Vedic *Samhitâs* and were used by a particular class of Brâhmins [21] for a variety of different ceremonial occasions and purposes. For example, the *Aitareya* and *Kausitaki* (or *Sankhayana*) *Brâhmanas* came attached to the *Rig Veda* in which part of their purpose included, justifying the deities who were addressed and the sacrificial materials that were used, prescribing the proper ritual acts, and much more detailed ritualistic information.[22] The *Brâhmanas* of the *Samaveda* include the *Pancavimsa, Jaiminiya, Sadvimsa*, and a series of minor *Brâhmanas*[23]; from the less independent *Yajurveda*, which followed the ritual closely, we have the *Maitrayaniyas* and *Taittiriyas*; and from the *Atharvaveda* came the *Gopatha-Brâhmana*.[24] The *White Yajurveda*[25] contains the *Shatapatha-Brâhmana* and exist in two recensions; the *Madhyandina* and the *Kanvas*.

When interpreting the sacrificial ceremonies these ritualists employed certain Vedic texts to suit the purpose of their own symbolic explanations. At times this meant going beyond the "original design of the text."[26] Anyone familiar with the New Testament authors' use of the "Old Testament" will recognize this same type of hermeneutical freedom.[27]

The *Shatapatha-Brâhmana* found universal acceptance as the most important text of the *Brâhmanas*. It is the most extensive and well known. The SB serves not only as a paradigm of the high literary achievement that developed in Vedic religion but also sheds light on "the gradual transitions, in contents, style, and composition from the traditional ritual discussion to the philosophical speculations of the *Upanishads.*"[28] The SB provides an eclectic format that captures the intensifying spirit of Vedic sacrifice.

The heart of Vedic sacrifice comes to light through the SB as it discusses the indispensible sacrificial rites and explains their origin and meaning. J. Gonda said:

> the contents of the *Brâhmanas* may be classified under the heads of sacrificial directions, explanations and exegetical, 'mythological', polemical or 'philosophical' speculations on the great rites and their 'connections', and the advantages to be gained by means of the rites.[29]

Here again the SB best illustrates this general feature of the *Brâhmanas* since it was always made to fit a ritual framework.[30]

The SB contributes a major source of data concerning the problem of transcendence and immanence in Vedic ritual. Although this shall be discussed in detail later, a couple of examples here will help set the stage for the next chapter. The Vedic view of transcendence and immanence are embedded in the whole sacrificial milieu. The SB makes clear that the sacrificial ritual itself was viewed as a vehicle to reach the heavenly world (Svarga Loka). "The Agnihotra sacrifice is a ship bound for heaven. The ahavaniya fire and the garhapatya fire are the two sides of that heavenly bound ship, the agnihotra. The captain of the ship is the priest who offers the milk oblation ksirahotri."[31] Even the gods themselves reached the Svarga Loka through the sacrificial ritual. "By means of this the gods went to the world of heaven; one who desires the world of heaven should use it for reaching the world of heaven."[32] This exemplifies the trenchant desire of Vedic worshippers to be linked up with the transcendent realm.

The paradox of both having to come in contact with the "Heavenly World" and the dilemma of such immanent proximity also finds expression in the SB. This too resulted from further speculation on an old idea. The *Rig Veda* hymn of the primordial giant, Purusha, (Purushasukta, RgV. 10. 90), whose dismemberment accounted for the animals, the liturgical elements, the social classes, the earth, the sky, and even the gods themselves. This cosmogonic sacrifice also includes the notion of transcendence and immanence. Strophe three reads, "all creatures are a quarter of him; three quarters are what is immortal in heaven."[33] Eliade said that, "Purusha is at once transcendent and immanent, a paradoxical mode of being but one that is typical of the Indian cosmogonic gods.[34]

The SB continued this line of thought by giving special attention to the construction of the fire altar that corresponded to the re-creation of the universe. This reveals a special link between the two realms. One that was only possible through the transformation of the mundane one. The SB also identified the sacrificer with the gods, "He who is initiated approaches the gods and becomes one of them."[35]

Thus the *Brâhmanas* in general and the SB in particular portray the growing articulation in Vedic religion concerning transcendence and immanence through their intricate and elaborate prescriptions for the sacrifice. We shall see that these texts show how the notion of transcendence and immanence came into conflict with one another precisely in the ritual act.

The *Upanishads* stand as a clear signpost in the transition of Vedic religion. This transition moved the center of Vedic religion from the ritual act to a type of inner reflection and mysticism that stemmed from the ritual texts. Nonetheless, the mythology of the ritual remained important as did the very texts of the Veda. The new philosophical system that emerged in the *Upanishads* was built on the old sacrificial system. Kees Bolle said that, "Among other things, the Upanishadic mysticism arose from a sense of puzzlement over the ritual; it was in relation to the ritual that the Vedic hymns were handed down."[36]

Early speculation in the *Upanishads* did not recognize Vedic sacrifices as the only means of salvation. The two oldest *Upanishads*, *Brihadaranyaka* and *Chandogya*, relied on the earlier *Brâhmanas* and the esoteric forest texts, the *Aranyakas*.[37] The authors of the *Upanishads* still quoted from the earlier authoritative Vedic texts in order to substantiate their new teachings, but viewed these older texts as another form of revealed wisdom.[38] For example, the *Rig Veda* hymn 10. 129 speaks of "the One" (strophe 2, neuter) that was before anything else. This notion of "the One" as the first Being and as the "All" was known in the *Brâhmanas* as Prajâpati (Lord of Beings).[39] The first Being in the *Upanishads* came to be known as Brahman [40], who was the entire universe and the true self (Atman). "Like the Purusha of *Rig Veda* 10. 90, Brahman reveals himself to be at once immanent ("this world") and transcendent, distinct from the cosmos and yet omnipresent in the cosmic realities."[41] Those major religious themes that emerged from the earlier Vedic period continued to inspire the philosophers of the *Upanishads* and even later Hinduism. While the actual practice of sacrifice waned in the Upanishadic literary period the notion of transcendence and immanence certainly did not. Part of this has to do with something Kees Bolle has said: "Religion, and likewise mysticism, lives by reinterpretation. And often the reinterpretation acquires the greater importance. That was the case with the great Upanishadic reinterpretations of the Vedic texts."[42]

    As noted earlier the ritual *Sûtras* were not considered a part of Shruti and therefore did not carry the same authority as previous Vedic literature did. But the *Sûtras* did have an important practical function in the rituals and ceremonies of the Vedic *Samhitâs* and *Brâhmanas*. About the seventh century B.C.E. the *Brâhmanas* were accompanied by manuals that served as ritual handbooks. These *Kalpa Sûtras*, as they were named, gave precise rules for the proper order and mechanics of the ritual. The *Kalpa Sûtras* made systematic descriptions for both major divisions of Vedic sacrifices, the Srauta Sûtras (eighth to fourth century B.C.E.) and the *Smarta Sûtras*. The Shrauta sacrifices were the non-domestic elaborate ceremonies that required three fires and the employment of Brahmins or specially qualified priests. The Smarta sacrifices were based on Smrti and further subdivided into the Grhya or domestic sacrifice that required only one fire without the special services of the priests.

    More will be said later about the Shrauta and Smarta sacrifices. For the present time I have introduced the ritual Sûtras as one branch of Vedic literature because it will be cited later to demonstrate the rigid prescriptions that accompanied the already exacting system of Vedic sacrifice. The nature of the cautious preparation and performance of ritual can easily be illustrated in these ritual handbooks.

**1:2 Vedic Mythology**

This section provides a mythological basis for examining the problem of transcendence and immanence in the sacrifice. Only a few of the Vedic myths, gods, and concepts will be discussed here. However, one need not infer from this separate section on mythology that myth and ritual ought to be isolated from one another. Myth appears as one of the three forms that religions use to express the sacred. The words of myth share in expressing realities with sacred places or objects and ritual acts. Kees Bolle says that, "... human religious expressiveness in its threefold form of sacred speech, sacred acts, and sacred places remains essentially one, and the three forms we distinguish had best be considered as mere aspects visible to us; our differentiation between the three forms is external, conceptual, formal."[43]

The significance of Vedic mythology as a basis for examining the particular problem of transcendence and immanence in the sacrifice lies in the hermeneutical aspect of myths. Again I refer to Kees Bolle on this point.

> The chief reason why myths attract most scholarly attention is the medium itself: words. They can be expected to elucidate the entire religious life of a community, shedding light especially on the ritual acts and on sacred objects that by themselves do not speak at all, or certainly not as often, and not as clearly. For instance, a central temple or a sacred pole may be of paramount significance in the religious life of a community, yet a recorded myth is most likely to explain this significance, its origin, its basis, and the reason for its pivotal role in the community's religious life.[44]

The sanskrit word Rita occupies a key position in Vedic mythology. Rita is a past participle of the verb root r and occurs over 300 times in the *Rig Veda*. The verb r originally meant "to move; agitate; raise."[45] H. Lefever assigned two levels of basic meaning to the verb root r that carried the sense of both "to move" and " to fit or arrange."[46] Almost forty years earlier Able Bergaigne attributed the meaning of "to adapt oneself to" to the root r and suggested a more original meaning with, "what is adapted."[47] Rita has been translated as a past participle by "fitting, right; upright, honest; true", and as a noun by "established order; sacred ordinance, pious work, sacrifice, rite; divine law; truth, right."[48]

The quest for Rita's meaning within Vedic mythology has not come without disagreement and disappointments over the last century in the history of interpretation. The nineteenth century's contributions to philological studies remain useful for Vedic research while their mythological interpretations suffer from "cultural fashions"[49], positivism, historicism, and evolutionism. The religio-historical research of the nineteenth century equated the Indian gods with the powers of nature and reduced Indian mythology to a "primitive" mentality's response to natural phenomena. Nineteenth century scholars perceived Rita as "the regularity of the movement of the celestial bodies, of time sequences, the succession of the seasons, and so on."[50] An example of this purely "scientific" understanding can be seen in Bergaigne's etymological study on Dhaman, Dharman and Rita. He states,

> "Thus then, foundation, support and adaptation, such are the original meanings from which the meaning of law has issued in the case of the three words, Dhaman, Dharman, Rita. They express originally not a moral idea, but some particular material condition of the existence and the stability of the world."[51]

Even when Rita was viewed as governing the moral order it never went beyond a bias comparison with the moral grid of nineteenth century Western Europe.

The meaning of Rita need not be so elusive if we remove the above mentioned impediments. The first step should replace Rita in its mythological setting within the texts. Having done so we find that Rita participates in a particular range of relationships within Vedic religion as well as shares in a universal field of religiosity. This should not be understood to suggest that all religions are the same nor that specific religious phenomena or mythologies endeavor to do or say exactly the same things in exactly the same ways. It does confirm Joachim Wach's premise that we always find the universal embedded in the particular.

The universal in the case of Rita will be seen to touch on our notion of transcendence and immanence. The specific Rig Vedic texts that locate the meaning or use of Rita within Vedic mythology demonstrate three basic mythological thoughts that center on the juxtaposition of transcendence and immanence: 1) The link between Rita and the two worlds, heaven and earth; 2) the link between Rita and the sacrifice; 3) the link between the gods and human beings in their mutual roles and responsibilities to maintain Rita through the sacrifice.

Although the Vedas addressed no hymns to Rita, nevertheless, Rita provided a fundamental axiom that functioned within Vedic mythology. As such, Rita helped to form the paradigmatic character of specific myths and concepts, for example the Purusha myth and Dharma respectively. Its influence can be traced from the *Rig Veda* to Hinduism.

Rita establishes the most basic notion of the link that exists between Heaven and Earth in Vedic mythology. *Rig Veda* hymn X.36.2 says that Dyaus and Prthivi (Heaven and Earth) are true to Rita. As "cosmic order"[52] Rita governed both the transcendent world of heaven and the mundane world. Both Heaven and Earth are said to "dwell in close union in the womb of Rita."[53] Rita gave the blueprint for the earth that was drawn in heaven, and it also provided the celestial plan.[54] All activities, laws, and the unchangeable order of the earth must follow the design of Rita. Jeanine Miller has some helpful observations on this point.

> First, Rita as it manifests itself in heaven which, metaphysically, connotes the domain of the gods, their interaction and influence, hence the first differentiation of the transcendental Rita. If 'heaven' is considered in its physical sense of sky, then this domain of Rita pertains to the zodiac.
>
> Second, Rita as it manifests on earth in the orderliness of the natural processes, the time sequences, the balance of nature, the vast sweep of evolving life...
>
> Third, Rita manifests itself in human life both in so far as its socio-ethical norms and its religious life are concerned, the latter expressed by the words 'obeisance' (namas) and 'piety' or 'adoration' (Aramatih)..In obeisance and worship he aligns himself to the universal order, pays his tribute to the one Law and becomes himself whole, integrated, true.[55]

Rita covers all spheres of human and divine activities and thus not only shows a connection between earth and heaven but also between the religious and social. Eliade said, "The creation is proclaimed to have been effected in conformity with Rita, it is repeatedly said that the gods act according to Rita, that Rita rules both cosmic rhythms and moral conduct."[56] Rita connects the two worlds as their common standard of order and activity. This link between two distant realms, one transcendent and unmanifest the other mundane and visible, does not exist by mere accident nor is it left arbitrarily to maintain itself. The link between the two worlds and the dynamics to maintain this union can be seen more lucidly in the role of the god Agni.

Agni represents the two worlds.[57] "They magnify with adoration that priest efficacious at sacrifices, Agni the Hotri, who has spread himself over heaven and earth according to Rita."[58]. Agni is the messenger to the gods on behalf of men and gods and hence Agni has access to both realms being referred to as the "charioteer of the Transcendent."[59] "The head of heaven, the navel of the earth is Agni; he has become the stewart of both worlds... Agni has been established among the tribes of men..."[60] The *Rig Veda* also proclaims that Agni was born in Rita[61] and that Agni "places himself under the yoke of Rita."[62] Agni acts in accordance with Rita as he carries out the sacrifice for men and the gods. The two worlds are also linked together because of the inseparable bond between Rita and the sacrifice.

The link between heaven and earth through Rita as "cosmic or universal order" extends to another important part of Indian mythology involving Rita. The majority of Rig Vedic hymns have to do with sacrifice, and the most frequent use of Rita comes in connection with the sacrifice. "Rita then signifies, in the sphere of sacrifice, the ordered course of the sacrifice."[63]

In Vedic mythology universal order must be maintained. Bergaigne said that, "the law has been described as being observed so also it is described as maintained."[64] Just as Rita conveyed a force and order upon the cosmic and human realms for the good, so also the forces of Anrita and Adharma, (meaning that which is "contrary to law"), and Maya, (to "negate good order" [65]), oppose Rita. Even the ancient divine family, the Asuras, who battled the gods, the Devas, worked to reverse Rita (Dharma).[66] The Vedic texts prescribed only one course of action to maintain universal order. Sacrifice maintained Rita and overcame the inimical universal forces that attempt to undo Rita. "Le sacrificant sacrifie toujours pour lui-meme, quel que soit le resultat attendu et meme s'il s'agit avant tout d'assurer l'ordre universel."[67] The whole universe either suffered from the erosion of Rita or benefited from the work (Karman), of the sacrifice.[68]

Because of the notion that sacrifice maintained Rita we also find Rita identified as the sacrifice.[69] In these cases Rita as the sacrifice itself symbolizes the universe and its interconnection with the world in the act of sacrifice. This is no where more clearly recognizable than in the previously mentioned cosmogonic Purusha hymn.[70] The sacrifice of the Cosmic human that resulted in establishing the world and its order also provided a paradigm for all sacrifices in which the world and the cosmos were renewed. In this respect Rita and Yajña, "sacrifice", are inseparable. J. C. Heesterman said in this context that," when we turn to the Vedic conception of sacrifice, it is striking to notice that it is regularly connected with unbroken universal order."[71]

Again it will help to elucidate the link between Rita and sacrifice by looking at specific texts in which Agni and Rita appear together. As we have seen, Agni's relationship to Rita and his movement between both worlds exemplifies the necessary link between heaven and earth. Part of Agni's role in the sacrifice brings the gods to humans and humans' gifts, prayers and the dead to the world of the gods. This dimension of Agni's role in sacrifice captures the inherent concern for transcendence and immanence in early Vedic mythology and later brahmanism.

> How shall we sacrifice to Agni? What words, agreeable to the god, shall be addressed to him, the luminous one, who, being immortal and righteous, the Hotri, the best sacrificer, conveys the gods to the mortals.[72]

> Thee, O Agni, the Ritvig, the Hotri, they magnify at the sacrifices. Shine as the guardian of Rita in thy own house. May He, the banner of the sacrifices, Agni, come hither with the gods, anointed by the seven Hotris for the sake of the man who offers sacrificial food.[73]

> Agni goes thrice around the sacrifice, like a charioteer, conveying the enjoyment to the gods.[74]

Since Agni is the "charioteer of the high Rita,"[75] and because he is the "knower of Rita" who "performs the Rita,"[76] Agni can therefore make "the sacrifice acceptable to the gods through the path of Rita,"[77] having "carried out the sacrifice according to Rita."[78] Later the SB also understood sacrifice as the supreme means to maintain universal order.[79] The SB identified the primordial Purusha with Prajâpati, the god whose creative activity expended himself and had to be resuscitated. As in the case of Rita, sacrifice or Agni restored Prajâpati, who in turn became identified with Agni. The very construction of the fire altar meant the building up of Prajâpati or of the universe.[80]

Rita found its fulfillment in the sacrifice and this through the mediation of Agni. The role of Agni in the sacrifice illuminated the downward movement of the Transcendent and the upward ascent of the world of human beings. The link formed between the two worlds through Rita and the sacrifice maintained both worlds and hence became a necessary union of the sacred and the profane. Sacrifice, while maintaining universal order, also nourished the gods and assured humans of the sustenance of life. Human beings and the gods found themselves in a type of partnership ordained by Rita and perpetuated by the need to sacrifice.

The importance of sacrifice continued in later Hinduism even though many changes took place. J. Miller said, "There is no gulf stretching between the Vedic Rita and the Hindu Karma and Dharma; both the latter are the Hindu equivalent of the Rigvedic Rita."[81] Sacrifice had imprinted itself on Indian culture so deeply that much of the subsequent philosophical vocabulary and thought of Hinduism can be traced back to the Vedic sacrificial texts.

The nineteenth century had arrived at the opinion that the Vedic gods were dependant on the sacrifices of humans. But in actuality, both humans and the gods were interdependent upon one another according to Vedic mythology. The maintenance of Rita required both to participate in the sacrifice. The first sacrifice in primordial time had established this standard. Rita was thought to have been present at this paradigmatic sacrifice. Therefore the two worlds, no matter how distant or different, had to unite in the performance of the sacrifice.

Notice the idea expressed in *Rig Veda* X.130 concerning the link between heaven and earth and the mutual participation of men and gods. This hymn used the imagery of the weaving of the sacrifice.

> The sacrifice that is spread out with threads on all sides, drawn tight with a hundred and one divine acts, is woven by these fathers as they

> come near: 'Weave forward, weave backward,' they say as they sit by the loom that is stretched tight.
>
> The Man (Purusha) stretches the warp and draws the weft; the Man has spread it out upon the this dome of the sky. These are the pegs, that are fastened in place; they made the melodies into the shuttles for weaving.
>
> That was the model for the human sages, our fathers, when the primeval sacrifice was born. With the eye that is mind, in thought I see those who were the first to offer this sacrifice.
>
> The ritual repetitions harmonized with the chants and with the meters; the seven divine sages harmonized with the original models. When the wise men looked back along the path of those who went before, they took up the reins like charioteers.[82]

The action of sacrifice moves in both directions, "weave forward, weave backwards," as the gods and humans participated in the sacrifice they attained "nearness." Miller puts it this way: "This is the bond that binds man, the earthly being, to heaven. At the level of ritualistic religion man shares in the universal work in so far as he re-enacts the primordial sacrifice sacramentally as symbolic of the cosmic life."[83]

The *Rig Veda* makes explicit reference to the god's relationship to Rita. For example:

> When the gods deprived of food enjoy themselves in that udder : the abode of Rita, then may the great Agni, to whom oblation is brought with homage, approach the sacrifice, endowed as he is with the nature of Rita.[84]
>
> They, the Rudras, grew in the abodes of the Rita through the streams, like through red ointments.[85]
>
> These sons of Aditi, the mighty, the infallible, have grown up in the house of Rita.[86]
>
> By means of Rita you both (Mitra and Varuna) govern all the world.[87]
>
> This Indu has lighted the darksome nights, O Indra, at morning and at evening, along the years. Him alone they established as the landmark of the days. He made the dawns to be born in splendor.

> This has illuminated resplendent the somber (worlds). This has caused to shine the numerous (dawns), by means of Rita.[88]

According to Vedic mythology the gods were only one part of the manifestation of creation, e.g., "The gods appeared later by this world's projection."[89] Hymn X.72 of the *Rig Veda* spoke of the birth of the gods while vacillating between paradoxical statements like, "existence" was born from "non-existence", and "Aditi" was born from "Daksha" and "Daksha" from "Aditi." Rita, on the other hand, was not created. On the contrary, the gods followed the Rita.[90] More importantly, the gods shared an "interlinkedness... Manifesting as their solidarity, their essential righteousness, their concerted activity, is their peculiar feature and one that eminently marks them as the agents of the law of harmony, Rita, by which, through which and in which they live and perform their varied functions..."[91]

This inherent "interlinkedness" between the gods and humans has been established by their need to act (Karman) together in mutual responsibility for the sacrifice. And just as the gods were dependent on Rita and the sacrifice so also are humans. Rita, as we have seen, had to be maintained within the specific context of sacrifice; and the sacrifice had to be performed with the cooperation of both men and gods. Lafever said, "Rita as the actual order realized in the world, is a product of the activity of gods and men, an activity directed in accordance with the transcendent Rita."[92] For example, the ancient seers (Rishis) of Vedic literature received their vision through the help of Agni and Soma e.g., "The strong bull with sharp horns and seed a thousand fold has a mighty and double tone. As one reveals the hidden footprint of a cow, Agni has declared to me the inner meaning."[93] Soma gave the "vision of Rita and to the inspiration of prayer;"[94] "We have drunk the Soma; we have become immortal; we have gone to the light; we have found the gods."[95] The vision of the Rishis contained the most essential knowledge. The vision or revelation of Rita came to the gods and to the Rishis for the sake of the sacrifice and how to perform it.[96]

This partnership between the gods and men helps us realize the relationship between the gods and human beings as well as the very operation of the universe. To put it another way, one can not know the essence of either world apart from the relationship that the gods and men shared in the act of sacrifice. Another hymn reads, "the altar is the farthest end of the earth; this sacrifice is the navel of the universe."[97] Transcendence and immanence were built into the very structure Vedic mythology through the ritual relationship held between humans and the gods. Lefever said of Rita:

> It is transcendent as the governing principle of all life and activity in the sphere of space, time, and will. To this sphere belong both Gods and men. Hence it is said, "All share thy divine name, while in their accustomed ways they keep the Rita" I.68.2). Rita is, on the one hand, the law of their own nature and so is immanent, while on the other hand, it is the law which they must obey and yet are free to disobey, and so is transcendent.[98]

To understand the integral relationship shared in the sacrifice between the gods and human beings permits us to move away from the myopic label of "magic" that still plagues the discussion of Vedic sacrifice. Heesterman acknowledges that, "...Vedic ritualism is generally considered the hallmark of the magic-bound Hindu world."[99] Aguilar also resists the haphazard use of the term magic. He cites Renou as a prime example of one who misused this word in reference to Vedic liturgy. Renou said, "the distinction between sacrifice and magical act is slight."[100] Part of Aguilar's response to the attribution of magic in Vedic sacrifice goes like this:

> In our view the question here is not to discriminate between what is magic and what is not magic in the Vedic liturgy, but rather to be able to understand the infinite efficacy of the sacrifice, on account of its ultimate identity with the supreme Rita, which enables it to be used even for the sake of magic, however much this might be against the spirit of the Shruti...[101].

Although Aguilar's statement does cast doubt on the general use of the term magic for Vedic liturgy it fails to criticize the hermeneutical weaknesses of using the label "magic."

Historically magic has been applied to primitive cultures as one evidence of a low stage in their evolutionistic development. The irony of labeling some of the practices of these "primitives" as "magical" was the fact that it was an assumption rather than a conclusion; the researcher's methods were beset with blinding nineteenth century theoretical presuppositions. This was coupled with the fact that there was as much confusion in the scholastic community concerning the nature and purpose of magic as there was bewilderment over the very practices that they were labeling with this enigmatic term "magic."

Perhaps the most influential of the early group of social scientists that saw magic in primitive cultures was Sir James Frazer (1854-1941). Frazer divided magic into two types ("homoeopathic" and "contagious") under the main heading of "sympathetic magic." Homoeopathic magic attempts to produce a desired effect by imitating the result, "like produces like." The second type of magic bases its effectiveness on the principle of material contact having power over a person's enemies. Frazer based both types or "principles" on the "association of ideas" in the primitive's "undeveloped mind." Thus magic was a form of primitive science without the guide of proper logic. Frazer said, "In short, magic is a spurious system of natural law as well as a fallacious guide of conduct; it is a false science as well as an abortive art."[102]

Frazer, Durkheim, and Robertson Smith thought it best to separate magic from religion while G. van der Leeuw said that magic is religion. Marcel Mauss thought that magical acts belonged to phenomena outside of the "organized cults." The study of magic itself has gone through a revitalization in the last few years, especially under the auspices of anthropologists. Whereas the nineteenth century tended to define magic pejoratively distinguishing it from "true religion", scholars today label religious phenomena as magical in a more inclusive manner. Magic and religion are seen as intertwined. Magic belongs to religion as a way of tapping into divine forces for various purposes. Magic may be used to injure an enemy, procure healing, or gain special knowledge. The use of "black" and "white" magic has fallen into disrepute as a result of the modern obsequious approach to the broader definition of the term.

Without going further into the disagreements and foibles of the history of interpretation over magic it should suffice to say that the term does not elucidate the mysteries of sacrifice. In truth the use of magic as some type of all encompassing grid for both social and religious speculation remains just that -speculation. Concerning the issue at hand, namely Vedic sacrifice, the most fruitful studies will come from the realization that the Vedic sacrificers understood their responsibility to participate in maintaining Rita.[103]

Therefore the older magical characterizations of ritual forces us into an unnecessary psychologism and away from careful consideration of the texts. The Vedic text's emphasis remains clear; one must sacrifice if the world as he knew it was to continue and if he himself were to benefit from the protection and blessings that keeping the sacrifice promised. In cooperation with the gods, human sacrificers followed the cosmogonic paradigm that renewed the world from the beginning.

Throughout Vedic literature we find an inherent link between the gods and human beings. This link between the sacred and the profane comes to light in the sacrifice. But this union that was necessary to sustain and re-create the cosmos also created some problems. The absolute obligation of joining the two worlds in the act of sacrifice violated a fundamental reality in Vedic mythology. How do "sinful humans" and "sinless gods" come together without devastating consequences? To begin to deal with this question we shall first consider sacrifice in general and then examine how Vedic religion attempted to solve the problem of transcendence and immanence.

## ENDNOTES FOR CHAPTER ONE

[1] See Jan Gonda, *Die Religionen Indiens*, vol. 1 Stuttgart, W. Kohlhammer Verlag, 1960, p. 6.

[2] Raffaele Pettazzoni has demonstrated that the meeting of the Indo-Europeans, a pastoral and patriarchal civilization, with the indigenous Mediterranians, an agricultural and matriarchal civilization, produced one new civilization. This also happened to be the case in the development of other great civilizations such as, " de l'Egypt, de l'Anatolie, de la Mesopotamie, de L'Indie, de la Chine, de l'Amerique precolombienne." See *La Religion Dans La Grece Antique*, Paris, Payot, 1953, p. 21.

[3] See Louis Renou, *L'Inde Classique*, Tome Premier, Paris, Payot, 1947. According to Renou, "Les cadres qu'on a adoptes pour leur classement sont notoirement insuffisants et contesables : ainsi la distinction qu'on fait entre les religions dites primitives ou animistes, et L'hindouisme, suggere des notions inexactes:," p. 44.

[4] L. Renou in *Hinduism,* George Braziller, New York, 1961, p. 17; and A.L. Basham, in "Hinduism", *The Concise Encyclopedia Of Living Faiths*, ed. by R.C. Zaehner, Beacon Press, Bosron, 1959, p. 226; are a part of those scholars who maintain that some aspects of pre-Aryan religion "survived" the Aryan invasion and found their way into Hinduism. An example would be the early cult of Shiva based on an early seal with four animals that looked like a later seal of Shiva. Evidence for this identification does not present a conclusive case. Rudra in the Vedic texts becomes identified with Shiva in later Hinduism.

[5] Mircea Eliade, *A History Of Religious Ideas*, trans. by Willard Trask, Chicago, The University of Chicago Press, vol. 1, 1978, p. 196.

[6] Ibid., p. 196.

[7] See M. Eliade, *The Sacred And The Profane*, trans. by Willard Trask. Harper & Row, Publishers, New York, 1961, pp. 38-47. Jonathan Z.

Smith has correctly criticized Eliade for over generalizing the connection between the Australian Arunta tribe's sacred pole (in reference to its function as a "sacred center") and the great temples of ancient India and the Near East. Cf. Jonathan Z. Smith, *To Take Place Toward Theory in Ritual*, University of Chicago Press, Chicago, 1987, p. 2 and footnotes #2 and #3 on p. 122. The historical details do suggest that one should use more caution in drawing conclusions from such comparisons than exercised by Eliade in this particular instance. However, the notion of "sacred centers" as places religious humans set apart to make contact with the divine realm need not be jettisoned too hastily. Davîd Carrasco's excellent analysis of function of sacred centers in Mesoamerican religions represents one example the usefulness of Eliade's basic concept. See Davîd Carrasco, *Religions of Mesoamerica*, Harper Collins, San Francisco, 1990, pp. 21-23; 40-45; 70-77.

[8] L. Renou *(L'Inde Classique*, p. 52) said "le terme de langues 'aryennes' qu'on trouve parfois employe au mene sens est impropre."

[9] H. Oldenberg pointed out that before the Vedic texts reached their written form, "they encountered, in the course of great periods of time, many and manifold misfortunes." (*Ancient India Its Language And Religions*, Calcutta: Punthi Pustak, 1962, p. 19. Originally published in the Deutsche Rundschau of Berlin in 1890.) Oldenberg's remark here should not mitigate the meticulous effort that priestly families made to conserve the oral tradition as their sacrifices became more elaborate. L. Renou in, *L'Inde Classique*, p. 270, said, "Toute cette litterature, ou du moins la majeure partie, a ete (quoiqu'on en ait parfois doute) conçue et conservée oralement. La chose, a peine imaginable, s'explique par l'immense effort que demandent a la memoire et qu'en obtiennent des hommes façonnés de génération en génération à cette discipline."

[10] Eliade, *A History Of Religious Ideas*, vol. 1, p. 189.

[11] Gonda says that, "Aus einer Verglichung von Veda und Awesta ergibt sich, dass das Feuer schon im indo-iranischen Kultus und religiosen Denken eine bedeutende Rolle gespielt hat." See *Die Religionen Indiens*, vol. 1, p. 71.

[12] Jan Gonda, *Vedic Literature*, Wiesbaden, Otto Harrassowitz, vol. 1, 1975, p. 367.

[13] Sri Aurobindo, *On the Veda*, Pondicherry, Sri Aurobindo Ashram, 1956, (Originally published in the ARYA Journal from 1914 to 1920.) vol. 5, p. 5.

[14] For a discussion on the other mandalas see J. Gonda, *Vedic Literature*, vol. 1, pp. 11-14. While one distinct family of Rishi composed mandalas II through VII and IX, mandalas I, VIII, and X were not.

[15] Gonda seems to accept the proposal by Yaska that the codification was the result of a decline in the power of oral reproduction. See ibid., p. 15.

[16] *Rig Veda*, I.1.1.

[17] This notion appears in T. Hopkins, *The Hindu Religious Tradition*, Belmont, Wadsworth Publishing Company, 1971, p.3; as well as others.

[18] Most Vedic authorities echo what Gonda says here of Vedic religion, "Diese Religion ist jedoch mit allen möglichen Anschauungen uber Leben und Welt und in der Praxis mit vielem, was wir Magie nennen wurden, unloslish verbunden." See *Die Religionen Indiens*, p. 15. See alsoH. Oldenberg, *Ancient India its Language and Religions*, pp. 48-83. See below pp. 25-26.

[19] Kees W. Bolle, "Wendy Doniger O'Flaherty in Retrospect," *Religious Studies Review* 10, (1984) p. 23.

[20] *L'Inde Classique*, p. 288. Sylvain Levi also gives this two-fold classification of the *Brâhmanas* in, *La Doctrine Du Sacrifice Dans Les Brâhmanas*, ed. Ernest Leroux.Paris: Bibiotheque De L'Ecole Des Hautes Etudies Sciences Relieuses, 1898, p. 3.

[21] See Ramachandra Ghosha, *A Brief Survey of Sanskrit Literature*, New Delhi, Classical Publications, 1977, p. 65. The *Brâhmanas* were also assigned, as it were, according to the Veda that best suited their particular interests. For example the *Brâhmanas* of the *Rig Veda* were used for the intention of the Hotri, those of the *Yajurveda* for the usage of the Adhvaryu, those of the Samaveda for the Udgatr, and the *Brâhmanas* of the *Atharvaveda* appear to have been imitations of the earlier *Brâhmanas*. Also see L. Renou in, *L'Inde Classique*, p. 289.

[22] The first six chapters alone of the *Kausitaki* were devoted to the founding of the sacrificial fires(Agnyadhana). The prescriptions for the Brahmin priest concerning the Agnihotra, Full and New Moon sacrifices, as well as for special sacrifices are also found in this Brâhmana. See Gonda, *A History of Indian Literature*, vol.1, pp. 344-345.

[23] See L. Renou, *L'Inde Classique*, p. 291.

[24] Renou mentions the "lost *Brâhmanas*", cf. op. cit., p.291.

[25] The *White* or "clean" *Yajurveda* is a collection of mantras that were to be recited at the sacrifices and were free from explanations - hence collected separately in the SB. See Gonda, *A History Of Indian Literature*, p. 327. See also Julius Eggeling's translation of, The *Shatapatha-Brâhmana*, in *The Sacred Books Of The East*, ed. F. Max Muller, Oxford, Clarendon Press, 1894, SB. I, p. XXVII.

[26] Gonda, op. cite, p. 371.

[27] Recently New Testament scholars have been focusing on Jewish midrashic methods of interpretation in the New Testament and especially in light of Qumran. The Pesher method of interpretation is of particular interest because it declared that "this" event surrounding Jesus Christ "is that" which the prophets promised. See, Acts 2.16 and also C.H. Dodd, *The Old Testament in the New*, Facet Books Biblical Series - 3, ed. John Reumann, Philadelphia, Fortress Press, 1963. See also H.

Shires, *Finding the Old Testament in the New*, Philadelphia, The Westminster Press, 1974.

[28] Gonda, *A History of Indian Literature*, Vol.I, p. 353. Gonda also says that the SB provides a link between Vedic culture and the India of the great Epics and ancient Buddhism. See p. 355.

[29] Ibid., vol. 1, 1975, p. 341.

[30] The first nine books of the Madhyandina recension covers the Full and New Moon sacrifices, the founding of the sacrificial fires, the Agnihotra, seasonal sacrifices, other Haviryajnas, the Soma sacrifice, and the construction of the fire altar. See Gonda, op. cit. pp. 351 ff.

[31] See SB 2.3.3.15.

[32] Quote taken from Brian Smith's article ,"Gods And Men In Vedic Ritualism: Toward A Hierarchy Of Resemblance," which appeared in *History Of Religions*, May 1985, vol. 24, Number 4, pp. 293,295. The quote was originally taken from SB 2.3.3.15 and Pan. Br. 2.6.2. respectively.

[33] From Wendy O'Flaherty's, *The Rig Veda*, New York, Penguin Books, 1981, p. 30.

[34] *A History of Religious Ideas*, p. 224.

[35] SB 3.1.1.8, quoted from Eliade op. cit., p. 221.

[36] Bolle, *The Freedom of Man in Myth* , p. 126.

[37] The Aranyakas began differentiating between physically performing the ritual and merely contemplating its meaning. Their teachings gave the individual a new place in the scheme of Vedic religion because the gods were thought to be concealed with in oneself. This basic notion gave rise to the "transition of the sacrificial system (Karma-Kanda) of the *Brâhmanas* to the primacy of metaphysical knowledge (Jnana-

Kanda) proclaimed by the Upanisads." See Eliade, *A History of Religious Ideas*, vol. 1, p. 232. On the general subject of the *Aranyakas* see Renou, *L'Inde Classque*, pp. 294 ff., and Hopkins, *The Hindu Religious Tradition*, pp. 38 ff.

[38] See Gonda, *Vedic Literature*, pp. 48-53.

[39] SB 5.1.1.1.

[40] *Chandogya Upanishad* 3,14; 2-4.

[41] Eliade, *A History of Religious Ideas*, vol.1, p. 242. Ramachandra Ghosha makes the statement that, "The *Upanishads* from beginning to end, consist of texts which in some cases teach that God is the one spirit, which is the substance of the universe; that creation is nothing else than a multiplication and development of himself:" From, *A Brief Survey of Ancient Sanskrit Literature,* p. 75.

[42] Bolle, *The Freedom of Man in Myth*, pp. 125-126. In an article entitled, "A World of Sacrifice", The History of Religions, The University of Chicago Press, vol. 23, No. 1, August 1983, p. 58, Bolle also says, "...The *Upanishads* and the *Bhagavadgîtâ* did not set out to reject the brahmanic ritual, nor did they ever intend such a thing; instead they reinterpreted what was going on in the sacrifice in an inner, sometimes devotional manner."

[43] Kess W. Bolle, "Myth," *The Encyclopedia of Religion*, ed. in chief Mircea Eliade. New York: Macmillian Publishing Company, 1987, vol. 10, p. 262.

[44] Ibid., p. 262.

[45] A.A. Macdonell, *A Practical Sanskrit Dictionary*, Oxford: Oxford University Press, Reprinted 1979, p. 56.

[46] H. Lefever, *The Vedic Idea Of Sin*, Nagercoil: London Missionary Press, 1935, p. 1. Lefever also mentions Rita's Indo-Iranian background and its equivelent, asa, p. 2.

[47] Able Bergaigne, *Vedic Religion*, translated by V. G. Paranjpe. Delhhi: Motilar Banarsidass, 1978, vol. 4, chapter 3, pp. 216 ff. Eliade notes that Dharma later replaced Rita. *The History of Religious Ideas*, vol. 1, p. 201.

[48] Macdonell, *Sanskrit Dictionary*, Rita, p. 57.

[49] "Cultural Fashions and the History of Religions," *The History of Religions: Essays on the Problem of Understanding*, ed. by Joseph M. Kitagawa with the collaboration of Mircea Eliade and Charles H. Long (Chicago: University of Chicago Press, 1967), pp. 21 ff.

[50] Jeanine Miller, *The Vision of Cosmic Order in the Vedas*, London: Routledge & Kegan Paul, 1985, p. 43. Miller has also quoted Max Müller on this point. It reads on p. 43, "this Rita meant originally the firmly established movement of the world, of the sun, of morning and evening, of day and night the spring of that movement was localized in the far East...its manifestation was perceived in the path of the heavenly bodies...that right path on which the gods brought light out of darkness became afterwards the path to be followed by man, partly in his sacrifices, partly in his general moral conduct."

[51] Bergaigne, *Vedic Religion*, vol. 4, chap. 3, p. 221.

[52] I shall use J. Miller's translation of Rita from, *The Vision of Order*.

[53] *Rig Veda* X.56.8b, ibid., p. 40.

[54] Cf. *Rig Veda* V.62.1.

[55] Ibid., pp. 40-41.

[56] *A History of Religious Ideas*, vol. 1, p. 201.

[57] *Rig Veda* III.61.7.

[58] *Rig Veda* V.1.7., translated by Hermann Oldenberg, *The Sacred Books of the East*, ed. by F. Max Müller, Oxford, Clarendon Press, vol. XLVI, Vedic Hymns, 1897.

[59] Oldenberg translates adbhutasya rathih in *Rig Veda* I.77.3. as "charioteer of the mysterious", see S.B.E., vol. XLVI. Miller translates the genitive of Adbhuta as "transcendent," op. cit., p. 254. Also see Macdonell, *Sanskrit Dictionary*, p. 9, where his first choice for Adbhuta is "transcendent."

[60] *Rig Veda* I.59.2a.; III.5.3. Unless otherwise advised all translations of *Rig Veda* shall be from S.B.E.

[61] I.144.7; 189.6; 65.10.

[62] I.143.7.

[63] Lefever, *The Vedic Idea of Sin*, p. 3.

[64] Bergainge, vol. 4, p. 229.

[65] Bergainge, p. 271. Eliade said that Dharma took the place of Rita later in Vedic mythology. Eliade also spoke of the development of the Sanskrit word Maya, "to change", that had both a good and evil aspect. The "good" aspect of Maya was considered its creative forms, while its evil counter part meant a destructive change that negated good order. *A History of Religious Ideas*, vol. 1, pp., 200-201.

[66] M. Biardeau says, "Pour prendre la place des dieux, les asura doivent renverser le dharma; ils s'incarnent alors sur terre comme princes et oppriment les brahmanes, bouleversent les regles sociales, suppriment la pratique normale des sacrifices." From Madeleine Biardeau,Charles Malamoud, *Le Sacrifice Dans L'Inde Ancienne*, Paris, Presses Universitaires De France, 1976, p. 25.

[67] Ibid., p. 19.

[68] Originally Karman was used for the ritual. This was indeed the primary use of the term until it later came to denote types of human activity.

[69] Bergaigne said, "In fact the idea of the sacrificial rites and that of the world order appear to have been thus several times identified in the same passage by using some one of the four words." *Vedic Religion*, p. 233.

[70] See *Rig Veda* 10.90.

[71] J. C. Heesterman, *The Inner Conflict of Tradition*, Chicago, The University of Chicago Pess, 1985, p. 84. "The vedic intuition, I would say with my own words, is that the ultimate 'stuff' or 'structure' of the universe, or of reality is precisely sacrifice. It is not "God' or Being', but Action and more concretely the sacrificial act. The real is dynamic and its ultimate dynamism is the sacrifice, i.e. that urge, movement, spirit, energy, which encompasses God and all the creatures, and which consists precisely in letting the real be and in maintaining the balance keeping the tension between all the very poles which constitute the real." R. Panikkar from the introduction of H. Aguilar's, *The Sacrifice in the Rigveda*, Delhi, Bhartiya Vidya Prakashan, 1976, pp. VI-VII.

[72] *Rig Veda* I.77.1.

[73] *Rig Veda* III.10.2,4.

[74] *Rig Veda* IV.15.2.

[75] *Rig Veda* IV.102.

[76] *Rig Veda* V.12.2,3.

[77] *Rig Veda* X.70.2.

78 *Rig Veda* X.12.2.

79 SB 3.6.3.1.

80 See SB, Sixth Kanda, the Agnicayana, or building of the fire-altar.

81 Miller, p. 160. Lefever in places too much stress on the decline of Rita in the *Brâhmanas*. His argument sounds some what frivolous when he maintains that Satya replaces Rita, and that no real distinction existed between these two terms. His point is, however, well taken on the heightened importance of sacrifice in the Brâhmanas and that Rita and Satya became synonymous in later texts.

82 *Rig Veda* X.130.1,2,6,7.

83 J. Miller, p. 214, 215.

84 *Rig Veda* IV.7.7.

85 *Rig Veda* II.34.13.

86 *Rig Veda* VII.60.5.

87 *Rig Veda* V.63.7.

88 *Rig Veda* VI.39.3,4. These translations taken from Aguilar's, *Sacrifice in the Rigveda*. Aguilar states that, "Numerous are the texts depicting the Vedic gods as born of Rita. Agni, concretely, is called so about eleven times, Soma and the Maruts twice, the Adityas, Brhaspati, Visnu and possibly Indra once," p. 58.

89 *Rig Veda* X.129.6; Miller's translation.

90 *Rig Veda* I.65.2; IV.42.4.

91 Miller, p. 71.

[92] Lafever, op. cit., p. 18.

[93] *Rig Veda* IV.5.3; O'Flaherty translation, p. 113,114.

[94] Miller, p. 27.

[95] *Rig Veda* VIII. 48.3; O'Flaherty translation, p. 134.

[96] See *Rig Veda* IX.102.1,8.

[97] *Rig Veda* I.164.35.

[98] Op. cit. p. 13.

[99] Heesterman, *The Inner Conflict of Tradition*, p. 98. Here he mentions Hermann Oldenberg's classification of Vedic ritual thought as " vorwissenschaftliche Wissenschaft" and also reminds us of Max Weber's emphasis on priestly magic. (Gesamelte Aufsatze zur Religionssoziologie [Tübingen, 1920], 2: p. 136.)

[100] Taken from Aguilar, *The Sacrifice in the Rigveda*, p.74, fn. 55.

[101] Op. cit., p. 75.

[102] Sir James G. Frazer, *The Golden Bough*, New York, The Macmillan Company, 1922, p. 9.

[103] See Lucien Levy-Bruhl, *Primitive Mentality*, trans. by Lilian A. Clare, New York, Macmillan, 1923. I do not intend the notion of humans participating in the sacrifice in the same manner as French sociologist and philosopher L. Levy-Bruhl (1857-1939) who located "primitive man's" participation in the cosmos in his "mystical" mentality. Such characterizations of ethnic peoples by the nineteenth-century continue to plague the general study of religions in very subtle ways. The mystical aspect of human religious experiences and expressions should not be labeled as "irrational" in terms of ones

inability to reason. Religious documentation refutes the phenomenon of religion as the product of underdeveloped mentalities. See chapter 2.

# CHAPTER TWO

# INTERPRETING SACRIFICE

The following treatment on sacrifice participates in an ongoing attempt to better understand this religious phenomenon in the wake of late nineteenth and twentieth century theories on the subject.[1] I shall touch on the central ideas that came out of the early works on sacrifice as a precursor to our consideration of Vedic sacrifices and sacrifices in the Old Testament as they relate to the Christian Eucharist. This chapter also introduces the reader to more recent works that have significantly influenced our perception of sacrifice. I hope to make it increasingly clear that these very different sacrifices from different religious traditions belong to the universal symbolism of religious humans.

The new discoveries of ancient civilizations from the east in the eighteenth century and the ethnological data from tribal and ethnic peoples in the nineteenth century fascinated scholars and the general European community. By the end of the nineteenth century many of the texts of the ancient East had been translated, and many of the so called "primitive" customs of the American, African, Australian, and Melanesian nations had been described and interpreted. One of the topics that had captivated both the scholars who worked with the ancient texts and also those who gathered and studied ethnological data was sacrifice.

Sacrifice provided researchers with a type of instrument they felt could help them decipher the world of these folks who performed such strange deeds. Some scholars began to see a connection between themselves and different ethnic peoples by virtue of basic human interests; even though it was thought that the "primitives" operated on a much lower level. For example, these peoples, whether ancient or contemporary, gave a great amount of attention to economic matters. In the case of economics a system of exchange or gift giving could easily be discerned and illustrated in sacrifice between the community and their deity, according to E.B. Tylor (1832-1917). There were those scholars, such as Emile Durkheim (1858-1917), who saw in sacrifice the community's way of defining and preserving their own social order through a totemic identity with their deity. Others wanted to find the justification for psychological interpretations in the abundance of new religious phenomena. Psychological interpretations claimed to argue their point from assuming that "primitive psychology" resulted in a uniform operation of the unconscious mind. Similar religious phenomena from different parts of the globe were explained by humans' Elementargedanken (elementary ideas), see Adolf Bastian (1826-1905). Völkerpsychologie continued the quest for a purely objective approach to religious phenomena. Even Freud (1856-1959) could not resist the seducing proposition that sacrifice represented access to the irrational human psyche.[2] Since Freud, several psychoanalytical studies of sacrifice have been made.[3]

It now appears quite evident that nineteenth century scholars were more interested in their own contemporary theories than in the merits of the documents alone. The nineteenth century's venture sought to trace the development of its own economics, sociology, and psychology as particular aspects of human culture that had evolved from something as "primitive" as sacrifice and other "barbarian" customs.

Economical, biological, and sociological factors certainly have something to do with sacrifice because humans are economical, biological and social beings. But humans also leave evidence of their religious experience in symbolic texts, rituals, and artifacts. Cultural fashions can obfuscate our understanding of sacrifice if the specifically religious dimensions are mitigated by a zealousness to locate the origins of popular concepts in the documentation.[4]

E. B. Tylor's staunch evolutionistic approach to sacrifice shows up in the titles of some of his works, "*The Religion of the Savages;*" "*The Condition of Prehistoric Races, as inferred from Observations of the Modern Tribes,*" (here was evidence for "survivals" from the prehistoric past still to be found in the modern tribes of "savages"); and, "*The Philosophy of Religion among the Lower Races of Mankind.*" For Tylor the old notion of "do ut des" (I give that you may give) meant primarily that the god's favor was won and his wrath averted. Even Tylor's theory of sacrifice evolved into three stages: "gift," "homage," and "abnegation."[5] Abnegation was the latest and therefore attributed to the "higher" forms of religion, viz those which were monotheistic and adhered to high moral standards.

In 1889 William Robertson Smith referred to sacrifice as a communion between men and god during a sacramental meal in *Lectures on the Religion of the Semites: The Foundational Institutions*. Smith concluded that the animal's blood and flesh constituted a communion since the animal that was sacrificed and eaten during this ceremony was sacred. This variation of the gift theory presupposed a totemistic form of religion and also ascribed totemism to one of the earlier forms if not the earliest occurrence of religion. From here Smith determined that higher forms of religion retained this sacramental character in communion with their gods.

But problems arose in Smith's theory because of the misleading conjectures he aligned with totemism. Totemism, for example, is neither one of the earliest manifestations of religion nor can it be assigned to all religions, especially among the Semites. Hence totemism does not address those religions which were never totemic yet do sacrifice.[6]

Smith's basic idea of communion between the deity and the ancient Semitic cult demonstrated a central aspect of sacrifice that, as we saw earlier, figured into the relationship between Rita and Vedic sacrifice. For example, Smith argued that the act of communion, which was the most elementary form of sacrifice, sought to re-affirm the union between the social group and their deity. Signs of a deterioration or break in the community's vital link with their deity such as a famine, plague, or a disaster was cause to reunite with the deity, thus to sacrifice. Hecht, commenting on Smith's communal scheme, said that "The death of the sacrificial-totemic animal is at one time a shedding of tribal blood and a violation of the sanctity of divine life that is transfused through every member of the world because the same blood connects man, animal, and the transcendent."[7] The idea of connecting humans and the transcendent through the blood of the sacrificial animal meant that expiation became a part of the earliest sacrificial communion. So the importance of communion between humans and their gods in Semitic sacrifice stood out preeminently in Smith's research.

Smith also noticed that making the transcendent immanent through the mediation of the victim in the sacrificial meal also required the other concomitant idea of atonement. But his observations on Semitic sacrifice left some questions unanswered concerning the ambivalent nature of the sacrifice that portrayed a community eagerly seeking out the much needed presence of their deity while having an equal concern to provide expiation for this visitation. Smith drew attention to matters such as the Hebrew laws concerning materials and instruments used in their sacrifice (sin-offerings), and the disposal of sacrificial body parts after the ritual. He observed that "the flesh and blood of the sin-offering is a sanctifying medium of extraordinary potency; whosoever touches the flesh becomes holy."[8] Smith continued by taking note of the fact that the garments soiled by sacrificial blood "must be washed in a holy place" and that even the vessels having come in contact with the sacrificial flesh "must be broken or scoured to remove the infection of its sanctity."[9] With regard to disposing of sacrificial flesh Smith prefaced his observations with, "...the victim was so holy that no part of it could be treated as mere waste;"[10] and after citing similar concerns and practices among other Semites he added in reference to the Levitical ritual that, "...the sacred flesh must not be left exposed to human contact."[11]

Smith's explanation for all this special treatment of the sacrificial materials that occurred after the sacrifice, began by describing the Hebrew religion as having an unparalleled "doctrine of the consuming holiness of God" among Semitic peoples.[12] However, he did find similar examples from even non-Semites who treated their sacrificial materials and vessels with similar ritualistic procedures when it came to disposing of sacrificial flesh. Part of the problem with Smith's interpretation of these phenomena lies in his failure to explain the notion of holiness as it related to those sacrificial items that became sacred in the sacrifice. Why was it that humans could not come in contact with the very things and animals that he daily handled once they became part of the sacrificial ritual? Instead of addressing the problem of holiness Smith launched the totemism theory again.

This time totemism was used to account for the animal's sacred nature in kindred relationship to humans so as to explain why the sacrosanct animal ceased to be eaten except by priests as a part of the sanction of the sacred ceremony. According to Smith, after the oldest stage, when the "savages" ate the animal's flesh and blood, humans began to rationalize that such behavior was not fitting for their totemic relationship and therefore it became necessary to place tabus on certain aspects of the sacrificial communion. When these new rules of the sacrifice meant that some animal parts would be leftover the sacrificers had to find another way to dispose of the flesh.[13] Hence Smith attributed the idea of holiness to the scheme of totemism as the sacrificial system evolved. In fact, the evolution of the sacrifice that Smith characterized as some type of desacralization, in essence, became just the opposite. But he could not adequately explain away this inconsistency in his theory. Why, for example, "as time went on", did "the feeling that the victim is too holy to be eaten or even touched" still persist even after the "special holiness of the victim has gradually faded away...", and after "the idea of full kinship of men with their cattle began to break down" (especially when people were hungry)?[14] Smith even admitted that the concept of holiness in the sacrifice intensified with the piacula (expiatory) type.[15]

Smith's treatment of expiation and atonement remained loosely connected to the idea of holiness or the notion of the deity's presence in the sacramental meal. Ironically, his quest for religious origins usurped any consideration of the symbolic religious character of sacrifice. Holiness and its relationship to the profane realm eluded Smith's consideration of the problem of sin or impurity and forced a social evolutionistic scheme of expiation rites as well as rites of disposing of the sacrificial materials. Notice the following example of Smith's brazen detour from any problematic sense of holiness or the presence of God with humans at the communal meal.

> Gradually this rule is modified, partly because it is difficult to insist, in the face of growing civilization, on the rule that even bones, skin and offal must be devoured, and partly because there is increasing reluctance to partake of the holy life. This reluctance again is connected with the growth of the distinction between degrees of holiness. Not every man is holy enough to partake of the most sacred sacraments without danger. What is safe for a consecrated chief or priest is not safe for the mass of the people. Or even it is better that the most sacred parts of the victim should not be eaten at all; the blood and the fat are medicines too powerful to be taken internally, but they may be sprinkled or daubed on the worshippers, while the sacrificial meal is confined to the parts of the flesh in which the sacred life is less intensely present. Or, finally, it is most seemly and most safe to withdraw the holiest things from man's use altogether, to pour out the whole blood at the altar, and to burn the fat. All this applies to ordinary sacrifices, in which the gradual concentration of the holiness of the victim in its fat and blood tends to make the rest of the flesh appear less and less holy, till ultimately

> it becomes almost a common thing. But, on special occasions, where the old ritual is naturally observed with antique rigidity, and where, therefore, the victim is treated at the altar as if it were a tribesman, the feeling of sacred horror against too close an approach to things most holy extends to the whole flesh, and develops itself, especially in connection with actual human sacrifice, into the rule that no part of such victims may be eaten, but that the whole must be reverently burned.
> It is quite possible that the use of fire began among the Northern Semites in connection with ordinary sacrifices, simply as a means of dealing with such parts of the victim as were not or could not be eaten, and yet were too holy to be left undisposed of.[16]

We are left in the lurch as what to make out of Smith's observations. What do "degrees of holiness", "danger from the sacred and safety through ," "sacred horror against too close an approach to things most holy," and "too holy to be left undisposed of" mean in the context of sacrificial ritual in general and Semitic mythology in particular? Smith would have us believe that "The use of fire in sacrifice, as the most complete and through means of avoiding putrefaction in whatever part of the victim cannot or may not be eaten, must have suggested itself so naturally wherever fire was known, that no other reason is necessary to explain its wide adoption."[17] Such utilitarian explanations leave the most interesting problems of sacrifice untouched. One gets the impression that holiness, expiation, and atonement were things on the peripheral of Semitic sacrifice and only related in a mechanical manner to totemism. But if we remove totemism from the central scheme of Semitic sacrifice then how should we understand these precautions in the contact with the deity and the sacrificers?

In short, Smith's totemistic theory undermined his helpful information concerning the communion that was established between the Semites and their deity at the sacramental meal. All of the document's concern for holiness, atonement, expiation, and the proper disposal of sacrificial utensils and materials ended up as being secondary to Smith's concern for a popular theory on the origins of religion. In the final analysis, Smith obscured the difference between Semites and their deity.[18]

Another important work in the history of interpretation is Henri Hubert's and Marcel Mauss', *Essai sur la Nature et la Function du*

*Sacrifice*, 1898 (E.T. *Sacrifice: Its Nature And Function*). Hubert and Mauss dealt with the structure of sacrifice by concentrating primarily on the Sanskrit and Hebrew texts. They found a similar sacrificial structure in both the Vedic texts and the Torah, a similarity they were willing to extend universally to every rite of sacrifice. Hubert and Mauss went so far as to speak of the "astounding likeness" of the Christian sacrifice.

> We do not claim to examine here how the Christian ritual of sacrifice was built up, or how it is linked to earlier rites. We believe, however, that in the course of this work we have sometimes been able to compare the ceremonies of the Christian sacrifice with those we have studied. It must suffice here simply to recall their astounding likeness, and to indicate how the development of rites so like those of the agrarian sacrifice could give rise to the concept of a sacrifice of redemption and communion of the unique and transcendent god. In this respect the Christian sacrifice is one of the most instructive in history. By the same ritual processes our priests seek almost the same effects as our most remote ancestors. The mechanism of consecration in the Catholic Mass is, in its general form, the same as that of the Hindu sacrifices.[19]

Their work is important to the present book for the obvious reason that they compared Indian and Hebrew sacrifices and also because they saw a similar connection to the structure of the Christian Mass. However, it should be pointed out that they lived in a time when similarities between religions took the foreground of comparative studies to the near exclusion of their differences. Most of these similarities were based upon the influence of neighboring cultures and the popularly held notion that such religious folks operated from a uniform mental pattern. The influence of surrounding cultures played a major part, for example, in the study of the Hebrews and their near eastern neighbors as well as that of the early Christians and their Hellenistic environment.[20]

Hubert and Mauss represent an even greater break from earlier theoreticians than some today acknowledge. Their emphasis on the examination of those religious texts that contained the most complicated and yet best defined instances of sacrifice (Vedic animal sacrifices) reflects a significant departure from the likes of Frazer, Tylor, and others for whom the texts stood as childish obstacles to the "real" meaning of sacrifice. Comparing the Vedic texts with the less complicated yet substantially descriptive Hebrew texts allowed these sociologists to focus on the essentials determined by the texts themselves and not by the rudiments that were stipulated by predisposed theories or arbitrary labels. For example, when Hubert and Mauss criticized the sundry classifications of sacrifice as "vague, confused, and often indiscernible"[21] and opted rather for a "unity" of sacrifice they did so from the conviction of having studied the texts.

I want to call attention to some of those features in Hubert's and Mauss's work that exhibit their emphasis on the texts. Many of these observations were presented as an aside to the main thrust of their thesis, and hence contain little or no explicit interpretation of sacrifice. These discussions, and especially their footnotes, do offer valuable information on the mechanics and structure of sacrifice. The descriptive portions of their work made a landmark addition to the study of sacrifice. Yet, one must also understand that their work did suffer from the ubiquitous gift theory. Consequently their thesis failed to go much beyond the description of the consecrated intermediary object of the sacrifice. They too, like Roberson Smith, have left some questions unanswered concerning sacrifice that the present book wishes to investigate. Yet their work deserves special consideration because it postulated a fundamental, universal structure of sacrifice. Kees Bolle said, "I think that the most stimulating quality of their work, and the principal reason why readers often rediscover Hubert and Mauss, is their insight into the effectiveness of ritual...They looked for its symbolic life rather than for an unchanging cause."[22]

The undeniable focus of Hubert's and Mauss' study converges on the subject of consecration. They begin by differentiating between sacrifice and consecration. They made the point that while every sacrifice involves some form of consecration not every consecration is the same. Unlike consecration, sacrifice always alters beyond the thing or person consecrated.[23] Sacrifice also establishes a link between the sacred and profane worlds, according to Hubert and Mauss, in which the intermediary plays a paramount role. They defended the unity of sacrifice based upon its universal structure rather than trying to determine its origin.

Like Robertson Smith, their work lacked a definitive treatment of holiness or any attempt to elucidate the idea of sin and impurity in the specific context of sacrifice. The great deal of attention that they paid to consecration, and rightly so, would have been more illuminating had they also treated the paired yet incongruent ideas of holiness and sin, sacred and profane, purity and impurity, not to mention transcendence and immanence. These concepts related directly to consecration rites within the framework of the sacrifice. Why was consecration so vital for sacrifice and why did they spend so much time on references to the preparation and conclusion of sacrifices?

Recently, several have taken Hubert and Mauss to task for their attention to sacrificial consecration. Luc de Heusch thinks that their focus on the concept of consecration is an example of "Indo-European ethnocentrism."[24] E.E. Evans-Pritchard had already criticized Hubert and Mauss based on his work with the Nuer people in eastern Africa in which substitution seemed more central than consecrated mediation between the sacred and the profane. But the most significant challenge to Hubert and Mauss came from Marcel Detienne and Jean-Pierre Vernant who pointed out that sacrifice in ancient Greece did not require a transition to the world of the sacred. Humans found their place (social standing) between the gods and the animals through sacrifice. However, Detienne and Vernant characterize sacrifice along similar lines with Robertson Smith in which the gods commune with humans during a meal. This meal ultimately results in establishing an impassable distance between the two realms.[25] Mediation, substitution and consecration, though semantically different and not always appropriate in all sacrifices, nonetheless involve the ritual's problem of bringing two ontologically distinct worlds together through ritual consecration.

The Vedic and Hebrew texts seemed to converge on the necessity of consecration. Based on this insight they devised a structural scheme for the entire sacrificial act. In Hubert's and Mauss' chapter on, "The Scheme of the Sacrifice," they presented a threefold structure of sacrifice. The first phase of this structure they called "the entry." The purpose of the entry, as they saw it, was to transform the profane to the sacred and thus make contact with the two worlds possible.

> Sacrifice is a religious act that can only be carried out in a religious atmosphere and by means of essentially religious agents. But, in general, before the ceremony neither sacrificer nor sacrificer, nor place, or victim, possess this characteristic to a suitable degree. The first phase of the sacrifice is intended to impart it to them. They are profane; their condition must be changed.[26]

Using the example of the Dîkshâ, the consecration rite for the sacrificer of the Soma sacrifice in India, Hubert and Mauss showed how several rites of purification were necessary before the sacrificer could actually experience the sacrificial act. A special hut had to be built for him, "for the dikshita is a god and the world of the gods is separated from that of men."[27] After mentioning other special rites of purification, eg. shaving, bathing, new linen clothes and anointings, the Dîkshita was dressed in a black antelope skin symbolizing his new birth as a god. In this transformed state, "He must have no contact with men of impure caste, nor with women; he does not reply to those who question him; he must not be touched."[28]

"The sacrifier," taken from the etymology of the word that meant consecrated, was used in their scheme to illustrate the entrance into the sacrifice by means of the changed condition of the sacrificer, viz. the Dîkshita. Hubert and Mauss saw the role of the priest in general cases where, "one does not venture to approach sacred things directly and alone; they are too lofty and serious a matter."[29] The priest was "more familiar with the world of the gods," "he can approach it more closely and with less fear than the layman, who is perhaps sullied by unknown blemishes."[30] The special consecrated character of priests represented a type of security for all participants in the sacrifice for Hubert and Mauss. The texts warned of a real danger for all the participants in the procession of consecration rites or "the entry" that moved closer and closer to the ultimate moment in the sacrifice when contact was actually made with the deity.

The priests served as intermediaries or guides that ensured the proper ritual prescriptions for the sacrifice by virtue of their special heritage, knowledge, and sanctity. Thus the dangers associated with sacrifice and the prospect of the failure of the sacrifice were subsequently diminished. Nonetheless, these more pure, divine like, sacrificial guides could not come into direct contact with the deity. Only the victim could make direct contact with the deity, and this was only after both the sacrificial place and instruments were consecrated. The victim held the place of greatest importance in the entire scheme of sacrifice for Hurbert and Mauss. The victim was the central focus of a series of "concentric magic circles" that included the consecrated place and instruments as the entry rite moved inward towards the victim and greater degrees of sanctity.[31] In other words, the closer the sacrificial act moved towards the moment of contact between the victim and the deity the greater the degree of holiness and hence danger for everyone involved.

The second stage of their scheme was simply called "The Victim." The Victim stage of the ritual represented the highest point of the sacrifice when victim and deity met. The victim maintained contact with mankind while it continued to move upwards to the world of the gods through "principles of magical and religious sympathy."[32] Ultimately the victim made a clean break from the profane world and took on a new divine nature. But the task of linking all of the participants, human and divine, was accomplished through the intermediary role of the victim.

Hubert and Mauss dealt next with the victim's remains. Having described several instances from both Indian and Hebrew texts that described how the victim's remains were discarded they commented that:

> These precautions were designed to prevent the remains of the victim, now consecrated, from coming into contact with profane things...Even those remains of the cremated offering that could be neither destroyed nor put to use were not thrown away at random. They were deposited in special places protected by religious prohibitions.[33]

The third phase of their scheme of the sacrifice - "The Exit" - involved returning all of the sacrificial participants, place, and instruments back to the profane world. The Exit was a part of the same sacrifice that united the sacred and profane worlds. Hubert and Mauss mentioned that the rites of the exit were "the exact same counterparts of those we observed at the entry," but they did not expound any further on the necessity of returning to the profane world or the reason for breaking the "bonds that joined priests and sacrifier to the victim in the act of sacrifice."[34]

Hubert's and Mauss' scheme of sacrifice points to an absolute condition of sanctity that had to be attained by all persons and things involved in the sacrifice. Since nothing impure could come into close proximity, and certainly could not come in contact with the deity, the sacrifice began by anticipating the moment of contact between the victim and the deity with rites of consecration. The sacrifice itself can be seen to serve as an expiation and sanctification as the victim established communication between the two worlds. But the vital union attained in the sacrificial act had to be separated by returning those things sanctified in the sacrifice back to their profane realm. This too was an important aspect of the sacrificial ritual.

As a religious phenomenon, did sacrifice involve no more than communication with a deity in order to "magically" appropriate a desired result or gift? "The two parties present exchange their services and each gets his due."[35] Hubert and Mauss went on to make other curious statements such as, "There is no need to explain at length why the profane thus enters into a relationship with the divine: it is because it sees in it the very source of life."[36] This over simplification of the mythological nature of the sacrifice seems to have satisfied Hubert and Mauss. Apparently their structural explanation of sacrifice precluded any specific treatment of the glaring religious questions even though they referred to a "religious frame of mind" in the performance of sacrifice. This was true for them to the extent that their questions reveal a pragmatic interest in their own findings on sacrifice. They asked, "But how is it that the profane only draws nearer by remaining at a distance from it (the divine)? How does it come about that the profane only communicates with the sacred through an intermediary"[37]? Again they turned to the role of the victim and said that, "Thanks to it, the two worlds that are present can interpenetrate and yet remain distant," and that, "Because the victim is distinct from the sacrifier and the god, it separates them while uniting them."[38]

If Hubert and Mauss had asked why instead of just "how it is that the profane only draws nearer by remaining at a distance from the divine," then perhaps the whole notion of consecration and the role of the victim would have led to a discussion of the religious notions that surfaced as a result of the sacrifice. Such considerations delve into the function of both myth and ritual within the symbolic universe of sacrifice. For example, the whole notion of the intimate presence of the sacred with humans in the act of sacrifice would have necessarily required a treatment of the Vedic and Hebrew concept of sin and holiness as well as atonement. The value of their study on sacrifice languished when, having stressed the religious act of consecration, they still omitted an explanation of the "religious environment" that involved things "too holy and serious" for the sacrificers. Again I acknowledge that their descriptive work on sacrifice has been invaluable. Yet the general scope of this work fell short of addressing the obvious questions of which I have raised only a few. Notice their concluding interpretation of the function of sacrifice.

> Now this character of intimate penetration and separation, of immanence and transcendence, is distinctive of social matters to the highest degree. They also exist at the same time both within and outside the individual, according to one's viewpoint. We understand then what the function of sacrifice can be, leaving aside the symbols whereby the believer expresses it to himself. It is a social function because sacrifice is concerned with social matters.[39]

In the final analysis Hubert's and Mauss' work suffered from an inherent methodological weakness. A purely sociological interpretation of sacrifice, and especially one that in the final analysis abrogates sacrificial symbolism can not adequately address sacrifice in its complex cultural environment. It may seem somewhat prosaic, yet necessary, to note that the sociological grid Hubert and Mauss imposed on sacrifice could only partially account for the universal symbolic structure they discerned within two different religious traditions (not to mention the Eucharist). Sacrifice has something to do with the social order of religious humans because the mythological paradigm of sacrifice informs both worlds, and both worlds are therein affected by the sacrifice. The necessity of bringing both worlds together represented an insurmountable religious problem that only myth and ritual could solve. Failing to address this aspect of sacrifice means missing the central mystery that the sacrifice itself faced head on.

The legacy of Durkheim's functional approach to the study of religion resonates in the works of many sociologists and social anthropologists today who make no distinction between religion and the social structure it legitimizes. While such approaches remain important for serious students of culture and religion they also trivialize the view of religion as something specific within society. Collapsing the religious aspects of sacrifice to mere products of psychosocial forces makes it frivolous to suggest that religious apperception and apprehensions could have played a significant role in shaping sacrifice. Discerning the socio-functional similarities between sacrifices must be held in tension with the religio-historical details that helped produce the symbolic structural and patterns of sacrifices.

As noted above, many from the nineteenth century had already assumed that such similarities existed based on the structure of the mind. One still finds this type of conjecture, for example, in the modern structuralism of Lévi-Strass. But the tendency to manufacture a convenient universal methodology based on the unconscious operations of the human brain begins a circuitous journey that leads away from the documentation.

## 2:1 Violence and the Quests for Origins: Burkert, Girard, and Heesterman

Walter Burkert links sacrifice to the struggle for survival among Paleolithic communities.[40] Based on research from ethology that stipulated ritual communication preceded language, Burkert concurred that ritual behavior would have been one way for early humans to develop "successful strategies" needed for existence.[41] Burkert speculates with others that ritual, as a part of the continuous evolutionary process, served to communicate indispensible survival tactics through "imprinting."[42] Social order would gradually develop in concert with both "imprinted" and "learned" behavior experienced through rituals. Eventually, as the theory goes, religion evolved out of this sociobiological marsh in which ritual functioned as an unconscious apparatus to maintain the fragile social unit.

In the scenario configured by Burkert sacrifice evolved from basic human needs, especially those formulated through hunting. According to Burkert the hunt not only led to hominization and sacrifice but also to "pure religion." He thinks that the cooperation and communication necessary for hunting large game and the subsequent distribution of the meat account for the development of human communities.

He further regards the act of killing animals as having had more than mere nutritional value for the Paleolithic diet. Burkert also gives a psychological stroke to his portrait of hunting. Although early humans acquired a fondness for eating meat it must have left a bad taste in their mouths. Because the "aggression" involved in hunting brought about "remorse" for killing and the subsequent desire to render "compensation."[43] According to Burkert, sacrifice dealt with this psychological crisis and established the Neolithic period's practice of sacrificing domesticated animals.[44]

Burkert finds evolution a useful tool not only to unearth the origin of religion in ritual but also to revitalize functionalism. In the former case prehistory offers little or no evidence for the sacrifices imagined by Burkert; and in the latter, one must speculate about the contingent connection between animal rites and religious rituals performed exclusively by humans. Spanning the gap from present research on rituals among certain animals to the earliest human communities' development of successful strategies seems more tenable than deciphering animal sacrifice in Jewish, Greek, and Roman religion from the theorized practice of Paleolithic hunting and sacrifice. Conjectures about rituals as a part of the evolutionary process do not present the same type of problems that one encounters in Burkert's origin of sacrifice and religion. Working backwards from the bulk of diverse materials found in eastern Mediterranean religions to Burkert's version of Paleolithic "sacrifice" seems reminiscent of Hansel's and Gretel's dilemma. In order to supplement the lack of any hard evidence for the origins of sacrifice Burkert can only offer a crash course in Paleolithic psychology.

Besides providing invaluable information on Jewish, Greek and Roman religion Burkert has also raised an important question with regard to ritual and sacrifice. He wonders if the advent of human language incorporated into rituals radically transformed the ritual so as to have "lost all connections with what was there before, especially "animal" ritual."[45] Experts speaking on the origins of language have noted quite emphatically that "there is not simply a quantitative but a qualitative and indeed unbridgeable, gulf between the abstractions and complexities of language and the most abstract and complex of known mammalian systems."[46] If indeed religious rituals, including religious sacrifices, take on their own distinctive nature under the transforming impact of language then the quest for origins seems better separated from the study of religious phenomena as we have it, especially in those cases where only the texts remain.

Réne Girard's classic work, *Violence and the Sacred*,[47] is a fascinating interplay between literary interpretation and psychoanalysis. The implications Girard makes for understanding human society based on violence are no less pretentious than Freud's psychosocial theory founded on the repressed sexual libido. According to Girard, sacrifice represents the key that unlocks the dilemma of human violence as well as the mysteries of the sacred itself. In his scheme sacrifice exposes the unconscious operations of society driven by human passions. Rage outweighs reason when it comes to the forces that shape the world. Sacrifice springs from the blind impulses of anger that seek out and always find a victim.

Girard claims that an instinctive mechanism developed in human communities that not only satisfied the desire to act out inevitable violence but also subsequently protected society from this same rage and self destruction. He called this the "scapegoat mechanism." The process begins with the random selection of a "surrogate victim" or "scapegoat" that substitutes for the community at large through sacrifice. Sacrifice channels violence away from the community to its surrogate victim which in turn gets replaced by a "ritual victim."[48] Girard says that "the purpose of sacrifice is to restore harmony to the community, to reinforce the social fabric."[49]

Some degree of awareness results from the scapegoat mechanism, although it must remain shrouded in confusion for it to be effective. The delusional community recognizes that killing the victim results in peace. Sacrifice actually represents the ritual repetition of the original scapegoat mechanism as a mimetic response to "nonconscious" social forces. Based on the primordial act of violence, sacrifice consigns an ambivalent nature upon the victim in the mind of the community. The victim is at once a presumed evildoer and savior. The overall experience is a collective process and becomes identical with the experience of the sacred from which develop concomitant religious ideas. As with Burkert, sacrifice gives birth to myth.[50]

Girard has become the easy target of criticism for suggesting a uniform explanation for the complex and diverse phenomenon of sacrifice.[51] But in fairness to Girard, sacrifice remains subordinate to his task of literary criticism and social analysis. His quest for the primordial moment and its affect on society predetermines his interest in sacrifice. Girard does not need to investigate the different types of sacrifices nor pay close attention to historical changes in order to make his hermeneutical grid coherent. Although he focuses on the notion of substitution in sacrifice as it suits his psychosocial theory, he does not reduce all of religion to the passions of violence. Substitution and the ambivalent nature of the scapegoat victim reveal a central part of the sacrifices he examines. But these sacrifices represent historical developments in religious traditions far removed from the original violent moment that Girard thinks forged the collective psyche. Girard stresses the continuity of ritual killing with later sacrifices at the expense of the documentation that suggests the opposite.[52]

J. C. Heesterman's latest work on sacrifice in Ancient India, *The Broken World of Sacrifice,* expands on his previous treatments and reflects similarities to Burkert and Girard.[53] He too prefers to view sacrifice in regression, beginning with extant texts and then peering back to an earlier time (the "preclassical" period). As with Burkert and Girard, Heesterman finds the conundrum of sacrifice lodged in violence. Sacrifice began in the "preclassical" age as a spinoff of warrior activities. As such, it reflects the warrior's acquisition of goods through contests, raids and battles coupled with the necessity of killing animals as offerings to the gods. But sacrifice centers on violence as a necessity to real life. Heesterman believes this original phenomenon of the warrior-sacrificer went through a decisive transformation at the hands of the Vedic ritualist. The Vedic texts portray a much different world according to Heesterman because the priesthood ritualized sacrifice. That is to say, the Brahmins eliminated the chaotic rivalry of the preclassical sacrifices and isolated the new version from society at large. Heesterman writes, "The exclusive emphasis on the individual sacrificer not only desocialized sacrifice but, more importantly, placed it in a transcendent realm of its own."[54] This model of sacrifice paved the way for the individual sacrificer to internalize the ritual and ponder the immortal Self.

Heesterman's conclusions about Vedic sacrifice suggest a rite beaming with religious symbolism that reveals ambivalence and transcendence. The ritual's ambivalence surfaces from the residual experiences of life and death that once characterized the warrior's affairs. Transcendence develops in the ritualization of sacrifice that made it retreat from everyday life in the surrounding world. Heesterman thinks Vedic sacrifice became something radically different than what it was before. The transformation from social realities to metaphysics, materialism to spiritualism, and sacrificial conflict to ritual serenity seem over played in Heesterman's scheme. If the first sacrifices involved offerings to the gods then ambivalence and transcendence may have just as easily hinged on religious expressions that developed along with the other aspects. I find no justification to make a radical break between preclassical sacrifice and Vedic ritual. How is it that priests could have wrestled control of sacrifice away from the warriors? Why was the king considered just another sacrificer during the ritual?[55] In other words, how could religious symbolism usurp and transform previous sacrificial forms if the religious dimension had not always been central to the entire enterprize?

## 2:2 Transcendence and Immanence in the Sacrifice

Rudolf Otto's book, *Das Heilige*, (1917), English translation, *The Idea of the Holy*, appeared twenty-eight years after Hubert and Mauss published their work on sacrifice.[56] Otto's book had wide sweeping influence in Europe and continues to make its influence felt, especially among historians of religions. Otto's immediate contribution to the study of religions consisted in addressing one's experience of the holy. Otto said that humans had two basic impressions of "the altogether different" (das ganz Andere) holy. This twofold "numinous" experience he characterized as a sensation of terror (mysterium tremendum), which followed later with a feeling of attraction to this same numinous power (mysterium fascinans). The human encounter with God did not primarily involve a moral connotation but rather hinged on an experience that was simply altogether different from one's "natural" experience of reality.[57]

I have introduced Otto's famous work here because it provides an essential aspect in the discussion on sacrifice. The "altogether different" nature of the holy and religious humans' quest to be linked with it stands out foremost as that phenomenon which best characterizes religious experience. The knowledge gained from this experience serves as an authoritative model of behavior and standard of ultimate truth. Thus religious humans integrate their experience of the holy into the fiber of their mundane existence. Accordingly one does not find a "pure" or distinct form of religion because religious phenomena are not completely isolated from their general cultural milieu. This is true even when the religious stands out as being primary in relationship to its general social context. American anthropologists, in particular, have insisted that they do not always find a sharp distinction between the sacred and profane in human cultures. At times religious and profane matters come so closely packaged together in societies that they defy any label exclusive of the other. Kees Bolle has helped clarify this issue with a discussion of the role of the king in ancient civilizations. The king combined both religious and political aspects of his office into what Bolle calls an example of the "murkiness of religion."[58]

Since not all religious expressions conform to Otto's basic premise about the "altogether different" nature of the holy, how then are we to apply his elementary suppositions? Should Otto's notion of the holy be dropped from the prevalent discussion of socio-religious matters and be confined only to theological issues? In other words can we discern Otto's "altogether different" in the testimony of religious documents; and if so, should we separate it from those "murky," less distinctive socio-religious human phenomena? Or is it profitable to consider both aspects together?

The case of sacrifice deserves special attention in this exchange. Sacrifice often includes political and economical concerns within its structure while making use of terrestrial objects to symbolize transcendent realities. Yet at the same time sacrifice reminds the participants of the difficulty and danger of crossing the boundaries between this world and the other. The barriers that humans confront in the sacrificial act are specifically related to the difference between humans and god. This pervading reality must always be reckoned with when the two come in contact with one another in the sacrifice. The central issue for the sacrifice lies in the problem of transcendence and immanence, or the presence of god and humans together. But before elaborating on the essential nature of this problem we need to examine how Vedic religion dealt with the presence of the gods and humans; and why the gods and humans had to be periodically brought together through the extraordinary means of sacrifice.

Otto's approach to the notion of the holy allows us to discuss the problem of humans in the presence of the sacred without reducing it to mere moral depreciations. He said, "When once it has been grasped that qadosh or sanctus is not originally a moral category at all, the most obvious rendering of the words is 'transcendence' ('supermundane', überweltlich).[59] Otto admitted that this "altogether different" character of the numen is "purely ontological" and does not lend itself to other attributes of the numen that inspire respect and praise. But this in no way attenuates the paradoxical phenomenon of one being drawn to the transcendent out of sheer cultic necessity.[60] Otto's conceptualization of the holy also enables us to begin to address the issue of sin in the Vedas separately from its classical Christian use in the West.

The act of sacrifice created a visual drama in which the plot revolved around the "altogether different" difference between the two main characters, God and humans. The role of the victim, priest, and other mediators portrayed the radical nature of the difference between the sacred and profane. This difference does not lessen such theological statements as one being created in God's image, as in the case of Jewish and Christian religions, or those myths in Vedic religion where humans and the gods were at one time not different. In each case where humans are metaphorically compared to God, or God is described anthropomorphically, the texts never retract the essential ontological and epistemological differences between God and humans. Something always remains hidden and outside of one's conceptualization of the holy. This is true even in the case of divine revelation, whether the mode of revelation came through a mystical vision or an incarnation of the god. No decent Christian theologian would ever maintain that the incarnation of God in Jesus Christ left a vacuum in Heaven. The Bhagavadgita also made it clear that no mortal could bear to see the fullness of God. Such was the case where Arjuna pleaded with Krishna to return to his "normal" divine form after momentarily revealing a transcendent form human beings could not grasp. Here the manifestation of God in both traditions not only revealed God but also conveyed that there is still more to the reality of God. The incarnation does not solve the mystery of God nor exhaust his fullness.

Any notion of the "altogether different," transcendent nature of God should be checked against those areas of religious phenomena where no sharp distinction can or should be made between sacred and profane. The point of ancient kingship is well taken. Yet we should also keep in mind that religious humans integrate the transcendent into their phenomenal world. Religious humans' symbolization discloses their link with the what they perceive as "altogether different." This fact perhaps more than any other makes the study of religious phenomena so difficult. But this also makes it necessary to examine both the less distinctive aspects of religious phenomena together with those that highlight the "altogether different" aspects of the sacred so as to distinguish it from its murky environment. Sacrifice is an example of the latter type.

Otto's category of the "altogether different" nature of the holy must be used with caution.[61] The particular details of religious phenomena show that the purely religious simply does not exist. The religious intersects with its historical frame of reference. Eliade said that,

> There is no such thing as a 'pure' religious datum, outside of history. For there is no such thing as a human datum that is not at the same time a historical datum. Every religious experience is expressed and transmitted in a particular historical context. But admitting the historicity of religious experiences does not imply that they are reducible to non-religious forms of behavior. Stating that a religious datum is always a historical datum does not mean that it is reducible to a non-religious history--for example, to an economic, social, or political history.[62]

Yet Otto's transcendent value of the holy still finds an important place in the history of religions because the documentation requires a particular category and specific treatment in order to adequately deal with the complexity of religious phenomena. Bolle has said that, `"The religious," whatever it is, does not permit its own dissolution into something else."[63] The sacrificial act exhibits religious humans' experience and impression of the "altogether different" in a manner that clearly differentiates between God and human beings. The distinction humans perceive between the profane and sacred works itself out in the very structure of the sacrifice. The sacrifice encapsulates both human and divine characters but never ultimately blends the two together so as to make them indistinguishable from one another. As we have noted, the profane must undergo transformation that sanctifies it before contact with the sacred is possible. Futhermore, what has become sacred through the sacrifice and has been left behind must not be left in contact with the profane. It must be properly returned to the profane or protected from causal identification with the profane realm. These precautions involve more than an utilitarian map of the sacrificial act. Such ritual procedures call attention to the dynamic tension between opposites that are brought together in the sacrifice. The presence of the sacred in the confines of the sacrifice with humans presented problems that threatened to create a frightening scenario in which the mythological distinctions between humans and the sacred became blurred. Clouding these distinctions would have meant obliterating ontology and cosmology in one secularizing act. But Vedic sacrifice always included provisions that re-established the transcendence of God and humans' dependence on the sacrifice.

While continuing our general discussion on sacrifice it may not be superfluous to remember that sacrifice is a religious ritual performed as part of the cult. According to S. Mowinckel, ritual is not a separate area of religion but is a main aspect thereof (Hauptaspeckt), from which all of a religion's phenomena can be considered [64]. Sacrifice stems from the community's or individual's need to enter into or continue a relationship with their deity.[65] But, as in the case of rituals in general, not just everyone is permitted to participate in the sacrifice. The ritually impure or uninitiated may not come into the presence of the sacred powers. Participants in the cult must also attain a certain degree of holiness and purity through purification or expiation rites. Once sanctified, the initiate may participate in the cultic ceremony.

The special condition of sacrifice within cultic life emerges in the intensified efforts to consecrate everything and everyone that is to participate in the sacrifice. Sacrifice most often requires special priests, places, utensils, materials, and a victim so that the sacrificer and God may join together under these exceptional circumstances. For this reason sacrifice always involves some form of consecration of these elements.[66] For example, the sacrificer takes on a transformed nature that, at times, results in a "new birth." Such was the case of the Dîkshâ ceremony in India. The measure of preparation and degrees of holiness for the participants may vary depending upon the type of sacrifice, but the basic issue remains constant for sacrifice; namely, how to accommodate the union or contact with two "altogether different" beings. Therefore sacrifice concerns itself with the notion of sin and holiness, as well as impurity and purity. These terms point out the elementary differences between humans and God. Nothing intensifies the contrast between these notions as does the encounter between humans and God in the ritual act. The sacrificial structure must then deal with "sin" and "impurity" regardless of how a particular religious tradition might understand these terms. The death of a victim often handles the dilemma of bringing humans and God together in the sacrificial act. A. Schimmel noted, "Ein Tier oder Mensch kann, als pars pro toto, die Sünden der Gemeinschaft auf sich nehmen und sie so vernichten order vertreiben."[67]

Once again, sacrifice created a special condition in which sinful humans and a holy God to came together and thus solved the initial problem of the God's distance from the profane world. But with this union another problem surfaced that also had to be addressed. Sacrifice had to account for the presence of God with humans. Thus sacrifice involves extraordinary circumstances that clearly distinguished its environment from everyday social standards and experiences which themselves might have been fashioned by the religious.

Since the problem of transcendence and immanence in the act of sacrifice converged on the differences between humans and God, consecration attempted to nullify the otherwise volatile consequences of bringing elements of the two worlds together. It does not attempt to eradicate these differences. Bolle says that:

> They transform a more encompassing circle of reality than the concepts of purity and impurity, which influences primarily the division of society. Of course, there are no absolute separations here. The pure and impure cannot function meaningfully or for long in isolation, apart from the ritual, and sacrifices could not be performed without them.[68]

The new reality that the victim, priests, and sacrificer entered during the sacrifice enabled them to surpass the barriers of their mundane condition. As we shall see, this new reality created in the sacrifice only temporarily transformed the profane condition. Another aspect of the sacrifice had to return the participants who were exposed to the transforming powers back to their profane world.

The anthropologist Mary Douglas has helped elevate the discussion on ritual beyond the nineteenth century's `primitive psychology' and its general disdain for ritual. After almost complete neglect of the subject by anthropologists in the first part of the twentieth century her treatment of purity and impurity deserves special attention. Douglas should also be credited with studying these concepts in context of the total structure of their thought. In other words, she has included the religious in her examination of social categories. Her consideration of purity and pollution appears all the more important in light of Preston's statement that, "The purification of religious pollution is a major religious theme because it forges a path of expiation, healing, renewal, transcendence, and reintegration, establishing harmonious triangular links among the individual, the cosmos, and the social order."[69]

I would also like to use this as an opportunity to clarify the importance of religious symbolism for the study of religious rites. In the first place we need to distinguish between the specifically religious conditions created during the act of certain rituals and their social ramifications. This simply means paying attention to the temporal conditions of sacred time and space created during the ritual act, and realizing that neither sacred time nor space carry the same acute regulations once the ritual has concluded. More specifically this means recognizing the difference between how particular religious traditions handle transcendence and immanence. Rituals will require the appropriate liturgical measures where the sacred's contact with the impure realm poses certain theological and mythological problems. The symbolic value of these liturgical provisions carries over to the social realm as a pedagogical and structural model for the community. But the ritual itself still encompasses a different level of experience. Preston determined that "the definition of religious pollution cannot be limited to social, psychological, or physiological domains alone. The definition of the "sacred" also involves issues of spiritual pollution."[70]

Douglas' primary work, *Purity And Danger*, 1966, describes the "primitive world view" as discerning the universe with a type of dualism, viz. "order" and "disorder," "being" and "non-being," and "form" and "formlessness." According to Douglas, the natives felt that these concepts came from powers that were operative in the universe and visible on the social level, although not entirely distinguishable from their "external environment." For Douglas "dirt is essentially disorder" and cleansing means reordering.[71] In fact, no clear distinction would exist between "sacred and secular,"[72] in her scheme of things, without reflection on dirt. Yet, once humans made this all important distinction, their "rituals of separation" both demarcated the boundaries between the sacred and secular and elucidated their entire "structure of thought" within their social patterns.[73] "Ritual recognizes the potency of disorder," according to Douglas, and, "Danger lies in transitional states, simply because transition is neither one state or the next, it is undefinable."[74]

In her example of the Hebrew concept of holiness Douglas used the root meaning of Qadosh (separateness) to show that, "Holiness means keeping distinct the categories of creation," so that, "Incest and adultery (Lev. XVIII, 6-20) are against holiness, in the simple sense of right order."[75] The following paragraph gives a good example of her view on pollution and its relationship to the sacred.

> Now is the time to identify pollution. Granted that all spiritual powers are part of the social system. They express it and provide institutions for manipulating it. This means that the power in the universe is ultimately hitched to society, since so many changes of fortune are set off by persons in one kind of social position or another. But there are other dangers to be reckoned with, which persons may set off knowingly or unknowingly, which are not part of the psyche and are not to be bought or learned by initiation and training. These are pollution powers which inhere in the structure of ideas itself and which punish a symbolic breaking of that which should be joined or joining that which should be separate. It follows from this that pollution is a type of danger which is not likely to occur except where the lines of structure, cosmic and social, are clearly defined.[76]

The point of clarification I would like to make with regard to Douglas' work may appear on the surface to be only one of emphasis, though I think it goes much further. Some of her observations concur with the general structure of Vedic sacrifice that we have covered above. For example, Douglas has recognized a basic pattern of ritual in which the sacred and profane are not clearly differentiated except in the case of pollution, as "a type of danger." But in this case the structure becomes "clearly defined."[77] She continually down plays the role of magic and emphasizes ritual exactitude that publicly establishes "rules of avoidance." These rules, in turn, mark off the boundaries between sacredness and impurity that must be respected in order to appropriate the desired results. For her too, the difference between the sacred and the "unclean" was not based on a moral category but on the powers of good order inherent in the cosmos.

The discrepancy I find with Douglas revolves more around her methodology than her conclusions. Douglas has approached religious symbolism from an almost purely external perspective. Even while drawing upon specific religious rites and saying, "To talk about a confused blending of the Sacred and Unclean is outright nonsense"[78], she still favors bringing it all together under a socio-political symbolic grid. She imposes this symbolic grid on religious documents which often results in emptying them of their specific symbolic value.

In her chapter on, "The Abominations of Leviticus" [79], she drew heavily upon the text and came closest to citing the relationship between the mythological and social symbolic structures. Granted, the Hebrew notion does affirm that "Holiness is an attribute of the Godhead." I also agree that it served as a socio-political symbol from Israel's altar to their table fellowship. In this manner it thus helped distinguish Israel from her neighbors. But how should the mythological and the sociological be placed in perspective? The last paragraph of this chapter has an insightful but troublesome conclusion.

> If the proposed interpretation of the forbidden animals is correct, the dietary laws would have been like signs which at every turn inspired meditations on the oneness, purity and completeness of god. By rules of avoidance holiness was given a physical expression in every meal. Observance of the dietary rules would thus have been a meaningful part of the great liturgical act of recognition and worship which culminated in the sacrifice in the Temple.[80]

Douglas' predilection for the cultural manifestation of "holiness" makes good sense of Israel's dietary rules. She has not tried to make them the product of an arbitrary, legalistic priestly code, but rather the "physical expression" of God's holiness. Yet she moved so quickly from the religious notions of God's "order," "holiness," and "wholeness" that one wonders how other importance mythological and theological ideas could have provided paradigms for the social order. For instance, the Hebrew notion of sin and atonement are conspicuously lacking. It appears to be yet another case where the religious dimension has been circumvented for some "more objective" method might be applied to religious texts.

She conspicuously glossed over Hebraic sacrifice where holiness, pollution, and danger carried ultimate significance for most of Israel's history. An examination of the religious symbolism surrounding the Temple cult would have broadened the historical and epistemological scope of the "rules of avoidance," "pollution," "danger," and "holiness."

Part of the problem with her method lies in the fact that she examines the sociological patterns derived from the religious cult as if they both operated on the same level of reality at all times. In other words, it is as if the new or transformed reality created during in the ritual act was merely carried over into everyday life of the community in its entirety. But the "danger" one encountered from violating dietary rules did not bear the same consequences that the high priest faced when he entered the Holy of holies on the Day of Atonement.

The religious symbolism of the cult established and perpetuated part of the social structure. Therefore, social behavior based on a religious model will in turn reveal something of that particular religious tradition as in the case of Israel's dietary rules. But caution should be exercised when using social symbolic behavior to totally explicate the phenomena of religious rituals. The results often end in psychosocial interpretations in which case social conditions are reconnoitered as producing the peculiarities of the cult.[81] For example, Douglas thinks that one way societies protect the efficacy of their religion "is to make ritual efficacy depend on difficult conditions. On the one hand the rite may be very complicated and difficult to perform: if the least detail gets into the wrong order, the whole thing is in valid."[82] This is a very important observation. But again she chose to look outside the ritual instead of thinking that the ritual itself might have provided meaning. The immediate context of the difficult and complicated conditions of rituals arise from the juxtaposition of the impure and the sacred.[83]

Rituals, shrouded in the mystery of religious symbolism, involve seemingly unrelated realities during their performance. But the sacred and profane bifurcation created by the ritual act serves first to help integrate the distinctions within society and then legitimize the prevailing social order. But again, ordinary social categories alone can not adequately address the transcendent matters that were originally invoked in the religious ritual. For this reason Douglas' work ignores the sense of mystery we find so prevalent in religious documentation. Everything mysterious in the ritual has been given an antidote of social science semantics in order to make the religious innocuous.

Such is also the case, for example, when she discusses the question why dirt can be made sacred on specific occasions.[84] Here she approaches a specifically religious problem of dirt or pollution "in the nature of dirt itself." She proceeds to sketch an "attitude" towards dirt that developed through two stages until dirt lost its "danger" through lack of differentiation. The absurdity of this type of theorizing lies in its convenient disregard for the documentation. I am not suggesting that we ignore the sociological and anthropological import to notions of pollution, etc. How else could we understand some of the historical changes in religious symbolization? But Douglas weakened her own attempt to understand purity and pollution in society by failing to give them the same symbolic function that their particular culture did. How helpful or scientific can it be to investigate the sociological, political, or anthropological aspect of a culture's "attitude" toward something "religious" without giving adequate attention to its religious symbolism; especially when the phenomenon was conditioned in part if not predominately by its mythology? In Douglas's scheme the religious determines social categories and marks the boundaries for the sacred and impurity. But the relationship between the social and the sacred remains blurred in the case of the ritual act.

Recent scholarship evidences a growing number of scholars have abandoned the attempt to determine the meaning of religious texts and phenomena.[85] This symptom of our modern age goes back to a few intellectuals in the seventeenth century that rejected certain cosmological assumptions of the Roman Catholic Church. The Church had received its cosmological data from her own "scientific" clergy, her astronomers. Since then the West has placed more and more distance between anthropology and cosmology in its search for "pure science" and "objectivity." Gerardus van der Leeuw thought that the nineteenth century had forfeited a sense of the meaning of the world because of the misappropriate influences of the natural sciences. He felt that in this respect our own century had followed the preceding one and, in fact, had reduced the world to a mere object for one to decipher.[86]

Structualism is one example of efforts to give a scientific basis for the objective study of human cultures. Structuralism claims to determine the original code behind different aspects of human culture. Its methodology is based upon the premise that all social phenomena reveal an unconscious inner logic of the mind that can be traced through language and ritual.

Structualism has exerted its influence upon students in virtually all disciplines that deal with human documentation. Lévi-Strauss has been credited with deciphering much of cultural beliefs and rituals that seemingly would not have come to light without his structural anthropology.[87] Lévi-Strauss sets out "not to show how men think in myths, but 'how myths think in men, unbeknownst to them.'"[88] Structural linguists echo the same basic position when they say that their task is not to determine 'what' the text means, but rather 'how' it is text, and 'how' it is meaningful for its own sake.[89]

Part of this search for objective methodologies has to do with an uncertainty with the scientific method itself to recover meaning. In this case many have decided to let others take on the `subjective' task of finding `what it means'. In other words, they attempt to remain within the confines of their particular descriptive disciplines and simply gather the information. This approach does recognize the limitations of fact finding but at the same time it suffers from the delusion that subjectivism plays no part in the actual process of gathering and describing their findings. For certain others, no method can possibly appropriate a documents original meaning. The text can convey meaning but only in a relationship with each individual reader.

Frits Staal believes that religion can and should be studied objectively with an adequate methodology. He chides scholars of religion for missing a chance to develop a contemporary scientific discipline instead of relying on a "pseudo-methodology," viz. phenomenology, existentialism, and hermeneutics. He thinks religious studies could have overcome a "non-scientific" methodology by adopting linguistics.[90] Anthropology, according to Staal, recognized the importance of language but lapsed into the same methodological malaise with religious studies because of an unjustified "emphasis on meanings and symbols."[91] Staal's methodology sounds impressive with his claim to utilize linguistics and ethology. But his work suffers from inconsistencies that appear form his selective use of these disciplines.[92]

In an article entitled "*The Meaninglessness of Ritual*," Staal said, "A wide spread but erroneous assumption about ritual is that it consists in symbolic activities which refer to something else."[93] Staal studied Brahmins who performed the three thousand year old Vedic Agnicayana ritual in 1975 to help illustrate his thesis. He also depended almost exclusively upon the ritual manuals, the Shrauta Sûtras, for the bulk of his textual support. He concluded from these sources that Vedic ritual's "primary concern, if not obsession, is with rules."[94] Stall cites the most frequent reply of the priests when asked why they performed this ritual as simply "because of our tradition (Parampara)."[95] The ritual manuals overriding emphasis on 'orthopraxy' also led Staal to imagine nothing counted more than the correct performance of the rite.[96] He pointed to the Shrauta term Tyâgâ as a "contradiction" in Vedic ritual that indicates the ritual's meaninglessness. Tyâgâ was used for the renunciation of the fruits of the ritual which Staal interpreted as the sheer lack of meaning and example of the solitary emphasis on ritual performance.[97]

Staal feels that various theories on ritual miss the mark because they assume rituals convey meaning outside of the ritual itself. For example, he criticized the theory in which ritual causes a transition from the profane realm to that of the sacred. His criticism on this point begins with the terms "sacred" and "profane." According to Staal, if "sacred" and "profane" are used to distinguish between the status of persons or objects before and after a ritual in terms of the ritual itself then "ritual cannot be defined in terms of sacred and profane."[98] Staal notices that sacred and profane mean very little outside of the realm of the ritual and therefore do not tell us anything aside from the confines of the ritual. Staal continued by saying:

> On another interpretation, this theory would assume that the distinction between sacred and profane is already established and known from elsewhere. For example, in the realm of divinity, "sacred" might have been shown to be the domain of the gods, and "profane" that of men. But a satisfactory distinction of this kind is not easily found, especially outside the realm of the ritual. Moreover, the terms do not introduce anything new. The theory would merely claim that ritual effects a transition from the realm of the gods to that of men (or a communication between the two). As a matter of fact, the Vedic ritual offers an immediate contradiction. During the soma rituals, a transition is effected from the "Old Hall" (prâcînavamsa) to the "Great Altar" (mahâvedi). The former is said to be the abode of men, and the latter that of the gods. Thus a transition from the domain of men to that of the gods is effected within the ritual. The distinction therefore cannot serve as a concept in terms of which the ritual itself may be defined.[99]

I agree with Staal's basic observation that the use of "sacred" and "profane" within ritual addresses a specific, predetermined notion of the differences between humans and god that do not apply equally to the general situation outside of ritual. It can again be stated that in rituals where "sacred" and "profane" are used to differentiate between humans and god special consideration should be given to the realities created within ritual as opposed to those outside and after the ritual act. We have already seen the failure to make this distinction among those who have dealt with ritual and sacrifice. This oversight has caused confusion between the heightened sacred environment established only in the ritual encounter between humans and god and the extended influence that religious ritual makes on every level of society. So the activities and realities that occur within ritual must be distinguished from life outside of the ritual's immediate performance. For this reason I suggested Otto's concept of the "altogether different" nature of the holy could still be helpful if used cautiously when dealing with the sacrificial act.

It would seem that Staal finds little use for the terms "sacred" and "profane" essentially because they are religious terms with symbolic meanings which are almost exclusively limited to a specific religious context. He objects to the notion that "sacred" was already distinguished from "profane" in the ritual by virtue of the distinction between the "domain of the gods" and "that of man." He reasons that such a distinction falters when, for example, in the Vedic soma ritual the transition to the domain of the gods from that of humans actually occurs within the ritual. This will not suffice as a means to define the ritual because, for Staal, ritual cannot define itself. In other words, "sacred" and "profane" do not provide the proper "concept" to objectively define ritual from the outside. In order to do this he turned to structuralism.

Having presented a structural analysis of Vedic ritual from the combination of several rituals Staal said, "What is important is that the existing rituals can be analyzed in the same manner as the model with regard to the structures in which we are interested."[100] Staal admitted twice that his structural diagrams did not correspond to any existing ritual. But from these paradigmatic models he proceeded to postulate toward the end of his argument that ritual was the "origin of syntax."

To define ritual in its own terms and on its own terms means accepting the religious symbolism it created, full of meaning. This does not preclude using scientific tools and methods nor does it prevent going outside of ritual itself to examine and compare it with rituals in other religious traditions. In fact it seems to require all of this.

If we consider the transition from the "Old Hall" to the "Great Altar" as a symbolic act in the ritual drama that served to bring the two worlds together on the ritual's terms then we realize that the ritual has excluded any determination outside itself. Vedic rituals are replete with such symbolic journeys to heaven as well as the gods coming to the "Great Altar." But such symbolic journeys and visitations would not have been possible unless the ritual grounds, materials and participants had experienced purification and consecration rituals. In this manner the ritual not only distinguished both sacred and profane within its own realm but also created a closed environment to anyone or anything that did not conform to the sacred standards of the ritual. These standards came to light through the rigid rules of the ritual's performance which, for the most part, involved purification and consecration rites. The ritual determined the difference between sacred and profane as a precautionary measure against confusing or mixing the two.

We should remind Staal that the Agnicayana ritual involved the construction of an bird shaped altar that was used with various Vedic sacrifices. The stated purpose of all sacrifices performed on this altar was to take the sacrificer to the world of the gods through the mediation of Agni. Once that trip or link to the heavenly world had occurred several other things happened. The building of the fire altar resulted in the re-creation of the cosmos and all life. The sacrificer was said to have become immortal.

> As to this they say, 'For what object is this fire (altar) built?' 'Having become a bird, he (Agni) shall bear me to the sky!' so say some, but let him not think so; for by assuming that form, the vital airs became Prajâpati; by assuming that form, Prajâpati created the gods; by assuming that form, the gods became immortal: and what thereby the vital airs, and Prajâpati, and the gods became, that indeed he (the Sacrificer) thereby becomes.[101]

In this text the mythology of Prajâpati and Agni extended the rudimentary performance of the ritual to include a host of symbolic results that effected the entire cosmos.[102] Prajâpati, the lord of all creatures, and Agni, the one who restored Prajâpati, enabled what human priests and the sacrificer did through their ritual performance to transcend the limitations of the profane realm. Without the symbolic role of the gods the ritual would have never reached beyond the mechanical performance of the humans and their world.

All of the authoritative Vedic texts (Shruti) tied the mechanical performances of Shrauta rituals to Vedic mythology. It would be impossible to detect a time in Vedic religion where the performance of any sacrifice was not accompanied by mythology. This is not to say that Vedic rituals were simply the performance of myths, or conversely that myths came about to explain rituals. It simply means that the two always appear together in the documentation. Therefore, we have no performance of Vedic ritual, regardless of how simple or complex, that is not at the same time given a symbolic framework. In fact, the stringent ritual manuals (Sûtras) were not given the same authority as the mythological texts of the Vedas. Consequently, there can be no doubt that these rituals always involved symbolic activities that referred to something else. The question then arises in view of Staal's thesis: did ritual mean anything outside of the ritual itself?

Vedic religion provides examples that address the issue of meaning outside of ritual's immediate performance. The Râjasûya, the inauguration of a king, had obvious political implications for all those under the king's rule. Many people in our day take great interest in the "secular" inauguration ceremony for the president of the United States because of what the "new era" might possibly mean to them. On one level everyone knows that not much will change because a new politician shall hold this office. But on another level we all hope that somehow there might be something behind all the rhetoric. The symbolism of the inauguration ceremony helps strengthen these hopes. The Ashvamedha, or horse sacrifice, was also performed by a king for his benefit and for the good of all the people in his kingdom. The same process of symbolization in the ritual that excluded outside contamination or determination also enabled the ritual to extend its influences to the socio-political realm. Ritual has the ability to both shut out and infiltrate the profane.

A simpler yet more graphic example or ritual's ability to extend its self-determined standards and meanings outside of its own realm can be seen in initiation rites. This is especially apparent in cases where the initiate has received physical markings during the ritual. Ritual circumcision occurs during the ceremony and its meaning is confirmed therein. But this act retains both its physical and symbolic significance outside of the ritual itself where it helps determine the social structure. Another problematic ritual phenomenon for Staal's thesis centers on leftover ritual materials. As we shall see, materials and instruments that have been consecrated for contact with the sacred must be properly disposed of within the control of ritual. If the ritual is meaningless outside of its realm then such caution would not be expected with regard to the leftovers. Ironically, Staal devised a hypothetical situation of a Brahmin priest lighting his cigarette with the same stick used to produce the sacred fire for the ritual. He advocated that the priest could never do this because the two realms can never be mixed. This point is well taken. But his axiom also illustrates exactly how much power ritual symbolism has for the outside world. Even if the priest could not answer why he would not light his cigarette with that stick we are still left with a meaningful distinction that has spilled over into everyday life that has been established by the ritual. The stick means something outside of its use in ritual performance. Although the religious symbolism of ritual prevents the mixture between the two realms it does not simply vanish outside of ritual but rather persists as a symbolic reminder. In cases where one renounced the fruit of the ritual he was merely acknowledging that he had participated in something greater than the acquisition of his own personal desires. The performer knew that the ritual also had cosmic consequences and therefore he said, "This is for Agni not for me."

Generally speaking, western theorists have expunged the meaning religious rituals have for the participants in order to objectively analyze its social function. Catherine Bell thinks that the whole enterprize of western scholarship has inadvertently imposed a type of subjectivism upon the documentation in an attempt to interpret rituals objectively. She writes that "the descriptions of how rituals work have been constructed according to a logic rooted in the dynamics of theoretical speculation and the unconscious manipulation of the thought-action dichotomy is intrinsic to this construction."[103] Scholarship begins by differentiating between the acting object and the thinking subjects. This leads to the "opposition between the theoretician and the object of theoretical discourse," according to Bell.[104] She says of performance theories that deny any validity to indigenous claims: "The meaningfulness of ritual that such interpretations attempt to explicate has nothing to do with the efficacy that the ritual acts are thought to have by those who perform them.[105] Not everyone interested in the social context of religious rituals wants to eliminate the vertical dimension. S.J. Tambiah reminds us that "the cosmological constructs are embedded in rites," and also that rituals have a "duplex existence" that "symbolically represents the cosmos and at the same time legitimatizes and realizes social hierarchies."[106]

Another part of the problem of "meaning" in the study of religious phenomena also has to do with the Jewish and Christian view of history that has in turn influenced the study of mankind. Many wish to get beyond the confines of understanding history as part of a divine plan of salvation. Karl Löwith said, "It is not by chance that we use the words "meaning" and "purpose" interchangeably, for it is mainly purpose which constitutes meaning for us. The meaning of all things that are what they are, not by nature, but because they have been created either by God or by man, depends on purpose."[107] In the recent departure from theology dealing with the study of history and anthropology we have witnessed the removal of a truly human element of our documentation. When, for example, religious ritual becomes "pure act" apart from one's desire to live in communication with the sacred then we have turned full circle and submit our documents to a new type of subjectivism.

Consideration of the Vedic notion of sin helps us clarify the problem of transcendence and immanence in Vedic sacrifice. We must return to the *Rig Veda* and to Rita. "So those who cleave to Rita are held righteous by all mankind" and, "The wicked travel not the path of Rita."[108] What does it mean to "cleave to Rita" and "not to travel the path of Rita"? In the first place the texts state that, unlike humans, the gods follow the ordinances of Rita and are "faithful to rta" (Ritavarî)[109]. For example, Varuna observes Rita (*Rig Veda* IV.42.4), Brhaspati upholds Rita (*Rig Veda* II.23.17), and the Adityas are "true to Rita" (*Rig Veda* II.27.4). Lefever said, "The gods are sinless (Anagas) because they are uniformly faithful to the Rita (Ritavarî), whereas humans, through wickedness, passion, etc., often acts contrary to the Rita."[110] When the poet prayed, "Whatever vrata of thine, O Varuna' we, men as we are, daily violate, give us not up to death or to thy fierce wrath when angered" (*Rig Veda* I.25.3); or when he pleaded, "Aditi, Mitra, Varuna, have mercy if we have committed sin (âgas) against you" (*Rig Veda* II.27.14), his trespass or sin was not so much an offence against the gods as it was a breach of the Rita that the gods were responsible for guarding.[111]

Vedic worshippers failed to "cleave" to Rita or consistently keep Rita because they were human and not God. The Vedas use several terms to describe man's "sinful" behavior [112] and the Rig Veda euphemistically expresses sin as being in the "noose of Varuna" or as the "chain of Yama."[113] We also find the idea in the Vedic texts that disease resulted from Anrita or going contrary to Rita. "To be diseased, to be sinful, to be caught in Varuna's nooses or by Varuna himself etc. all these ideas are conceptually one and the same."[114]

Anrita, or that which opposes Rita, continued to express the idea of sin in the Brâhmanas where Satya (truth) had replaced Rita.[115] In this case the term Svitra (left behind) was used for one who could not reach heaven because of Anrita. Miller said, "What is not Satya is also against Rita."[116] So whatever the particular offense might have been and regardless of whether it was committed consciously or not, Vedic sacrifice made it impossible for one to escape Anrita, or more simply stated, to ignore one's lot as a human being. In fact, it was thought that the Vedic sacrificer was born owing a debt (Rna) to the gods.[117] B. Smith described this situation in Vedic ritualism as follows:

> "Perfection" (samrddha or sampanna) is an attribute of the gods, not men. The human condition is often portrayed as the exact opposite of the divine. In contrast to the perfection that characterizes the gods and their heavenly locale, the earthly and human (mânusya) is said to be "imperfect" or "unsuccessful" (vyrddha) (SB 1.4.1.35). "What is 'no' for the gods is 'yes' for them," says another Brâhmana (AB 3.5) by way of emphasizing the utter difference between the two ontological ritual exactitude, is a quality of the gods, while anrta ("error" or "disorder") is the distinguishing quality of things human (SB 1.1.2.17., 3.3.2.2, 3.9.4.1).[118]

The Satapatha-Brâhmana states the predicament very succinctly, "Verily the gods are satya and man is anrta" (SB 1.1.1.4).

But did this difference between the gods and humans rest solely upon their given natures? Visah translated as, "we men," or, "men as we are," and Purusatvata, which can be read as, "in human manner," were used in the confession of sins.[119] However the issue does not appear to be merely one of sinful human nature but rather of sinful human behavior.[120] Once again from the SB we read, "Man is impure. He speaks untruth and, therefore, he is impure within."[121] The gods, as we have already seen, are free from all sin and irreproachable, Anavadya.[122] Here too, the "sinless" condition of the gods ensued from their action. The action referred to here is none other than the act of sacrifice.

A few lines from the SB offer some indication of how this distinction was made by virtue of the gods speaking Satya.

> Now, then, the discussion of the Samishtayagus (oblations). The gods and the Asuras, both of them sprung from Prajâpati, entered upon their father Prajâpati's inheritance, to wit, speech--truth and untruth, both truth and untruth: they, both of them, spake the truth, and they both spake untruth; and, indeed, speaking alike, they were alike.
>
> The gods relinquished untruth, and held fast to truth, and the Asuras relinquished truth, and held fast to untruth.

Now that same truth, indeed, is this threefold lore. The gods said, "Now that we have made up the sacrifice, let us spread out this truth!"[123] This text not only shows the mythological distinction made by "speaking the truth" but it also firmly places the context of this act in the performance of the sacrifice.[124] "Speaking the truth" was no mere arbitrary moral duty that simply meant the opposite of telling lies. The identification of speaking the truth or Satya with the sacrifice provided a transcendent model for sacrifice. Prâjapati himself established this model which in turn assured the maintenance of the universe because the gods and humans were required to sacrifice as it was done from the very beginning. This was also the case with the identification of Rita and sacrifice in the Rig Veda. Here the sacrifice of the Purusa or primordial man, (*Rig Veda* X.90), served as the raison d'être for sacrifice.[125]

In Vedic religion people had a variety of possible sins that they could succumb to e.g., arrogance, trickery, adultery, incest, evil thoughts, murder, anger, the slaying of an embryo, letting the sacrificial fire go out, etc. Even the love of women was considered an evil according to the *Jaiminîya Brâhmana*.[126] But the most offensive and critical trespass was simply not to sacrifice at all.[127] This most critical offence failed to adhere to the example of the gods and therefore jeopardized the maintenance of "universal order" which belonged to the sacrifice. The *Brâhmanas* deemed not sacrificing as a type of non-reality since spreading or performing the sacrifice accounted for all reality in Vedic mythology.

The next most serious "sin" resulted from ritual mistakes. Lefever noted that, "The majority of offenses mentioned are those incurred in the ritual."[128] Several texts testify to the arduous task of ritual precautions that accompanied sacrifice in order to insure the success of the sacrifice by means of proper guidelines. Ritual texts also emphasized the performance of the sacrifice according to its mythological parameters since the sacrifice was traced back to Vedic myths. The execution of the sacrifice meant high costs and certain risks that were outweighed by the sheer necessity to sacrifice. Therefore nothing that involved the sacrifice was as mandatory as the concern for doing it correctly, without mistakes, right down to the most infinitesimal detail.[129] All this indicates that what happened during the act of sacrifice marked the epitome of cultic experience. As M. Biardeau said, "...toutes les opérations du sacrifice brahmanique ont pour but de faire venir les dieux àcette table servie qu'est l'autel..."[130] Miller put it this way, "The whole sacrificial rite was conceived as a bringing together of gods and men so as to enact dramatically the cosmic order."[131] The fact that the majority of offenses occurred in the sacrifice symbolized not only how radical the essential difference between huamns and gods was as they drew close to one another, but it also accentuated how important it was to reconcile each trespass. Every time a mistake happened during the ritual the sacrificer was reminded of his precarious situation. The sacrificer faced the peril of death as well as the ever looming possibility that the sacrifice, if performed improperly, would fail.[132]

The essential difference then between the gods and humans came to light as the two parties approached the sacrifice. This difference centered on the portrayal of humans' inability to keep Rita and to speak Satya which, as we have seen, the texts regarded as sin (Anrita). Sin also resulted from mistakes made during the sacrifice. One committed these ritual mistakes simply by failing to adhere exactly to the prescribed ritual format that demanded perfection throughout every detail of the sacrifice. The distinction between God and humans far surpassed any mere equivalence to ethical contrasts and involved an altogether different realty that could only be experienced in the sacrifice where the Vedic worshipper came into actual contact with the numinous powers.[133] In other words, just being in the presence of the gods resulted in sin for the Vedic sacrificers unless they could avert ritual errors and transform their sinful human condition in general. We shall now address the texts solution to these problems.

## 2:3 The Sacrificial Solution

So far I have stressed the difference between the gods and humans in the specific context of Vedic sacrifice in order to discuss the Vedic notion of sin. But how can we reconcile those texts that speak of humans becoming one of the gods in a preliminary rite? For example, "He who is consecrated goes near to the Gods, and becomes one of the Gods."[134] If one became a god how could that same individual commit sin in the sacrifice and why would they still face danger? And how should we understand the human gods, or Brahmins, who also received an oblation or sacrificial fee (Dakshinâs)?[135] Why did these priests as human gods need to be consecrated? The answer to these questions lies in the Vedic solution to the problem of transcendence and immanence in the sacrifice where the presence of the gods was necessary for the completion of the sacrifice but potentially disastrous for sinful humans.

Some scholars continue to understand the transformation of one into a god and all other purification rites connected with the sacrifice as a type of magical manipulation of the gods. For example J. Gonda said,

> Part of the practices and prescriptions to the Vedic ritual can be cogently explained by the theory that it contained a 'magico-ecstatic' element which aimed at the attainment of control over powers and potencies conducive to the benefit of the sacrificer, his family and possessions. The dietetic regulations, austerities and abnegations involved in the Vedic Dîkshâ point in the same direction.[136]

The texts never tell us implicitly or otherwise that the gods must be "magically" controlled in order to appropriate the desired results in the sacrifice. However, the texts do emphasize that obstacles and dangers confronted one in trying to sacrifice or reach the world of the gods. Again this was part of differentiating between the sacred and the profane. The *Mâitrâyani-Samhitâ* says, "The world of man is separated from the world of the gods" (3.6.1.). The difficulty for the sacrificer lay not in finding the correct magical remedy to appease capricious gods but rather in the fact that one had to abide by the proper ritual procedures to sacrifice successfully. Even then, ambivalence shrouded the sacrifice. Once again, the task centered on solving the primary difference between humans and the gods who came together in the sacrifice. Why else did the Dîksitâ receive a new body as he prepared to be transported to the world of the gods? Levi said, "Le procédé consiste àfabriquer un corps nouveau à l'usage du sacrifiant; presque toutes les pratiques sont des symboles de conception et de naissance."[137] Magical manipulation of the gods does not adequately describe the scheme of Vedic sacrifice in either the Vedas or Brâhmanas. The sacrificer merely accepted the reality of Rita and Satya that was built into the universe with regard to his status and responsibilities in the sacrifice.[138] One aspect of this reality meant that the gods likewise adhered to the sacrifice and consequently Vedic worshippers could expect certain results from the gods; that is of course if they performed their part of the sacrifice correctly.[139] The concept of mutual responsibilities in the sacrifice and the interdependence of both worlds on the sacrifice carried more importance than "magic" for Indian cosmology. The apparent equivalence between the sacrificer and the gods ,in actuality, underscored the rudimentary distinction between the two.[140] Accordingly, the Rishis set out to solve the problem of finding a way to bring humans and the gods together, and then they sought to solve the problem created by this volatile contact. Therefore, the problem of transcendence and immanence makes the Vedic notion of sin most intelligible in the specific context of the sacrifice.

The sacrifice itself was said to atone for sins that were committed during the sacrifice. Here are a few examples from the SB:

> Now, Indrota Daivâpa Saunaka once performed this sacrifice for Ganamegaya Pârishita, and by performing it he extinguished all evil-doing, all Brahman-slaughter; and, verily, he who performs the Ashvamedha extinguishes (the guilt incurred by) all evil-doing, all Brahman-slaughter.[141]
>
> The righteous Pârikshitas, performing horse-sacrifices, by their righteous work did away with sinful work one after another.[142]
>
> If any part of the sacrifice were to fail, let him make an oblation with regard to that same deity for whom he may have intended (that part), on the Ahavanîya, if it is during the initiation and the Upasads ; on the Agnîdha, if it is at the soma-pressing ;for whatever then is the deity in that (part of the sacrifice) through that deity he heals the sacrifice, through that one he makes the sacrifice complete again.[143]
>
> He (Saukeya) said, 'If at the time when thy fires are taken out, and the sacrificial vessels brought down, thou wert going to offer, and the offering-fire were to go out, dost thou know what danger there is in that case for him who offers?' 'I know,' he replied; 'before long the

eldest son would die in the case of him who would not know this; but by dint of knowledge I myself have prevailed.' 'What is that knowledge, and what the atonement ?' he asked. 'The breath of the mouth has entered the upward breathing such (is the knowledge) ; and I should make the offering in the Gârhapatya fire that would be the atonement, and I should not be committing that sin.'[144]

Lefever noted that, "the most characteristic feature of the Brâhmanic doctrine of sin concerns the measures adopted for its removal. In this connection, the sacrifice or holy verse is all powerful, whether the sins be ritual or moral offenses."[145] Another example was the Prâyascittih rite that atoned for ritual mistakes and removed guilt that was thought to "break" the sacrifice.[146] The *Kâtyâyana Shrautasûtra* has a complete section on expiatory rites that cover any imaginable flaw in the performance of the sacrifice from too little done to too much done.[147]

As we have seen a large portion of the sacrificial enterprise encompassed measures to prepare one for contact with the sacred in the highest moment of the sacrifice. According to Hubert and Mauss, "All these purifications, lustrations and consecrations prepared the profane participant for the sacred act, by eliminating from his body the imperfections of his secular nature, cutting him off from the common life, and introducing him step by step into the sacred world of the gods."[148] The texts taught that the sacrifice could free one from Pâpam (evil) and atone for ritual mistakes. But another aspect of the sacrifice also endeavored to solve the problem of transcendence and immanence through preparation or consecration rites. Purification played a significant role in these rites as well as in the total scope of what Hubert and Mauss labeled the "entry". After the "entry" purification did not cease. The victim or animal required special purity (Medhya) for the sacrifice because it went "near to god" (SB III.8.1.15) and obviously had to be made fit (SB III.7.4.4). It is no wonder that Heesterman referred to Vedic sacrifice as, "...the domain of absolute purity."[149]

The notion of purity can be traced far back into Vedic literature where we find it said in the *Rig Veda* that, "By Rita I purify both heaven and earth by the sacrificial rite I purify Heaven and Earth."[150] The liturgical text of the *Taittirîya-Samhitâ* says, "All the gods who purified themselves for the sacrifice prospered. He who knowing thus purifies himself for the sacrifice prospers also. Having purified him without he makes him go within. Verily having purified him in the world of men, he leads him forward purified to the world of the gods..."[151] The SB is permeated with a concern for purity. The Sautrâmanî sacrifice, for example, was encouraged for Brahmins because, "the Sacrificer is the body of the sacrifice, and the officiating priests are its limbs ; and wherever the body is pure there the limbs are also pure ; both of them, indeed, purify him, and both of them repel the evil from him:" (XII.8.1.17b); and, "...But, surely, he who is consecrated by the Sautrâmanî moves away from this world" (XII.8.3.21a). In fact, the Brâhmanas reveal a heightened concern for purity as sacrificial ritualism developed. This does not mean that the Rigvedic period did not know of an elaborate rite with detailed concern for consecration.[152] It does show, however, that as the cult grew more and more elaborate in the Brâhmanic age, the theological mystery surrounding transcendence and immanence continued to pervade Indian religion specifically through the sacrifice. This was no less the case even later in the Upanishads where Brahman-Atman finally replaced Brahman-Satya as the Absolute. In other words ritual continued to be the most important source of knowledge for Vedic sacrificers.[153]

Purification rites included a lucid system of symbolism within Vedic initiation and consecration rites that conveyed knowledge. G. van der Leeuw saw purification in its relationship to "power" as the "release from evil and the induction of good."[154] The positive affects that van der Leeuw attributed to purification rites in general can be applied to the Vedic idea of purification in the specific context of the sacrifice where the "impure" or "profane" had to be transformed before making contact with the divine. For instance, the twelve day Dvâdasâha gradually purified the sacrificer (Yajamâna) so that "By means of various gifts representing the parts of his body he disposes of his impure self. Thus he is reborn pure out of the sacrifice."[155]

Water played an important part in purification throughout the cult in India. The universal symbolism of water was understood in light of its particular mythological background in Vedic religion. Krick noted that already in the Rigvedic period water was considered the original stuff (Urstoff) and the basic feminine principle (Grundprinzip) of the cosmos.[156] Both the sacrificial fire and Prajâpati were born from the divine mother, that is "the waters." With this new ontological status derived from myth water could help prepare the sacrificial grounds for the sacred fire,[157] or ritually wash evil from the sacrificer's past thus enabling him to go, as it were, bach to the beginning.[158]

Several other materials were used for purification such as special sacrificial grass, dung, butter, salt, sand, ashes, etc. It is of particular interest to recognize the symbolic value of these elements in the sacrifice. As in the case of water, we find that these other purifying agents could transform the profane or impure based upon their mythological ability to unite the two worlds or enable them to come into contact without disastrous results. For example, sand was strew out in order to prepare the ritual ground and make the fire hearth useful. Sand's transforming powers came from its mythological identification with the "ashes of Agni," or with the mythological claim that the gods were made pure by being sprinkled with water and sand.[159] As the "ashes of Agni" sand provided protection from divine contact in the sacred fire with the ordinary soil that laid under the sand of the Gârhapatya hearth.[160] According to this text the protection resulted from the fact that Agni could not "scorch" himself. Sand now had a transcendental referent in its mythological association with the god Agni that, in turn, allowed it to accomplish what no ordinary or profane substance could. In other words the mythological referent first transformed sand and then it became part of the transforming, new reality that the sacrifice was creating. Salt was also used in various aspects of the sacrifice for purification and its transforming effect.

> And again why he scatters saline soil. Prajâpati created creatures; he created them with different kinds of ammonium: they did not agree together. He desired, "May they agree together!" He made them to be of the same (kind of) ammonium; hence even to this day, being of equal ammonium, they agree together. And he who offers, offers thinking, "May I be (born) with the same (kind of) ammonium as the gods!" and when he scatters saline salt (in the hearthsite) he thereby becomes of equal ammonium with the gods.[161]

Salt gained ritual significance from its mythological alliance with heaven and earth. Salt was sent to Earth from her husband in heaven when the two became separated. Salt allowed heaven to continue to receive communication from earth during sacrifice despite of the great separation between the two.[162] Later salt and water became ritual agents that insured sacrificial purity for both the heavenly and earthly altars.[163]

Only Agni played a more important role in Vedic sacrifice than Soma. Soma bore both the meaning of a plant that produced an intoxicating juice capable of granting immortality humans and the gods who inspired Vedic poets with visionary powers. Soma enjoyed a close relationship with Agni and Rita as each carried out their important function in the sacrifice. Soma was born in heaven yet Rigvedic hymns IV.26 and 27 emphasize his descent to earth. Here we see one of soma's key mythological roles was to unite both worlds. As the fiery elixir that came from the "mountains" (heaven) Soma was poured out on the "sacrificial altar" (the center of the earth). In this regard soma had a purifying power that enabled the union of men and gods.[164] A scholar by the name of K. R. Potdar thought soma might have brought perfection to the sacrifice as a later development of sacrifice in the Rig Veda.[165]

The god Agni continued to play a paramount role in the sacrifice with regard to purification.[166] Vedic mythology employed Agni at every key juncture in the ritual. This made Agni's influence and control over the sacrifice far reaching. In the first place Agni's presence in the scope of the sacrifice was ubiquitous. The texts speak of Agni as belonging to all three realms and having three births, one in the waters, one in the plants, and one in Heaven. Agni, whose name means "fire,"[167] was both the sacrificial fire itself and one of the gods in the Indian pantheon. As the sacred flame Agni carried the offerings to the gods and was known as the "High Priest" of the sacrifice who made the sacrifice acceptable to the gods. As the "Messenger" of the gods Agni not only took the sacrificial offerings to the heavenly realm but also brought the gods to the sacrificial altar of humans. Agni was also called the "wide striding Visnu" the one who, like Visnu, could traverse the earth and atmosphere to reach the "highest step." Agni had access to the "Highest" place in Heaven and was referred to as the "nearest" god to humans, from whom all sought protection. "Mayest thou, O Agni, who knowest Varuna, deprecate for us the god's anger...As such, O Agni, be for us the lowest (god) with thy help, our nearest (friend)" *Rig Veda* IV.1.4,5. The gods consumed the sacrificial offerings through the mouth of Agni. Therefore both the gods and men were dependant on Agni in the sacrifice.

This type of mythological scenario made Agni indispensable for the sacrifice. The emphasis on Agni's ability to move and mediate between the two worlds points predominately to the need to unite both worlds in the sacrifice. Krick said of this mediating ability:

> Agni ist als der unsterbliche, zu den Sterblichen herabgekommene, der den Opferbund zwichen Diesseits und Jenseits aufrechterhält, als auch der Urlebensträger, durch den die Wesensunion zwichen Göttern und Menschen (d.h. deren Feuerseele jîvah, âtmâ, purânah purusah) besteht.[168]

Through Agni the two worlds could come together without harm to either one and without violating Rita. Nothing profane, evil, or sinful threatened the highest of all realms because of Agni. "Agni is the light, the burner of evil, he burns away the evil of this sacrifice and the latter becomes a light of prosperity and glory in this and a light of bliss in yonder world."[169] Agni was "sinless" (SB VII.4.1), could forgive all sins of the one sacrificing (*Rig Veda* III.7.10; IV.10. 7), and all the sacrifices were performed in him (SB IV.5.1.13). *Rig Veda* IX.66.19 called Agni the "purest of life's powers" while the *Mânava-Srauta-Sûtra* (258) compares Agni's purity to that of the Dîkshitâ who must remain isolated. The sanskrit term Pâvaka, "purifying pure"[170], often belongs to Agni. Even the profane fire was kept separated from the three sacred fires.[171] Agni made the sacrifice perfect according to *Rig Veda* VI.10.1; and VII. 17.3,4. This purifying aspect of Agni's mythological role dealt directly with the problem of transcendence and immanence in the sacrifice.

Since Vedic mythology rendered one sacrificially impure, purification must be seen in light of the religious symbolism that surrounded the sacrifice. Purification was one way that the sacrifice attempted to come to terms with the differences between humans and god, a distinction determined by the authority of myth. So the powers of transformation and purification that enabled the two worlds to come into contact during the sacrifice resulted not from magic but from the mythological process of identification that was integrated into the sacrifice itself.

## 2:4 Sacrificial Leftovers And Reestablishing Transcendence

Just after human beings and god came into contact with one another in the height of the sacrificial act they were quickly and decisively returned to their separate stations.[172] Once the sacrificer endured the laborious preparations and dangers that confronted him as he made his symbolic journey to heaven he then faced new dangers even after having safely arrived. All of the precautionary consecration and purification measures that were followed in the preparation rites did not alleviate the new threat. At this point of the sacrifice the sacrificer could no longer depend on the mediation of the victim through whom contact was actually made with the deity. Even his own transformed nature, acquired by virtue of his new birth in the Dîkshâ, only guaranteed a one way trip and hence made no provisions for a lasting divine status. The term Sarvatâti, or "the state of one who is safe and sound" [173] could not be used for the sacrificer at this juncture in the sacrifice.

We recall that this part of the sacrifice came under the heading of the "exit" in Hubert's and Mauss' work. They noted that the "exit" rites were the "exact opposite" of the preparation or "entry" rites.[174] Yet long before Hubert and Mauss made this observation the *Kausîtaki Brâhmana* stated with regard to the preparatory and concluding rites: "He who makes them equal to one another, just as one can make a journey as desired by driving a chariot with two sides, so safely he reaches the world of heaven."[175] Concluding rites showed concern for every element used in the sacrifice. The materials, place, vessels, and participants had to properly be returned to the profane realm. Here we find the leftover elements from the purification rites, which facilitated the union between the two worlds, continued to be the objects of further ritual action.[176] But this time they were employed to separate the two worlds and return the temporarily consecrated back to its profane condition.

Water and fire also played an especially important role in this operation. Hubert and Mauss said that, "All that remains of the sacrifice is plunged into the water;" and, "All that remains of the offerings is destroyed by fire, and the utensils are cleansed and taken away after having been washed."[177] Gonda recounts that one reason why a vessel was thrown into the fire after the sacrifice was "to prevent the demons from enjoying it."[178] The strew of grass that covered the altar and upon which the gods sat around the altar was thrown into the fire. The Svâru or chip of wood used in conjunction with the animal sacrifices along with the ointment used for anointing part of the fire altar was likewise disposed of in the fire.[179] Leftover sacrificial butter was sacrificed in the fire. The balls of rice leftover from the Srâddha sacrifice were thrown into the water. The disposal of these elements as well as others were often accompanied by special prayers.

Perhaps the best known concluding rite was the Avabhrtha that followed the soma sacrifice. The Avabhrtha rite seems to have reversed the conditions established by the Dîksâ ceremony. In the Avabhrtha ceremony the sacrificer and his wife immersed themselves into the water.[180] The antelope skin that they wore during the sacrifice along with the utensils that came in contact with the Soma plant were also thrown into the water while reciting verses addressed to Varuna. Scholars disagree as to the purpose of this ceremonial bath. Thite thinks that the "sins" that the sacrificer asked Varuna to remove were none other than "ritual sins" or mistakes made during the performance of the ritual.[181] Keith took the position that Oldenberg postulated in the late nineteenth century.[182] Keith said concerning the meaning of the Avabhrtha:

> The bath itself is addressed as the cause of the removal of sin. But these forms are obviously mere cloaks for the fact that the washing is the chief thing, and that it concerns itself with the removal of the mysterious potency, which has clung since the Dîkshâ to the sacrificer and his wife, rendering them unfit for normal human life. That this was realized by the priest is clearly proved by the language of the rite : the waters are distinctly said to remove the consecration and the Tapas, and it is stated that the sacrificer takes the consecration with him into the bath.[183]

Thite's interpretation does fail to do justice to the text's language concerning consecration. Ritual mistakes may well have still been a real concern at the end of the sacrifice but certainly not the primary one. The language of the texts gives evidence that the sacrifice had progressed to a new scene in the drama. The structure of the language indicates that the ritual had reached its goal of uniting both worlds and now was separating and descending towards earth. Oldenberg and Keith grasped this focus of the texts. The effects caused by the union of the two worlds made it impossible to simply return to "normal life." But was this merely an arbitrary scheme built into the sacrificial structure in order to magically ward off the dangers of the "mystical powers" that clung to the participants? Obviously both Oldenberg and Keith thought this of the Avabhrtha, but they also felt that the sacrifice became more and more "magical" throughout the Brâhmanas.

Ancient India did appear to think that powers could be transferred by different means of contact.[184] Accordingly, we find admonitions to sacrifice without touching[185] along with the notion that certain places and things in the sacrificial sphere carried more sanctity than others. Brahmins had a special holiness among humans for the purpose of sacrificing. The sacrificial site (Vihara) was sacred but the place of the altar (Vedi) was even more sacred. On certain occasions the Ahavaniya fire was held to be more sacred than the other two sacred fires.[186] The victim had such a degree of sanctity that even the sacrificer, who himself had taken on a special form of consecration, could not touch it without danger. These differentiated degrees of sanctity coincided with the proximity of person and things to the deity during the sacrifice. Those that actually made contact with the gods would bear the greatest degree of sanctity. For this reason Agni held the highest degree of sanctity and purifying powers in the world of men.

The notion of removing the effects of having made contact with divine powers and returning to the profane realm did not have to do with perfunctory magical duties. The significance of the Avabhrtha, as well as other concluding rites, stems from its perpetuation of the mythological concerns that developed in the sacrifice.

Agni's ashes rendered a significant role in the sacrifice[187] and especially at the end of the day's sacrificial activities. Agni's ashes were returned each day from the altar to the waters. No doubt that part of this ceremony had to do with the mythological notion of Agni's three forms, fire, lightning, and Sun, which enabled him to dwell in the three worlds and to manifest himself on the earth in the waters and plants. This guaranteed that Agni would return to the plants-wood from which he could be re-kindled, that is after he was taken back to his birth place in the waters. "When you enter in your mothers, the waters, do not forget, O Agni, the return and that you, staying in the distance, were (formerly) here."[188]

Agni's ashes present a problem at the close of the sacrifice because they represent the actual contact and transmission of the sacrificial offering to the gods. The ashes are all that remained of the victim that was charged with such sanctity at the height of the sacrifice. To simply leave this sacred material to come in contact with the impurities of the profane world was impossible at both the liturgical and mythological level. But neither could these ashes be left in contact with the gods because they shared in the profane nature of all humanity. The SB approached the problem this way:

> Now, then, as to the taking down of the ashes (to the water). Now, the gods at the time threw out the ashes (from the pan). They said, 'If we make this, such as it is, part of our own self, we shall become mortal carcasses, not freed from sin; and if we cast it away, we shall put outside of Agni what therein is of Agni's nature : find ye out in what manner we should do this!'
>
> While meditating, they saw this, 'Let us take it down to the water; for the water is the foundation of this universe : having settled it on that wherein is the foundation of this universe, we shall reproduce in this (heap of ashes).' They then took it down to (and threw it into) the water; and in like manner does this (Sacrificer) now take it down to the water.
> 'O divine waters, receive ye this these ashes, and put them in a soft and fragrant place!' that, being consumed (matter), has run its course (is useless).
>
> 'Having settled in the womb, as ashes, in the waters, and the earth, O Agni,'- by his ashes he is, indeed, settled in the womb, that is, both in the waters and in the earth; 'having united with the mothers, thou hast again, brightly shining, seated thee;' that is, 'Having joined thy mothers, thou, the shining one, hast again seated thyself (in thy home).'
>
> Having taken some of the ashes, and returned, he throws it into the fire-pan, and stands by (the fire) worshipping it; for when he throws Agni into the water he does what is improper; he now makes amends to him so that he may not injure him. With two (verses) relating to Agni (he worships), for it is to Agni that he makes amends,...[189].

Returning Agni's ashes to the water not only assured his return for humans in the sacrifice but it also re-established the mythological boundaries between the profane world and sacred. Left on the altar these ashes, that symbolized the union between the gods and humans in the sacrifice, might communicate a permanent merger. Agni went to his earthly home in the waters taking the terrestrial side of his nature to be absorbed back into the plants. Some of the ashes thrown in the water (now again purified) were put back into the fire pan signaling Agni's return to his heavenly home. The sacrificial cycle could now be repeated.

This aspect of the sacrifice as well as other concluding rites re-established the transcendence of the gods and reminded one of the altogether different nature of the two separate worlds. In other words, everything that had come in contact with the divine world in the sacrifice could not simply be discarded in the profane world. To do so would have fostered an incongruent mythological notion that the symbolism of the sacrifice had so painstakingly avoided. Those things that had shared in the sinless, pure nature of the gods through consecration and contact with the sacred could not themselves come into contact with the profane world. They first had to change their symbolic value so as not to obscure the differences between the two worlds. The symbolism of the concluding rites provided the necessary information. This aspect of the sacrifice also perpetuated the needed partnership between humans and the gods in order to maintain the universal order (Rita). In this way the desires of the worshippers and the gods were continually realized in the sacrifice and sacrifice persisted as an essential fact of life for Ancient India.

Vedic sacrifice became the medium of Indian speculation of ultimate Truth and Being. The basic mythological and philosophical issues taken up in the sacrifice concerning transcendence and immanence continued to develop in later Hinduism and Buddhism in regard to human conceptualization of the Absolute. Even the ambivalence that surrounded the sacrifice remained embedded in the philosophical discussions; something we would expect when dealing with the nature of transcendence and immanence.

## ENDNOTES TO CHAPTER TWO

[1] For a helpful survey and criticism of these works see Richard Hecht's dissertation, *Sacrifice, Comparative Study and Interpretation*, The University of California, Los Angeles, chapters 1 and 2, 1976. Hecht's thesis also provides a new approach to the problem of understanding sacrifice. He discusses sacrifice as a "perfect history" in which humans participate in recreating the cosmos in contradistinction to the gift theories and psychological interpretations.

[2] See, *Totem and Taboo*: Some Points of Agreement between the Mental Lives of Savages and Neurotics (1913). Translated by James Strachey. New York: Norton, 1950.

[3] See R. Hecht, *Sacrifice*, fn. 2, p. 418. These works came in addition to the general volumes on ethnopsychology, see, *Zeitschrift für Völkerpsychologie und Sprächwissenschaft*, ed. H. Steinthal and M. Lazarus; also see W. Wundt's ten volume, *Völkerpsychologie*.

[4] Richard Hecht has convincingly shown how cultural fashions operated on the interpretation of sacrifice. Hecht pointed out that basically only one theory of sacrifice emerged in the late nineteenth and early twentieth centuries, and that this one dimensional theory had two variations. The perennial "gift theory" understood sacrifice as essentially a gift made by humans to a deity. Some preferred to search for the origins of sacrifice (Tylor, Robertson Smith, and Frazer), while others (Hubert, Mauss, and Van der Leeuw) investigated the structure of sacrifice. But everyone essentially viewed sacrifice as a gift.

[5] Ibid., p. 50.

[6] See J. de Vries, *Perspectives in the History of Religions*, pp. 199-200; and R. Hecht, op. cit. pp. 55-58.

[7] Op. cit., p. 56.

[8] W. Robertson Smith, *Lectures on the Religion of the Semites*, London, Adam and Charles Black, 1914, pp. 348-350.

[9] Ibid., p. 349.

[10] Ibid., p. 369.

[11] Ibid., p. 372.

[12] Ibid., p. 350.

[13] Ibid., p. 369.

[14] Ibid., pp. 350-354.

[15] Ibid., pp. 350-387.

[16] Ibid., pp. 385-387.

[17] Ibid. p. 387.

[18] See Joseph Henninger who describes Smith's theory on Semitic sacrifice, "In this rite, recipient, offerer, and victim were all of the same nature; sacrifice was thus originally a meal in which the offerers entered into communion with the totem." "Sacrifice," trans. from German by Matthew J. O'Connell. *The Encyclopedia of Religion*, Mircea Eliade, ed. in chief, New York: Macmillan, 1987, vol. 12, p. 551.

[19] Hubert and Mauss, *Sacrifice: Its Nature and Function*, trans. by W. D. Halls, Chicago, The University of Chicago Press, 1964, pp. 93-94.

[20] For a concise treatment of the Myth and Ritual School and the Heilsgeschichte Schüle in the late Nineteenth and early Twentieth centuries involving the Hebrews and the early Christians see Samuel Terrien, *The Elusive Presence*, New York, Harper & Row, Publishers, 1978.

[21] Ibid., p. 14.

[22] Kees Bolle, "A World of Sacrifice," *History of Religions*, The University of Chicago, vol. 23, no. 1. August 1983, p. 55.

[23] Ibid., pp. 9-13. Eliade said that, "It must be understood that the consecration of unterritories is always a consecration; to organize a space is to repeat the paradigmatic work of the gods," *The Sacred and the Profane*,p. 33. This point shall become important in the general understanding of the sacrifice's all inclusive work of consecration; and specifically with regard to the ancient Indian's practice of preparing the ground for the sacrifice.

[24] De Heusch treats sacrifice as a structuralist in which ritual reenactment of death and rebirth stem from socialorder thus resulting in social utilities. Sacrifice is a "debt" paid to an ancestor that wards off death through the notion of sacrificial substitution. All sacrifices revitalize the generative powers that were released through the "man-god's primordial immolation." See Luc De Heusch, *Sacrifice in Africa. A Structuralist Approach*, trans. L. O'Brien and A. Morton (Bloomington: Indiana University Press, 1985), p.5).

[25] See Jean-Pierre Vernant (with Marcel Detienne), *The Cuisine of Sacrifice Amoung the Greeks* (Chicago: Chicago University Press, 1989).

[26] *Sacrifice: Its Nature and Fuction*, pp. 19-20.

[27] Ibid., p. 20; they cite, TS VI.1,1,1.

[28] Ibid., p. 21.

[29] Ibid., pp. 22-23.

[30] Ibid., p. 23.

[31] The inward direction during the sacrificial ritual symbolizes the upward direction to the transcendent world of the gods.

[32] Ibid., p. 31.

[33] Ibid., pp. 40-41.

[34] Ibid., p. 46.

[35] Ibid., p. 100.

[36] Ibid., p. 98.

[37] Ibid., p. 98.

[38] Ibid., pp. 99, 100.

[39] Ibid., p. 102.

[40] See *Homo Necans : Interpretation altgriechischer Opferriten und Mythen*, Berlin, 1972.

[41] He shares a similar view with V. Reynolds who claims that, "while religions cannot be understood as caused by natural selection working on genes, they nevertheless have implications for natural selection." See *The Biology of Religion*, V.Reynolds, R.E.S. Tanner Longman Group Limited, N.Y. 1983, p. 5. Burkert says "ritual behavior must have been a major factor in evolution," *Violent Origins*, Walter burkert, René Girard, and Jonathan Z. Smith on Ritual Killing and Cultural Formation. Edited Robert G. Hamerton-Kelly. 1987 Stanford University, Stanford, p. 152.

[42] Imprinting refers to a type of conditioned behavior acquired through vivid experiences in early childhood and among animals in contrast to learned behavior acquired by trial and error among humans.

[43] Burkert cites similar reactions among Siberian hunters' ritual, see, *Violent Origins*, p. 150.

⁴⁴ Jonathan Z. Smith took Burkert to task for postulating a theory of ritual killing when the evidence in both Lower and Middle Paleolithic periods simply does not exist. See *Violent Origins*, pp. 202-3.

⁴⁵ IBID, p. 154.

⁴⁶ Derek Bickerton quoted by Hans Penner in "Language, Ritual, and Meaning", *Numen*, Vol. XXXII, Fasc. 1, 1985, p. 8.

⁴⁷ Réne Girard, *Violence and the Sacred*, trans. by Patrick Gregory, Baltimore: Johns Hopkins University Press, 1977.

⁴⁸ Ibid., pp. 101-2.

⁴⁹ Ibid., p. 8.

⁵⁰ See Girard in *Violent Origins*, p. 92.

⁵¹ See J.C. Heesterman, *The Broken World of Sacrifice, An Essay in Ancient Indian Ritual*, Chicago, The University of Chicago Press, 1993, pp. 10-11. Girard also has some defenders, see Raymund Schwanger, S.J., *Must There Be Scapegoats? Violence and Redemption in the Bible*, translated by Maria L. Assad, San Francisco, Harper and Row, 1987, pp. 25-42; and James G. Williams, *The Bible Violence and the Sacred, Liberation From the Myth of Sanctioned Violence*, San Francisco, Harper Collins, 1991, especially chapters 1 and 7.

⁵² A.E. Jensen made a major distinction between ritual killing in agricultural societies and later sacrifices in ancient civilizations, see *Mythos und Kult bei den Naturvölken*, Wiesbaden, 1951.

⁵³ See especially, *The Inner Conflict of Tradition*, Chicago, University of Chicago Press, 1985. *The Broken World of Sacrifice*, 1993, op. cit.

⁵⁴ *The Broken World of Sacrifice*, p. 5.

[55] Heesterman says that "Under its leveling law even the royal Ashvamedha sacrificer is just a Yajamâna like any other," ibid., p. 187.

[56] Even G. van der Leeuw writing on sacrifice twenty-one years after R. Otto's *Das Heilige* did not think it expedient to incorporate Otto's insights concerning the "altogether different" nature of God. For van der Leeuw sacrifice was a mystical power attached to a gift that established communion between man and god in which reciprocal blessings resulted.

[57] Rudolf Otto, *The Idea of the Holy*, E.T. by John W. Harvey, London, Oxford University Press, 1981, cf. Chapters 1-4. I agree with Wayne Proudfoot that religious experience can not be separated from beliefs, practices and other forms of historical conditioning, see *Religious Experience*, Los Angeles, University of California Press, 1985.

[58] Bolle discusses how the conquest of Alexander the Great rendered the poleis no longer socially, politically, or religiously self sufficient. Alexander was seen as divine figure, to many he was Dionysus, who provided universal appeal to individuals looking beyond their own polis. Bolle also discusses ancient kingship in Egypt, including the non-Egyptian Ptolemies, Kingship in ancient Israel, Japan and India. Bolle made these comments during a lecture at U.C.L.A. in 1986.

[59] *The Idea of the Holy*, p. 53.

[60] Eliade observed, "Yet we must note that even when the celestial gods no longer dominate religious life, the sidereal regions, uranian symbolism, myths and rites of ascent, and the like, retain a predominate place in the economy of the sacred. What is "above," the "high," continues to reveal the transcendent in every religious complex. Driven from the cult and replaced in mythologies by other themes, in the religious life the sky remains ever present by virtue of its symbolism." *The Sacred and the Profane*, p. 128.

[61] Evan M. Zuesse, who is one among many finding flaws in Otto's concept of the holy, points to Otto's failure to mention the use of Qadosh

with reference to common or profane things. Yet this fact does not invalidate Otto's main point concerning the identification of the god of the Hebrews and Jews as "altogether different" or Luther's god for that matter. Besides, the fact that something profane can be temporarily transformed into something holy through ritual also demonstrates why such consecrated things had to be treated with great care and why they were returned to the profane realm.

[62] Eliade, "History of Religions and a New Humanism," in *History of Religions*, vol.1, 1961, p. 6.

[63] Bolle, "*A World of Sacrifice*," p. 55.

[64] In, *Die Religion in Geschichte und Gegenwart*, "Kultus," Tübingen: J.C.B. Mohr, third edition, vol. 4, 1960, p. 121. Mowinckel said that, "Die allgemeinste Kultus handlung ist das Opfer, ein Sammelwort, das einen sehr verschiedenartigen Inhalt deckt und oft sowohl sacrifizielle wie sakramentale Elemente einschließt."

[65] Zuesse based his definition of ritual on Otto and Eliade's premises that "religious persons seek to live in continual contact with those realities" gained from their experience with the "numinous"/"sacred." Zuesse defined ritual as, " those conscious and voluntary, repetitions and styled symbolic bodily actions that are centered oncosmic structure and/or sacred presences." See "Ritual" in *The Encyclopedia of Religion*, vol. 12, p. 405. Zuesse also stipulates that all rituals can be divided into two types, "confirmatory" and "transformatory." Among other things the first type, "brings the transcendental and ordinary realms into relationship while preserving each;" "distinguishes the various species of the sacred from each other;" and "contrasts the polar modes of the sacred, pure, impure" pp. 414-416. The latter type of rituals "serve to bridge the various divisions;" "result from the need to renew;" and "if possible brought into direct contact with transcendence" p. 416. Zuesse's division seems to be unnecessary in view of the fact that neither type could get along with out the other in a religious cult that links up to the transcendent. Zuesse did say in the midst of his description of both

types of rituals that, "Both must exist in any system" p. 414. But he failed to explain why.

⁶⁶ A. Schimmel in, *Die Religion in Geschichte und Gegenwart*, "Opfer," third edition, vol. 4, p. 1638, wrote: "Es versteht sich von selbst, daß die im O. verkörperte Macht nur bestimmten Eingeweihten zugänglich ist: O. darf nicht unbefugt verzehrt, oftmals auch nicht aus dem O. bezirk hinausgenommen werden. Vielfach dürfen nur Männer die O. zerermonien ausführen, und dies nur nach langer sorgfältiger Vorbereitung; daraus hat sich der spezielle Stand des mit allen tabu-Vorschriften vertrauten O. priesters entwickelt."

⁶⁷ Ibid., p. 1637.

⁶⁸ *A World of Sacrifice*, p. 46.

⁶⁹ J. Preston, "Purification," *The Encyclopedia of Religion*, vol. 11, p. 91.

⁷⁰ James Preston, "Purification," *The Encyclopedia of Religion*. vol. 11, p. 95.

⁷¹ Mary Douglas, *Purity and Danger*, pp. 2 ff. See also, "Deciphering a Meal," in C. Geertz, ed., *Myth, Symbol and Culture*, New York, Norton, pp. 61-81, where she draws an association between the table and with the individual in Israel and the nation as symbolic of the distinction between clean and unclean.

⁷² Ibid., p. 40.

⁷³ Ibid., pp. 41 ff.

⁷⁴ Ibid., p. 94 and 96 respectively.

⁷⁵ Ibid., pp. 49-53.

⁷⁶ Ibid., p. 113.

[77] I would insist that the ritual made the lines "clearly defined."

[78] Ibid., p. 159.

[79] Ibid., chapter three.

[80] Ibid., p. 57.

[81] Zuesse reminds us that, "Sociologists and anthropologists who favor such a contrast between ritualistic and rational behavior are usually interested in ritual's socio-cultural functions, in which religious values shrink to social affirmations." Op. cit., p. 405.

[82] Ibid., p. 175.

[83] Preston states that "Anyone who approaches the divinity, either as an intermediary or in a state of deep reverence, is required to perform rites of purification," "Purification," p. 95.

[84] Ibid., pp. 159 ff.

[85] See, Hans H. Penner, "Language, Ritual and Meaning," *Numen*, XXXII, Fasc. 1, 1985, pp. 1-16.

[86] Gerardus van der Leeuw, *Der Mench und Die Religion*, Basel: Haus zum Falken. 1941, pp. 11-17.

[87] See Claude Lévi-Strauss, *Structural Anthropology* (Penguin Books, 1972). Lévi-Strauss applied a method similar to those used in linguistics to study human cultures. His essential method did not vary from the examination of one aspect of social life to another. Also see David Pace, "An Exercise in Structural History: An Analysis of the Social Criticism of Claude Lévi-Strauss," in *Structuralism An Interdisciplinary Study*, edited by Susan Wittig. Pittsburgh: The Pickwick Press, 1975, pp. 38-55.

[88] Terence Hawkes, *Structualism and Semiotics*, Berkeley and Los Angeles: The University of California Press. 1977, p. 41.

[89] See *Signs And Parables, Semiotics and Gospel Texts*. Translated by Gary Philips, The Entrevernes Group, Jean Calloud et. al. Pittsburgh. The Pickwick Press, 1978. See also, *Semiology and Parables*, ed. Daniel Patte. Pittsburgh. The Pickwick Press. 1976. Patte says, "Semiology, the science of signs, aims studying texts and other cultural phenomena in terms of linguistic paradigms as opposed to historical paradigms which characterize traditional exegetical methods. A sentence is meaningful because its linguistic elements are interrelated in a specific way," p. VI, VII.

[90] Staal, *Rules Without Meaning*, New York, Peter Lang, p. 258.

[91] Ibid, p. 451.

[92] Ivan Strenski recently took Staal to task for his inappropriate analogies between human and non-human animal behavior as well as his premise involving the role of evolution in human rituals. See *What's Rite? Evolution, Exchange and The Big Picture*, in *Religion, 21*, 1991, pp. 219-225.

[93] Staal, "The Meaninglessness of Ritual," in *Numen, International Review for the History of Religions*, ed. by M. Heerme Van Voss. Leiden: E. J. Brill, 1979, p. 3.

[94] Ibid., p. 3.

[95] Ibid., p. 4.

[96] Staal defines ritual as, "a system of acts and sounds, related to each other in accordance with rules without reference to meaning," see *Rules Without Meaning*, p. 433.

[97] Ibid., p. 6.

⁹⁸ Ibid., p. 8. This is the problem for Otto's "altogether different" category of the holy.

⁹⁹ Ibid., p. 8.

¹⁰⁰ Ibid., p. 17.

¹⁰¹ SB VI. I.2.36.

¹⁰² We have already discussed the connection between Rita and the sacrifice and the maintenance of the cosmos, see supra, chap. 1.

¹⁰³ Catherine Bell, *Ritual Theory Ritual Practice*, New York, Oxford University Press, 1992, p. 25.

¹⁰⁴ Ibid, p. 25.

¹⁰⁵ Ibid, p. 43.

¹⁰⁶ Stanley.J. Tambiah, "A Performative Approach to Ritual." *Proceedings of the British Academy* 65, 1979, pp. 120, 142 respectively.

¹⁰⁷ Karl Löwith, *Meaning in History*, Chicago. The University of Chicago Press, 1949, p. 5.

¹⁰⁸ *Rig Veda* V.67.4; IX.73.6. Quoted from H. Lefever in, *The Vedic Idea of Sin*, p. 5.

¹⁰⁹ *Rig Veda* I.62.2. Ibid. p. 10.

¹¹⁰ Ibid., p. 22.

¹¹¹ See op. cit. p. 21.

¹¹² See, Pâpam, "wicked;" Agah, "sin;" Arâti, "non giver;" Asatya "untruthful," "unfaithful;" Dureva, "evil lives;" Enah, "sin" (act of aggression); Pâka, ignorance; Rip,"deceit;" Hvr, "to be crooked" (with

Pari "to be entangled"); Dhvarah, "deceitful;" and Anrita, "untruthful," "against order." See Lefever, pp. 17 ff. and Bergaigne, Vol. 3, pp. 184 ff, for text references and discussion of these terms. Lefever also said, "There is in the Rigveda three pairs of contrary terms, by which the distinction between right and wrong is normally expressed. The distinction is viewed as one between "straight" and "crooked," "single" and "double," and "true" and "false." It is evident that these are simply three different modes of expressing the distinction between action which is in conformity with the "straight path of rita" and that which is opposed to it." p. 31.

[113] *Rig Veda* X.97.

[114] Thite, p. 61.

[115] Lefever said concerning this point that, "Just as in the *Rgveda* action contrary to Rita could rightly be termed "sin," so in the *Brâhmanas* the term can be applied to action contrary to the Transcendent Reality, - satya." p. 61. Later he commented that, "In the three terms, Rita, Satya, and Brahman, the basic conception is the same. They represent different stages of an attempt to envisage the principle of the universe" , p. 73.

[116] Miller, p. 556.

[117] SB I.2.3.4.

[118] Brian Smith, "God and Men in Vedic Ritualism: Toward a Hierarchy of Resemblance," *History of Religions*, Vol. 24, Number 4, May 1985, p. 294.

[119] See *Rig Veda* IV. 54.3; X.15.6.

[120] Lefever said, "The idea of sin that is found in the Upanishads then, may be described as that of a "failure to be real," i.e., to be one's true Self- as against the more familiar conception of sin as merely a "failure to do right" p. 86. Lefever here seems to lessen the force of sacrifice as

an important concept in the Upanisads. They place of Atman must be understood as a transcendent model fashioned after Rita and Yajña.

[121] Quoted from, Thite, p. 121.

[122] Cf. *Rig Veda* VII.57.5; X.13.4.

[123] SB IX.5.1.12,13,16a,18.

[124] The SB equates "truth" (Satya) with the Vedas. See Eggeling's footnote on verse 18, p. 258, vol. XLIII, *Sacred Books of the East*.

[125] We remember that Prajâpati in the *Brâhmanas* took the place of the Purusa in the *Rig Veda*, see Eggeling's introduction to *The Sacred Books of the East*, p. XV. Miller says that Rita was present in the primeval Yajña, op. cit. p. 207. Panikkar said that, "The sacrifice of the Cosmic Man signifies divine transcendence investing humanity." R. Panikkar, *The Vedic Experience*, London, Darton, Longman & Todd, 1977, p. 348.

[126] Levi thought that the Brâhmanas revealed a "moral tendency," op. cit. p. 21. It would perhaps be more consistent with the total scope of the notion of sin in Vedic literature to say that these type of sins distracted one from the sacred texts and the performance of the sacrifice and later on inhibited meditation.

[127] *Rig Veda* 1.147.4; 1.150.2.

[128] Op. cit. p.66.

[129] Cf. SB. XII.6.1ff.

[130] *Le Sacrifice dans L'Inde Ancienne*, p. 157.

[131] *The Vision* of *Cosmic Order*, p. 203. Lefever wrote, "The sacrifice being, normally at least to the gods, mans contact with this mysterious power is regarded as contact with the gods." p. 63. Miller said this was, "direct contact with his god," op. cit. p. 215.

[132] See SB. XI.5.3.8-12.

[133] This follows Joachim Wach's premise that religious cognition does not fully exist prior to its cultic expression.

[134] SB III.1.1.8,10 ; also cf., III.1.1.1.

[135] See SB 2.2.2.6.

[136] J. Gonda, *Change and Continuity in Indian Religion*, London, Mouton & Co, 1965, p. 336.

[137] Sylvain Lévi, *La Doctrine du Sacrifice dans Les Brâhmanas*, ed. Ernst Leroux. Paris, 1898, p. 103.

[138] Sacrifice was considered one of the main manifestations of Rta according to Max Müller, see *Sacred Books of the East*, vol. XLVI, p. 328, note 2 on *Rig Veda* IV.3.4. "Thou who art well-intentioned, give heed to this our toiling, to this Rita, O Observer of Rita!"

[139] The Brâhmanas show a tendency to de-emphasize the importance of the gods in the sacrifice. Such a case does not interfere with the notion of mutual responsibilities between humans and the gods to sacrifice, nor does it mitigate the importance of transcendence and immanence in the sacrifice. The demands of ritual exactitude and purity became even greater in the Brâhmanic period. See SB XI.2.6.13-14 where the "self-offerer" surpasses the "god-offerer" because of his "new body" formed by the "sacrifice."

[140] B. Smith wrote in connection with this idea that, "...despite first appearance, men and gods were kept ontologically distinct within a hierarchical order of mutually resembling, but fundamentally separate, forms. The divine self and the resembling counterparts were unconstricted prototypical models, not true equals ofthem." From his article in the *History of Religions*, vol. 24, no. 4, 1985, p. 292.

[141] SB XIII.5.4.1b.

[142] SB XIII.5.4.3b.

[143] SB XII.6.1.2.

[144] SB XI.5.3.7; 8-12.

[145] Lefever, p. 68.

[146] See SB XII.6.1.2ff.

[147] KSS XXV.

[148] *Sacrifice: Its Nature and Function*, p. 22.

[149] J. C. Heesterman, *The Inner Conflict of Tradition*, p. 27.

[150] See I.133.1a. "The verb Pû, 'to purify', is used with both the word Yajña and Rita as reflected in the sacrifice." This verse from the *Rig Veda* was quoted from Miller op. cit. p. 221.

[151] TS.1.2.2.1, quoted from *Change and Continuity*, p. 363.

[152] Most scholars think that the Dîksâ entered the corpus of Vedic rituals at a late date. However, Gonda, says that initiation rites similar to the Vedic Dîksâ are to be found elsewhere in the Indo-Iranian sources. Gonda also believes that the Dîksâ existed in the age of the *Rig Veda* see *Change and Continuity*, p. 349 ff.

[153] See Alfred Hillebrant, "Ritual-Literatur Vedishe Opfer und Zauber," *Grundiss Der Indo-Arischen Philogie Und Altertumskunde*, G. Bühler, vol. 3, no. 2. Strassburg: Verlag von Karl J. Trübner, 1897, p. 1.

[154] *Religion and its Manifestation*, vol. II, p. 343.

[155] Heesterman, p. 27.

[156] See X.21.7. Krick, *Das Ritual der Feuergründung*, Wien, Verlage: Der Österreichischen Akademie Der Wissenshaften, ed. G. Oberhammer, vol. 399, no. 16, 1982, p. 119.

[157] See SB VII.2.4ff and *Mâitrâyanî-Samhitâ* III.2.3; 18.6-10.

[158] MS III.6.2.

[159] See SB VII.1.1.9-11. For more information on the use of sand and other sacrificial materials see Krick op. cit. chapter 4, in reference to sand see pp. 120-123.

[160] See SB VII.1.1.9. See Eggeling's note on this verse.

[161] SB VII.1.1.7.

[162] See Krick op. cit. p. 123.

[163] See Krick who said that, "Die Wasser sind der opferwürdige, reine (Besitz) der Erde, sie wurden jene (Wasser des Himmels; im Mond?). Die Saltzerde ist der opferwürdige, reine (Besitz) des Himmels, sie wurde diese (Salzerde auf Erden)." Ibid., p. 129.

[164] *Rig Veda* IX.83.1a; VII.13.3.

[165] Potdar, *Sacrifice in the Rigveda*, Bombay, Bharatiya Vidya Bhavan, 1953, p. 100.

[166] When the Vedas are compared to the Avesta scholars have found that the ritual fire played an important role even in the Indo-Iranian cult. See Gonda, *Die Religionen Indiens*, vol. 1, p. 71.

[167] Agni or, Ignis in Latin, Ogni in Slavic.

[168] Op. cit. p. 317.

[169] SBE, The *Sutta-Nipata*, vol. 12, p. 315.

[170] Gonda, *Vedic Literature*, vol. 1, p. 234.

[171] See Krick p. 278.

[172] Smith said, "The human sacrificer does not end the ritual at its highest point but rather embarks on the second half of the procedure, regarded as a descent from this world the sacrificer has so laboriously won. Heaven, having been attained, is quickly renounced," op. cit. p. 297.

[173] Bergainge, vol. 3, p. 165 ff. This term was used in reference to those who sought "liberation" from the "nooses of Varuna," the phrase that expressed the idea of sin in the Vedas. See, *Change and Continuity*, p. 317.

[174] Op. cit. p. 46 ff.

[175] See KB VII.7, quoted from B. Smith op. cit. p. 294.

[176] Special places were set aside for vessels and materials that were used in the ritual from day to day. Since these elements possessed a sanctity they had to be protected from contact with the profane realm until the end of the sacrifice. Renou said, "Des places fixes sont prévues pour le brahman, le yajamâna et son espouse, ainsi que pour les euax <<amenees>> et pour le tetre qui reÇoit les rebuts." See *L'Inde Classique*, p. 349.

[177] Op. cit. p. 47, 46. As part of the Haviryajñâh Somâh the Darsa ritual purified sacrificial utensils and the consecrated water was carried from the Gârhaptya fire to the Ahavanîya fire, see Gonda, *The Haviryajñâh Somâh*.

[178] *Vedic Ritual*, p. 172.

[179] See A. B. Keith, *The Religion and Philosophy of the Veda and Upanishads*, vol. 31 in, The Harvard Oriental Series, ed. Charles Rockwell Lanman, Cambridge, Harvard University Press, 1925, p. 286.

The spits that held the victim's sacrificial parts were not burned but secretly buried because it "must not be laid on the earth or water," p. 286.

[180] See SB IV.4.5.9-10.

[181] Thite op. cit. pp. 171-173.

[182] Hermann Oldenberg, *Die Religion des Veda*, Berlin, Wilhelm Hertz, 1894, cf. pp. 407-410. Part of his argument reads, "...dass nach dem ursprünglichen Sinn es nicht Sünde und Unreinheit, sondern die anhaftenden Spuren übernatürlicher Potenzen waren, von denen das Bad lösen sollte.," p. 408.

[183] Keith. *The Religion and Philosophy of the Vedas and Upanishads*, Vol. 31, p. 303.

[184] See Gonda, *Vedic Ritual*, chap. 4, where he discusses this phenomenon with examples of transferring powers, good or bad, by means of the hands, through garments, eating certain substances etc.

[185] SB I.2.5.4.

[186] The Ahavavnîya fire was called the world of the gods, (cf. SB. VII.3.1.10), and the Gârhapatya fire was related to the world of humans, (see SB. VII.3.1.10; IX.2.3.14).

[187] Ashes were used to purify the sacrificial utensils and transferred a special power. See Gonda, *Vedic Ritual*, pp. 171ff.

[188] *Taittirîya Samhitâ* VI.6.4.2, quoted from Thite, op. cit., p. 129.

[189] SB VI.8.2.1 ff.

## CHAPTER THREE

# THE EXAMPLE OF THE ASHVAMEDHA

The Ashvamedha or Horse sacrifice in Ancient India illustrates the problem of transcendence and immanence in the ritual act.[1] Special attention shall be given to the role of the religious symbolism in the Ashvamedha as this ritual intersected with its social and political constituents.

The textual sources for the Ashvamedha include a variety of ancient witnesses in India as well as other Indo-European societies.[2] The Horse sacrifice first appeared in Vedic literature in the *Rig Veda*, Hymns I.162 and I.163, as a complex ritual but somewhat different from the accounts in later texts.[3] The most obvious variation found showed that the *Rig Veda* did not give a long list of victims but only mentioned the goat and the horse.[4] An expanded form of this earlier sacrifice ultimately held a significant position in the *Taittirîya-,*[5]*Kathka-, Vâjasaneyi-,*[6] *Maitrâyana-Samhitâ.*

The *Black* and *White Yajurveda* give evidence of the different schools that incorporated the Ashvamedha into their canons of Shruti.[7] The Ashvamedha in the *White Yajurveda* takes up a major part of the *Vâjasaneyisamhitâ* and the *Shrautasûtra* of the *Kâtyâyana* while including many other sacrifices as well. The *White Yajurvedas* carefully separated Mantra and Brâhmana and in several cases preferred the *Rig Veda's* recension. On the other hand, the *Black Yajurveda* placed the Mantras and *Brâhmanas* together in many instances and did not follow the *Rig Veda* closely.[8] P. E. Dumont had also recognized a basic difference in the style between the *White* and *Black Yajurvedas.*[9]

The *Shatapatha-(*XIII), *Taittirîa-* and *Pancavinsa-Brâhmana* (XII-XXV) provided mystical explanations for this sacrifice that had become extremely complicated in the Brahmanic period. Both the *Jaiminîya-*(II.266 ff.) and *Tândya-Mahâ-Brâhmana* (XXI.4.1 ff.)

classified the Ashvamedha as a Trirâtra-sacrifice or modified Soma sacrifice that lasted three days.[10]

The *Sûtras* of the *Yajurvedas* as well as the *Vaitana Sûtras*[11] *of* the *Atharvaveda* devoted themselves to the description of various minute details of the Ashvamedha. The *Kâtyâyana Shrauta Sûtra* of the *Yajurveda*, for example, described the Ashvamedha sacrifice from the view point of the Adhvaryu priest.[12] The *Sutra* of the *Yajurveda* are particularly interesting because this Veda provided so much elementary information about the Shrauta sacrifices.[13] The accounts of the sacrifice in the *Sûtras* agreed with the *Yajurveda* and the *Sâmaveda* and were even closer in agreement to the *Samhîtâs*. The *Rig Veda*, while different, does not represent an all encompassing change.[14] Renou said of the relationship between the *Rig Veda* and later accounts of the Ashvamedha that, "Sans doute y a-t-il un accord général entre les Sûtra d'une part, les Brâmana ou même le Yajurveda de l'autre. En revanche, le ritual contemporain du Rig Veda, celui les que hymnes laissent inférer, devait être quelque peu different du ritual des Sûtra."[15]

Thus the Ashvamedha represents the development of Vedic sacrifice over several centuries and contains many of Ancient India's most common rites. The variety of Indian literature that undertook some aspect of the Ashvamedha reveals that this archaic religious tradition not only sought to know exactly how to perform the sacrifice but also pondered every element in the sacrifice as if it had a direct correlation to the ultimate mystery behind the universe. In essence these two concerns, the former liturgical and the latter mythological, represent one symbolic quest that was characteristic of Vedic religion. The desire to align all of life with the transcendent Rita, Satya, and Brahman by means of the sacrifice permeated every level of Ancient India's culture. In this manner the sacrifice helped shape the notion of Dharma and its long history of concern for proper duty or custom.

The Ashvamedha falls under the category of the Shrauta or solemn sacrifices and therefore differs from the Grihya or domestic sacrifices. In the first place the Shrauta sacrifices required three sacred fires in contrast to the one fire of the domestic rite. The Gârhapatya fire was the only fire that was perpetually kept and served both the domestic and solemn ceremonies. Fire was taken out of the Gârhapatya altar to ignite the other two sacrificial fires. This fire served to prepare food for the sacrifice. The spherically shaped Gârhapatya fire altar represented the earth. The four cornered Ahavanîya altar was used to receive most of the prepared offerings. This fire represented the four directional sky and the fire of heaven. The Dakshina fire served to ward off evil spirits and sometimes conveyed offerings to dead ancestors. The Vedi altar had a rectangular shape with convex sides and was situated between the other altars, most likely to protect it from profane contact. The Vedi received obligatory substances of which the gods came to eat while seated around the Vedi on special grass (Barhis). This sacrificial grass facilitated the purpose of protection against contact with the profane.

The relationship between the Gârhapatya and Ahavanîya occupied a significant place in the symbolic framework of sacrifice at large. Offerings ceremoniously taken from the Gârhapatya altar and moved eastwardly to the Ahavanîya fire served to symbolize the transmission of gifts from earth to heaven. The vital link between both worlds and the essential trip to heaven took place in this basic symbolic gesture as well as through other more particular parts of the entire sacrifice.

During a major Shrauta ritual the four altars mentioned above stood to the west of the sacrificial grounds and formed a part of a very complex sacrificial compound. These compounds were prepared especially for a particular sacrifices such as the Ashvamedha. To the east, north and south stood special stations along which the qualified participants ceremoniously traveled while carrying out their particular liturgical duties. These specialized duties conformed to the various prescribed rites. The sacrificial compound also contained important sheds that seated different participants that at times included the sacrificer's wife. In this manner those who aided in the performance of the ritual could be set apart from the profane world that remained outside the parameters of the sacrificial grounds. Special containers also housed sacrificial materials while they were not in use. Here again, the concern was to protect sanctified elements, whose profane nature had been transformed for use in the ritual, from any illicite contact with unconsecrated objects. At the far eastern end of the compound stood the "high altar" (Uttaravedi) that was built during the Agnicayana ceremony. This altar had from five to seven courses or layers of bricks built in the shape of a bird. Like the sacrificial compound that contained this great altar every part of its construction and final form took on an important mythological interpretation in the *Brâhmanas*. For example, the bricks numbered three hundred and sixty to represent the year. Furthermore, the construction of the layers symbolized the creation by Prajâpati and his restoration by Agni. The actual layers themselves stood for the relationship between the earth, the atmosphere and the heavenly realm.[16] The significance of the sacrificial compound abided both in the symbolic positions and dimensions of its components and also in the dynamic movement in specific directions from one area to another. The Rshis gave great attention to directional movements in the ritual.[17] The importance of these symbolic gestures stems from their correlation to mythological motifs. Many of the gestures and directional movements of Shrauta rituals symbolized the ascent to heaven.[18] Many other such procedures directed towards the east were patterned after the course of the sun. These typical directional movements were often accompanied with *Mantras* or *Brâhmanas* that mentioned the distance, whether near or far, the sacrificer was to a particular deity or the world of heaven. Such ritual organization, division, and making endless categories contitutes what Brian K. Smith calls "classifing the universe."[19]

In the domestic rites the head of a household could perform the sacrifices,[20] whereas only highly trained priests were allowed to officiate in the solemn rites. In some cases priests numbering up to sixteen managed different parts of the sacrifice.[21] The Shrauta sacrifices developed with greater attention to detail along with the priesthood from early Vedic religion. Initially the Hotri priest was the most important priest in the ritual because he recited mantras during the performance of the rite.[22] These mantras based upon the Rig Vedic hymns were believed to carry the power of Brahman. This neuter term was thought to be that very force that caused the sacrifices to be effective. As emphasis on the performance of the sacrifice increased so did the role of the Advaryu priest who carried out the manual tasks of the sacrifice. The Advaryu's function came to incorporate the recital of prose verses during his ritual procedures that later produced the *Yajurveda Samhitâ*. Another priest called Udgatri specialized in singing the precise sounds of the Sâman during Soma sacrifices which produced the *Sâmaveda Sanhitâ*. At the height of Vedic sacrifice, during the Brâhmanic period, a Brahmin priest supplemented these three priests. The Brahmin supervised the entire sacrifice from a vantage point seated near the sacred fires and only intervened when ritual mistakes occurred.[23] In this case the Brahmin performed the required expiation for such offenses.[24] He thus received his name from the neuter term Brahman (see above) that designated this sacred power.

The role of the priests in the solemn ceremonies served to insure that every possible precaution had been taken to successfully gain the world of heaven for the sacrificer. Therefore, the primary concern for these priests involved the preparation of an environment suitable for the gods who needed to be present at the sacrifice.[25] The importance of these priests became increasingly evident as the demands for their own purity grew with the complexity of the sacrifices.

The Shrauta sacrifices were divided into various types. The simplest Shrauta sacrifice was the Agnihotra that priests daily performed at dawn and at twilight.[26] Other basic Shrauta sacrifices included seasonal rites, the Câturmâsya, first-fruits ceremonies, the Agrayana, and the praise to Agni held once a year in the spring, the Agnistoma. Besides serving as manuals for the sacrifices the Shrauta sûtras had also established distinctions between the Shrauta sacrifices. The Ishti[27] sacrifice was a non-animal type that used milk, butter, cereal, and cakes. The Pasubandha sacrifices used animals[28] and the Soma[29] formed yet another type of Shrauta sacrifice. Keith stated that, "Each sacrifice is divided into Pradhânas, the characteristics which mark it out as a special offering, and Añgas, the auxiliary parts which are common to many sacrifices, and which build the framework, Tantra, which serves to maintain the sacrifice."[30] A major ritual such as the Ashvamedha would have included all three types of these vedic rituals in their assorted forms.

## 3:1 A Description of the Ashvamedha

The total ceremony of the Ashvamedha lasted over a year with the actual rites surrounding the sacrifice of the chosen horse taking only three days.[31] The Ashvamedha was one of three royal sacrifices in Ancient India.[32] Performance of this great sacrifice required a victorious king, his three wives, hundreds of attendants, a swift steed with special markings,[33] the special sacrificial grounds near a large quantity of water supplied with a myriad of ritual utensils and materials. The Horse sacrifice also required all four types of priests mentioned above. Only the victorious king could perform the Ashvamedha.

If we view the Ashvamedha as a symbolic journey that began on earth and gradually moved to heaven by means of the sacrifice we find that not only the king and his realm but also the gods benefited from this journey to the heavenly world. Along the way multifarious rites emphasized the difference between the two worlds and the difficulty of attaining the world of heaven. This difficulty was evidenced in part by the purification demands of everyone and everything involved. Yet at the same time the texts convey the necessity of going to the trouble to perform this costly sacrifice. Nothing was rushed or overlooked as the profane aligned itself with the sacred. Every step to unite the two worlds was judiciously taken according to sacrificial protocol. Finally, and again by further ritual actions, this union was just as decisively abrogated and both worlds returned to their respective stations with no depletion of the distance that stood between them a year earlier. Just as the Ashvamedha had to be performed on this occasion it would have to be repeated. But not because the sacrifice had failed, on the contrary, it persisted precisely because it had been successful.

In order to fully appreciate the symbolic scheme of the Ashvamedha we should see it in relationship to its preparation and concluding rites. In other words, to view it within its entire sacrificial structure and not as some conglomerate of Shrauta rites arbitrarily attached to the Ashvamedha. Although the Ashvamedha served a particular purpose in Ancient Indian life it also participated in the grand or cosmic scheme of Vedic religion and therefore shared much in common with the design of other Shrauta rites. Eggeling said that, "Like the Râjasûya, or inauguration of a king, the Ashvamedha is not a mere sacrifice or series of offerings, but it is rather a great state function in which the religious and sacrificial element is closely and deftly interwoven with a varied programme of secular ceremonies."[34] I hope to illustrate these points with the following description of the Ashvamedha before attempting a specific interpretation.

The Sâmgrahani Ishti introduced the entire ritual, and like all of the new or full moon ceremonies this rite had a special significance for the events that followed.[35] The rite involved giving boiled rice to the priests, the king, his four wives, and their four hundred attendants. The king shaved his hair, cut his nails and beard, washed his teeth, bathed, and put on a new garment before he participated in this rite. That night the king was required to remain at the Gâhapatya fire with his queen but in sexual abstinence.[36] During the Ishti offering a Brahmin lute player sang verses he composed about the victories won by the sacrificing king and concerning the nature of the gifts.[37] At sunrise the Brahmaudana occurred.[38]

The *Kâtyâyana* claimed, on the basis of Shruti, that one should perform a sacrifice only after specific new or full moon rites.[39] By this same authority the establishment of the sacred fires could only follow new or full moon rites (cf. *Kâtyâyana Shrauta Sûtra* 7.1.1). The rites of the new and full moon symbolized the "chariot of the gods" by which the sacrificer "safely" attained the world of heaven (cf. AB 2.37; JB 1.129f; KB 2.6.; 5.10; 7,7). "One should not perform a Soma sacrifice unless one has already performed the sacrifices of the full and new moon."[40] Take note of the concern for purity in these few lines from the *Taittiriya Samhitâ*:

O Agni, guard the offering. Let the god Savitr purify you, with a filter that has no flaw, with the rays of the bright sun. Ye divine waters, that go in front and first purify, forward lead this sacrifice, place in front the lord of sacrifice.

I sprinkle you agreeable to Agni, to Agni and Soma. Be ye pure for the divine rite, for the sacrifice to the gods. The Raksas is shaken off, the evil spirits are shaken off.[41]

Futhermore, the *Shatapatha Brâhmana* stipulated that only after a new or full moon sacrifice could one free oneself from evil,[42] and thus qualify to participate in the ritual. This Ishti preparation rite helped make the world of heaven accessible by beginning the consecration that would gradually intensify throughout the ritual until heaven had been attained. The fact that other Shrauta rites could only be performed after the Ishti shows the increasing standard of sanctity required as the ceremony proceeded to the height of its sacredness when the victim actually made contact with the deity. The Ishti rites marked off the beginning moment of the ritual when time was itself transformed from profane to sacred time.

The next morning the chosen horse was bound and led to a body of water. The binding of the horse had an important symbolic purpose. It intentionally corresponded to the myth of the first horse sacrifice that Prajâpati produced[43] where the Ashvins bound the horse.[44] The rope used to bind the horse measured twelve cubits which represented the months of the year plus one additional cubit to identify the Ashvamedha with the bull.[45] The twelve cubit rope of the Ashvamedha incorporated all seasons of the year and the additional thirteenth cubit made a complete sacrifice by identifying this sacrifice with the bull.[46]

The SB identified the symbolism of the rope as part of the an indispensible "formula" that helped make the first horse sacrifice "successful" and therefore had to be repeated if subsequent horse sacrifices were to have the same results. The SB reads:

> Now, unsuccessful in the sacrifice, assuredly, is what is performed without a formula. "This rope did they take, at the first age of the truth, [the sages, at the rites : it hath been with us at this Soma-sacrifice, declaring the course in the gaining of the truth]," he takes the halter of the horse in order to supply a formula for the success of the sacrifice. It (the rope) is twelve cubits long,- twelve months make a year : it is the year, the sacrifice, he secures (XIII.1.2.1.).

This mythological identification of the rope with the first Ashvamedha in which the sacrificer secured the sacrifice was yet another of the many preparation rites.[47] The rope not only served to limit the movement of the horse while it went through further consecration[48] but it also served to proscribe the boundary in which time itself was consecrated for the performance ritual. The same notion of the rope was applied spatially to "all the quarters" in order to symbolically demarcate the extent of the sacrificer's influence through the Ashvamedha.[49] The text also attached a special purifying property to this rope. "The rope consists of Darbha grass (Poa Cynosuroides) ; -for Darbha stalks are a means of purification : he thus purifies that (horse), and immolates it as one purified and meet for sacrifice" (SB XIII.1.1.2). The Rhsis of the Brâhmanic period patterned all of these preliminary, symbolic actions after the same "truth" that the gods followed in the first horse sacrifice.[50]

After tying the horse at the water hole the priest sprinkled the horse while it stood in the water.[51] The sprinkling was done in the names of several gods in association with all four compass directions and in the names of all of the gods in association with all three realms, earth, atmosphere and heaven.[52] The horse was thus prepared or consecrated for all directions and realms. This universal scope of the horse's influence over all was matched by all creature's and the god's dependence on the horse sacrifice. The texts presented a portrayal of the Ashvamedha in which the entire cosmos depended upon this sacrifice according to the texts.[53]

During this rite a peculiar thing happened. A man from a low class killed a "four-eyed dog" with a club made of Sidhraka wood. The most prevalent idea among the various modern explanations for this strange part of the ceremony at the pond equated the four-eyed dog with evil threatening the sacrificer from all four directions of the cosmos.[54]

This conception of the four-eyed dog seems to best fit the general concern for "order" that so characterized Vedic thought and the performance of sacrifice.[55]

After the above dedication and consecration of the horse to Prajâpati and the other gods it was released in a north-eastern direction.[56] The horse then wandered throughout the country side for an entire year. The horse's release and subsequent meandering about for a year may sound like the ritual proceedings had reached some type of sabbatical in which the horse's activities became totally independent from the ritual compound and its activities. In actuality nothing could be have been further from the truth. Before the horse embarked on his journey he was led back to the sacred fire where Ishti offerings were made to Savitri for three more days. The *Shatapatha Brâhamna* interpreted these offerings to Savitr as a means to be able to find the horse.

They (the Ishtis) belong to Savitri; for Savitri is this (earth): if any one hides himself thereon, if any one goes elsewhere, it is on this (earth) that they find him; for no one (creature), whether walking erect or horizontally (like an animal), is able to go beyond it. Their belonging to Savitri thus is in order to find the horse (XIII.1.4.2.).

It would seem logical that this rite was meant to provide an additional measure of protective, magical control over the horse. But the fact that four hundred youths of equivalent rank guarded the horse during its wandering and four hundred horses also accompanied it from the moment it left the sacrificial grounds makes the notion of magical control somewhat superfluous.[57] The central reason for performing these Ishtis rested on the fact that Prajâpati had originally found the horse by performing Ishtis.[58]

Before the horse left the Adhvaryu also instructed it to, "Go along the way of the Adityas!", because the Adityas protected the four quarters and would therefore guard the horse in every direction it wandered.[59]

Once on its way the horse was the subject of constant ritual activity at the sacrificial compound. For example, priests performed Dhrti offerings in the evenings to protect the horse during the night.[60] The *Shatapatha Brâhmana* referred to these Dhrtis offerings as the "horse's chain" so that "whence the horse, when let loose, does not (entirely) abandon its chain."[61] In this way the ritual extended a perpetual link with the horse which not only sought its safe return at the end of the appointed time but also made sure that every movement of the horse came under the auspices of the ritual or heavenly control, ie. Prajâpati's primordial horse sacrifice. During each day of that year the Adhvaryu offered three Ishtis in the morning, mid-day, and in the afternoon.[62]

The young men were armed with various weapons for protecting the horse as it rambled about without a rider. But they also had specific instructions that went beyond the ordinary safety of the horse. For example, they were not to allow the sacrificial horse to have intercourse with any mares. They were also to prevent this horse from getting into the water.[63] Such provisions must have been aimed at maintaining the special sanctity that the horse received from the consecration rites performed prior to its departure from the sacrificial grounds.[64] The consecration of the horse played an essential part in its travels throughout the country side because the horse was also symbolically correlated to the entire cosmos. Consequently, this sanctified horse could not come into contact with anything that would reduce the power of its mission within the total scope of ritual and its purposes.

Another important ritual activity that happened at the sacrificial compound while the horse wandered was the telling of the Pâriplava stories. The priests and the sacrificer sat on golden thrones while the Hotri told tales of ancient kings, retold myths, recited Vedic poetry, taught traditions of the Vedas, and spoke of other ancient mysteries to a crowd of visitors.[65] These narratives lasted ten days and were then repeated in cycles for the remainder of the year.[66]

The particular mythological themes of the ten days are worth mentioning here. On the first day the Hotri told of King Manu Vaivasvata whose father was Sûrya, the sun.[67] The ancient race of kings in India could trace their ancestry back to the sun[68] as a part of valorizing the king during the Ashvamedha. Manu was also known as the name given to the fourteen progenitors of the human race who each ruled a period of time called Manvantara. By the time of the Ashvamedha the universe had already gone through six periods of destruction and creation. This cosmic destruction usually came about from a great flood from which Manu Vaivasvata escaped with the help of a fish.[69] The rich mythological heritage surrounding Manu gave the priest an assortment of texts to share and relate to the king in Ashvamedha. The first day also provided another important mythological theme of recreating the cosmos through destruction and death in which the solar kings had always played a crucial role.

117

The second day of the Pâriplava cycle told of yet another key mythological figure by the name of Yama.[70] "'King Yama Vaivasvata,' he (the Hotri) says, 'his people are the Fathers, and they are staying here; old men have come thither : it is these he instructs.'"[71] Since Yama was the first human born in the age of perfection when all humans lived to be one hundred years old, he became the first human to die. As such Yama was considered the lord of the dead and the one who knew the way to the afterlife.[72] The second day drew attention to the honor of the ancestors and the desire of long life, both of which the Pâriplava rite tied to the Ashvamedha.[73]

The third day highlighted the young as "King Varuna Aditya spoke.[74]

The fourth day's Pâriplava legend followed three offerings. This happened everyday and continued with the same opening exchange between the Hotri and the Adhvaryu. This particular day dealt with the beautiful mythological maidens called the Apsaras. The imagery seemed to involve the association of opposites since the Apsaras were water vapors that rose toward the sun.[75] One narrative told how Urvasi, an Apsara, was rescued by a mortal king, Purûravas, and who then fell in love with her.[76] One night the king lost Urvasi through the trickery of the Apsaras' companions, the Gandharvas. Upon eventually finding her again the king was given one request by these same beings who had originally separated the two lovers. The king asked to live with Urvasi for all time. But this request amounted to an impossibility because King Purûravas was not a Gandharva. A fire sacrifice ultimately solved the problem in this legend and reinforced the applicability of the sacrifice for the audience at hand.[77]

The fifth day concerned the "Knowledge of Serpents" which was thought to have been associated with certain ancient medicines used for healing.[78] Even these "healing powers" came under the scrutiny of the ritual. The ability to heal or the knowledge to work "charms" belonged to the same cosmological forces that the sacrifice produced, restored and maintained.

On the sixth day instructions were given about Devaganavidyâ, or demonology.[79]

The seventh day centered on the Asuras who opposed the gods and were known from the *Rig Veda* as those who tried to impair the sacrifice.[80] The sixth and seventh days encompassed the evil forces which also fell under the universal authority of the sacrifice.

On the eight day the priest retold legends about kings and gods.[81] One of these kings of the Matsyas by the name of Dhvasan Dvaitavana offered an Ashvamedha following his victorious battle.[82] The king offering the Ashvamedha had to be a victorious ruler.

King Târkshya Vaipasyata appeared in the stories of the ninth day.[83] Ancient mythology had personified Târksya as the sun in the form of a bird and horse.[84] The horse had long symbolized the sun in Ancient India and was thought to have been the source of the fire.[85] The Ashvamedha horse represented the swift solar steed who was first mounted by Indra and subsequently by all earthly kings who offered an Ashvamedha.[86]

The tenth day of the cycle of legends introduced Srotriyas or theologians who in all likelihood discussed and debated various meanings of the previous days' stories and their relation to the Ashvamedha.[87]

The Pâriplava cycle integrated several popular stories into the daily rites that occurred all year long while the horse roamed free. Aside from mere entertainment, the Pâriplava ritual served to connect the king with his glorious and victorious lineage of the past. The present victorious king could in turn extend his beneficial influences over all his realm and further through the auspices of the Ashvamedha. Thus the sacrifice covered every vital aspect of social and political life by linking the world of men with the heavenly world. The Pâriplava ritual used mythology to indicate the intricate relationship between the socio-political entities and the transcendent mysteries that took place during the course of the Ashvamedha. Even the seemingly meaningless wanderings of the horse had some significance for everyone under the domain of the king.

Clearly the sacrificial compound remained a busy place the entire time that the horse wandered. The ritual activities during that period deliberately followed the myth of Prajâpati and the primordial horse sacrifice. The rites centered at the sacrificial compound served to link the daily movement of the horse on earth with its transcendent model. This symbolic connection between what happen in primordial time with the horse's movements on earth made the ritual participation of the king and his entourage indispensible. The horse never escaped the authority and sphere of the ritual's guidelines even while outside of the physical parameters of the sacrificial center. The horse, the ritual participants, and the world of Heaven all continued together in mutual cooperation during the interlude of the horse's absence.

When the horse returned to the sacrificial compound further preparations took place before the actual horse-sacrifice occurred. These preparation rites focused on the sacrificer, the construction of the high altar or the Agnicayana, and the horse. All three of these central ritual elements formed an important symbolic portrayal of the essence behind the Ashvamedha.

The Dîkshâ associated with the Ashvamedha lasted seven days and included Vaisvadeva and Audgrabhana oblations in addition to the Agnicayana on the seventh day.[88] The sacrificing king underwent the Dîkshâ ceremony which consecrated him for the sacrifice.[89] Up until this point in the ritual the king had been identified with his ancient linage of human kings. But through the transforming powers of the Dîkshâ ceremony the king was now declared to be with the gods, and soon afterwards the king would be identified with Prajâpati himself.

The king's identification with the great Prajâpati occurred just before the ritual approached the height of its sacredness; viz. in the three days of Soma pressing at which time the horse was killed and offered upon the high altar.[90] The *Brâhmanas* make it perfectly clear that the sacrificer followed Prajâpati's example in the course of the Dîkshâ. Just as Prajâpati had offered the Vaisvadeva in order to "gain the Dîkshâ" so did the king.[91] These texts also indicated that the sacrificer could establish himself in all three worlds and be elevated to Prajâpati by means of these offerings.[92] By transforming the king the Dîkshâ had brought him to a new level of reality and prepared the ritual for its ultimate moment.

The elaborate Agnicayana ritual formed part of the Ashvamedha.[93] Here again water played an important part in the construction of this central altar. Water not only served the practical purpose in the making of bricks but more importantly it was used in the ritual's cleansing and purification.[94] The priests carried Agni's ashes back to the water each day as a symbolic gesture that set the sacred fire and altar apart from their profane surroundings. At night a white horse protected the altar site from hostile forces that would threaten to pollute the sanctity of this most holy place within the sacrificial compound. The heads of sacrificial victims were placed on stakes as a warning not to trespass on this sacred ground that was being prepared for the altar and eventual sacrifice.[95]

These ritual precautions belonged to the rich symbolism behind the Agnicayana. The Agnicayana ritual elucidated the need for such purity and consecration. The Agnicayana's shape, the manner of its construction, and its purpose to transport the sacrificer to the heavenly world as well as to receive the gods at the altar all displayed how the Agnicayana excluded the profane by symbolically creating its own sanctified environment. It was here upon the high altar that the horse, the sacrificer and the gods came into contact.[96]

After a special ceremony that selected the clay for the fire pan, the fire was said to be born there. At that time an Adhvaryu prayed for the birth of a gifted Brahmin and victorious king as well as other desired worldly items that would enhance all areas of life for everyone in the realm.[97]

Following the Agnicayana, another ritual, called the Upavasatha, further prepared the altar and then marked it off as the central area of the sacrificial compound. By placing twenty-one stakes into the ground the sacrificer was thought to have gained the heavenly world through the Upavasatha.[98]

When the Dîkshâ, Agnicayana, and Upavasatha rituals had concluded the king and the sacrificial grounds stood ready for the three days of Soma pressing. The first day of the Soma sacrifice fell on the full moon of Vaiçyâkha.[99] The Hotri addressed Agni, Usas, and the Ashvins with stanzas from the *Rig Veda* before offering Soma in the morning, midday and that afternoon. The Adhvaryu then followed that same evening by offering food oblations into the fire in order to please particular gods and ward off evil beings or Raksasas just as Prajâpati had defeated the demons who sought to ruin the first Ashvamedha.[100]

The second day of the Soma sacrifice once again brought the horse back into the center of the ritual activities. Up until this point, after it returned, the horse had been kept in an enclosure that the priests built specially for the horse during its year away from the sacrificial compound.[101] Now the horse was directed from this temporary structure back to the sacrificial compound. Once there, the Adhvaryu took the horse by the tail with the following explanation by the *Shatapatha-Brâhmana*:

Now, the gods did not know the Pavamâna at the Ashvamedha to be the heavenly world, but the horse knew it. When, at the Ashvamedha, they glide along with the horse for the Pavamâna (-stora), it is for getting to know (the way to) the heavenly world; and they hold on to the horse's tail, in order to reach the heavenly world; for man does not rightly know (the way to) the heavenly world, but the horse does rightly know it.

Were the Udgâtr to chant the Udgîtha, it would be even as if one who does not know the country were to lead by another (than the right) way. But if, setting aside the Udgâtr, he chooses the horse for (performing) the Udgîtha, it is just as when one who knows the country leads on the right way: the horse leads the Sacrificer rightly to the heavenly world.[102]

After this confirmation of the sacrificer's dependence upon the Ashvamedha they yoked the horse to a chariot with three other horses and led back to the adjacent pond.[103] Once there, the Adhvaryu made the sacrificer recite a formula[104] and hold on to the horse while the Adhvaryu sprinkled it. Part of the formulas recited during this sprinkling ceremony read as follows:

"Thou shall not die here, neither suffer harm," he thereby cheers it; "on easy paths thou goest to the gods," he thereby shows him the paths leading to the gods; "where dwell the pious, whither they have gone," he thereby makes it one who shares the same world with the pious; "thither the god Savitri shall lead thee," it is, indeed, Savitri that leads to the heavenly world. Whilst whispering "I sprinkle thee, acceptable unto Prajâpati," he then holds (the sprinkling water) under (its mouth)."

"Agni was an animal; they sacrificed him, and he gained that world wherein Agni (ruleth): that shall be thy world, that thou shalt gain, drink thou this water! "As great as Agni's conquest was, as great as is his world, as great as is his lordship, so great shall be thy conquest, so great thy world, so great thy lordship. This is what he thereby says to him."[105]

The prohibition against letting the horse bathe during its journey assured that the effects of its initial consecration were not diminished. After the horse returned, it was once again cleansed from any possible defilement that it might have acquired outside the sacrificial compound. But the second sprinkling ceremony also prepared the horse for an even higher level of sanctity just as the sacrificer and the sacrificial grounds had experienced an elevated consecration in the Dîkshâ and Agnicayana respectively.

Still during the second day of Soma pressing the horse returned from the pond where the chief queen, the Mahisî, anointed it. The least esteemed queen did not take part in this anointing.[106] Then the first three wives of the king weaved one hundred and one pearls into the tail and mane of the victim.[107] While the weaving took place the queens were required to pick up any hair that fell out of the horse. "But even as some of the offering-material may get spilled before it is offered, so (part of) the victim is here spilled in that the hair of it when wetted comes off."[108] Not even a hair of the victim could be left discarded outside of the strict domain that the ritual had established for it.[109] Once fully consecrated, the horse no longer belonged to the profane world but to its sanctified and purified environment that the ritual had gradually created.

The Adhvaryu then offered the horse remains from the previous night's oblation. If the horse did not eat all of the leftover oblation another rite ensued. This leftover portion was in turn taken to the waters and ritually disposed with a formula.[110] Here again, nothing could be left outside of the auspices of the ritual. That which the ritual purified and placed in contact with the sacred fire could not merely be abandoned to the profane realm.

The horse was then tied to the central stake where the Adhvaryu attached other staked animals to different parts of the horse by a rope.[111] The king also made his entry into the sacrificial grounds that now may have contained over two thousand officials.[112]

After a year of necessary preparations the horse was finally killed along with the other designated victims. Only the priests and queens that formed the procession to the sacrificial post continued at this point in the ritual. The king and all the others stood back and watched as the horse was sprinkled one last time before being suffocated. At the moment the horse was "quieted" the priests offered two Paripasavyâ oblations and three additional oblations just after its death. While the horse lay upon a piece of gold placed between two cloths, the queens went around the corpse nine times, three times right to left, then three left to right, and three final circles towards the left.[113]

Following these rites, the queens, their four hundred female attendants and a curious "fifth maiden" brought water to wash the horse's feet.[114] Next occurred perhaps the most peculiar of all the rites of the Ashvamedha. The horse laid on the Târpya-cloth after it was suffocated and then the Adhvaryu folded this large cloth over the horse.[115] The Adhvaryu then helped the Mahisî, or consecrated queen, to climb under the Târpya-cloth with the horse where the horse and queen mated. A mysterious succession of statements followed during their concealment beneath the cloth. The Udgâtri, Brahmin and Adhvaryu all addressed the queens and their female attendants.[116] Notice the following dialogue between the Adhvaryu and the Mahisî:

"Do you both envelop yourselves in the heavenly world?" He thus makes her (the Mahisî) go to the heavenly world.

As she puts the Sepha (the sexual organ of the horse) on her lap says, "I will urge that which produces the embryo; urge thou that produces the embryo." The embryo, surely, means offspring and cattle.[117]

Here are a few statements that were made by the Udgâtri and the Brahmin:

The Udgâtri says concerning the king's favorite wife, 'Raise her upwards, the Ashvamedha, doubtless, is that glory, royal power: that glory, royal power, he thus raises for him (the Sacrificer) upward.[118]

The Brahmin addresses the queen consort, "Thy mother and father," the mother, doubtless, is this (earth), and the father yonder (sky): by means of these two he causes him to go to heaven; 'mount to the top of the tree,' 'to the top of royal power', doubtless, is glory: the top of royal power, glory, he thus causes him to attain; saying, "I pass along, thy father passed his fist to and fro in the cleft, 'the cleft', doubtless, is the people; and the fist is royal power; and royal power, indeed, presses hard on the people; whence he who wields royal power is apt to strike down people."[119]

Concluding this symbolic intercourse between the horse and queen, she and her two subordinates went to the pond to be purified.[120] Upon their return the queens busied themselves with the task of diagraming the horse's hide for dissection. The queens used needles made of different precious metals that represented the three worlds. Again it was said that this rite made it possible to "know the way to the heavenly world."[121] The SB recorded, "When they prepare the knife-paths, the Sacrificer makes for himself that passage across, a bridge, for the attainment of the heavenly world."[122]

Once more the Adhvaryu took control of the sacrificial proceedings with the words, "Who cuts you, who divides you? Prajâpati cuts thee, Prajâpati divides you."[123] As the Adhvaryu cuts the horse along the "knife-paths" other priests began to recite verses or Mantras from the Vedas that requested healing and regeneration for the horse.[124] The other animals were cut with knives made with iron and copper while a golden knife was reserved for the horse.[125] The Brâhmana texts had previously explained the events that led up to the actual sacrifice of the horse as being a repetition of the primordial horse sacrifice by Prajâpati. Here again the

Brâhmanas delineated the connection between the visible acts at the altar with their unseen counterparts in the heavenly world. Thus the Adhvaryu recited:
"It is Prajâpati who cuts you." The Adhvaryu continued by saying, "After he had created the creatures, Prajâpati, through love, entered into them; but he could not disengage himself from them and re-assemble his parts together. He said: 'He shall prosper who shall disengage me from these, and restore him to unity.' They then prospered. Whosoever offers the horse sacrifice, he restores Prajâpati and consequently prospers."[126] Yet again the king followed the example of Prajâpati and drank two servings of Soma called the Mahiman draughts.[127]

All of these activities on the second day had set the stage for the next part of the sacrificial drama that took place at the central sacrificial post. Here the Hotri and the Brahmin began a "theological discussion" referred to as a Brahmodya. While the Hotri sat on the left side of the post and represented Agni the Brahmin seated himself on the right and represented Braspati.[128] A series of proper theological responses followed each of the questions and served to reiterate the spiritual explanations that stood behind the symbolic acts of the sacrifice. For example, the Hotri asked, "Who was the great bird?", and the Brahmin answered, "the great bird, doubtless, was the horse: vital power he thus secures for himself."[129]

At the end of the second day of the Soma sacrifice several blood oblations from the horse and other animals were offered into the sacred fire.[130] These blood oblations followed the Svistakrt offering and included various plant offerings that lasted through the evening.

The third and final day of Soma sacrifice was called the Atirâtra day. The priests presented several more offerings and recited hymns that occurred in conjunction with the ceremonial bath, the Avabhrtha.[131] The rites of this day and the days that immediately followed concluded the Ashvamedha.[132]

Each aspect of the Atirâtra concerned itself with purification. For example, the Adhvaryu offered three oblations of clarified butter, two of which claimed special purifying powers. The Bhrûnahatya was supposed to remove transgressions from the sacrificer even if some member of his family had actually murdered a Brahmin.[133]

Clarified butter was also offered to Jumbaka. This strange rite used a leprous man with protruding teeth and reddish brown eyes. The priest made the offering upon the white-spotted, bald-head of this man for the stated purpose that the sacrificer "redeems himself from Varuna."[134] Many have understood this rite in terms of pure magic.[135] But as indicated in the previous chapter the "nooses of Varuna" signified sin and, subsequently, "being loosed from Varuna" was the equivalent to the removal of sins in Vedic mythology. This rite removed any possible sin or ritual errors that may have transpired during the three days of Soma sacrifice when the sacrificer first became identified with Prajâpati.

After these purification rites the priests performed nine Anûbandhyah sacrifices involving nine white barren cows consecrated to Sûrya. The sacrifice of cows, who represented the "all-mother Aditi," went back to the *Rig Veda* and symbolized new life. The Anûbandhyah sacrifices usually served to form or re-new the basis for the next year of sacrifice. Krick said that the Anûbandhyah belonged to the protectors of Ritam, the world, and sacrificial order, par excellence: Mitra and Varuna.[136] These cow sacrifices can be understood as one aspect of the ritual's return to the profane. The sacrifice did not simply end and the world of normal operations automatically begin. Without the further assistance of the "exit" rites the transformed realities created during the ritual could not convert back to their original profane realm. But even the return to the profane did not remove the world from the transcendent universal order of Rita.

The Avabhrtha ceremony itself provides the clearest example of the ritual's return to the profane or its "exit." The notion of purification associated with this bath must come under some scrutiny. If the sacrificer, the altar, the horse and all the utensils had already undergone consecration, why then should an additional bath of purification have been required?[137] The sacrificer and all that had been consecrated for contact with divine powers in the sacrifice had to be returned to the profane. Again this indicates the need to differentiate and separate the sacred from the profane.

The Câtvâla is an example of the careful attention that was given to the sacred objects used in the ritual after they had served their purpose in the sacrifice. Priests used the Câtvâla, or special pit, to contain such sacrificial objects as the black antelope skin, the royal chair, the sacrificer's belt and, in general, everything that had come into contact with Soma during the ritual. Dumont took note of the fact that the removal and temporary storage of these items was to be accomplished without touching them with the hands, "sans se servire ses mains."[138] The Câtvâla isolated these leftover objects until the final processional to the Avabhrtha waters.[139]

Having left the sacrificial compound, the priests, the sacrificer and his wives, all proceeded together to the Avabhrtha ceremony. They each carried along the objects stored in the Câtvâla. Once at the pond the sacred objects were thrown into the water and a priest chanted a hymn to Varuna asking that the bond of Varuna be broken. The priests, sacrificer and his wives then bathed completely in the waters.[140] The Adhvaryu offered an Ishti to Varuna and Agni.[141] This time the offering was made in the water and not in the fire. When the sacrificer had emerged from the waters all those people who had "committed sins and not observed vows, should take a bath in the water."[142]

The Avabhrtha removed the sacred nature of everyone and everything that had participated in the sacrifice and that had consequently undergone transformation in the ritual.

### 3:2 The History of Interpretation

The general approach to the Ashvamedha has been somewhat predictable given the lasting presuppositions of late nineteenth century scholarship. Indologists have mainly attempted to establish the origin of the Ashvamedha. Consequently, their interpretations concerned themselves with details that also seemed to indicate an evolutionary development of the Ashvamedha. Such interpretations focused on aspects of the Ashvamedha that drew primary attention to a magical-fertility denouement for the entire ritual.

The following examples depict the strong sway that the above mentioned scholarly fashions exerted over different interpreters.

Late in the nineteenth century Hermann Oldenburg saw the Ashvamedha as a sacrifice in which the king received his greatest desires.[143] According to Oldenburg, the Ashvamedha was the highest expression of royal power and glory. The horse was the most acceptable animal from which the king could magically appropriate strength through its sacrifice. For Oldenburg the origin of the Ashvamedha went back to an association with warfare. Originally the sacrifice was offered to Indra, the great slayer of the Vrtra, and only later became identified with Prajâpati.

Oldenburg did notice the emphasis on consecration that was associated with the Ashvamedha. But he chose rather to emphasize the fertility and power that resulted from the "original" sacrifice. The role of

Indra overshadows that of Prajâpati in Oldenburg's treatment of the Ashvamedha even though the Brâhmanas center on Prajâpati.

Julius Eggeling included an interpretation of the Ashvamedha in the introduction of his translation of the *Shatapatha Brâhmana* in 1900.[144] Unlike Oldenburg, Eggeling placed great significance on the connection between Prajâpati and the Ashvamedha. His reasoning for this emphasis was quite clear. He said Prajâpati had always been connected with sacrifice in the Brâhmanic sacrificial system. Moreover, Eggeling noted the horse's identity with Prajâpati.[145] However in the same spirit of Oldenburg, Eggeling sought to establish the origin of the horse sacrifice. In this regard Eggeling believed that the Ashvamedha was substituted for the Purushamedha.

In 1898 Sylvain Lévi had also resolved that Prajâpati played an indispensible role in Brâhmanic sacrifice.[146] Lévi traced the origin of the mythology surrounding Prajâpati to the creation of the entire cosmos as he studied the Brâhmanas. In Indian cosmology the concept of creation followed the verbs Srj, "to emit" and Nir-ma, "to construct" and differed from the popular notion of the Church Fathers that God created Exnihilio. Lévi pointed out that the order of creation began with nothing or "non-being" followed by "heat" and then creation. He associated this basic pattern with Brahman, for in the beginning there was only Brahman, then Brahma, who meditated in silence with breath (esprit), and this breath became Prajâpati. Hence, Lévi said that nothing could have existed without Prajâpati.[147]

Lévi's began to indicate the identification between Prajâpati and the sacrifice. His purpose for drawing attention to these associations also stemmed from a vested interest in discovering the origin of the Ashvamedha as some type of mechanical procedure that was self-explanatory. He said, "Prajâpati, qui est le sacrifice même, est naturellement l'origine du sacrifice."[148] Prajâpati's identification with Brâhmanic sacrifice in general and with the first Ashvamedha in particular formed part of a rather rigid appraisal of sacrifice. Lévi composed a typical magical function for the sacrifice by using only particular details of the sacrifice. He too understood the role of magic to appropriate the desired results.[149]

A. B. Keith deviated only slightly from his predecessors' interpretation of the Ashvamedha. Although Keith admitted that the original impetus behind this rite was "somewhat obscure" he nonetheless arrived at what he confidently referred to as the "most attractive alternative" to other views. Keith's own opinion of the origin of the Ashvamedha was, in his own words, undoubtedly the acceptance of the sun as the sun horse, offered originally to the sun as a spell to strengthen it, and the chief difficulty in that view is merely the fact that the sun is not the recipient of the offering, in any measure.[150] Keith felt that this view of the horse sacrifice remained the most plausible and rejected the interpretation drawn from a comparison with the October horse sacrifice at Rome which concluded that the horse sacrifice in Ancient India had originated from a vegetation rite. Keith likewise rebuffed the claim that said the horse sacrifice came about from a rite in which offerings were made to the sun who was conceived as a horse. This particular theory found support from a vague mythological comparison between Indra, who defeated the Asuras with his horse, and the human king, who defeated his enemies with the help of an earthly horse. Keith found the connection between Indra and the horse unwarranted because Indra never had this association in Vedic or even pre-Vedic myths.[151]

Keith's rejection of these other views did not mean that he was apathetic towards the cultural fashions of the day as his own quest for the origin of the Ashvamedha indicates. What appears even more frustrating with Keith's interpretation is the fact that his predisposition for "origins" caused him to merely mention aspects of the Ashvamedha that he himself thought were important. For example he noted in passing that the redemptive powers of the sacrifice and the ceremonies using water to bath the horse were "points of importance."[152]

P. E. Dumont gave little attention to the interpretation of the Ashvamedha. The vast majority of his work on the Ashvamedha went towards translating[153] and describing it.[154] Like those before him, Dumont had to come to terms with Oldenburg's work. With only minor disagreements with Oldenburg, Dumont proceeded to characterize the Ashvamedha as a magical charm that ensured victory, sovereignty, and glory to an already victorious, sovereign and glorious king. According to Dumont, the magical powers of this rite were also thought to produce fecundity. He too claimed that the Ashvamedha was a manifestation of a solar cult that identified Prajâpati with the solar year. The new perspective in Dumont's interpretation of the horse sacrifice dealt with the Mahisî. On this subject he used the sanskrit term Sakti to indicate what he called, "la forme féminine de la puissance divine," and "la forme féminine de la puissance royale" for this queen's role in the Ashvamedha.[155] Dumont continued the search for what made up the original horse sacrifice and how it had evolved to its form in the later texts. Therefore, he spoke of the less complicated (moins compliqué) Ashvamedha in the Rig Vedic period as compared to that described in the *Brâhmanas*.[156]

Ganesh Thite closely followed a popular interpretation of the Ashvamedha as a fertility rite that preserved the king's victory and prosperity.[157] He amplified this basic theory with the suggestion that many fertility rites belonged to the Ashvamedha. But Thite also suggested that the primary aspect of the Ashvamedha was not a fertility sacrifce.[158] At this point he departed somewhat from the otherwise obvious influences of Oldenburg and other indologists. For Thite, the Ashvamedha was "first a victory-celebration and then a fertility rite."[159] Thite gave no particular reason for this conclusion except to say that it was a device of the Brâhmana-texts to "elevate a sacrificial rite by showing its connection to many results."[160] He listed several of these "results" from the texts but never expounded upon the nature of their "connection" to the "victory-celebration." Thite merely linked what he called "results" to the Ashvamedha as a victory celebration. For instance, Thite said, "Wherever, this sacrifice is performed, everything is obtained; everything becomes distinct; everything becomes served; everything becomes abounding in food; everything becomes sapful; the *Brâhmana* is born as rich in brahman-splendor; the Râjana is born one excelling in hitting (the mark); a wide tract of forest-land will be provided; everything becomes fit and proper; everything becomes firmly established."[161]

All of this, according to Thite, served to "elevate the rite." Once more he failed to articulate exactly how this elevated the rite, and he never made it clear just what he meant by "elevate." His interpretation seems to rest more upon an utilitarian view of human culture than on the Brâhmana-texts themselves. As noted before, obvious changes had occurred in the Brâhmanic presentation of the Ashvamedha and especially in the connection with Prajâpati,[162] and no doubt the rite had become more complicated and sophisticated in every aspect of its performance, mythology, and socio-political ramifications during the Brâhmanic period. But it is questionable if the primary import of these developments resulted from some type of systematic effort in the *Brâhmanas* to rise above a crude ritualism to a new type of ritualism that included spiritualism.[163] It was, however, the avowed purpose of Thite's work to make this very point by examining the sacrificial rituals in the *Brâhmanas*.[164] Yet in the process of demonstrating that "spiritualism" had co-existed with "ritualism" in the Brâhmanas he reduced the Ashvamedha to a type of evolutionary precursor of "higher spiritualism" in the *Upanishads*.

Thite's interpretation of the Ashvamedha exemplifies a case of rushing over the texts in order to arrive at a preconceived thesis. Thite ended his treatment of the Ashvamedha with these words:

> The Brâhmana-texts have elevated the Ashvamedha along with its popular rites. Though originally a popular feast of victory-celebration and fertility, the Brâhmana-texts have added many aspects to it, have connected it with Prajâpati, Gods, Soma-sacrificial-institute, made historical references to its performances and have even praised it. And thus, the Brâhmana-texts have elevated, established it in the Shrauta-ritual and have given a good status to it.[165]

In Thite's scheme of things the Ashvamedha attained a "good status" only when these aspects, which were not originally part of the "fertility rite," were added. Thite's "added aspects" end up sounding themselves conspicuously western in an anti-ritual sense. He has thus construed an unnecessary tension between ritual action and spiritual reflection. Thite would have us believe that Vedic spiritualism began in the *Brâhmanas*, reached fruition in the *Upanishads*, and resulted from a conscious effort to elevate the status of rituals such as the Ashvamedha.[166]

But can such an assumption be made on the basis of recognizing new aspects of the Ashvamedha in the *Brâhmanas*? The subtle anti-ritualism of Thite's theory of elevated rituals undermines the whole concept of the actual performance of the ritual. How should we understand statements from the *Brâhmanas* that say the sacrificer actually has no life until he performs the sacrifice,[167] or those that say truth (Satya) is the performance of the sacrifice? Do these lines demonstrate a mechanical ritualism that was permeated with magical conceptions of the cosmos? Or can they stand on their own merit without looking for causes and effects to make them comprehensible for a society that sees no redeeming value in ritual? Were there no spiritual aspects the Ashvamedha prior to its 'elevation' in the *Brâhmanas*? The whole notion that "spiritualism" only accompanied the "elevated rituals" of Brâhmanism bases itself on the supposition that prior to their elevation all Vedic rites were magical fertility rites. Thite used the Ashvamedha as an example of "spiritualism" in the Brâhmanas but only after its elevation to a "victory celebration." In arguing for the connection between "ritualism" in the Brâhmanas and "spiritualism" in the *Upanishads* Thite has intravertently perpetuated a bias against ritual that empties it of any philosophical meaning and spiritual qualities.

The Indo-Europeanist, George Dumézil, added a new dimension to the study of the Ashvamedha. Dumézil compared the Ashvamedha to the Roman October Equus for the purpose of showing that the tripartite Indo-European structure also manifested its common pattern in rituals.

Indo-European scholars who dealt with the Ashvamedha followed an equally myopic model of interpretation. G. Dumézil's ideological theory involving a tripartite "function" of Indo-European society, among other things, has also influenced the interpretation of the Ashvamedha. In this case the Ashvamedha served to illustrate the Indian version of the triple structured Indo-european paradigm that collectively represented Indian society. Here again a fashionable theory eclipsed the full scope of this intricate ritual.

Since the basis for his comparative work with the Indian and Roman horse sacrifice went beyond a purely descriptive approach, Dumézil entered the precarious world of hermeneutics. In fact, Dumézil was criticized for not pointing out the important differences between the Roman and Indian sacrifices.[168] Dumézil's interest in these two rituals should be coupled to his notion of "ideology" (Idéologie). Dumézil said, "Souvent cette idéologie n'est qu' implicite et doit être dégagée par analysis de ce qui est dit en clair des dieux et surtout de leurs actions, de la thélogie et surtout de la mythologie, ce qui conduit à restaurer dans une certaine mesure la primauté de ce genre de documents."[169]

It is no wonder why Dumézil had such a fascination with "ideology." According to Dumézil, "ideology" functioned within the basic tripartite division of Indo-European societies as a determining factor over every characteristic element of these particular civilizations. In part this meant that rituals were no less important than any of the other "elements of a religion" ("theology, mythology, sacred literature, sacred organization") since they too were subordinate to this "ideology."[170]

This equality that ritual held in relation to the other aspects of religious symbolism should be understood against the backdrop of his conflict with Max Müller and his students who advocated myth as the supreme element of religion. In the final analysis, everything was subordinated to his concept of "ideology." Ironically, his own characterization of "ideology" functioned very much like myth. He obviously realized this himself and subsequently attempted to distinguish "ideology" from its mythological attachments.

Dumézil's decision to utilize rituals appears to be, at least in part, an effort to substantiate his general tripartite theory consciously different from certain influences of the Nature Mythologists, and to view ritual from a sociological perspective.[171] But the separation he made between myth and "ideology" was contrived, and furthermore, his hierarchial scheme that placed this "ideology" prior to other elements of religion was unwarranted. Thus, his comparative work concealed much of the Ashvamedha's historical distinctiveness. Additionally, Dumézil made no real effort to address the meaning of the Ashvamedha since any meaning would have been the product of sociological forces which were in turn determined by his mysterious and illusive "ideology."

The prolific Indologist Jan Gonda made a significant step towards understanding the Ashvamedha by emphasizing the symbolism of the king and the horse.[172] Gonda held the concept of Virâj, that is "one who rules far and wide," to be central to the symbolism of the Ashvamedha.[173] Gonda pointed out that in Ancient India the Virâj brought benefits to the kingdom through his participation in the Ashvamedha. In other words, the benefits of the actual Ashvamedha were extended to the king and his kingdom. The purpose of the horse's wandering about, according to Gonda, was:

> ...on the one hand to bring the country into contact with its own divine power, and on the other to extend the rule and power of the king, or rather to re-establish his claims of overlordship and to re-invigorate his power, which involved: to strengthen the potency of kingship, to enhance welfare and fertility all over the country and to bring about the other consequences of prosperous sovereignty.[174]

Perhaps more than anyone else Gonda has demonstrated the socio-political aspects of the Ashvamedha by examining it from, as he put it, "a religious point of view." Gonda has shown the vital link between the transcendent world of the gods and the mundane world of men by concentrating on the symbolic role of the king and horse. Gonda's work allows for the integration of these two aspects of the Ashvamedha and confronts us with the necessary "murkiness of religion" that K. Bolle has so aptly coined.

Mircea Eliade treated the Ashvamedha as a rite having a cosmogonic structure which both regenerated the entire cosmos and reestablished every social order during its performance. Originally, Eliade thought, the Ashvamedha was most likely "a spring festival, more precisely a rite celebrated at the time of the New Year."[175] The symbolism of the horse seemed to unlock much of the Ashvamedha's essence for Eliade. He noted that both the Rig Vedic and Brâhmanic texts had stressed the connection between the horse and the primordial waters. This connection he understood as a clear sign of the cosmogonic element in the Ashvamedha. Eliade also emphasized the horse's symbolic role in representing royal power, Kshatriâ, which could be seen as a type of substitute for the king.[176]

Richard Hecht rejected the Indologist's and Indo-Europeanist's reduction of the entire Ashvamedha to a magical-fertility sacrifice. Hecht recognized the contributions made by earlier interpretations of the Ashvamedha but felt that too much had been made of the sexual intercourse between the horse and the Mahisî. The magical-fertility approach to understanding the sacrifice had excluded "other important elements of the ritual which seemingly have nothing to do with the question of fertility."[177]

Hecht made use of Gonda's concept of ancient kingship in India and Eliade's works dealing with the symbolism of the horse in order to understand the Ashvamedha as an example of what he labeled, "the concreteness of history."[178] According to Hecht, the symbolism of the king and the horse demonstrated the most important aspects of the sacrifice. Everything that was crucial to the proper structure of the world became perfect through the sacrifice.

Hecht used this "concreteness" of the Ashvamedha as a further example of what he called "perfect history." In Hecht's scheme, sacrifice, as "perfect history," requires participation in each particular religious tradition. In the Vedic tradition the king and horse participated in the Ashvamedha to re-enact the mythic acts of Prajâpati in primordial time.

Hecht's insights help establish the importance of viewing the Ashvamedha in the totality of its socio-political and religious context. His interpretation has restored to the primary documents much that had been lost through over simplistic schematizations that were bent on proving popular cultural fashions.

### 3:3 The Ashvamedha: A Summary

Certain details of the Ashvamedha's description have already been related to the problem of transcendence and immanence in this chapter. These final deliberations shall summarize this great sacrifice as a specific example of Vedic rituals that deal with the problem of transcendence and immanence. This interpretation also understands the Ashvamedha as sharing in a similar universal structure of all rituals that deal with the problem of transcendence and immanence. I would like to go one step further and conclude that this universal structure represents what I believe to be most central to the Ashvamedha within the general scope of Vedic religion. I do not deny the importance of the other aspects of the Ashvamedha nor do I mean to mitigate its unique character among other Vedic rituals.

The primary texts reveal that the Ashvamedha was primarily concerned with what Hecht called "the concreteness of history," that is, the major concerns of order in the world on every level of social, political and biological life. For the realization of these concerns the Ancient Indians performed the sacrifice. As noted earlier, the performance of the Ashvamedha should not readily be dismissed as some type of perfunctory cure-all for a culture steeped in superstitions. This stereotype of the Ancient Indians conjures up an image of half wits who believed in magical sacrifices that offered the only solution for a people lacking the benefits of modern science. Such an approach relies too heavily upon a pseudo-psychology and too lightly upon historical documents.

The task of interpreting the Ashvamedha must, at some point, recognize the interplay between Vedic religious symbolization and its socio-political context. Yet, with few exceptions, the history of interpretation has disguised the specific role of the Ashvamedha's religious symbolism as the product of more influential psychological and sociological factors. If "primitive" minds invented magical-fertility rites, why delve any further into the nature of the symbolism that expressed such child like conceptualizations of the world? If something more profound stood behind the religious elements that can and should be isolated from the religious, why then seek to understand the influence that religious symbolization might have had on societies such as in Ancient India? These procedures have tended to preclude serious consideration of the religious symbolization involved in such rituals as the Ashvamedha.

Ultimately, the historical documents suffer and the quest for understanding a phenomenon like Vedic sacrifice becomes squelched.

The task of interpreting the Ashvamedha should also recognize its poignant religious aspect. The religious runs through the whole gamut of human activity and concerns in Ancient India so as to make a definitive separation between religion and politics, or and social organization impossible. But the case of the sacrifice presents an exception to the rule of Vedic culture at large. The same religious symbolization that integrated the sacred and the profane into a working alliance also served to distinguish the two in the sacrifice. The Ashvamedha made a consorted effort to both unite and then differentiate the sacred and the profane.

Interpreting the Ashvamedha requires patience. If the history of interpretation has taught us anything it should caution us towards making the ritual always have a utilitarian cause and effect. Some things are best left to stand as the texts present them, as mysteries, incomprehensible in terms of human reason. However, this does not mean complete silence concerning the "altogether different" since some texts invite meditation, speculation, and commentary upon their greatest mysteries. In such cases our task is to always remain within the parameters set by the religious symbolization itself. When we reduce religious symbolism to our own social or economic categories we forfeit the essence of what the text was trying to communicate.

As we have seen, the king performed the Ashvamedha in order to realize several desired results that affected his entire kingdom. According to the Brâhmanic texts, the obtainment of everything that the king and his realm wanted resulted from attaining the heavenly world. Time and time again the texts clearly state that the sacrificer attained the heavenly world through the successful performance of the Ashvamedha. "He performs oblations successively increasing one by one, for single, indeed, is heaven: singly he thus causes him (the Sacrificer) to reach heaven. Straight away he offers in order to the winning of heaven; for straight away, as it were, is heaven."[179] Without a successful sacrifice, that is a sacrifice in which the king reached the world of heaven, none of the other desires could be obtained.

The symbolism of the sacrificial horse played a crucial part of the sacrificer's attainment or journey to heaven by means of the Ashvamedha. The Rig Vedic hymns concerning the horse sacrifice began by stressing the horse's ability to reach the world of the gods. For example:

> When you whinnied for the first time, as you were born coming forth from the ocean or from the celestial source, with wings of an eagle and the forelegs of an antelope - that, swift Runner, was your great and awesome birth.
> They say you have three bonds in the sky, three in the waters, and three within the ocean. And to me you appear, Swift Runner, like Varuna, that is to be your highest birth.
> Your body flies, Swift Runner...
> The racehorse has come to the slaughter, pondering with his heart turned to the gods.
> The swift runner has come to the highest dwelling-place, to his father and mother. May he go to the gods today and be most welcome, and then ask for the things that the worshipper wishes for.[180]
> When, as the ritual law ordains, the men circle three times, leading the horse that is to be the oblation on the path of the gods...
> You do not really die through this, nor are you harmed. You go to the gods on paths pleasant to go on.
> Let this racehorse bring us good cattle and good horses, male children and all-nourishing wealth...Let the horse with our offerings achieve sovereign power for us.[181]

The Brâhmana texts continued with the significance of the horse as a means of attaining the world of heaven. We recall that the texts said the horse knew the way to the heavenly world while neither men nor gods did. The horse could lead the "Sacrificer rightly to the heavenly world"[182] and therefore ensure that the sacrificer obtained his wishes. The *Shatapatha Brâhmana* says that even the queen's intercourse with the horse caused the sacrificer to go to the heavenly world; and in that same section the text said that the trip to heaven secured royal powers.[183] This mysterious act of copulation between the queen and the horse primarily represented the union of the two worlds. The horse at this point in the ritual represented Prajâpati and linked the transcendent with the king's realm. This union promised in turn to promote fertility and political power as the result of the intimate fellowship gained in the sacrifice between humans and god, and not because of magic that controlled capricious gods.

The horse symbolism in the Ashvamedha that served to link the phenomenal world of humans to the transcendent world of the gods also appeared through other identifications.[184] Parts of the horse's body were identified with important parts of the cosmos. For example the *Taittirîya Samhitâ* says:

> The head of the sacrificial horse is the dawn, the eye the sun, the breath the wind, the ear the moon, the feet the quarters, the winking

the day and the night, the joints the half-months, the joining the months, the limbs the seasons, the trunk the year, the hair the rays of the sun, the form the Naksatras, the bones the stars, the flesh the mist, the hair the plants, the tail the trees, the mouth Agni, the open mouth Vaisvânara, the belly the sea, the anus the atmosphere, the testicles the sky and the earth, the Membrum Virle the pressing stone, the seed the soma. When it chews there is lighting; when it moves about there is thundering; when it makes water there is rain; its speech is speech.[185]

This type of symbolic identification between the cosmos and the horse underscored the necessity of linking the two worlds together through the medium of the sacrifice. If any benefits were to be gained, the human world had to come into contact with the heavenly world, and the only way to accomplish the impossible was through the sacrifice.

Because the union of these two worlds secured political, social, and fertility blessings, it was said of the Ashvamedha, "Verily, this is the sacrifice called Obtainment: wherever they worship with this sacrifice, everything indeed becomes obtained."[186]

The description of the Ashvamedha enabled us to take note of the ritual's abundant use of purification rites. The necessary union between the sacred and the profane in the sacrifice required the consecration of everything from the terrestrial side involved in the ritual because the sacrifice itself was seen as a vehicle that transported the sacrificer to the gods, and the gods themselves came to the sacrificial altar. As in the case of other Vedic sacrifices Agni played a very important part in the purification and linking of the two worlds.

The sacrificer and the horse underwent the most intense consecration because of their intimate encounters with the transcendent during the quest for heaven. The *Rig Veda* said, "The gods receive the horse who has been sacrificed, worshipped, consecrated, and sanctified with the cry of 'Vasat!'"[187] The *Shatapatha Brâhmana* says concerning the consecration of the horse, "I sprinkle three (so as to be acceptable) to Prajâpati." "I sprinkle three, acceptable to Indra and Agni." "I sprinkle thee acceptable to the All-gods."[188] Not only the horse but also everything had to be made acceptable to the gods through preparation rites. Thus the ritual began with consecration and purification rites that symbolically portrayed the sacrificer's ascent to heaven. The sacrifice reached its "height of perfection" or "holiness" when the gods consumed the horse in the sacred fire. From beginning to end these purification rites guarded the ritual from contact from the profane or unconsecrated by transforming the entire ritual environment and its participants.

The Ashvamedha also made claims to expiate sins. Whether sin meant ritual mistakes or intentionally violating a recognized code, the message of atonement stands out clearly throughout the history of the Ashvamedha. The *Rig Veda* mentioned an "atoner" in one of the two horse sacrifice hymns, and in that same hymn it reads, "Let Aditi make us free from sin."[189] The *Brâhmanas* stated, "Thereby the gods redeem all sin, yea even the slaying of a Brahmin they thereby redeem; and he who performs the Ashvamedha redeems all sin, he redeems even the slaying of a Brahmin."[190] Still later in Indian history a sage told Yudhistira, after he had slayed many kinsmen in the epic war between the Pândava and Kaurava princes, "...the Ashvamedha, O king of kings, cleanses away all ill-deeds: by performing it thou wilt without doubt become free from sin."[191]

The history of interpretation has virtually ignored the notion of sin and atonement in the Ashvamedha. Eggeling seemed compelled to add a footnote after the statement in the SB saying that the Ashvamedha "redeemed all sins." His note reminded readers that the "greater stress is laid in the *Brâhmana* on the efficacy of the ceremonial in ensuring supreme sway to the king, and security of life and property to his subjects."[192] In essence his note reminds us that he was one among many at the time who accepted the magical "gift theory" for sacrifice. Eggeling as well as others did not know what to do with the notion of sin and atonement in Vedic religion. Even though they used a vocabulary loaded with Jewish and Christian theological overtones when translating the texts they avoided any lucid comparison and contrast with the Jewish and Christian traditions. The main reason for this aversion stemmed from the predominance of magical-fertility presumptions of the Ashvamedha which on the surface seemed to exclude any deeper examination of the notion of sin and atonement.

As we shall see, sin and atonement in Vedic religion must be distinguished from the Jewish and Christian religions in their particular historical details. The king did not perform the Ashvamedha for the sole purpose of redeeming himself and the extended community from sin and, thereby, restoring their relationship or covenant with a holy God. The forgiveness of sins in the performance of Vedic sacrifice came as one of many results, but again not merely as some type of magical manipulation of the gods through a gift.

Clearly one aspect of atonement in Vedic sacrifice came from the sacrificial prerequisite to transform the profane before contact with the holy gods. Thus participating in the sacrifice itself resulted in changing one's status from a "sinner" to one "redeemed" by the sacrifice. In other words, the mere act of sacrificing brought about "forgiveness" through the transforming powers of the ritual. The sacrificer, having been consecrated, was now considered fit to participate in the ritual and also receive the benefits of the sacrifice. The ritual transported the king to mythical time where he temporarily became free from the greatest incumbrance that would prevented his gaining the heavenly world, namely his being human. Here the notion of sin and atonement belonged to the structure in Vedic religious symbolization that took into account the problem of transcendence and immanence. Both ritual and myth in Vedic religion operated from this reality.

Consequently, the notion of sin and atonement in Vedic religion make no sense without understanding their relationship to the concept of universal order (Rita), truth (Satya), and sacrifice (Yajña). Sin opposed universal order, truth, and ultimately the sacrifice at every level in Vedic culture simply because the sacrifice maintained and restored universal order and truth. So any sin was understood as a deviation from universal order and a hindrance to sacrifice. The most basic idea of sin in Vedic religion was simply Anrita, that is "without universal order."

An important aspect of universal order included the concept of partnership between humans and the gods who jointly shared in the responsibility to perform the sacrifice. For this reason not performing the sacrifice meant sin, non-truth, and non-being. Here too, the concept of sin and atonement belonged to the very structure of Vedic sacrifice. A structure that required the transcendent world of the gods, in all of its perfection, to join with the human world in order that both orders continued as a part of the one, universal order.

In the case of the Ashvamedha, the king's participation rendered benefits not only to himself and his realm but also, on an even grander scale, to the transcendent world from which the Ashvamedha originated in holiness. "He who preforms the Ashvamedha makes Prajâpati complete, and he (himself) becomes complete; and this, indeed, is the atonement for everything, the remedy for everything."[193] The "completion" or restoration of the creator Prajâpati marks the Ashvamedha's restoration of the entire cosmos. The *Brâhmana* associated the Ashvamedha's act of universal restoration to universal redemption. Human redemption can not be separated from the restoration of Prajâpati and all things, viz Rita. Redemption in Vedic religion came with the undoing of Anrita, or the re-establishment of Rita, or more simply stated, the performance of the sacrifice. Therefore when the king performed the Ashvamedha it was said that "everything became fit and proper" and "everything became supported (firmly established)."[194] All that the sacrifice accomplished for the cosmos was possible only because its mythological attachment to the holy world of the gods. The myth of Prajâpati's horse sacrifice in the beginning of time had both given the model to follow and made the Ashvamedha an indispensible part of the cosmos. Thus it was also said of the Ashvamedha, "Verily, this is the sacrifice called Abounding in holiness."[195]

Another central aspect of the Ashvamedha's structure existed in its demarcation between the human world and the heavenly world throughout the ritual. The ritual's demanding preparation rites reminded the sacrificer of the great distance between himself and the gods. Yet having brought the two worlds together, the ritual decisively separated them through a series of "exit rites." Just like the exit rites of other Shrauta sacrifices those of the Ashvamedha were designed to return everything that had been set apart for the sacrifice back to the profane. The Avabhrtha ceremony played a paramount role in re-establishing the boundaries between the two worlds.

The Ashvamedha's ability to distinguish between the sacred and profane during the ritual and to separate them at the conclusion of the sacrifice also relates to the notion of "holiness" in Vedic religion. The transcendent continued to be "altogether different" as the direct result of the sacrifice. The social, political, and biological realities created in the sacrifice did not exist apart from their alignment with the transcendent world. Had the mundane world ultimately assimilated the transcendent in the sacrifice then the entire structure of Vedic religion would have collapsed. Without the all important distinction and separation between the two worlds the king could not have celebrated his victories or extended any benefits to his realm because there would no longer have been any need to sacrifice.[196]

Rather it was said of the Ashvamedha that, "Verily, this is the sacrifice called Distinction: wherever they worship with this sacrifice, everything indeed becomes distinct. Verily, this is the sacrifice they called Severance: for wherever they worship with this sacrifice, everything indeed becomes severed."[197]

In this way the Ashvamedha helped extend the influence of sacrifice throughout India's history.

## ENDNOTES FOR CHAPTER THREE

1. Brian K. Smith commenting on the substitutional aspect of sacrifice says, "The theology, metaphysics, and ontology created by the Vedic ritualists presume the inaccessibility of transcendent prototypes and the necessity, therefore, of ritual action using counterparts or "symbols" for the "real thing." See, *Reflections on Resembalance, Ritual, and Religion*, New York, Oxford University Press, 1989, p. 176.

2. A full description of the Ashvamedha is not possible or necessary for the purpose of this examination. Eliade cited traces of horse sacrifices among the ancient Germans, Iranians, Greeks, Romans, Armenians, the Marsagetae, and the Dalmatians. See *A History of Religious Ideas*, Translated by Willard R. Trask, Chicago, The University of Chicago Press, vol.1, p. 218.

3. See also the *Brahmodya* I.164 which represented the last part of the Rgvedic period. Gonda raised the problem between the use of the *Rig Veda-Samhitâ* for the ritual and the relations between the hymns and stanzas. He saw no clear evidence that the Rig Veda hymns were used for specific rites, and thought that the exact opposite was in fact true, see *Vedic Literature*, vol. 1, pp.83-85. Elsewhere Gonda said, "Moreover, as already intimated in the *Brhaddevatâ* (5, 95), cases are not rare in which there is a disagreement (Visamvâdah) of the words of the Rig Veda with the ritual context in which they are applied, i.e. with their Viniyoga. The acts may even run counter to the sense of the mantras." See, *Hymns of the Rigveda not Employed in the Solemn Ritual*, Amsterdam: North-Holland Publishing Company, 1978, p. 10.

4. See A. B. Keith, *The Veda of the Black Yajus School*, in the *Harvard Oriental Series*, ed. by Charles Rockwell Lanman, Cambridge: The Harvard University Press, vol. 18, 1914, p. CXXXIII.

5. The *Taittirîya Sanhitâs*, also commonly called the *Black Yajurveda*, agree verbally at times with the mantras taken from the Rig Veda. The *Taittirîya* arranged a special section for the Ashvamedha.

6. This text forms a part of the *White Yajurvedas* and was arranged with a collection of mantras that were recited at the sacrifices. These mantras were free from the explanatory matter that was collected separately in the Brâhmanas.

7. Keith drew a close relationship between the school that produced the Mantras of the *Taittirîya* and those of the *Kâthaka*, the *Kapisthâlâ*, and the *Maitrâyanî Sanhitâs*, see op. cit. vol. 18, pp. lxxxv-lxxxvi.

8. Keith thought that for these reasons the *Taittirîya* texts were both superior and earlier to the *Vâjasaneyi* texts. Cf. ibid., pp. lxxxvi-lxxxvii.

9. P. E. Dumont, *L'Asvamedha: Description du sacrifice sonennel du cheval dans le culte védique*. Paris: Paul Geuthner, 1927, pp. II, VIII-IX. Dumont used primarily the White Yajurveda for his work on the Horse sacrifice The *Shatapatha-Brâhmana* and the *Taittirîya-Brâhmana* belong to the *Yajurveda* and like all the *Brâhmanas* of the *Yajurveda* they follow the ritual closely. The *Pancavimsa Brâhmana* belongs to the *Sâmaveda* and interpreted the Soma rites, see Gonda, op. cit., pp. 350-355. Eggling noted that the *Aitareya-Brâhmana* took no account of the Horse sacrifice at all, nor did the *Kausîtaki-Brâhmana* which also ignored the *Râjasûra*, see SBE, pp.XV-XVI. The *Aitareya Brâhmana* did list eight kings that were said to have performed the Horse sacrifice. However, this *Brâhmana* did deal with the *Râjasûra* which found acceptance into the *Brâhmanas* easier than did the Ashvamedha.

10. See G. U. Thite, *Sacrifice in the Brahmana-Texts*, Poona: The University of Poona, 1975. "Its first day is Catustoma-Agnistoma; the second day is Ekavimsa-Uktha and the third day is Sarvastoma-Atiratra (TMB XXI.4.1.).", p. 96. The actual Ashvamedha lasted more than three days.

11. This text was compiled at a comparatively late date yet Eggeling thought it to be older than the *Gopatha-Brâhmana*, cf. op. cit., pp. XVI-XVII.

12. This *Sûtra* covered all three categories of the Shrauta sacrifices that were divided into the following categories: Ishti, Pasu, and Soma. See, *Kâtyâyana Shrauta Sûtra*, Translated by H. G. Ranade, Poona, SMS Letter Press, 1978, pp. I-VIII.

13. Gonda said with regard to the sûtras of the *Yajurveda* that they, "tended to become a sort of ritualistic encyclopaedia rather than aide-memories as the srauta sûtras of the other Vedas have been called." Gonda believes that the *Sûtras* originated in *Yajurveda* circles and laid the foundations of "the literary developments of Vedic religion and ritual in general." See *A History of Indian Literature*, vol. 2, "The Ritual Sûtras," p. 490.

14. The use of technical terms and the mention of the priest's role in the sacrifice signified a sophisticated ritual to Keith. He noted that the Brahmin, who was the overseer of the whole sacrifice in later texts, did not function as such in the *Rig Veda*. The Garhapatya fire appears only in name in the *Rig Veda* an the used only one altar contrasted with the two altars (Vedhi and Uttaravedhi) of later rites, cf. *The Harvard Oriental Series*, vol. 31, 252-254. In this same volume Keith said that, "The imperfections of the record of the *Rigveda* renders it necessary in any account of the Vedic ritual to deal with the ritual, as it stands in the later *Samhitas* and the *Brâhmanas*, and as it is set out in full detail in the *Sûtras*, while using the *Rig Veda* whenever possible to explain in how far the views of that collection agree with the ideas later prevalent.," p. 256.

15. L. Renou, *L'Inde Classique*, vol. 1, p. 345.

16. For a chart of this compound refer to Dumont's L'Asvamedha, op. cit., p. XXXV; and for a description and interpretation of the Agnicayana see Naama Drury, *The Sacrificial Ritual in the Shatapatha Brahmana*, Delhi, Shri Jainendra Press, 1981, Chapters IV-VI.

17. Drury noted the *Shatapatha Brâhmana's* representations for compass directions in the sacrifice and said, "...the East was the region

of the gods (III,1.2), the North was the region of men (III,1.1.2), and at the North-east, between the region of men and gods, was the gate of heaven (IV,6.2.4). The region of the Pitrs ("fathers") was to the South (III.1.1.7), and the West was the region of cattle (XIV,2.2.28) and snakes (III,1.1.7)." See op. cit. p. 16.

18. The fact that the ground chosen and prepared for the Soma sacrifice was to be the highest in that region can be regarded as being most suitable for ascending to the worlds of the gods. Gonda also holds this view, see *The Haviryajñah Somah*, Amsterdam, North-Holland Publishing Company, 1980, p. 10.

19. Brain K. Smith, *Classifying the Universe*, New York, Oxford University Press, 1994. Smith's primary attention to this activity of classifying has to do with the origins of caste in India. But the caste system began with the Varna system and its ritual connection.

20. The Upanayana rite was a very typical puberty initiation ceremony for a boy of arachic societies. An Indian boy passed into Brahmanhood through the Upanayana. Of the domestic rites that were based on smurti, "what is heard," this ancient rite held the highest place of importance. (See Atharvaveda 19.17). The domestic rites also comprised Samskarâ (sacraments), one daily Mahâyajña (great sacrifice), and seven Pakayajña (cooking) sacrifices. According to J. Gonda the domestic rituals were based on the solemn rites, see *Vedic Ritual, The Non-Solemn Rites*, Leiden, E. J. Brill, 1980. Also see L. Renou in *L'Inde Classique*, pp. 352 ff.

21. The *Kauysîtakins* required seventeen.

22. Eliade called the hotri the most important priest without qualifying the changing role and significance of the Adhvaryu, see, *A History of Religious Ideas*, E.T. Willard R. Trask, Chicago, The University of Chicago Press, vol. I, 1978, p. 215, fn. 1.

23. This symbolic position gained prowess from its proximity to the sacred fires since both Agni and Soma bore purifying and illuminating powers. No doubt this function of the Brahmin priests is related to the development of Dharma and the emphasis on "saving knowledge" in later Hinduism and Buddhism.

24. According to the SB II.3.1.39 the gods would not permit the Ucchista, the remains that were left in the ladle and pot of the Agnihotra, to merely be discarded or drunk by just anyone. "None but a Brahmin must drink it for it is put on the fire and therefore none but a Brahmin should drink it."

25. See Charles Malamoud in, *Le Sacrificedans L'Inde Ancienne*, with Madleine Biareau, Paris, Presses Universitaires de France, 1976, esp. chap. 4. Here Malamoud discusses the importance of studying the persons, the materials, and the successive moments of the sacrifice. The persons have certain responsibilities with regard to the sacrificial materials and the order of the sacrifice. He thus emphasizes the central place of the priests whose job it was to bring the gods to the sacrificial table with man. Notice Biareau's statement on page 21 : "Mais, quoique le brâhmane soit considéré comme un dieu sur terre, la différence entre eux reste essentielle : c'est celle d'une rupture de niveau de réalité, le passage de ce que l'on hésite à appeler le profane au sacré. On n'entre en communication avec les dieux que sur l'aire sacrificielle."

26. Bodewitz understands the meaning of the Agnihotra as some kind of "sun charm" by which a weakened sun was transported at the end of the day through the darkness, coolness and danger of the night into Agni. In Agni he saw the sun revitalized by the "heated milk" on the Garhapatya.(Another rite called the Pravargya that was incorporated into the Agnistoma and also functioned to strengthen the sun after the rainy season). According to Bodewitz the Agnihotra later evolved into the daily worship of the sacred fire. See, *The Daily Evening and Morning Offering(Agnihotra) According to the Brâhmanas*, Leiden, E. J. Brill, 1976, pp. 2 ff. This typical magical approach to the Agnihotra bypasses the import of the texts themselves which clearly state that the "Agnihotra

is the sun" (SB II.3.1.1-9) and the sacrificer gained the world of the gods through it (*Sankh Brah.* 2.9). The sacrificer followed the same primordial order (Rita) that the gods did in the beginning in a conscious effort to continue the maintenance of both the fire in heaven i.e. the sun, and the earthly fire through sacrifice. In this way the Agnihotra also perpetuated the use of the sacred fires for all sacrifices. Therefore the JB 1.4. could say, "...the one performing the Agnihotra thus performs all." The TB II.1.2. reads, `In the evening the performer pours water round all three fires with the formula "I pour truth round thee, order." In the morning "I pour order round thee, truth" order is Agni', quoted from Bodewitz, p. 52.

27. The Prakrtih and the Vikrih sacrifices were full and new moon sacrifices that the Ishti type were based upon. The Prakrtih was the model for the Vikrih.

28. The animal sacrifices formed the basis for offerings to Agni and Soma. According to Keith, op. cit. p. 324, the sutras made a distinction "between the animal sacrifices as an independent offering and the sacrifice as connected with the Soma sacrifice." The animals used in these sacrifices were goats, bulls, cows, sheep, and horses.

29. Several rituals belonged to the Soma type. For example the Agnistoma was the fundamental form of the Soma sacrifices, cf. Keith, H.O.S., vol. XXXII, p. 313. The Mahavrata, the Vajapeya and Rajasuya ceremonies also used the Soma sacrificial system. The Agnicayana also associated with the Soma system but it was not obligatory part of it, see Eliade, op. cit., p. 217.

30. Keith, op. cit. p. 314. Here Keith called the most important division of the sacrifice as that between the Soma offerings and those offerings that sometimes were classified as Haviryajñas. The essential difference was that the latter did not employ the Saman singers, p. 316.

31. Since the horse sacrifice lasted for more than one day it was classified as an Ahîna sacrifice.

32. The Râjasûya and the Vâjapeya formed the other two parts of the royal Vedic cult. The Ashvamedha appears to have had some difficulty getting accepted in certain schools. See Thite, op. cit., pp. 89 ff., where he discusses the removal of "objections" to the Ahsvamedha.

33. The horse was to be black in front and white in back with a dark mark, see SB XIII.4.2.4.

34. J. Eggeling, trans. *Shatapatha Brâhmana*, in the *Sacred Books of the East*, ed. by F. Max Mueller, vol. XLIV, 1900, p. XV.

35. According to the *Kâtyâyana Shrauta Sûtra* (20.1.2), the ritual began with rites on the eight or ninth day of the month of Phâlguna while other ancient authorities taught the Ashvamedha should begin in the summer. (See, SB XIII.4.1.4.) The *Taittirîya Brâhmana* places the initial rites on the day of the full moon in the month of Caitra thus making it a mid-spring ceremony.

36. The *Kâtyâyana Shrautasûtra* (20.1.17) says that the king, "...sleeps observing celibacy to the west of the Garhapatya between the thighs of the Vavata with his head pointing to the north." Also see SB XIII.4.1.9).

37. The purpose of these songs was said to obtain the desires of the sacrificer, see SB XIII.1.5.6; 4.2.8.

38. TB 3.8.2. The Brahmaudana ritual involved offering boiled rice and was also employed to restore the Gârhapatya fire; see Krick, op. cit. pp. 232 ff.

39. The *Darsapurnamasau*.

40. Quoted from Gonda in, *The Haviryajñah Somah*, p. 8.

41. TS I.1.4t, 1.5a, b, e, f; Keith's translation, *The Harvard Oriental Series*, vol. 18.

42. See SB VI.6.2.2.19.

43. See SB XIII.1.1.3 ff. Here the horse is identified with Prajâpati.

44. The Ashvins were the Advaryus of the gods in this primordial sacrifice, see Richard Hecht, *Sacrifice, Comparative Study and Interpretation*, Doctoral Dissertation, the University of California at Los Angeles, 1976, p. 225. I have made special use of Hecht's chapter on, "The Ashvamedha and History." His interpretation of the Ashvamedha deserves special attention. We shall consider Hecht's treatment of the horse sacrifice later in this chapter.

45. SB XIII.1.2.2.

46. TB 3.8.3. Hecht said that this thirteenth cubit of the rope formed a "perfect" Ashvamedha, op. cit. p. 225. TB 3.8.1. suggests that the sacrificer obtained the year by means of these twelve cubits.

47. Eggeling said that, "The ceremonies treated in the first six chapters (*Brâhmanas*) refer to the setting apart of the horse for its sacred office, a year before the sacrifice, and to the intervening period during which the horse is allowed to roam about," op. cit., p. 274, fn. 1.

48. SB said the horse was sprinkled in order to make it acceptable to Prajâpati, see XIII. 1.2.5 ff.

49. See, SB XIII.1.2.3.

50. I take "truth" here to be the same as Rita or the universal that the Brahmins interchanged for Satya, see chapter two.

51. The *Kâtyâyana Shrautasutra* specified "non-flowing" water, 20.1.35.

52. The sprinkling was done in the name of Prajâpati from the east; in the name of Indra and Agni from the south; in the name of Vâyu from

the west; in the name of Visvedevâh from north; and in the names of all the gods and the earth, atmosphere, and sky from above and below, see, TB 3.8.19.

53. Notice the SB rendering of this notion: "Concerning this they say, 'Seeing that the horse is sacred to Prajâpati, wherefore (does he say), "I sprinkle thee" for other deities also?' Well, all gods are concerned in the horse-sacrifice; when he says, 'I sprinkle thee for all gods, 'he makes all the gods take a concern in the horse-sacrifice..." (XIII.1.2.9).

54. This was Eggeling's belief also, see. SB, vol. V, p. 279, fn. 1. Thite thinks this was one of the "popular" rites that the Ashvamedha "elevated" and used to signify that the sacrificer's enemy had been removed, also see, *Sacrifice in the Brâhmana Texts*, p. 91. Others saw the killing of the dog as a fertility rite. Richard Hecht suggested that the dog was a real danger to the king because it physically represented "that which is opposed to order," op. cit., p. 468, fn. 14.

55. Sin, disease and Anrita would have been considered threats to the success of the sacrifice. See chapter two on Rita.

56. The north-eastern direction symbolized the gate of Heaven, see Hecht, op. cit., p. 469, fn. 21.

57. See, SB XIII.4.2.5.

58. TB 3.19.13 held that the horse could only be found by performing Ishtis.

59. SB XIII.1.6.2.

60. The Dhrtis offerings were performed on the Ahavanîya altar just after the sun set, see, SB XIII. 1.4.3.

61. XIII.1.6.2.

62. Both the Dhrtis and these Ishtis were Soma sacrifices.

63. See, KS 20.2.12,13.

64. Keith also felt that these measures were part of protecting the sanctity of the horse's powers, see, *The Harvard Oriental Series*, vol. XXXII, p. 334. If any of these protective measures failed and something happen to the horse atonement had to be made. If the horse died the entire ritual had to be started again, see, SB XIII.1.6.3 and TB 3.8.9.

65. This all took place near the Vedi altar with the story teller himself, the Hotri, stationed closest to this most holy spot while he addressed the Adhvaryu who responded, (see, SB XIII.4.3.1,2). The rite of telling the Pâriplava Legend shows the continuing importance of the Vedas for all the people under the king's rule. "'King Manu Vaivasvata,' he says; 'his people are Men, and they are staying here;-householders, unlearned in the scriptures, have come thither : it is these he instructs; 'The Rik (verses) are the Veda : this it is;' thus saying, let him go over a hymn of the Rik, as if reciting it" (SB XIII.4.3.3 a). Drury reminds us that the root of King Manu's name, "man," means "to think," see, *Sacrificial Ritual in the Shatapatha Brâhmana*, p. 45.

66. See SB XIII. 4.3.3 ff. This scene may have been similar to that of the sacrifices when the ancient Vedas were in their oral stage.

67. The sun, Sûrya, was once in the form of a horse who produced children with Sannâ while she had the form of a mare. See Alfred Hillebrant, *Vedic Mythology*, E.T. Sreeramula Rajeswara Sarma, Delhi, Motilal Banarsidass, vol. I, 1981, see, Sûrya.

68. A lunar race also existed that descended from a seer by the name of Atri. The Kauravas and Pândavas found in the *Mahâbhârata* were, for example, from this Lunar heritage, see, Drury, op. cit., p. 45.

69. See SB I.8.1.1-6.

70. SB XIII..4.3.6.

71. SB XIII.4.3.6.

72. SB X 13.4; 14.15; 14.2.

73. Drury said that each day a different part of the community was honored, see, op. cit., p. 48.

74. SB XIII.4.3.7. Varuna in Vedic times exerted great power over men and nature. We recall that he also was associated with maintaining the Rita, see chapter two.

75. See Hillebrandt, *Vedic Mythology*, vol. II, pp. 251 ff, "...the waters conceived as women are the Apsarases." Also see Drury, op. cit., pp. 50-51.

76. SB XI.5.1 ff.

77. See Drury for more details on this legend, op. cit., p. 51. The fire sacrifice imparted knowledge to the king that enabled him to attain his desire.

78. SB XIII.4.3.9.

79. SB XIII.4.3.10.

80. SB XIII.4.311. See Hillebrandt, op. cit., vol. I, pp. 11 ff. Drury thinks that the Asuras represented the "negative aspect of the community" (see, op. cit., p. 53). This does not do justice to the sacrificial context of this instruction. The text speaks of the forces that opposed the sacrifice and consequentially had to be overcome if the sacrifice was to succeed.

81. SB XIII.4.3.12. These stories came from the Itihâsas.

82. See XIII.5.4.9.

83. SB XIII.4.3.13.

84 Hillebrandt, *Vedic Mythology*, vol. II, p. 246.

85. Hillebrandt said, "There was no intrinsic difference between the sacrificial horse and the solar horse." Ibid., p. 246.

86. See *Rig Veda* I.163. The Gods are said here to have fashioned the horse out of the sun, cf.,I.163.2.

87. Thite thinks that the Pâriplava legend was of "popular origin" and that its purpose was to amuse those present. See op. cit., p. 92.

88. The *Kâtyâyana Shrauta Sûtra* (XX.4.2-10) called these offerings Audgrabhana while the *Shatapatha-Brâhmana* (XIII.1.7.1) labeled them Vaisvadeva, cf. Eggeling's note, S.B.E., vol. XLIV. The Audgrabhanarites always preceded ordinary Soma sacrifices, see SB III.1.4.1. In the Dîksha of the Ashvamedha the Adhvaryu performed the Audgrabhana oblations on the first six days. The seventh day required the special offerings that applied to the Agnicayana, see SB VI.6.1.15-20; KSS XX.4.7. Like the Ishti rites before Full and New moon rites the Audgrabhana and Vaisvadeva rites which preceded the Soma sacrifices, as well as the rites that necessarily came prior to the Agnicayana ritual, seem to indicate an increasing level of sanctity as the ritual progressed upwards, so to speak, towards the heavenly world. Hence, the pressing of Soma was too sacred an act to perform without first taking proper ritual precautions.

89. For a detailed study of the Dîkshâ see J. Gonda, *Change and Continuity in Indian Religion*.

90. Refer to Keith, H.O.S., vol. 32, p. 344.

91. Prajapati practiced some form of austerity that produced heat, Tapas, and thus succeeded in gaining the Dîksâ, see, SB XIII.1.7.1.

92. See, TB 3.8.10. The SB XIII. 1.7.2b,3 reads, "He makes offering by dividing (each) deity into three parts; for the gods are of three orders, and of three orders are these worlds : he thus establishes himself in these worlds in prosperity and vital power. They amount to one and twenty (single invocations and oblations),-there are twelve months, five seasons, these three worlds, and yonder sun as the twenty-first,-that is the divine ruling-power, that is the glory : that supreme lordship, that summit of the fallow one (the Sun), that realm of light he attains."

93. The Prajâpati-Agni myths were an essential part of the Agnicayana ritual, see SB VI.1 ff.; X.1.ff.

94. "The sacrificial ground chosen for the Ashvamedha Sacrifice should have to its east a water-place having the water permanently" (KSS XX.4.14).

95. The bodies of these animals was placed in the water for brick making, see Drury, op. cit. p. 77.

96. The SB said that both the sacrificer and the king mounted the altar during the sacrifice.

97. A slight variation exists between the two lists of births given in these two *Brâhmanas*, see TB 3.8.13; SB XIII.1.8.1-10.

98. TB 3.8.19.

99. Keith noted the discrepancy of these rites during these days of the Soma sacrifice, H.O.S., vol. 32, p. 344.

100. TB 3.8.14,15.

101. This too was done in accordance with the mythological actions of Prajâpati who stood under an Asvattha tree for a year in the form of a horse to hide himself from the gods. The enclosure for the sacrificial horse was made out of Asvattha wood and thereby sacrificer repeated the primordial act of Prajâpati, see, TB 3.8.12.

102. SB XIII.2.3.1,2a; also see TB 3.8.22. Eggeling said that, "Pavamâna is the name of the pressed Soma while it is 'clarifying,'" S.B.E. vol. XLIV, p. 304, fn. 2.

103. The SB recorded a similar statement contrasting the gods ignorance and the horse's knowledge. The SB XIII.2.8.1a. reads: "Now the gods, when going upwards, did not know (the way to) the heavenly world, but the horse knew it: when they go upwards with the horse, it is in order to know (the way to) the heavenly world." Here the gods were totally dependent on the sacrifice.

104. See KSS XX.5.14.

105. SB XIII.2.7.12,13.

!06. SB XIII.2.6.7, see S.B.E., vol. XLIV, p. 312, fn. 1.

107. The Mahisî, the Vâvâtâ, and the Parivrktî, see, SBXIII.2.6.8. The SB explained this weaving rite as giving the sacrificer one hundred years of life.

108. SB XIII.2.6.8. KSS XX.5.16 says that the three wives weaved these gold-beads "in such a fashion that the beads do not fall out (and get lost)."

109. The SB also mentions the fact that the remaining food "from the cart for the horse" was taken down to the people (XIII.2.6.8). Eggeling said this was the material leftover from the Annahomas, see p. 314.

110. See KSS XX.5.18,19.

111. A hornless he-goat, a deer, three goats (one with a black neck) dedicated to Agni, two goats with hairy front legs dedicated to Tvastar and Dhâtar, a white he-goat dedicated to Sûrya, a he-goat dedicated to Pûsan, two more he-goats for Brhaspati, and one last he-goat dedicated to Indra and again Pûsan were all symbolically attached to various parts of the horse from different directions. Several hundred additional animals joined the horse in temporary confinement. Approximately fifteen domestic animals were bound to each of twenty-one stakes positioned around the horse, see SB XIII.2.2.1ff. Priests added two-hundred and eighty-two wild animals to stakes between the domestic ones. The SB explained that Prajâpati gained both worlds through the tame animals, which represented the terrestrial world, and the wild ones, which stood for the heavenly world, XIII.2.4.1. The wild animals were now to be sacrificed with the explanation that, "By (so doing) with the wild (beasts) the roads would run asunder, the village-boundaries of two villages would be far asunder, and there would come to be ogres, man-tigers, thieves, murders, and robbers in the forests," SB XIII.2.4.2b. In short the SB and TB (see 3.9.1) taught that the sacrifice of the wild animals would have meant "a violation of the sacrifice." The sacrifice of the tame animals brought order to the terrestrial world, (see SB XIII.2.4.2,4.). But the sacrifice of the wild animals disrupted cosmic order.

112. See Drury, op. cit., p. 55.

113. For this series of events see KSS XX.6ff; SB XIII.2.8.1ff.

114. SB XIII.5.2.1.

115. This cloth represented the world while the other cloth stood for the atmosphere and the piece of gold symbolized the sun. Eggeling suggested that the large blanket under the horse prevented any sacrificial material from spilling out, see S.B.E., vol. XLVI, p. 320. fn. 2.

166. KSS XX.6.20 says that only the queens' attendants responded to the priests' statements and not the queens themselves.

117. TB 3.9.6; see SB XIII.2.8.5.

118. SB XIII.2.9.2.

119. SB XIII.2.9.7.

120. Drury believes that the fifth maiden that came along with the four queens was in actuality a substitute for the Mahisî. The need for the queen's stand-in, according to Drury, was because the maiden would have become "too sacred to return to ordinary living," see op. cit., p. 56. His reason makes some sense and may have been the case for the SB where no mention was made of the queen's purification bath after her night with the horse. But in the case of the TB, for example, the bath served to remove the extraordinary sanctity from such contact with the holy animal. The queen's holiness would have made it impossible for her to have normal contact in the profane world. She would have, in fact, become taboo herself by virtue of her contact with the consecrated horse.

121. TB 3.9.6.

122. SB XIII.2.10.1

123. TB 3.9.6.

124. TB 3.9.6; TS 5.2.12 e,f.

125. KSS XX.7.3,4.

126. TB 3.9.8.

127. TB 3.9.10. According to the TB the purpose for drinking these two servings of the Soma drink was so that Prajâpati, and consequently the king likewise, would become a "great eater of food."

128. See SB XIII.2.6.10-17; TB 3.9.5. These accounts differ slightly in the two versions. The main difference being that the positions were reversed between the Hotri and Brahman. This Brahmodya resembled the discussion called by the same name in SB XIII.5.2.11 ff. where the four priests raise questions and answers just prior to the omenta offering. For a fuller treatment of the Brahmodya and its significance see R. Hecht, op. cit., pp. 234-236.

129. SB XIII.2.6.15. Eggeling noted that, "Mahîdhara, moreover, identifies the horse with the horse-sacrifice, which, in the shape of a bird, carries the Sacrificer up to heaven," see vol. XLIV, p. 315.

130. KSS XX.8.1-11.

131. The KSS made provisions for the performance of the Avabhrtha rite at the end of each of the Soma pressing days. However, the KSS stipulated that if an Avabhrtha rite followed the end of each day of Soma sacrifices the vessel used to contain the Soma juice must not be submersed in the water to the point that the remnants of the Soma touched the water. If the leftover Soma of the first two days did make contact with the waters of the purification bath then "the consecration-vows for the Sacrificer will come to an end," see XX.8.17-22. Only on the last day could the leftover Soma residue in the vessel come into contact with the water. Premature contact before the Soma pressing ended would have removed the special, consecrated nature of the Soma and sacrificer. Such an action would have violated the distinction between that which had been transformed in order to come in contact with the divine and that which was being returned to the profane.

132. Another Brahmaudana was performed that lasted for twelve days TB 3.9.18; SB XIII.3.6.6. These sacrifices were Ishtis as at the beginning of the Ashvamedha. According to TB 3.9.18 this rite lasted twelve days because the year has twelve months and thereby the sacrificer established himself in the year.

133. TB 3.9.15.

134. SB XIII.3.6.5.

135. Keith placed this ceremony with other magical practices in Ancient India that removed sins, see H.O.S., vol. 31, pp. 264-268. Thite, following a host of others,suggested that this rite removed the difficulties of vegetation, see, *Sacrifice in the Brâhmana Texts*, p. 94. One wonders about the context of the above concerns in light of the actual concerns in the texts.

136. Krick, *Das Ritual der Feuergründung*, pp. 577-578.

137. The anthropologist might say that the "holy" served as an "contagion" for the profane. See Mary Douglas, *Purity and Danger*, pp. 159 ff. Douglas is somewhat ambiguous as to the nature of this "contagion." Does "dirt" or the profane become sacred through contact with the Holy or does it merely become undifferentiated? Douglas thinks the latter only because "dirt" gradually loses it distinctive features for a society as "pollution." Dirt or the profane can then take on a sacred nature. But the problem for religious ritual is precisely the problem of nondifferentiation, there is no such thing as innocuous pollution in a purified environment or harmless sacredness in the profane world. Outside the ritual boundaries in the everyday life of society these distinctions become blurred, but not in the world createdby religious ritual that re-affirms the distinction.

138. Dumont op. cit. p. 226; V.S. 18.57.

139. According to Krick the Câtvâla represented the Primordial sea that once had contained the sun. She also thought that the Câtvâla served to purify objects, see op. cit. pp. 116, 119, fn. 309. The notion of purification may not best suit the function of this special pit. The objects used on the Vedi would have already have been purified for sacrificial use. This special pit rather served to protect the consecrated nature of these objects from profane contact or from merely being discarded haphazardly when not in use.

140. This was how Oldenberg described the ceremony: Zur Schlussceremonie, welche am Ende des Ophers der Dîkshâentspricht, steigt, man vom Opferplatz zum Wasser hinab. Der Opferer und seine Gattin haben das Antilopenfell und die Umgrürtung, die sie von der Dîkshâ her trugen, abgelegt. Diese Dinge werden in's Wasser geworfen; ebenso die Opfergefässe, welche mit Soma in Berührung gewesen waren. Auch die ausgepressten Somaschösslinge werden im Wasser untergetaucht. Zum Schluss steigen der Opferer und seine Gattin sowie die Peiester selbst in's Wasser. Mann und Frau reinigen einander den Rücken. Beim Heraussteigen legen sie frische Gewänder an. Die Opferspenden und Sprüche, welche diese Riten begleiten, richten sich vor Allem an Varuna, den Befreier von aller Schuld; die Bitte um diese Befreiung tritt in den verschiedensten Formen hervor. "Hundert und tausend Aerzte hast du; O König. Weit und tief soll deine Gnade sein. Treibe Hass und Untergang in die Derne. Auch die vollbrachte Sünde löse von uns." Und in einem Spruch, der an das personifieirte Reinigungsbad selbst gerichtet ist: "Du hast die von den Göttern gottbegangene Sünde hinweggeophert und die menschbegangene der Menschen. Aus deiner Weite schüze uns, O Gott, vor Schaden." See *Die Religion Des Veda*, p. 407.

141. Hillebrandt said that "The sacrificer who takes the Ashvamedha bath hopes to be forgiven for his grave sins."Op. cit. p. 246.

142. KSS XX.8.17.

143. *Die Religion Des Veda*, pp. 306-7, 407-9, 473-75.

144. S.B.E., vol. XLIV, regarding the XIII Kânda, pp. XLIV ff.

145. Eggeling also identified the horse with Varuna, or the sea of waters, because mythology said the horse came from the waters, see *Rig Veda* I.163.1.

146. See *La Doctrine Du Sacrifice dans Les Brâhmanas*, chap. 1.

147. Ibid. see pp. 13-15.

148. Op. cit., p. 28.

149. Lévi said "Si la vérité assure le triomphe définitif des deux, ce n'est pas par le prestige de la deux, mais par la vertu des prestiges magiques qui sont le sacrifice," ibid., p. 39.

150. H.O.S., vol. 32, pp. 346-7.

151. Ibid., p. 346.

152. H.O.S., vol. 18, p. CXXXIV.

153. See "The Horse-Sacrifice in the *Taittirîya-Brâhmana*," *Proceedings of the American Philosophical Society*, vol. 92, pp. 447-503.

154. See *L'Asvamedha: Description du sacrifice solennel du cheval dans le culte védique*. Paris, Paul Geuthner, 1927.

155. Refer to *L'Asvamedha*, p. XII.

156. Ibid., p. XIII.

157. *Sacrifice in the Brâhmana-Texts*, pp. 94-95.

158. Here Thite politely disagreed with K. F. Johansson, "Dhisanâ," *Äber die altindische Göttin Dhisanâ und Verwandtes*, Uppsala, 1919; and J. J. Meyer, "Trilogie," *Trilogie altindischer Mächte und Feste der Vegetation*, Zürich-Leipzig, 1937.

159. Op. cit., p. 94.

160. Ibid., p. 95.

161. Ibid., p. 95.

162. Thite also felt that the introduction of Prajâpati served to elevate the Ashvamedha, see op. cit., p. 95.

163. Few indologists today fail to see the connection between 'ritualism' in the *Brâhmanas* and 'spiritualism' in the *Upanishads*. Consequently, scholars have recognized a closer relationship between the major concerns of the *Brâhmanas* and *Upanishads*. Also see Gonda, *Change and Continuity*, p. 243.

164. Thite said, "In this thesis an attempt is made to see everywhere the latent connections of the Brâhmanical 'ritualism' with the Upanisadic 'spiritualisms.' " See op. cit., p. 6, also check p.329.

165. Op. cit. p. 97.

166. It has been a simple matter for many to understand Vedic ritual's development, or "new elevated status," to have logically led to a de-emphasis of ritual act.

167. Tat âhuhu kena juhoti kasmin hûyata iti. Prânenaiva juhoti prâne hûyate. Tat yad etad agnîn manthanti yajamânasyaiva tat prânân janayanti. "This is what they say: 'What does he offer, in what is offered (at the sacrifice)?' By means of life (breath) he offers, in life (breath) it is offered. Now they make (drill) the fires, thus they produce the life (breaths) of the one sacrificing." See *Jaiminîya Brâhmana* I,1; also see the translation of H. W. Bodewitz, *Jaiminîya Brâhmana*, Leiden, E. J. Brill, 1973, p. 19.

168. Jaan Puhvel, who sought to establish a Celtic connection to the Ashvamedha, found two significant discrepancies between the two sacrifices. One was the manner in which the horse was put to death, and the other being the absence of the "erotic element," see ibid., p. 242.

169. Ibid., p. 7. Dumézil's assertion that "ideology" can recapture the primacy sense of the documents implies that the original Sitz im Leben had produced a pure ideology which only later became incumbered with religious aspects. We have no evidence of this anywhere in human documents. At this point the historical record stands against Dumézil's hypothesis.

170. Dumézil, *Rituals indo-européens à Rome*, Paris, Libraire C. Klinksieck, 1954, p. 7. Without rejecting the role that fertility played in rituals Dumézil placed rituals on an equal level with the other elements of religion.

171. Here the influence of his old teacher E. Durkhiem can be seen, see S. Littleton, *The New Comparative Mythology: An Anthropological Assessment of the Theories of Georges Dumézil*, Berkeley and Los Angeles: University of California Press, 1966.

172. Gonda's work in general still reveals the influence of Oldenberg and Frazer's magical-fertility causes and effects for ritual.

173. Gonda, *Ancient Indian Kingship from the the Religious Point of View*. Leiden: Brill, 1969, p. 110.

174. Gonda. "The Sacred Character of Ancient Kingship," La Regalità Sacra: *Contributions to the Central Theme of the VIIth International Congress for the History of Religions*. Leiden: E.J. Brill, 1969, p. 177.

175. Eliade, *A History of Religious Ideas*, vol. I, pp.218-219.

176. Ibid., p. 214.

177. Hecht, op. cit., p. 243.

178. Ibid., pp. 249 ff.

179. SB XIII.2.1.5,b; also see XIII.1.3.3; 2.2.16; 1.3.1.

180. Hymn I.163.1,4,11,12a,13; Wendy O'Flaherty's translation in, *The Rig Veda, An Anthology*, New York. Penguin Books, 1981, pp. 87, 88.

181. Ibid., pp. 90-92; Hymn I.162.4,21,22.

182. SB XIII.2.3.2.

183. SB XIII.2.8.5; 2.9.2; 2.9.7.

184. Just as the sacrificial horse represented the human side of the link with heaven for the sacrificer so too Prajâpati represented the transcendent side of this symbolic connection.

185. TS 5.25.

186. SB XIII.3.7.3.

187. I 162.15.

188. SB XIII.1.2.5ff.

189. I.162.5, 22.

190. SB XIII.3.1.1.

191. Quoted from S.B.E., vol. XLIV, p. XXII, fn. 1.

192. S.B.E., vol. XLIV, p. XXVII, fn. 1.

193. See the myth of Prajâpati creating the horse from his eye which in turn was restored when the gods performed the Ashvamedha, SB XIII.3.1.1.

194. SB XIII.3.8.11,12.

195. SB XIII.3.7.8.

196. The absence of the sacrifice in India's history came only in the form of Buddhism's rejection of the authority of the Vedas.

197. SB XIII.3.8.4,5.

# CHAPTER FOUR

# THE SACRIFICIAL BACKGROUND OF THE EUCHARIST

The Eucharist continues to be a subject shrouded in mystery and controversy while still providing spiritual enrichment for many people. The academic community has also found the Eucharist an intriguing topic. Many specialists have undertaken different approaches to the Eucharist from its historical development, origin, social background, theologies, liturgies, texts, to Jung's psychoanalytical interpretation. Liturgists, New Testament scholars, patristic scholars, church historians, religious historians and theologians have all made valuable contributions to the study of the Eucharist. The sheer size and complexity of eucharistic studies requires such specialization. However, research on the Eucharist has become fragmented, leaving a somewhat distorted perspective of the multiple related aspects that combined to make up the Eucharist . Some scholars stress liturgical considerations at the expense of textual concerns. A few traditio-historical exegetes have deemed the Eucharist so similar to ancient Mediterranean cultic meals that its distinctiveness as a religious phenomenon has evaporated. Still others fail to acknowledge that the Eucharist shared religious symbolism in common with other religions.

The first part of this chapter contains the history of interpretation on the Eucharist as an example of the type of problems biblical specialists have faced when confronted with eucharistic texts in the New Testament. The following brief survey of the history of interpretation also reveals how scholars have practically ignored the religious symbolization in the New Testament texts in favor of an almost exclusively textual and philological examination. The search for eucharistic origins has subsequently eclipsed much of the liturgical, the sacramental, and especially the sacrificial aspects of the Eucharist in the

New Testament. New Testament historical and philological works remain crucial to the study of the Eucharist but not in isolation from comparative studies. The present approach takes into account the significance of the Eucharist's religious symbolism as something universally shared but at the same time recognizing its own particular historical development and expression.

The remainder of the chapter covers the general historical background that led to the inception of the Eucharist in early Christianity. This historical sketch gives particular attention to the role of sacrifice in Israel and Judaism as a determining factor in the early church's celebration of Jesus Christ's death and resurrection in the Eucharist. Hellenism's influence on the religious matrix of Judaism can not be ignored, but neither can the Mystery Religions. The symbolism that surfaced in the religions of the Hellenistic period had a clear influence on the Christian cultic meal.

### 4:1 The History of New Testament Interpretation

The classic work of Darwell Stone in 1909 on the Eucharist made it clear that the church had focused almost exclusively on the theological issues of Christ's presence, the elements and their consecration, and of course, the eucharistic sacrifice.[1] The older treatises on the Eucharist looked at the presence of Christ in relationship to the elements of the bread and wine. The medieval doctrine of transubstantiation articulated a centuries-old concept of the elements changing into the actual body and blood of Christ during the Eucharist. Roman theologians thought of the substance of Christ's body displacing the substance of the bread and wine. In contrast to the doctrine of transubstantiation, Luther spoke of the co-existence of the substance of Christ and the elements (consubstantiation) based on the ubiquity of Christ's humanity. However, Christ remained in heaven for both Zwingli and Calvin.[2]

The notion of Christ's presence was closely related to the claims for a sacrificial nature of the Eucharist throughout the older treatises. Many sought to understand the relationship between the Cross of Christ and the eucharistic offering of Christ expressly since the classical liturgical traditions presented the Eucharist as a sacrifice. The Council of Trent (1545-63) displayed the Roman concern for the true understanding of the sacrifice of Christ in view of the Protestant rejection of Christ's sacrifice in the Eucharist. Notice Joseph Jungmann's comment on the sacrifice in the Roman Mass in light of the Council of Trent:

> But how is this presence of the sacrifice of Christ to be understood? There must be something more here than just a representation of the oblation that took place once upon a time, something more than the memoria passions as we see it commonly exhibited by the separate presentation of the Body and the Blood of Christ. On the altar a sacrifice truly takes place, but it is a sacrifice which in many respects coincides with the sacrifice of the Cross. For the Council of Trent says of it: "There is the same oblation, and the same Person who now makes the oblation through the ministry of the priests and who once had made an oblation of himself on the Cross. Only the manner of the offering is different."[3]

These questions have preoccupied Christianity in the West up until the nineteenth-century when modern historical research began to offset the more purely theological and liturgical interests. Modern historical criticism has concentrated on textual problems in the New Testament sources for the Eucharist. Other efforts of modern research attempt to trace the historical development of early liturgical sources that produced the major traditions in the East and West.

The name of Albert Schweitzer (1875-1965) surfaces in the discussion of modern research on the Eucharist because his work marks the changing methodological trend in eucharistic studies. Schweitzer's work, originally published in 1901 as *Das Abendmahlsproblem auf Grund der wissenschaftlichen Forschung des 19. Jahrhunderts und historischen Berichte,* did not convince most of his colleagues. But it did help to establish a critical historical precedent for the study of the Eucharist in the New Testament. He tried to find a historical connection between Jesus' "Last Supper"[4] and the "Lord's Supper" of the early church. Schweitzer argued that Mark's gospel represented Jesus' own intentions and therefore was the authentic source for the Eucharist.[5] Schweitzer decided to depart from the traditional approaches to the Eucharist. Instead of following the Reformers or Roman Catholics of the past who sought to understand the Eucharist from the symbolic words of the institution, "this is my body"..."this is my blood;" Schweitzer approached the Lord's Supper through the historical Jesus problem.[6] In other words, one could avoid the unprofitable "pure symbolic interpretation" or the "crass realistic interpretation" by separating the historically authentic intention of Jesus from the artificial "words of institution."[7]

Schweitzer believed the original intention of Jesus at the Last Supper (Mark 14: 22-25) was to reveal the "secret" of his suffering as the Messiah to the disciples. Schweitzer proposed that the only way to arrive at this historical understanding of the Last Supper was to examine the "general pattern of the life of Jesus."[8] He said, "The problem of the Lord's Supper is the problem of the life of Jesus!"[9] The "general pattern of the life of Jesus" that Schweitzer used to understand the Lord's Supper rested on his judgment regarding Jesus' messiahship. He believed Jesus depicted himself as the Messiah during his ministry. Schweitzer felt that this self-characterization of Jesus was especially illuminating with regard to the messianic banquets foretold by the Jewish prophets. Schweitzer referred to the feeding of five thousand in the sixth chapter of Mark as an example of the prophesied messianic meals and in fact called it the "first Eucharist."

The revelation of Jesus' suffering and death was only part of his secret at the last supper, according to Schweitzer. Jesus also revealed to the disciples that shortly after his death he would unite with them again in the kingdom of God (Mark 14:25). Thus Schweitzer gave the last supper an eschatological treatment that he felt others had neglected.[10] It was this eschatological component that provided Schweitzer with his connection between the historical last supper and the early church's continuing celebrations. The importance of this connection for Schweitzer went back to Schleiermacher's observation that Mark's account did not command that the rite be repeated. So the early church, according to Schweitzer, continued to celebrate the meal out of expectation of the messianic feast with their risen Lord. These earliest thanksgiving meals were built around the eschatological expectation of the return of Jesus and fellowship with one another. Schweitzer thought that the Apostle Paul had placed the command to repeat the rite in the mouth of Jesus (1 Corinthians 11:23, 25). Schweitzer also took Paul's so-called sacramental use of the bread and wine to mean fellowship with Christ's body and blood so that as eschatological expectation waned the "meal-celebration" became a "distribution-celebration."[11]

Schweitzer's name has fallen almost completely from current critical works on the Eucharist, yet the basic problems he addressed continue to beget controversy today among New Testament specialists.[12] Like Albert Schweitzer these scholars delve into eucharistic origins and developments. Their studies involve both evidence from the New Testament texts and sources from the church fathers, the early church liturgies, and the religious and social environment of late antiquity.

Two names continue to emerge in critical works on the Eucharist. One is that of Hans Lietzmann and the other is Joachim Jeremias. Lietzmann's work was originally published in 1926 in German as *Messe und Herrenmahl* and was later published in English under the title of *Mass and the Lord's Supper* with the addition of a supplementary essay by Robert D. Richardson.[13] Jeremias' work, *The Eucharistic Words of Jesus* was originally published in 1935 as, *Die Abendmahlsworte Jesu* with Jeremias' own revisions in the English editions up to 1964.[14] Both men were eminent New Testament scholars who made exemplary use of modern historical science and added their own unique contributions to eucharistic studies.

Lietzmann gathered and described an invaluable collection of ancient liturgical texts. He worked back from families of existing rites that he had classified under four main types[15] until he arrived at an "early Egyptian" and a "Western" type.[16] Lietzmann then traced these two types back to the liturgies of Hippolytus (early third century) and Sarapion (mid-fourth century).

According to Lietzmann's investigations, the Egyptian types stemmed from the Sarapion liturgical source which in turn was based upon the *Didache* (chapters IX-X). Lietzmann further stipulated that the *Didache* text ultimately went back to the early church's continuation of Jesus' table fellowship that he practiced with his disciples during his lifetime. The *Didache* preserved the "breaking of bread" that signified Jesus' table fellowship and subsequently that of the early church. Thus Lietzmann also referred to this as the "Jerusalem type." However, the *Didache* witness lacked the "cup of blessing" at the end of the meal. Lietzmann also noticed that the book of Acts (2:42) likewise mentioned the "breaking of bread" without any reference to the cup. He concluded that the "breaking of the bread" meals did not derive from the last supper and did not use the symbolic cup of wine. Lietzmann identified this "breaking of bread" as the Jewish festive meal shared with a group of friends called the Habûrah.[17] Liturgies based on the Egyptian type of "breaking the bread" meals were known only to the Palestinian churches that celebrated this rite in joyful anticipation of their risen Lord's return.

Lietzmann then conjectured that the church considered these fellowship meals as sacrifices early on in their development. He specifically attributed the sacrificial element in the Eucharist to Hellenism. Nonetheless, this "non-Jewish" influence ultimately resulted in a concept of "sacrifice" that had atoning powers just as those sacrifices in the Old Testament. The elements were also regarded as "holy" food from which the participant could receive eternal life if one "approached without defilement."[18] Lietzmann thought that the Jerusalem type would have eventually added the cup from the influence of Jewish customs.

Lietzmann attached the "Western" type to the Hippolytus rite and extended it back to Paul in I Corinthians, chapters 10 and 11. Here too, the rite in Paul's churches took place within the general context of a Habûrah meal after which the "Last Supper" would have also been patterned.[19] Lietzmann regarded the Hippolytus Church Order as the primary source for the early Christian love feasts or agape meals.[20] The Western type differed from the Egyptian rites according to Lietzmann's scheme because of Paul's own innovations. For Lietzmann, Paul's "Lord's Supper" did not continue Jesus' table fellowship meals but rather used the liturgical "breaking of the bread" at the beginning and "blessing of the cup" at the end of the meal to remind the church of the death of Christ. The "Pauline" type used the metaphor, "This is my body", as a liturgical device but need not be attributed to Jesus own words.[21] The sacrifice of Christ sealed the "new covenant" and the Lord's Supper proclaimed this truth until their Lord returned. According to Lietzmann, Paul had modeled the sacrificial element of the rite after Hellenistic funeral banquets "held as memorials to great men, founders of religious communities."[22] At the same time he considered the Lord's Supper a sacrificial meal that established communion with Jesus as in Hellenistic and Jewish rites.

The gist of these "two main types" shows that Lietzmann differentiated between Paul's "Lord's Supper" or "agape meal" and the "breaking-of-bread" table fellowship meals from evidence within the New Testament itself. But Lietzmann also based his division between the two types on assumptions that he formulated from this internal evidence. Perhaps the most revealing of Lietzmann's presumptions came to light under the careful scrutiny of R. D. Richardson in his supplementary essay to *Mass and Lord's Supper*. Richardson compared Lietzmann's theory of the origins and development of the eucharistic liturgy with Westcott and Hort's theory of the origins and transmission of the text of the New Testament. The similarities between the two works were quite obvious to Richardson. Westcott and Hort discovered the existence of two types of texts behind the standard fourth-century Syrian (Byzantine) text used for the New Testament.[23] The first type they named the "Neutral" text. Westcott and Hort believed the Neutral text to have only originated in Egypt at the end of the second century. They further believed that the Neutral text was more "pure" than the second type or "Western" text that had a relatively early date but also possessed many corruptions.

Lietzmann followed the exact same development and transmission for his Egyptian rite from fourth century Byzantine liturgies back to the "general Supper-practice of Jesus and his Jerusalem disciples."[24] But Lietzmann's fundamental assumption that the texts of the New Testament and the eucharistic rites developed together in the same localities can not be substantiated by any example of the "interaction of rite and text upon each other."[25] Lietzmann copied an incomplete paradigm based on Westcott and Hort's textual hypothesis. Their preference for the "Neutral" text rested on documentary and internal evidence that could not account for important external factors such as the influence of doctrines and rites on the texts.[26] Lietzmann did recognize the influence of rites upon texts. He also saw the second century evidence for a Pauline type of bread-cup rite but gave little significance to these factors in comparison to his predilection for the bread rites of the "pure Egyptian rite."

Lietzmann's theory of two main eucharistic types has come under widespread criticism. Some have made revisions of his theory while others have rejected it outright. Ernst Lohmeyer merely supplanted it with his Galilean and Jerusalem types.[27] R. D. Richardson took his adaptation of Lietzmann's theory further still by suggesting that the Sarapion rite went back to an unique and independent source that had emphasized the symbolism of the bread and wine in relation to Jesus' body while the Hippolytus type represented rites where the words of the institution were central.[28] Oscar Cullmann rejected Lietzmann's theory on the grounds that the Jerusalem "breaking of bread" could not be traced directly back to Jesus' meals with his disciples.[29] Instead, Cullmann postulated that the Jerusalem "breaking of bread" originated from the accounts of the resurrected Christ appearing with his disciples at meals before his ascension. Also in opposition to Lietzmann, Cullmann saw a connection between the Jerusalem type and the Last Supper. Gregory Dix went so far as to say, "There is no evidence whatever that these (Lord's supper or agape and the eucharist) are really parallel developments of the same thing, a "Jerusalem type" of non-sacramental fellowship meal, and a "Pauline type" of eucharistic oblation, as Lietzmann and others have supposed."[30] Joachim Jeremias felt Lietzmann's division was overly subjective, and John Reumann mentions the fact that the idea of "two clear, antithetical types of meals" has today fallen from prominence.[31]

A brief look at the above mentioned work of Joachim Jeremias also makes clear the thrust of current topics surrounding New Testament studies on the Eucharist. Jeremias spent four of his five chapters in *The Eucharistic Words of Jesus* dealing with problems directly related to the textual accounts of the Eucharist in the New Testament. His largest chapter (chapter I) argued that the Last Supper was in fact a Passover meal as presented in all three synoptic gospels (Mark 15:42; Matt. 27:62; Luke 23:54).[32] The Gospel of John (18:28; 19:31) does not make this claim. In three additional chapters Jeremias carefully scrutinized the textual accounts of the Eucharist (Mark 14:22-25; Matt. 26:26-29; Luke 22:15-20; I Cor. 11:23-25; John 13:1-30). Jeremias deliberated on these passages in comparison to one another, in relationship to their larger contexts and the specific "words of Jesus," as well as the originality of each. Jeremias' reserved his last chapter to venture into the "meaning of the eucharistic words of Jesus" (chapter V).

The same type of problems surrounding the Eucharist that Jeremias set out to solve through literary, linguistic, textual, form, and historical criticism[33] did not escape the attention of his contemporaries or successors. For this reason his work serves both as a good example of modern critical science's treatment of the Eucharist and as a survey of the history of interpretation within New Testament studies on the subject.

Jeremias confidently defended the Last Supper as a Passover meal against all scholarly objections and continued to do so throughout his book's revisions.[34] But his arguments have far from persuaded all scholars.[35] Some still prefer the Gospel of John's date for the Last Supper[36] over the synoptics while others have explained the contradiction in chronologies between the synoptics and the Fourth Gospel by means of alternative Jewish calendars for eating the Passover in Jesus' time.[37] One argument suggests that the Passover meal would have been eaten earlier when the Passover itself fell on a Sabbath. Yet another proposes that controversies between the Pharisees and Sadducees concerning the proper time for offering the first fruits could account for the different dates.[38]

Anne Jaubert attempted to solve the chronological problem between the synoptics and the Fourth Gospel's account of Jesus death by suggesting the use of different calendars.[39] She compared the official calendar in Jerusalem with that of the Essene settlement at Qumran. The Qumran community rejected the established priesthood in Jerusalem and regarded their sacrifices in the Temple as impure.[40] This cryptic religious sect also followed another calendar similar to the one in the *Book of Jubilees*.[41] According to Jaubert, the Qumran solar calendar placed the day of the Passover on Tuesday evening each year and was used by the synoptics sources. On the other hand, the Gospel of John relied upon on the official Jerusalem calendar. None of these theories has gathered much support, Jeremias among the chief opponents. However, Jaubert has shown that the chronological problem cannot be solved by referring to a single calendar.

Others cannot accept the Last Supper as a Passover meal because of the sketchy and conflicting material in the synoptics themselves.[42] For example, it has been pointed out that Luke did not indicate a clear connection between his Last Supper account (22:15-18) and the Passover.[43] Mark's Last Supper account (14:1,2; 12-16), like the other traditions, provides paschal characteristics, e.g. the preparations, an evening meal setting, held inside the city, and accompanied by a closing hymn. But Mark's text also causes some chronological problems.[44] Paul's version also has clear Passover typology but lacks indisputable evidence to identify the Passover as the "Lord's Supper." Even the Fourth Gospel's Last Supper rendition reveals Passover characteristics while denying the meal was actually eaten on the Passover.[45] For the above reasons Delorme said:

But the relationship between the paschal meal and the last Supper remains vague. And the typology of the lamb, if it was used by Jesus, has left no trace in the tradition of the last Supper. It is difficult to see how the idea of a paschal last Supper came into being, when the liturgy did not encourage it and when the paschal typology in the proper sense did not apply to the Supper.[46]

Alternative views to a paschal Last Supper have explored the premise that the Last Supper was either one of several possible types of Jewish religious meals or an ordinary meal patterned after Jesus' table fellowship but given special significance by Jesus himself in the Upper Room.[47] These two general directions differ from Jeremias' arguments. Jeremias said that the early Christians did continue Jesus' table fellowship meals on a daily basis. But he maintained that these daily meals were not "originally repetitions of the last meal which Jesus celebrated with his disciples."[48] According to Jeremias, the early table fellowship meals were only gradually linked with the "remembrance of the Last Supper," which, of course, he defended as a Passover.[49]

Three possible Jewish ritual meals suggested for the Last Supper besides the Passover are: the Kiddish, Habûrah, and Qumran meals. Jeremias flatly rejected all three.[50] Jeremias said of the Kiddish that it was "neither a meal, nor a sacrifice, nor does it have sacrificial significance, but it is just a simple blessing."[51] The Kiddish[52] not only served to sanctify the beginning of the Sabbath but it was also a blessing that marked "the separation of the sacred period from the profane at its beginning, just as the Habdalah ("separation blessing" at the close of the Sabbaths and feast days) does at the end."[53]

The Habûrah meal has found more support than a mere Kiddish for the type of Jewish ritual meal held in the Upper Room by Jesus and his disciples. Following Lietzmann[54], many scholars have made use of the highly religious character of this meal to speak of the Last Supper and the early church's fellowship meals. The fact that the Habûrah convened on the eve of sabbaths or holy days and involved symbolic acts similar to the New Testament accounts of the Last Supper has drawn much attention from those looking for alternatives to the Passover hypothesis. Religious topics and even business matters were often discussed during the Habûrah. The most striking similarities between the Habûrah and the Last Supper involve Berakoth ("blessings"). These blessings were an integral part of the meal and were accompanied by special blessings over the bread and cup. The bread was broken and distributed among the participants at the beginning of the meal with the addition of a blessing over the cup at the end of this ceremony.[55] While the Habûrah meal has provided a convenient alternative to the Passover it certainly has not solved the problems surrounding the nature of the Last Supper or the origin of first Eucharists. Delorme warned against making too much of these parallels because of the limited information that exists for the Habûrah.[56]

The suggested Qumran source for the Last Supper must be viewed with even more pessimism. The fact that the members of this Jewish sect participated in a daily communal meal with a blessing over bread and drink has led some to identify Jesus' table fellowship as belonging to this Qumran model. Again, Jeremias has shown that the points of difference outweigh the similarities.[57] Qumran has become a valuable source for examining the religious environment in first-century Judaism and early Christianity, but a definite link to the table fellowship of Jesus has yet to emerge from the daily meals at Qumran let alone an identity between the two.

A number of scholars are steering clear from any strict identification of the specific origin and nature of the Lord's Supper. Joseph Fitzmyer, after considering a host of different contributors to the subject, said that, "The upshot is that we cannot answer the question when the historical Jesus ate the Last Supper or whether he ate it as a Passover meal."[58] Klaus Gamber does not think that the Passover solution is all that important anyway in view of the fact that the Passover merely distinguishes itself from other Jewish ritual meals by certain additions.[59] A. Verheul thinks Jesus either used the Passover setting or the Habûrah and gave new content to the meal. According to Verheul, the precise ritual meal that Jesus used does not matter because both are possible when viewed from the vantage point of the New Testament texts.[60] Gillian Feely-Harnik represents yet another who feels that the controversy cannot be resolved without further evidence. She has added an unique element to this discussion by suggesting that the Last Supper,

> was deliberately ambiguous in traditional terms. Early Christian writers seem to have chosen this opportunity to reinterpret several of the major feasts by which Jews expressed their relationship to other human beings and to God, stressing one or another according to their different circumstances and intentions.[61]

Feeley-Harnik went on to say that even though the Last Supper was meant to be ambiguous so as to refer to several sacrifices the "Passover sacrifice was the focus."[62]

James Dunn quickly moved away from the equivocal issue of the identity of the Last Supper. He focused instead on the development of "divergent traditions" within early Christianity that could have resulted in a standardized Eucharist.[63] Dunn cited three meals that could have influenced the development of the Eucharist. First, he named a "Jerusalem fellowship meal" from Acts 2: 42,46 as an example of an ordinary meal where only bread was used and no wine.[64] Secondly, Dunn proposed an annual Passover type meal including bread at the beginning or middle and wine at the end.[65] Finally he suggested a "complete meal in which the cup came first and the bread later."[66] Eduard Schweizer distinguished two types of meals that eventually led to the Lord's Supper. One was celebrated as part of the early Christian's table fellowship in which a high level of eschatological jubilation was present. The other type he referred to involved the sacrificial death of the Lord by which the celebrants received the benefits of his death. But neither type originally had anything to do the with the Lord's Supper.[67] In all, scholars have found a variety of possibilities for both the nature of the Last Supper and the types of meals that Christians may have celebrated in response to the tradition based on the Last Supper.

If the original setting in the Upper Room was not a Passover meal then either one of the Jewish festive meals or simply an ordinary fellowship meal served as the occasion. It would have been shortly thereafter that Passover typology began to appear in the early eucharistic traditions[68], unless of course the Last Supper Passover was gradually assimilated to the early table fellowship meals as Jeremias argued.[69] However, the sacrificial context of these early Christian liturgies has evaded no one.[70] Their importance stands out clearly in light of the christological symbolism that was attached to the Eucharist. For this reason the eucharistic sayings have also been scrutinized in their textual forms and literary developments. I offer here translations of the four texts to accompany the subsequent section covering the basic areas of New Testament research on these eucharistic passages.

## Mark 14:22-25

22) As they were eating, he took bread, blessed (it) and broke (it) and gave (it) to them and said, "Take (it), this is my body." 23) And when he had taken a cup and given thanks he gave it to them and they all drank from it. 24) Then he said to them, "This is my blood of the covenant that is poured out for many. 25) Truly I say to you that I will no longer drink of the fruit of the vine until that day when I drink it new in the kingdom of God."

## Matthew 26:26-29

26) As they were eating, Jesus, took bread and having blessed (it), he broke (it) and giving (it) to the disciples he said, "This is my body." 27) And when he had taken a cup and given thanks he gave (it) to them saying, "Drink of it all (of you), 28) for this is my blood of the covenant poured out for many for the forgiveness of sins. 29) I tell you that I will not drink from this fruit of the vine from now until that day when I drink it with you anew in the kingdom of my Father."

## I Corinthians 11:23-26

23) For I received from the Lord that which I have delivered to you, that the Lord Jesus on the night he was betrayed took bread 24) and having given thanks he broke (it) and said, "This is my body for you. Do this in my memory." 25) Likewise (he took) the cup after dinner, saying, "This cup is the new covenant in my blood. Do this in my memory as often as you drink (it)." 26) For as often as you eat this bread and drink this cup you proclaim the Lord's death until he comes.

## Luke 22:15-20

14) And he said to them, "I have greatly desired to eat this Passover with you before I suffer. 16) For I say to you that I will not eat this until it is fulfilled in the kingdom of God." 17) And having received a cup and given thanks he said, "Take this and share it among yourselves. 18) For I tell you that I will not drink from the fruit of the vine now until which (time) the kingdom of God comes." 19) Having taken bread and given thanks he broke (it) and gave (it) to them saying, "This is my body given for you. Do this in memory of me." 20) And likewise (he took) the cup after dinner, saying, "This cup (is) the new covenant in my blood, poured out for you."

As indicated earlier in association with the work of Jeremias, the investigation of the eucharistic sayings in the New Testament requires a comparative study of the textual accounts. Variations in the existing accounts have led most scholars to speculate that more than one liturgical tradition stood behind the accounts in the forms as they appear today. This research has also tried to determine the oldest and most original accounts of the Last Supper in the New Testament. Joachim Jeremias' name continues to appear in even the most recent works dealing with these particular textual issues. Thus once again, his work on the Eucharist provides a good starting point to survey the general approaches and conclusions in the history of interpretation on the New Testament sayings of Jesus at the Last Supper.

Jeremias set out to recover the oldest form of the eucharistic tradition. Part of his methodological approach to the eucharistic texts was to look at each gospel version (including the Fourth Gospel) in the larger context of its passion narrative. He did this to show that the Supper accounts were analogous to their larger narrative contexts in the respect that they "are related blocks of tradition composed out of very diverse elements."[71]

Jeremias endeavored to determine the oldest text by using a large portion of historical criticism's arsenal.[72] He relied heavily on the use of literary criticism to establish the age of the particular texts. In his mind, Mark's account provided the oldest linguistic tradition since it gave a number places where an Aramaic or Hebrew origin ("semitisms") most likely stood behind the Greek text.[73] Jeremias noticed that at times Luke and Paul had used a graecized form of a semitic original in order to clarify its meaning for a Hellenistic audience. But this did not necessarily indicate a later date. In these cases Jeremias took other factors into consideration. For example, Paul wrote his account of the "Lord's Supper" around the year 54 from a tradition he himself claimed to have received.[74] So Paul's account offers the earliest written tradition, taking into account that the synoptics were probably written between the years 75 and 90. From this Jeremias also suggested that Paul provided the eucharistic words of Jesus that the Antioch church began to use from sometime in the fourth decade.[75] He also believed Paul's account retained the more archaic meal setting of the Eucharist evidenced by the expression, "after supper" (I Cor.11:24). In other words, Jeremias drew attention to the fact that Paul's account still portrayed a meal between the breaking of the bread and the cup.[76] The meal only later disappeared from the eucharistic celebration, at which time the sayings over the bread and the cup were brought together as in Mark and Matthew.[77]

In similar fashion, Jeremias thought Luke also presented a part of the tradition older than Mark. He recognized in Luke's version of the words of interpretation a pre-pauline semitic source[78] and regarded Luke's graecizisms of the words of interpretation to a large extent as both pre-pauline and pre-lukan.[79] Jeremias offered Luke's double "eschatological prospect" as an example of its pre-marcan or "Urlukas" source.[80] He also spent a good deal of space on the age old controversy over the short and long (22:19-20) textual witness of Luke's Last Supper account.[81] Jeremias considered the longer reading of the Lucan text a primitive liturgical formula and therefore an original part of the evangelist's text.[82]

The topics of semitisms and the dates of the synoptic traditions on the Eucharist have continued to draw attention among biblical scholars. Joseph Fitzmyer, a leading Aramaic scholar cast some doubt on Jeremias' thesis that the Markan form represents the more Semitic and therefore more original linguistic formula. Fitzmyer went on to show how both the Markan and Lucan/Pauline forms could reflect an Aramaic substratum.[83] F. J. Leenhardt espoused the priority of the Pauline account because he regarded the saying over the cup as belonging to a pre-pauline source.[84] Haenchen felt that the question of whether Mark or Paul epitomized the older tradition was an over-simplification. Haenchen agreed with Jeremias in that in one place Mark has elements that are older and truer to the historical occasion than Paul and in another place Paul presents the purer form.[85] In Haenchen's view, the search for the oldest and most genuine eucharistic text as a whole unit wrongly assumed that each part of the whole is just as old as the other parts and that one part is equally original in its literary aspects as the rest of the text. Quite to the contrary, Haenchen suspected that the manner in which the tradition of the Last Supper developed made it impossible for any one account in the gospels or Paul to be the original (ursprüngliche).[86] In this regard Haechen believed that all parts of the eucharistic accounts already show changes. Haenchen's conclusions reveal a close proximity to the basic textual positions of Jeremias.[87]

As a result of his research, Jeremias envisioned two basic independent traditions for the eucharistic sayings in the New Testament that ultimately went back to a common eucharistic tradition.[88] The texts represent "two versions" of the primitive eucharistic words that have come down to us "in three lines of tradition": a Markan, a Pauline/Lukan and a Johannine.[89] Having assigned one tradition to Mark (and Matthew) he characterized the other as belonging to Paul and Luke.[90] Jeremias found that the division between these two traditions was discernable in two common motifs within the eucharistic sayings. He labeled one "eschatological." These "eschatological" sayings depict Jesus abstaining from the meal again until that time when the kingdom of God arrived (Mk.14:25; Mt.26:29; Lk.22:16,18; I Cor. 11:27).[91] In addition to this Jeremias perceived two traditions behind the eschatological sayings (one in Mark and another longer in Luke) and claimed each had a Semitic original.[92]

The other type of eucharistic sayings Jeremias used to differentiate between the two basic textual traditions involved the words of interpretation (Deuteworte) over the bread and cup (Mk.14:22,24; Mt.26:26,27b-28; Lk.22:19,20; I Cor.11:24,25). Jeremias compared the bread and cup sayings in Mark and Matthew with those in Paul and Lukan and discovered that the two groups of texts differed not only over the bread words but also over the cup words as well. Recently J. Dunn corroborated much of Jeremias' research concerning the words of interpretation. Dunn noted that the Markan account, "This is my body," probably provides the older tradition of the bread-word since the Pauline/Lukan versions show an almost certain liturgical development with the addition of "which is given for you."[93] Jeremias had taken account of the fact that Luke and Paul agreed most closely over the cup-word of interpretation and went on to notice that the most striking dissimilarities were to be found here between the Markan and Pauline/Lukan traditions. Dunn demarcated a Markan emphasis on the "blood" in the word of interpretation over the cup and a Pauline/Lukan emphasis on the "covenant." In this case Dunn decided on the Pauline/Lukan tradition as earlier for grammatical reasons.[94] Here too, Dunn's research and conclusions show Jeremias' influence.

New Testament research on the Eucharist has demonstrated both the quest for historical origins and a predilection for a scientific approach to the texts. However, the presuppositions behind the descriptive tasks of historical criticism have not openly disclosed their nineteenth-century origins and zeal for objectivity. For this reason the whole issue of a religious text's meaning continues to evade many scholarly agendas. Jeremias, to his credit, ventured to discuss the meaning of the eucharistic words after and as a result of his preliminary descriptive investigations. But one gets the feeling that Jeremias tried to strengthen the fragile historicity surrounding the gospel's formulation that resulted from the barrage of nineteenth-century historical science by a new type of universal authenticity he found in the form of historical science itself. This quest for the historical Eucharist has not resolved of all the difficult questions anymore than other historical quests in biblical research. The history of interpretation has reached multifarious conclusions concerning the Eucharist and continues to investigate this complex subject. The descriptive efforts of biblical scholarship have produced an indispensable source of information for future study and dialogue on a subject that continues to mesmerize a variety of scholars.[95] However, the challenge of understanding the Eucharist as a religious rite remains.

## 4:2 First Century Eucharists

As we have seen, virtually all scholars agree that the divergences in the accounts were due not only to the transmission of the eucharistic traditions (oral and written) but also resulted from an incontrovertible liturgical development.[96] New Testament researchers also concur with regard to the sacrificial nature of the Eucharist[97] and the communion attained between humans and God during this rite. As we shall see, these facts become increasingly evident as the Eucharist developed beyond the first century.[98] But first these three aspects of the New Testament Eucharist need further clarification.

James Dunn gave a summary of the development of the Eucharist within the first forty years in which he mentioned the liturgical, sacrificial and communal aspects of this development. He understood the development of the Lord's Supper in three basic stages: First of all, it would have developed from the context of a complete meal (Christian Passover). Secondly, the eucharistic ceremony started to come at the end of the meal. The third stage, as evidenced by Mark and Matthew, shows that the Lord's Supper may have already become a separate and distinct event.[99] With these developments in mind Dunn went on to suggest that the original understanding of the Last Supper also changed. The fellowship meals began to focus more on the elements of the bread and wine themselves rather than on the whole meal with its emphasis on covenant and eschatological hope in the kingdom of God. Dunn felt that this concentration on the elements transformed the fellowship meal into a "ritual act" subject to "magical interpretation."[100] According to Dunn, the covenant meal, expressed particularly by the common cup, soon started to emphasize the wine as a symbol of Jesus' blood and sacrifice. He said, "If so, the predominant note of a covenant fellowship enjoyed in the here and now would have begun to give way to the representation of an initiating sacrifice."[101] Dunn saw all this as the beginning of a process that made the center of the Lord's Supper a "divine-human encounter between God and the believers through Christ."[102] The liturgical, sacrificial, and the notion of divine-human encounter all represent central aspects of the Eucharist from a very early stage of it development. It may be more accurate to think of these aspects as belonging to the Eucharist from the beginning and having quickly taken on intensity through their cultic expression. We shall now direct our attention to this prospect.

Jeremias' literary criticism led him to conclude that all of the Last Supper accounts reverted back to a liturgical formula where the words had long since been fixed for cultic use.[103] These liturgical formulas explained many of the divergences in the texts for Jeremias.[104]

Regardless, he believed that a historical account originally stood behind the liturgy.[105]

The liturgy also had one other major influence upon the Eucharist in Jeremias' view. Beginning with the curious fact that the Fourth Gospel did not record the eucharistic words of Jesus, Jeremias proceeded to address the sanctity of the early eucharistic liturgy. Jeremias maintained that the reason for this silence or secrecy in John was to protect the sacred eucharistic formula from the profane. He found similar practices of secrecy existing in late Judaism and early Christianity. Jeremias also pointed to the influence of the Greek mystery religions, the esoteric teachings of Gnosticism, to the philosophic schools and magical practices to bolster his point.[106] Texts from Qumran likewise revealed that secrecy belonged to this sect.[107] According to Jeremias, the early Christians sought to protect the sacred character of their liturgical formulas by "isolating" the sacred from the profane. In other words, the eucharistic words were either abbreviated, as in the short version of Luke, or removed altogether as in the Fourth Gospel, or given a mere oblique reference such as "breaking bread" in the book of Acts. In Jeremias' own words this evidence from the first-century showed a concern "to protect the sacredness of the Eucharist and the eucharistic words from profanation..."[108] In this way Jeremias was also able to demonstrate the early liturgical influence on the eucharistic texts. But he did not explain why the Eucharist took on such a sacred nature or why it had to be protected from the profane. He merely gave the esoteric nature of the "sacred formula" as the reason for its concealment from the general public.[109]

One must concede the strong likelihood of Jeremias' theory that 'secrecy' protected the Eucharist and the sacred words of its liturgy from the profane. But several questions remained unresolved in regard to his vague sacred and profane dichotomy. If the early Christians had tried to guard both the actual words of the eucharistic formula as a type of special Christian knowledge or mystery and also to protect these esoteric words from misunderstanding, as Jeremias had suggested, then it can safely be assumed that these Christians were concerned for the entire ritual and not just for the spoken words. Concern over the words apart from their role in the ritual would imply that a magical scenario engendered the formulas. This would have been uncharacteristic of the early eucharistic meal celebrations as well as for Jewish rites and Greek mystery rituals.[110] Simply remembering that the Eucharists in the New Testament were religious rituals helps to clarify the ambiguity surrounding Jeremias' sacred and profane categories.

Prior to the fourth-century, emphasis was placed on what was done rather than on what was said in the Eucharists, although the words played an indispensible part.[111] Dix informs us that the "Ancients" spoke of "doing the Eucharist," "performing the mysteries" or "doing the oblation."[112] This proclivity towards ritual continues to jostle the modern western mind in the study of religions and especially the Eucharist. But the fact remains that the Eucharists in the New Testament reveal a plurality of liturgical expressions with no specific dogmatic conception. One rite had the capacity for many meanings through its symbolic acts and words. The basic symbolism of the liturgies would have conjured up different images and meanings for Jewish and Gentile Christians but without displacing the central thrust of the Eucharist. As it will be demonstrated below, the Eucharists all contained the symbols of Christ's sacrifice and presence, and although the influence of both Hellenism and Judaism touched the early Christians the Eucharist was neither reduced to just another type of Greek mystery ritual nor one of the strictly Jewish rites.[113]

Christians from different socio-religious backgrounds were experiencing the Eucharist as something already given while the various forms and formulas developed in the continuing act of cultic celebration. Theological reflections came secondarily as a result of what was celebrated in the Eucharist.

> Further, it is evident that the meals themselves were the important thing and not a theological purpose which they might be said to serve. The existence of such different theological emphases as those connected with the 'Lord's Supper' in the New Testament (ICor. 11) is an indication that the occasion has called forth the theologies, not the theologies the occasion. The practice of the early Christian community meals existed before there was a specifically Christian theology to give it meaning.[114]

One must take note of the distinction between liturgy and theology when considering the development of the Eucharist. As in the case of Mark's bare phrase, "Take this, this is my body," the act of sharing the bread in a liturgical manner preceded theological ramifications. Early Christian writers continued to reflect on Christ's presence at the eucharistic celebrations but they do not attenuate the liturgical act. The symbolism of the liturgy was already pregnant with meaning. Ritual action and theological or mythological contemplation represent an ancient universal pair. The command to "do this in my memory" has often been viewed by Protestant scholars only from the second half of the phrase e.g., "in my memory." The mystery of the act itself has often been overlooked in attempts to recover the original and theological meanings.[115]

The emphasis on the liturgical aspect of the Eucharist can be clarified further still by recognizing the sacrificial context behind this rite. The symbolic acts, elements, and words involved in the different forms and formulas of the Eucharists brought to mind Christ's sacrifice on the cross. The sacrificial symbolism of the Eucharist also invoked the notion of an encounter between sinful humans and a Holy God. This sacred and profane encounter caused the ritual to develop its own preparation or protection.

The sacrificial context of the Eucharists in the New Testament asserts itself in several ways. For example, the terms "body and blood" or "flesh and blood" (John 6:53) convey a sacrificial tone as well as the expression "poured out."[116] When read in their immediate context these terms suggest an even stronger association with sacrifice. "This is my body" in Mark and Matthew[117] followed by "which is given for you" in Luke 17:19 and "which is for you" in I Corinthians 11:24, clearly reveal the sacrificial intent behind them. The same can be said of, "my blood of the covenant which is poured out for many" (Mk. and Matt.), with the addition of "for the forgiveness of sins" in Matthew 26:28, and "the cup of the new covenant in my blood" (I Cor. 11:25 and Lk. 22:20), and with the addition "which is poured for you" in Luke 22:25).[118] Here not only does the association with the Passover stand out for the Last Supper but also the victim and the blood that ratified the covenant as in the Hebrew Bible. Fitzmyer said that, "The allusion to the Sinai pact, when Moses sprinkled the blood of the twelve sacrificed oxen, half on the altar representative of Yahweh and half of it on the people of the twelve tribes, as a conclusion of the covenant, is still clear in the Lucan formula."[119] John 6:51; I Cor. 5:7, 15:3; I Peter 1:18,19 describe the death of Jesus as vicarious sacrifice that served as an expiation for the Christian community.[120] Bultmann believed that the interpretations of Jesus' death as a covenant sacrifice and a expiatory sacrifice were current in earliest church.[121] Mann expressed confidence in his suggestion that the sacrificial content of the meal as well as its link to expiation for sin went back to Jesus himself.[122]

Rudolf Otto made a provocative comment on the eucharistic words concerning Jesus' sacrifice and the kingdom of God. According to Otto, the distribution of the broken bread, symbolizing Jesus, was an ancient ritual act that served to sanctify his disciples (Leqadesh Otham). This sanctifying act (Quaddush) "removed (them) from the profane realm" and having participated in Jesus' own holiness (through eating the broken bread) the disciples were "expiated," and thus "consecrated" to be his witnesses in the kingdom of God.[123] Otto recognized that the Eucharists in the New Testament retained older Jewish notions of the need for consecration in the ritual but in a new spiritualized form.

We have begun to see that the Eucharists in the New Testament reveal a sacrificial structure by virtue of the liturgical acts of breaking the bread and sharing the cup, reference to Christ own sacrifice, and the implied communion between God and the participants through the elements representing Christ. Before examining how this basic sacrificial structure developed in the second-century and beyond we will look briefly at some other sacrificial ideas that have influenced the Eucharist.

### 4:3 Israel's Sacrifices

The Eucharist originated in a highly complex religious environment of which sacrifices formed an indispensible part of eastern mediterranean cultures. As we have already seen, Judaism and the early Christian movement gave the Eucharist its immediate form of cultic expression.[124] But ancient Israel had left a remarkable legacy in the form of myths and rituals that continued to influence both Jews and Christians. Much had already changed during the course of the Hebrews' own religious development from the traditions of the Yahwists in the ninth-century B.C.E. to the writings of the Priestly Code in the sixth-century B.C.E. with regard to sacrifice.[125] Yet the fundamental notions concerning the holiness of Yahweh and the need for proper sacrifice remained intact down to the time of Jesus.[126]

The Hebrew scriptures introduce the patriarchs who worshipped a number of sky gods like El Elyon, El Shadday, El Roy, El Bethel, and El Olam.[127] The worship of sky gods has become a well documented phenomenon that indicates transcendence.[128] The Hebrew patriarchs conceived of divinity in transcendent terms even before the actual epiphany of Yahweh (Exodus 3:6-4:14). Yahweh's arrival in Israel's cult instigated a clear response to the notion of his transcendence. This response can perhaps be best characterized by the seer's protection of Yahweh's transcendence. These divine visitations with their thunder, smoke and other ominous visible signs actually concealed Yahweh. As Terrien put it, "In a Hebrew theophany, Yahweh is not really seen by man, but only heard..."[129] Although not seen, Yahweh was truly present, and that which was heard was truly his word. The revelation of Yahweh's word and obedience to his will inevitably held a higher precedent in Israel than the visual phenomena associated with his appearance.

Both the traditions from northern and southern Israel gave their own particular interpretations of Yahweh's appearances to the patriarchs.[130] The simple fact that these early accounts of Yahweh's epiphanies were interpreted from the context of Israel's liturgical life deserves mention. These conceptualizations of Yahweh's presence were not mere theological speculations that came out of thin air. The notion of God's transcendence developed in direct relationship with Israel's sacrificial rites. The patriarchal myths of epiphanic visitation were at one time narrated during the cultic celebrations of the seasonal feasts. These accounts were most likely delivered at Israel's shrines where the disclosure of Yahweh's appearance had inspired the construction of a sacrificial altar.[131]

The compelling importance of Yahweh's presence can not be overlooked. Even when Israel began to locate its worship in the Tabernacle and ultimately the Temple, the matter of Yahweh's presence continued to play an essential place in the cult. The priesthood that had witnessed Yahweh's glory, according to the Yahwist, now governed the Temple cult where Yahweh's presence in the Holy of holies formed the crux of the cult. The notion of Yahweh's presence gave all of the symbolism involved in the Temple and its cult a clear referent for the drama that brought man and God together in the sacrifice. Here too, Yahweh's transcendence was protected through an elaborate symbolic system that included the design of the Temple, its artifacts, the priesthood, the mythology and the sacrificial rituals themselves.

The well known account of Moses and the burning bush reveals the profound respect that Israel's seers had for the encounter between man and God. According to the text, Yahweh called out to Moses and told him, "Do not come near; put off your shoes from your feet, for the place on which you are standing is holy ground."[132] The same regard for Yahweh's presence in the company of man came later in the epiphany on Mount Sinai. Having recently been delivered from Egypt, Israel was to prepare themselves to meet Yahweh at the foot of the mountain. This preparation was tantamount to a consecration. Moses received instructions to consecrate the people for two days having them wash their clothes, having the men avoid contact with a woman, and setting boundaries around the mountain.[133] Yahweh included a stern warning with his instructions to Moses. No one was permitted to touch the mountain, not even an animal. Violating this provision meant certain death. If anyone touched the sacred mountain they were to be put to death. Moses added the provision that those who executed the violators were not even to touch them with their hands. For this reason the condemned were "stoned or shot" from a safe distance.[134] After three days had passed Yahweh "descended upon it (Sinai) in fire" and the people were warned once more to stay clear and the priests were reminded to consecrate themselves before coming near.[135] The purpose of this encounter was to enable Yahweh to enter into a covenant with Israel. The basic terms of the pact meant Israel had to obey Yahweh's word and Yahweh would in turn make them a "kingdom of priests and a holy nation."[136]

The ambivalence surrounding this divine encounter stands out profoundly. The terrible sights and sounds along with the warnings of grave danger came together with the promise of many blessings.[137] In fear of death the people stood "afar off" as Moses went into the "thick darkness where God was."[138] The word translated as "thick darkness" comes from the Hebrew 'Araphel. This word itself conveys a very ambivalent image of divine danger and blessing simultaneously.[139] The text here in Exodus seems to contradict itself. When Moses went into the "dark thickness," a symbol of divine presence, the text says that Yahweh spoke to Moses "from heaven."[140] But this paradoxical feature also belonged to the word 'Araphel.[141] Yahweh both reveals and conceals himself at the same time. His divine presence did not annul his transcendence. Yahweh remained hidden in the smoke and clouds, protected in the fire. "Fire" (Hebrew, 'ês) appeared in almost all of the Hebrew theophanies "as a way of representing the unapproachable sanctity and overpowering glory of Yahweh."[142] Thus Yahweh was in heaven and on Sinai at the same time. We see in these accounts of divine appearance that Yahweh's transcendence was protected both by ritual consecrations under the direction of the priest Moses and by the mythology surrounding Yahweh, the God who reveals himself in his divine hiddenness.

Israel's cultic life peers clearly through these accounts of Yahweh's theophanies.[143] Even here the remnants of a sacrificial structure are to be found. The God who came so near as to be heard and felt on the mountain by Israel remained exalted in heaven. Historically Israel narrated such theophanies at a great festival just prior to a sacrifice upon an altar of stones.[144] From a very early time sacrifice had made its impression upon virtually every aspect of Israel's knowledge and worship of God. Yahweh's presence in Israel's tabernacles and later temples revealed an even greater respect for his presence among humans.

Sacrifice brought the whole issue of Yahweh's transcendence and presence into sharp focus. Just as Yahweh's transcendence was not forfeited by his presence in the divine visitations so also Yahweh maintained his transcendence while being present at the sacrifice. Israel came to know Yahweh as the distant God who came near not only for their salvation in time of need but especially for the sacrifice.[145]

Israel performed three basic types of sacrifices and used many terms for the manner in which they were performed.[146] First, the "Communion" sacrifice (Hebrew, Zebach; Greek, Thusia) burned one part of a victim on the altar offered to Yahweh[147], gave one part to the priest and another portion to the sacrificer.[148] Here, as in all sacrifices, the victims as well as the participants had to be in a state of ritual purity.[149]

The second type was the "Holocaust" (Hebrew, 'Olâh). It got its name from the Hebrew root 'Alâh which means "to ascend." The sacrificial victim was burned in its entirety, except for the skin, and ascended to God through the smoke.[150] The sacrificer himself cut the victim's throat at a good distance from the altar, skinned the animal and then washed the entrails and feet.[151] The priest did not get involved in this sacrifice until the victim came into contact with the altar. Some scholars have thought that one form of the Holocaust sacrifices had an etymological connection with the Hebrew term for fire.[152]

The third type was the "Expiatory" sacrifice that belonged to several different rites. Both the Communion and Holocaust sacrifices developed a sense of expiatory value over time but did not initially have a clear expiatory meaning. The use of blood in these sacrifices on the altar[153], ritual vessels, and on behalf of the priests, nation or an individual became increasingly important. Leviticus reads, "For the life of the flesh is in the blood; and I have given it for you upon the altar to make atonement for your souls; for it is the blood that makes atonement, by reason of the life."[154] We can better understand sacrifice in Israel by now looking more closely at the concept of expiation or atonement illustrated in expiatory sacrifices. Expiatory sacrifices bring many other central elements of Hebrew and Jewish religion to the fore.

The Hebrew term Kippêr connotes both the meaning "rub off" and "cover."[155] It often appears translated as "expiate," "atone" or "forgive."[156] When used in the sacrificial ritual, God was never the object of this expiatory rite but rather the sanctuary and its ritual contents.[157] Here Kippêr was used in conjunction with the rite of smearing on the blood of Hattâ'th.[158] The ashes of the red heifer were likewise called Hattâ'th and whoever handled these ritual ashes had to be himself ritually "pure."[159] These "pure" ashes that had come into contact with God through the altar fire were then taken to a "pure" place outside the camp and put into water.[160] The "pure" man who disposed of the ashes could not come back to the profane or non-ritual confines of the people until he had taken a ritual bath. The ritual made provisions to protect Yahweh's holiness from profane contact at every stage.[161] The red heifer was consecrated prior to its contact with the altar. The sacrifice then reduced the victim to holy ashes from its contact with Yahweh through the fire.[162] The ritual provided continued separation from the profane by the exit rite that ceremoniously had removed the ashes to a holy place. These "pure" ritual leftovers could not be merely discarded without further distinguishing the sacred from the profane. The ritual bath also served to differentiate between the sacred and the profane. The water removed the holy contagion from the one who handled the holy ashes so that he could return to the profane.

Scholars have also noted that the word for "purity" (Tohar) regularly accompanied Kippêr in the ritual texts, and in these cases the predominate meaning of Kippêr carried with it the idea of "purge" or "rub off."[163] Ritual Kippêr purged sin from the sacrificial realm where Yahweh came to participate in the sacrifice. In the context of the sacrificial system, sin represented physical impurities that resulted from contact with the profane. However, it was believed that human sin ultimately caused the contamination of the sanctuary.[164]

Part of the Hebrew's own sinfulness rested on his or her inability to remain ritually pure, whether the sin was a conscious act against God or simply an inadvertent trespass against one of God's commandments.[165] In other words, Israel could never come before Yahweh to sacrifice without first expiating its own sin and that of the sanctuary with its ritual elements.[166] The consecrating preparation rites illustrate the increasing need for purity and holiness as the ritual moved into the sanctuary towards the "most holy place" or "Holy of holies" where the high priest would meet with Yahweh who was present above the Ark on the "mercy seat."[167] This scene presented all of the dangers and promises of the earlier divine appearances.

Ritual Kippêr demonstratively showed that the sacrificial realm belonged to the dominion of holiness. Yahweh's presence at the sacrifice demanded such scrutinizing maintenance of ritual purity (Tohar) for his holy (Qadosh) indwelling.[168] This materialistic holiness that the priestly cult linked to the concept and practice of purifying the sanctuary and everything else involved in the sacrifice served to differentiate the sacred from the profane apart from mere moral categories. Leviticus gave the cardinal job description for the priest, "You are to distinguish between the holy and the common, and between the unclean and the clean; and you are to teach the people of Israel all the statutes which the Lord has spoken to them by Moses."[169] So the notion of Yahweh's holiness developed along the lines of his transcendence in the specific context of the sacrificial act. Yahweh's holiness expressed his "altogether different" nature from the worldly or creaturely.[170] The profane, worldly, impure, sin, non-differentiated threatened Yahweh's transcendence.[171] The preparation rites, the actual sacrifice and entry into the sanctuary's most holy place as well as the exit rites all represented Yahweh's presence and at the same time preserved his transcendence.

The Day of Atonement or "day of purgation" that took place once a year on the tenth of Tishri provides another example of Israel's response to the tension between transcendence and immanence. In this case several related religious terms, acts and concepts came into view as they determined the sacrificial structure. This great sacrifice combined the notions of consecration, expiation, purity, impurity, sin and holiness together in one numinous drama. This sacrifice also delineated the relationship between humans and God. Sinful humans and a holy God came together symbolically through the mediation of a sacrificial victim without obfuscating the differences between the two realms.

The sixteenth chapter of Leviticus contains the account of Yom Hakkippurîm. The account begins with Yahweh instructing Moses to warn Aaron "not to come at all times into the holy place within the veil, before the mercy seat which is upon the ark, lest he die; for I will appear in the cloud upon the mercy seat."[172] This advise came after two of Aaron's sons had drawn "near" to Yahweh and consequently died.[173] From now on, Aaron was not to come into the "holy place without a young bull for a sin offering and a ram for a burnt offering."[174] Aaron also received instructions that he had to wear special ceremonial garments and take a ritual bath before putting on his holy costume.[175] Next Aaron was to take from the people two male goats for a sin offering and a ram for a burnt offering.

The bull was to be sacrificed for Aaron himself as a sin offering so that he and his house could receive atonement, or officiate at the sacrifice. The two goats were first placed in front of the door to the sanctuary where Yahweh chose one through the casting of lots as a sin offering to himself. The remaining goat was set aside while the sacrifice continued.

After Aaron sacrificed the bull for himself he was permitted to enter within the veil carrying a censer full of coals from the altar's fire.[176] He then placed the fire before Yahweh and put incense in the fire to create a cloud so that the mercy seat would be covered. According to the text, if Aaron did not perform this act he would have died. Exposure to Yahweh's presence was lethal without the proper ritual cover, even in Aaron's high state of ritual purity. While the cloud was in place Aaron went about his duty of sprinkling bull's blood before the mercy seat and then the goat's blood in the same manner.[177] Having completed the blood sprinkling on the mercy seat, sanctuary and altar, the text now declared that atonement/expiation had been made for the "holy place because of the uncleanness of the people of Israel."[178] It was now safe for Yahweh to make his appearance.

After Aaron came out from the Holy of holies he took off his ritual garments, stored them in a special place, and took a ceremonial bath in a "holy place." He then came out and offered yet another sacrifice for himself and the people.[179] Whoever led the goat out of the camp was also to bath in water before returning. Someone else took the sacrificial leftovers from the bull and the goat outside of the camp and burned them. Because Aaron had used the bull and goat for a sin offering and smeared their blood to make atonement in the Holy of holies, their disposal also came under the careful sanction of the ritual. The one assigned to burn these ritual leftovers washed his cloths and bathed himself before returning to the congregation.

For the year prior to this great sacrifice Israel had used the sanctuary and its altar for daily sacrifices.[180] By means of different sacrifices Israel had confirmed Yahweh's presence among them as his people throughout the year. Their sacrifices maintained their covenental bond with Yahweh in thanksgiving for his blessings and in obedience to his will. If expiation sacrifices were offered daily as a part of the sacrificial system why would this one great sacrifice have been necessary? In part this sacrifice was a response to Israel's neighbors who celebrated great yearly rituals of renewal.[181] The Day of Atonement had great significance for Israel because it secured Yahweh's continuing presence through cleansing the sanctuary and also reestablished his transcendent holiness by confirming the differences between cultic purity and impurity. The place of sacrifice functioned as the center of Israel's cultic life as a nation. But it was also the place that dealt with the sins of the people, the very thing that separated them from their God. Should Yahweh abandon his sanctuary because of the accumulation of sin then Israel would have ceased to exist as a holy nation.[182] Cleansing the sanctuary comprised a major part of this sacrifice. The result of this material cleansing reaffirmed the necessary theological distinctions between Yahweh and the profane. Therefore the need to sacrifice perpetuated itself. The Day of Atonement assured that Yahweh, their King,[183] remained with them because the sacrifice restored the terms of their relationship and consequently renewed Yahweh's rule and order over all his creation.[184]

Just as this sacrificial ritual had reestablished Yahweh's transcendent holiness so also the rite of sending the goat into the wilderness to Azazel reaffirmed Israel's place as a holy nation.[185] After the sanctuary had been cleansed, Aaron laid his hands upon the live goat's head and confessed all of the iniquities, sins and transgressions of the people so that the goat might carry all these sins away, and thus make atonement.[186] This "scapegoat" rite again distinguished Israel as a "holy nation." Aaron, who in the highest state of ritual purity or holiness himself, had also reaffirmed the priesthood and became qualified to lay his hands upon the medium that Yahweh had provided. Therefore through a series of expiation rites Aaron and his family, the sanctuary with its most holy place and the people were set apart for Yahweh whose presence and transcendent holiness had been simultaneously reaffirmed through the sacrificial ritual.

This sacrifice and its connection to the covenant between Yahweh and Israel graphically showed the responsibility that Israel had to perform the sacrifice. Even though Yahweh had provided the means of expiation Israel still had to do her part. In this manner, that is through the sacrifice, Yahweh and Israel renewed their bond and eventually began to look forward to a time when Yahweh's Messiah would extend the blessing of Yahweh's covenant to all the nations of the world.

### 4:4 Hellenism, Judaism, and Jesus' Table Fellowship

Hellenism had began to effect virtually every aspect of Jewish life three hundred years before Christians celebrated the Eucharist. The consequences of Alexander's victory in Palestine over the Persian Darius III in 333 B.C.E. initially meant only another change in foreign domination. But it did not take long for the repercussions of these new rulers to dramatically alter the Jew's way of life.

After Alexander's death in 323 B.C.E. the Ptolemies in Egypt continued this Hellenistic rule over Palestine until the Seleucids of Syria gained control around the end of the third century B.C.E.[187] The Jews finally overthrew the Seleucids around the middle of the second-century in the Maccabean revolt and established the Hasmonean monarchy. However, by this time Hellenism had made demonstrable inroads in the Hasmonean dynasty and continued to influence their successors, the Herods, during Roman rule.[188]

Hellenism first impressed the Jews with the same advanced methods of warfare that had captured the entire Mediterranean world. The Ptolemies started to restructure the political and economic life in Palestine soon after they secured the land by this superior military technology. They implemented a mixed government made up of Jewish aristocracy and Ptolemaic officials to whom the former were accountable. The noble Jews were responsible for tax collections and land management.[189] According to Hengel, the high priest in Jerusalem would have been responsible for the finance of Judea and the temple while serving under foreign supervisors.[190] This bureaucracy efficiently exploited the poor while sharing in the fortunes of their rulers.[191] The wealthy also had access to other of Hellenistic influences which eventually took shape in the cites of Palestine.

The next development in the hellenization of Palestine was subtle yet obvious. The arrival of Koinê, the new official universal language, opened the way for the full scope of Hellenistic life styles and virtues. A Jew living or working in the city could hardly have escaped exposure to the pervasive impact of this "common" Greek because it was used in business, law, treaties, letters, and the hallmark of Greek culture, education (Paideia).[192] Hengel pointed out that the Greek word 'Ellânîzien "primarily meant to 'speak Greek correctly'."[193] Perhaps the most lucid symbol of Hellenism's penetration into Jewish life in general was the translation of the Hebrew Torah into the Greek Septuagint around 250 B.C.E.[194]

Hellenistic education had a well organized institution for integrating the privileged into the upper ranks of society. This system began with a type of elementary school and advanced to the second and final level of education. The highest level of education emphasized physical and military training, music, and the study of Greek literature, primarily Homer.[195] This education took place at the gymnasium as did the worship of heros and the emperor. Hellenistic schools appeared in Palestine in the third century B.C.E. and a gymnasium was founded in Jerusalem in 175 B.C.E. as a part of an aggressive Hellenistic reform by the Seleucids.[196] The hellenization of barbarian subjects was not only important for the successful administration of the total political and economic program but also because it was indigenous to Alexander's vision of a united culture that lived on in Hellenistic cities' spirit of cosmopolitanism.

Ptolemaic hellenization had not fostered the radical response from Judaism that the Selucid program provoked. The tyranny of Antiochus IV struck specifically at the core of Jewish life by attempting to abolish the traditional Temple cult. The affluent Jewish aristocracy found themselves caught between their support of the Hellenistic reform and the growing rebellion of the priests, the tenacious Maccabean family, the Law-preserving Hasidim party[197], and most of the common Jews of the land. The thrust of the Jewish insurgence sought to renew Judaism by the strict observance of the Law. This resulted in great persecution from the Antiochus IV and eventually to the bloody war led by the Maccabeans. While the Maccabeans' swords brought liberation from the oppressors, the Jewish writers, schools and synagogues[198] responded with the liberating force of myth.[199] Just as Israel had once borrowed myths and given them new meaning[200] these pious Jews were using their ancient myths to address the present crisis. They persisted in claiming that a greater reality existed than the inimical circumstances which had been forced upon them; namely, Yahweh was still their God and the covenant was still intact.

The restoration of the Temple cult required more than a return to myth. The covenant relationship with Yahweh was founded on sacrifice and the observance of the Law. In this way the Jews had become a holy nation, set apart from the nations of the world. Thus an essential part of their response to Hellenism involved a return to cultic purity in order to clarify the distinction between the anointed people of Yahweh and the intruding Gentiles. The assumptions about Yahweh's holiness and his presence once again reiterated the importance of a ritual system that maintained absolute purity through elaborate preparation rites before coming into His presence, viz., the Temple. More than one religious group stresses this renewed emphasis on purity in Palestine. The fact that Temple was controlled by Jews who had compromised the Law and its regulations with regard to holiness meant that these different groups had to address the notions of holiness, purity and God's presence from outside of the Temple priesthood and its sacrifices.

The Pharisees began a purification program of daily life (Haberim) that made sharp distinctions between those who adhered to their particular views and rules on purity and the common Jews ('Am Ha-arets).[201] The Pharisees did not have special access to the Temple nor any control over the sanctity of its cult. However, "their fellowships and strict laws of table and ritual purity, had made the peasants into virtually an untouchable class."[202] Their insistence on punctilious observance to purity outside of the Temple cult may have been a way to circumvent the problem of impurities at the Temple without actually forsaking the Temple and its sacrifices. So by keeping what would have normally been "trivial"[203] purity laws concerning table fellowship the Pharisees attempted to keep everyone in a state of ritual purity because the Temple priesthood itself was impure. The Pharisees may not have been making a mountain out of a mole hill with their concerns for everyday purity regulations if they felt this was the only way to insure that a replacement to the Temple cult was acceptable to Yahweh. Impurity did not necessarily make one a sinner but it did prevent entrance into the Temple and participation in the cult. This resulted in a partial rejection of the Temple, specifically the part governed by an impure priesthood.

The community at Qumran also took issue with the problem of Hellenism and the impurity of the Jerusalem Temple cult. The Dead Sea Scrolls indicate just how important a place purity, holiness, pollution and expiation/atonement had in the community's life and worship. The Qumran community separated themselves from impurities, evil and falsehood in people and things. They not only shut themselves off from the world but from other impure Jews.

> Let him (i.e. the perverse man who has not entered into the covenant) not enter into the water to touch the Purity of men of holiness, for they shall not be pure except they have repented of their wickedness, for uncleanness (is) in all who transgress His word.[204]

Water played a crucial part in ritual cleansing from impurities, whether the objects of these rites were foods, utensils, garments, or members of the sect.[205] One specific occasion for ritual washing was the community meal at which only the fully initiated could participate. Only these members had access to the purified articles.[206]

This isolated desert community set many protective barriers around themselves in similar fashion to the divisions and degrees of purity that served to protect the Temple complex from contact with the profane. The community went so far as to use Temple imagery to describe itself. Some have understood Qumran as a community (Yahad)[207] whose secluded location and sanctified daily life provided an alternative sanctuary for the corrupted one in Jerusalem.[208] The sum total of their study and observance of the Law in addition to their strict purity rites equated to the presence of Yahweh.[209]

The Qumran sect did not despise the Temple or the Levitical ordinances for sacrifices. On the contrary, certain scrolls declare great reverence for the Temple while at the same time levying harsh criticism against the Jerusalem priests who did not observe the purity laws in their Temple duties. One of their writers said concerning this situation at Jerusalem that a "wicked priest did abominable deeds and defiled the sanctuary of God."[210] Convictions over the desecration in Jerusalem prevented the Qumran community from participating in the Temple cult. Another of their scrolls read:

> Let no man send to the altar burnt-offerings, meal-offerings, incense, or wood, by the hand of a man unclean with one of the forms of uncleanliness to permit him to defile the altar; for it is written, "The sacrifice of the wicked is an abomination while the prayer of the righteous is like an acceptable oblation.[211]

The community at Qumran had elevated their prayers to the level of acceptable, spiritual sacrifices. Spiritualization of the cult in Israel had occurred prior to Qumran. But it should be pointed out that it was only after the destruction of the Jerusalem Temple in 70 C.E. that non-cultic worship replaced the material sacrifices. As Clements has said, "This radical spiritualization of the cult, however, is not truly evidenced in the Old Testament, where the emphasis upon the spiritual meaning of cultic acts is not to dispense with these acts themselves."[212]

The Essene's[213] attitude towards the Temple naturally resembled that at Qumran. Josephus wrote that the Essenes kept themselves "from the public precincts of the Temple," professing "to have more pure lustrations;" but they did send "what they had dedicated to God into Temple."[214] The Essenes' purity-concerns extended into the ritual character of their meal. Again, Josephus recorded that everyone who participated in the meal had to purify themselves and wear special linen garments.[215] The preparations for these community meals followed the sacrificial meals of the priests.[216]

The above factions of Judaism all emphasized purity in response to Hellenism and its particular influences on the Temple. The Pharisees, the community at Qumran and the Essenes restricted their table fellowship to those who met the proper purity requirements that each sect had devised. The latter two groups ceased to sacrifice at the Temple because of the impurities caused by the Jerusalem priests. All appeared to have continued to respect the Temple itself as well as the importance of sacrifices to God. However, the Essenes and the sect at Qumran eventually began to substitute their sacred rituals for the Temple cult itself.

By the first century the Temple and Palestine had remained in very much the same situation that had instigated Judaism's reform sects. The only real political changes involved Herod over the Temple and Rome over all. Hellenism had suffered no real setback at the hands of the Maccabeans, as far as the main stream of society in Palestine was concerned. In fact, Hellenism found a quite vibrant host in the new bureaucracy of the Roman Empire. The same religious parties mentioned above continued to follow God's will, as they saw it, hoping that their efforts of purification might enable or incite Yahweh to rid the land, nation, and Temple of its foreign and domestic impurities once and for all.[217] Messianic expectations ran high among these religious sects as each waited for the coming Day of Yahweh and the restoration of his kingdom to Israel.[218]

The institutionalization of these various religious sects over time resulted in the creation of new centers of holiness outside of the Temple itself. But these alternative centers of holiness also instituted a certain perversity of their own in reaction to the impurities at the Temple. The reform movements distorted the symbolic paradigm that had developed from sacrifice as performed in conjunction with the Temple complex and its priesthood. In the first place the sects could not perform the elaborate sacrifices that the Law required in concert with the priesthood and the Temple. The sectarians' patterned their meals after the sacrificial meals of the priests, but these remained meals and not actual sacrifices.[219] These fellowship meals, though elaborate and rich in symbolism, still lacked the full symbolic force of Yahweh's ambivalent presence that the priesthood and Temple portrayed through sacrifice.

In the second place, requiring ritual purity on a daily basis, outside of the Temple complex and apart from the anointed priesthood eliminated the strict control that the sacrificial ritual provided. The Qumran sect's maintenance of ritual purity, a virtual state of consecration for Yahweh's presence outside of the Temple, could not reproduce the heightened temporary consecration of the priests and sanctuary during the great sacrificial festivals of old. In short, the sects had compromised the strict holiness code itself by circumventing what they believed was a compromising situation at the Temple. Furthermore, the sects had excluded everyone who would have normally had access to Yahweh through the sacrificial cult. The mediation of the high priest had once brought all the people into the presence of Yahweh.[220] But now access to God's presence was restricted to those who could meet certain requirements. The priesthood in Jerusalem could not offer pure sacrifices, and the sects outside the Temple could not offer actual sacrifices as required by the Levitical code. Consequently the purity movements altered the whole notion of God's forgiveness and mercy through the covenant by going outside of the context of the Levitical sacrifices where Yahweh himself provided the means for atonement.

In part, Jesus' practice of table fellowship represents both a response to the Temple in Jerusalem and to the purity-reform sects at his time. Riches interpreted Jesus' cleansing of the Temple[221] as "a demonstration intended to initiate a national renewal of prayer and dedication."[222] Riches perceived Jesus' attack as against not only the "rapaciousness and extortion of the Temple cult" but also against the Temple as a sacrificial institution, "carefully hedged about with regulations governing access to and participation in the cult."[223] According to Riches, Jesus rejected the notion that God was restricted only to certain places that protected his presence from the profane through careful regulations and rituals. Riches added that sacred and profane could be distinguished apart from the category of purity. Accordingly, Jesus rejected the notion of purity, in Riches' scheme, as a "means of regulating relations between men and God" and emphasized the "love and mercy of God for all men" as the true standard to adjudicate human relationships.[224] This was in contradistinction to the Pharisees' and Essenes' ritually enforced barriers that served to differentiate between members of a group and non-members, and between members within a group by means of purity laws.[225]

Jesus' practice of open table fellowship[226] symbolized access to Yahweh's forgiveness and mercy to all people. The gospels characterized Yahweh's presence through the rule or kingdom of God (or "of heaven") in Jesus' message and ministry.[227] This appears to have been the design of a new convention that understood the Temple as impure and temporary. John Dominic Crossan said concerning the message of Jesus that "it states that the Kingdom is at hand or near in the sense not of promise but of presence and that its power is made visible in the commonality of shared miracle and shared meal."[228] To this Crossan later added, "I think the symbolic destruction (of the Temple) was but the logical extension of the miracle and table conjunction, of open healing and open eating."[229] Thus, Jesus found the Temple unsuitable for Yahweh's cultic presence and in need of cleansing. But on the other hand, Jesus relocated Yahweh's presence from cultic activity to the activities of his own ministry, particularly his table fellowship. This open acceptance of all people, especially the poor, the ritually impure and sinners, also served to reject the Pharisees' and Essenes' practice of exclusion of these very types of impure people.

The influence of Jesus' table fellowship carried over into the early church (Acts 2:42,46). Norman Perrin thought that Jesus' pre-Easter fellowship meals with tax collectors and sinners (Matt. 11:16-19) inspired the early Christian table fellowship meals.[230] These joyful fellowship meals continued Jesus' practice of accepting the outcast as well as anticipated the expected Kingdom of God.[231]

The tradition of the Lord's Supper that Paul handed down to his churches also reveals a remnant from the original table fellowship of Jesus. Recently some scholars have approached the discussion of the Lord's Supper in I Corinthians from a sociological perspective and have noted a clear relation to one aspect of Jesus' table fellowship. Gerd Theissen understood what Paul meant by the "abuses" in the Corinthian's "Lord's Supper" as a type of social-segregation in which the privileged and rich members of the congregation arrived early and consumed all the food. In doing so these members excluded the group that arrived later from their private meal and only shared the sacramental bread and wine.[232] Stressing the socioeconomic divisions in the church, Theissen went on to submit that the early group that ate their fill were rich and "of noble birth." These rich members, according to Theissen, mirrored the protocol of pagan banquets in which ones social status was proportionate to the amount and quality of food given during the meal. Theissen thought that Paul's solution to this problem was to place the meal between the bread and the wine thus making it a common meal that destroyed social barriers. Theissen's interpretation implies Jesus' table fellowship provided the model for Paul's concern for mutual acceptance.

S. Scott Bartchy has shed new light on the subject of the Lord's Supper by locating the historical context of I Cor. 11:1734 and relating it with the practice of Jesus' table fellowships.[233] According to Bartchy, Paul had no intentions of separating the church's common meal together ("Agape") from the "Lord's Supper."[234] The Corinthian's common meal was meant to express the same themes of Jesus' table fellowship meals. "It is clear that Paul understood the death of Jesus as that act by means of which Jesus' forgiveness and reconciliation became available to all human beings."[235] In Pauline theology, Christian table fellowship (Agape-meal) and the Eucharist (Lord's Supper) form an essential unity that symbolically portrays God's redemptive work. The Eucharist represents God's forgiveness through Christ's death and resurrection while table fellowship conveys the continuing ministry of Jesus in the love and acceptance of all members (rich and poor, Jews and Gentiles, men and women, see Galatians 3:28) in "one body," the church.[236] Paul also characterized Christ's presence during the Agape-Eucharist as being in the body of believers, the church gathered together in Christ, and not in the Eucharistic elements.

As we shall see in the following chapter, the notion of Christ's presence during the Eucharist changed radically from Paul's early teaching. Suffice it to say for now that the changes brought about by Judaism's reform movements produced demonstrable influences upon Jesus' own table fellowship and ultimately upon the Eucharist. The old Hebraic emphasis on Yahweh's presence continued in the ritual meals. But the Jewish sects now offered access to Yahweh through channels independent from or in addition to the sacrificial cult. This basic change transformed other concomitant notions in Israel's religion. The new form of mediation between the transcendent and profane seriously undermined the old symbolic code and the political stature of the Temple among the growing numbers of sectarian members.

### 4:5 Greek Philosophy and Sacrifice

Judaism's reform movements represent but one force responsible for significant changes in Israel's traditional cult. Many Jews of the Diaspora, particularly those dwelling in Alexandria, were impressed by Greek culture but wanted to preserve their ancestral tradition as well. The results of their infatuation with Greek culture and simultaneous devotion to their Jewish heritage showed up in new interpretations of the

Septuagint. By the middle of the second century B.C.E. Jews in Alexandria began to use the allegorical method to interpret their scriptures. Allegory enabled them to assimilate Greek notions as if they had originated with Moses. Philo, who died in the middle of the first century C.E., lifted many "deeper" and "hidden" meanings from the Jewish scriptures through the allegorical method. Philo's interpretations revealed how one's soul could escape the lustful entrapments of the body and reach immortality, a major leitmotif of Greek religion in the Hellenistic era. These Hellenistic Jews focused most of their attention on obedience to the law stressing "monotheism and imageless worship, moral ideals and precepts for ethical conduct, sabbath observance, circumcision, and avoidance of swine meat."[237] On the one hand the sheer distance from the Jerusalem Temple cut many Hellenistic Jews off from the sacrificial cult, while on the other hand many found the new Alexandrian hermeneutics closer to the true spirit of the law than literal interpretations that required bloody sacrifices. For example, Philo used several Jewish rituals allegorically as symbolic vehicles for the soul to attain a "higher" philosophical plane through the powers of reason.[238] These tendencies to spiritualize Israel's cult were already at work in the tradition of the Jewish prophets.[239] Jews in the Diaspora synagogues did not perform actual sacrifices but considered their worship assembly as a sacrifice to God.[240] According to Beim, "both the ethical criticism of literal sacrifice and the coming of a figurative and mystical concept of sacrifice are to be found in Hellenistic Judaism."[241] The consequences of this spiritual perception of sacrifice had a ambiguous effect on early Christianity.

The Hellenistic period's impact upon Jews and Christians can not fully be appreciated apart from the Greek's basic concepts of sacrifice. Sacrifice had formed an essential part of life for the Greeks as it had for the entire East. In fact, the entire Greek religious system had been established by the first sacrifice of Prometheus.[242] The ancient Greeks performed several types of sacrifices, stressing purification rites, the presence of the deity at the altar and the worshiper's communion with the deity by means of the sacrificial ritual.[243] However, Presocratic, and later the Sophist's, criticism of the Homeric gods also marked significant changes in the traditional concepts of Greek sacrifices. For example, Socrates insisted that the desire of virtue brought favor from the gods. This has been understood as Socrates' rejection of the assertion that sacrifice could manipulate the gods. Plato definitely followed Socrates' thought with regard to his own criticism of sacrifice. The following quote from his *Republic* shows the changing attitude towards sacrifice among certain Greeks.

> Others, to show that men can turn the gods from their purpose, cite Homer: "Even the gods themselves listen to entreaty. Their hearts are turned by the entreaties of men with sacrifice and humble prayers and libation and burnt offering, whensoever anyone transgresses and does amiss." They produce a whole farrago of books in which Musaeus and Orpheus, described as descendants of the Muses and the Moon, prescribe their ritual; and they persuade entire communities, as well as individuals, that, both in this life and after death, wrongdoing may be absolved and purged away by means of sacrifices and agreeable performances which they are pleased to call rites of initiation. These deliver us from punishment in the other world, where awful things are in store for all who neglect to sacrifice.[244]

But Plato's criticism of sacrifice also indirectly reveals the importance that sacrifice continued to have for Greek life. For some, the gods' intervention into the affairs of this world remained crucial for mortals who needed, among many other things, the gods' forgiveness. Such Greeks willingly performed costly sacrifices along with their demanding purification rites.[245] The danger Plato testified to because of neglecting to sacrifice sounds reminiscent of the Vedic admonition. Vedic sacrifice made universal order the responsibility of both humans and the gods.

Other Greek writers continued to criticize the traditional sacrificial cult. According to Young, Aristotle suggested that sacrifice threatened to make the gods inferior to humans because sacrifice made the gods dependent on humans.[246] This logic extended into the Hellenistic period where the religious philosophers of Chance (Tùché), astrology, and the Stoics' impersonal Providence eliminated any possible disruption in the predetermined state of affairs. The Epicureans found sacrifices completely worthless for gods who had no concern for humans and their world.[247] The Stoic concentration on "morality" and the soul's "self-sufficiency" (Autarkeia) also served to free them from any need to sacrifice. The Stoic's "material pantheism or divine immanence" that obliterated the difference between God and the world dealt the most deadly blow to the traditional notion of sacrifice.[248] In this Stoic paradigm one did not need to bring together the two worlds; so naturally the necessity of sacrifice was eliminated. The Platonist rational assessment of the transcendent God and his unchangeable character also rejected the frivolous attempts to change him by sacrifice. Others followed with the conclusion that the gods did not have any need for sacrifices.[249] Young summed up the sentiment of these Hellenistic philosophies' attitude toward sacrifice by saying, "God needs nothing; he is everything and all things are in him. We should adore him by giving thanks."[250]

The Greek's efforts to replace material sacrifices with spiritual or rational sacrifices (Logikai Thusiai) had an eventual affect upon Jewish and Christian writers with regard to sacrifice and the Eucharist respectively.[251] But material sacrifices did not cease among the Greeks. In fact, sacrifices continued to thrive during this succession of philosophic criticism. Young reminds us that even the Stoics compromised their position on sacrifice in order to be reconciled with the state religion of Rome. "Even Marcus Aurelius frequently sacrificed to the gods."[252]

The Neoplatonists first entered the polemic surrounding sacrifice with Porphyry's moral objection to the killing of animals and his insistence that "to the Immaterial One everything material is impure."[253] Porphyry taught that the Highest God should receive the sacrifice of pure thought, through which man and God united with one another.[254] Porphyry's contemporary and fellow neoplatonist, Iamblichus, argued that the freer souls had less need of material forms of worship.[255] Nonetheless, both agreed that material sacrifices to the gods were necessary. Iamblichus reasoned that sacrifice did not affect the gods but rather enabled "lower orders of being" to "ascend to higher;" and he also believed that through sacrifice one united with the gods and consequently received salvation for his soul.[256]

The Hellenistic Mystery Religions comprise yet another part of the environment that helped shape the Eucharist.[257] A variety of opinions exist as to the extent that Christianity borrowed from the Mystery Religions. Generally speaking syncretism has always and everywhere represented one of the central features in the development of religions. The suggestion that Jesus Christ was no different than any of the other cultic heros of the Mystery Religions, Attis, Osiris, Mithra, simply ignores the historical and mythological distinctions surrounding

Christianity.[258] The Hellenistic Mystery Religions reveal a vast diversity of details and emphases.[259] Scholars today recognize that Christianity, like post-exilic Judaism,[260] had experienced different degrees of Hellenization but also resisted complete identification with other religions, especially in matters concerning the "true faith."[261] Benoit distinguished between the historical phenomenon of Christianity and its linguistic expression for the simple reason that Christians had adopted the terminology of the Mysteries in order better to express certain fundamental aspects of the Christian faith and cult without confusion and improper assimilation.[262] The fact that Christianity triumphed over the Mystery Religions does not mean the former persisted by virtue of a profound uniqueness. But Christianity most certainly interpreted its message as the true revelation of God in the person of Jesus Christ.[263]

The most common point of comparison between Christianity and the Mystery Religions lies in the religious matrix that each shared.[264] This same environment nourished some very old religious symbolism in the "new religions" of the Hellenistic period. In their new forms Dionysus, Isis and Osiris, the Eleusinian and Orphic Mysteries, as well as the others, all had experienced a popular following by the first century. The Mystery Religions usurped the ethnic and parochial character of their ancient eastern beginnings[265] and went on to challenge the sway of Greek rationalism by their powerful promises of personal salvation. Salvation from Destiny (Heimarmené) or Chance (Tyché; Latin, Fortuna) required initiation into one of the Mystery cults.[266]

The common attributes of these initiation rites illustrates a dynamic tension between transcendence and immanence that had survived from centuries past. Evidence of this primeval dichotomy appears in the fact that each mystery religion shared three basic elements in its quest for salvation through initiation.[267] All had rites of purification. Angus made the following comment with regard to the sense of sin and defilement that prevented the approach to the Divine. "Initiands must therefore submit to a cathartic process whereby the defilements of the flesh and ritual uncleanness were removed, and an expiation for sin duly made."[268] Secondly, all required the deity's mystical presence. Eliade spoke of the centrality of the deity's presence in initiation.[269] Thirdly, all claimed to provide union with their Saviour-God. D. H. Tripp noted that "the core of the rite was a unification of the worshipper with the god in a way not otherwise possible, i. e. a mystical union or bond."[270]

This threefold facet of the mysteries' initiation rites discloses an ancient core of religious symbolism that existed in both Greece and the eastern cults long before their mixture in the Hellenistic period.[271] Eliade interpreted the Minoan cult (2600-1400 B.C.E.) as "centered on the "mysteries" of life, death, and rebirth" and having a transcendent storm god in the symbol of a thunderbolt,[272] while noting that their Mycenaean conquerors left clear evidence of an elaborate sacrificial system.[273] The subsequent Hellenic tradition that resulted from the symbiosis of these two ancient civilizations and the entrance of the new Indo-European invaders (1200 B.C.E.)[274] reveals a religious tradition steeped in sacrifice and imbued with a mythology that contrasted transcendence and immanence.[275] Therefore the essence of this archaic religious symbolism, although changed through time, remained discernable down to the Hellenistic period. This persistent religious symbolism continued to address human beings' ultimate concerns in which the act of sacrifice played a crucial role. The Mysteries continued to perform a number of sacrifices.[276] But these sacrifices only made up part of the initiation rites and did not form the crux of the Mysteries' cultic expression. The Mystery Religions' initiation rites portrayed a primordial desire of homo religiosus to be linked with the sacred.

Not only did Christianity share a common environment with the Hellenistic Mystery Religions but it also followed a similar pattern of development that continued its aged desire to link up with the sacred. Again in similar fashion to the Mysteries, Christianity revalorized its ancient religious symbolism from its historical roots into the new forms that spread throughout the Roman Empire. Specifically, early Christianity conveyed its own basic threefold structure through the rites of baptism and the Eucharist. The importance of purification from sins, the presence of God and union with God through Jesus' sacrifice resounded the basic tones of ancient Israel's sacrificial cult.

The Eucharist, like the sacramental meals of the Attis and Mithra Mysteries, enabled its partakers to commune with a once dead and risen deity, Jesus Christ. Bultmann wrongly thought that the Apostle Paul had conceived of "the eucharistic meal as a representational rite (Dromenon) like the "acted rites" (Dromena) of the mysteries; the ceremony acts out the death of the Lord."[277] But even in

Hellenistic Christianity the death of Jesus Christ was conceived primarily as a sacrifice under the auspices of the Jewish Law.[278] Christians came to understand Jesus' death as the fulfillment of the Jewish Law, and thereby eliminating Levitical sacrifices in their entirety, "For Christ is the end (Télos) of the law to righteousness for everyone who believes."[279] Paul also wrote, "For Christ our paschal lamb, has been sacrificed."[280] The writer of Hebrews wrote:

> Thus it was necessary for the copies of the heavenly things to be purified with these rites, but the heavenly things themselves with better sacrifices than these. For Christ has entered, not into a sanctuary made with hands, a copy of the true one, but into heaven itself, now to appear in the presence of God on our behalf. Nor was it to offer himself repeatedly, as the high priest enters the Holy Place yearly with blood not his own; for then he would have had to suffer repeatedly since the foundation of the world. But as it is, he has appeared once for all at the end of the age to put away sin by the sacrifice of himself.[281]

Ancient Israel's notions of sin, Yahweh's presence and Levitical sacrifice determined the particular symbolization of Christ's sacrifice and formed the underlying premise for celebration of the Eucharist.

In general the early Christians also entered into the prevailing notions of how God was saving the world through his "Soter" Jesus Christ, the "Son of God."[282] Participation in the religious world of Hellenism required knowledge of its basic universal terminology that the Mysteries shared in common, but used for their own particular purposes. The Eucharist must be viewed against the backdrop of this common religious environment and development of ancient symbolization with the Mysteries. This resulted in a morphological similarity between the Eucharist and the cultic meals of late antiquity. Neither the similarities nor the differences between Christianity and the Mysteries can fully be appreciated without recognizing the influence that sacrifice continued to have on the Hellenistic perception of the cosmos and God.

The general religio-historical background of the Eucharist establishes the importance that the concept of transcendence and immanence played in sacrifice. Israel's religion experienced many changes throughout a long course of events while retaining the basic essence of its symbolism. The central features of Israel's sacrificial cult continued to dominate the religious sects of Judaism even when Jews ceased to perform material sacrifices. Not even the constraint of rationalism in the Hellenistic age could remove the Jew's sense of being a Holy nation poised for Yahweh's final act of deliverance. Only the material sacrifices ended, finally with the Roman destruction of the Temple in Jerusalem. Spiritual sacrifices accompanied the spiritually pure who worshipped in the presence of God and did his will or kept the Law. Jesus' ministry and early Christianity's proclamation of his sacrificial death extended the ancient agenda to a non-Jewish audience in terms familiar to the new age. The symbolism of communion with the body and blood of Christ in the Eucharist fulfilled the old sacrificial covenant of Israel that promised Yahweh's presence, expiation of sins and salvation in the sacrifice of Jesus Christ.

This brief historical survey has shown that sacrifice or sacrificial ideas persist as an indispensible aspect of understanding the background of the Eucharist. In the following chapter we shall look at examples in the historical development of the Eucharist to determine what place sacrificial symbolism played.

## ENDNOTES TO CHAPTER FOUR

[1] D. Stone, *A History of the Doctrine of the Holy Eucharist*. London, Longmans, Green, and Co., two volumes, 1909.

[2] See infra chapter five on the Reformation's impact on eucharistic doctrine.

[3] Jungmann, *The Mass of the Roman Rite*, trans by Francis A. Brunner. Westminster: Christian Classics, Inc., vol. 1, p. 183.

[4] The phrase "Last Supper" does not occur in the Gospels. Tradition has commonly held it to refer to the last meal Jesus had with his disciples on the night when he was betrayed. Paul called it the "Lord's Supper" in I Corinthians 11:20.

[5] See A. Schweitzer, *The Problem of the Lord's Supper According to the Scholarly Research of the Nineteenth Century and the Historical Accounts*, vol. I, "The Lord's Supper in Relationship to the Life of Jesus and the History of the Early Church," trans. by A. J. Mattill, ed. with an intro. by John Reumann. Macon: Mercer University Press, 1982, p. X. One of the basic conclusions Schweitzer reached in this work was that Jesus did not command his disciples to repeat this rite, since such evidence is lacking in Mark.

[6] Ibid., pp. 11, 52. In the nineteenth century the crisis developed over the reliability of the Bible as a document of revelation whose historicity had eroded under the stream of historical criticism. The most pressing question that historical science raised centered on the historical Jesus. How could Jesus Christ be the basis and content of Christian faith if historical science could not affirm with certainty the historical Jesus? See David F. Strauss, *The Christ of Faith and the Jesus of History*, trans. by Leander E. Keck, Philadelphia: FortressPress, 1977; originally published in 1865. Also cf. Martin Kähler, *The So-called Historical Jesus and the Historic Biblical Christ*, trans. by Carl E. Braaten, Philadelphia: Fortress Press, 1964; originally published in 1896. For a concise treatment on the subject see, John P. Meier, *A Marginal Jew: Rethinking the Historical Jesus*, New York, Doubleday, 1991,

Introduction and chapter 1. Schweitzer's best known work, *The Quest for the Historical Jesus* (1906 E.T. 1910) concluded that it was impossible to recover a historical account of the life of Jesus. Under the influence of the nineteenth century's historical criticism, many studies in the twentieth century have sought to reconstruct the historical origin of the last supper in the Gospels and trace the ensuing liturgical families.

[7] *The Problem of the Lord's Supper*, pp. 51, 52. C. S. Mann has recently said that, "In the whole history of interpretation, both of the Last Supper and of the Eucharist, the situation has constantly been obscured and even distorted (especially in Western Christendom) by a massive and often exclusive concentration on "This is my body and This is my blood." Unless we can divorce our minds from this preoccupation, we shall be in danger of isolating the Last Supper from the whole ministry of Jesus which gave it meaning." Cf. *Mark*, in, *The Anchor Bible*, ed. by William F. Albright. Garden City, Doubleday & Company, Inc. Vol. 27, 1986, p. 571.

[8] Ibid., p. 137.

[9] Ibid., p. 137.

[10] Geoffrey Wainwright has written on the history of the Eucharist from the standpoint of its eschatological framework, cf. *Eucharist and Eschatology*, op. cit. Wainwright also says that the eschatological element in the Eucharist has been over-looked in the history of interpretation, without mentioning A. Schweitzer's work on the subject.

[11] Ibid., 32.

[12] A good example of the on-going efforts to deal with critical questions on the Eucharist exists in Eduard Schweizer's article, "Abendmahl Im NT," in RGG, vol. I, third ed., pp. 10-21. Here, too, one sees how much of A. Schweitzer's work has evaporated under the light of new historical criticism.

[13] Hans Lietzmann, *Mass and Lord's Supper*. Trans. by, Dorthea H. Reeve, Introduction and Supplementary Essay by, Robert D. Richardson, Leiden, E. J. Brill, in 10 Fascicles, 1976.

[14] Joachim Jeremias, *The Eucharistic Words of Jesus*, Philadelphia, Fortress Press, 1966. As an example of Jeremias' continuing influence today upon New Testament scholars I offer the following quote from C. S. Mann: "Apart from the various commentaries on the individual gospels, this writer would say without hesitation that theone indispensible tool is the work referred to more than once above: *The Eucharistic Words of Jesus* by Joachim Jeremias. It has the supreme advantage of meticulous footnotes and a through examination of all the theological factors, New Testament and otherwise, which have combined to make the whole topic a matter of intense debate," cf. *Mark*, (The Anchor Bible, ed. by William F. Albright). Garden City: Doubleday & Company, Inc., 1986, 581.

[15] Lietzmann named the Syro-Byzantine, Egyptian, Roman and Gallican types. Lietzmann also discussed the relationships between these texts and the influence of the ancient Syrian and Egyptian upon the Roman development, cf. *Mass and Lord's Supper*, pp. XI-XII.

[16] Ibid., p. 142.

[17] The Habûrah or "confraternities" of Jewish men practiced rites of sanctification of bread and wine at their table fellowships, see J. Delorme, et al, *The Eucharist in the New Testament*: A Symposium. Trans. by E.M. Stewart, Baltimore, Helicon Press, pp. 24-25.

[18] Ibid., p. 205.

[19] Lietzmann said, "These Jewish table-customs represent in all points the exact prototype of the last meal of Jesus with his disciples." Ibid., p. 171. Lietzmann also recognized an eschatological element in this type.

[20] Richardson summed up Lietzmann's views on this point in the following manner: "The genuine agape is fully compared with the

Jewish meal which ushers in the Sabbath, in which the blessing and distribution of the bread (not of the first cup) marks the beginning of the actual meal, and sharing of "a cup of blessing" marks the end. In the *Church Orders* however the latter is omitted." Ibid., p. XVII.

[21] Ibid., p. 206.

[22] Ibid., p. 205. Though once popular this idea has recently come under fire by biblical scholars. For example "It is impossible--though the attempt has been made more than once--to attribute the idea of a vicarious, expiatory death to some supposed Hellenistic "savior god" myth utilized by Paul. Savior gods had never been a serious feature of Greek religion, and an attempted importation of such a motif among the predominantly Jewish members of Paul's congregations would have been an act of consummate folly." C. S. Mann, op. cit., p. 576.

[23] The Syrian text based on the fourth-century revision that began in Antioch produced the Received Text of the New Testament. See ibid., pp. 221-225. Also see Bruce M. Metzger, *The Text of the New Testament.* New York, Oxford University Press, 1968, pp. 129 ff.

[24] *Mass and Lord's Supper*, p. 222.

[25] Richardson went on to say concerning the longer Lucian text of the Eucharist (considered corrupt by Lietzmann) found in the "pure Egyptian rite": "From this it follows that not even as regards either the type or the place of their alleged corruption do the Egyptian text and rite illustrate each other." Ibid., p. 223.

[26] Hort relied heavily upon what he called "Internal Evidence of Readings" in similar fashion to Lietzmann's use of internal evidence for his work. We should mention in fairness to Westcott, Hort, and indirectly to Lietzmann, that the Chester Beatty papyri was not available to them at the time. This discovery would have shown that other texts were extant in Egypt during the second-century along with the Neutral text.

[27] Ernst Lohmeyer, "Vom urchristlichen Abendmahl," in *Theologische Rundschau*. Tübingen, Vol. 9, 1937, pp. 168-227; Vol. 10, 1938, pp. 81-99. Cf. E. Schweizer who said, "schon Lohmeyer hat darum die These Lietzmanns variiert, indem er im ersten den galiläischen Typus fand, der aus der Tischgemeinschaft des irdischen Jesus herausgewachsen wäre, im zweiten hingegen die jerusalemitische Art der Herrenmahlfeier." Op. cit., p. 16.

[28] Richardson's criticism of Lietzmann is helpful on this point, op. cit., XX ff.; and see his further inquiry into eucharistic origins, pp. 222 ff., 269, 273.

[29] Cf. Cullmann and F. J. Leenhardt, *Essays on the Lords Supper*. Richmond, John Knox Press, 1958, pp. 5 ff.

[30] Dix, *The Shape of the Liturgy*, Westminster: Dacre Press, 1945, p. 95.

[31] John Reumann, *The Supper of the Lord*. Philadelphia: Fortress Press, 1985, p. 49.

[32] Jeremias (pp. 42-61) made "fourteen observations" to prove the Last Supper was a Passover meal. He gavehis points from the content of the synoptic narratives themselves. Jeremias felt that the strongest of his fourteen points in favor of a Passover meal was number fourteen. Jeremias concluded that Jesus' "ritual" interpretation of the bread and wine was in fact the required interpretation in the Passover meal as the father responded to his son's questions. For this reason the words of interpretation have been preserved in a liturgical form in the Eucharist even though they do not reflect a Passover context, see pp. 55-61. For a brief summary of nine of Jeremias' fourteen points and a response to his Passover thesis see, Xavier Léon-Dufour, *Le partage du pain eucharistique selon le Nouveau Testament*. Paris: Éditions Du Seuil, 1982, pp. 348-351.

[33] Briefly: Textual criticism compares the variants in the text in order to determine the oldest or most original sources. Linguistic criticism takes into account that the Greek New Testament has both a Greek and

Hebrew background. Therefore many idioms and terms in the Greek text may best be understood from a semitic rather than secular Greek point of view, yet on other occasions Greek or nuances from Greek religions may provide the original meaning of the word. Jeremias made much of linguistic criticism by finding "semitisms" in Mark's account of the Eucharist which explained the awkward style and suggested a very early source behind the text. Literary criticism focuses on authorship, date, purpose of writing, recipients, style and sources. Form criticism attempts to recover the process that began with the original oral historical tradition and ended with the interpretive religious traditions in the written texts of the gospels (initially based on an oral tradition). Ernst Haenchen said of form criticism that "man verstand die Formgeschichte nicht bloß dahin, daß nach ihr alle Jesustradition durch den Filter der glaubenden Gemeinde hindurchgegangen war, sondern daß sie sogar von den Bedürfnissen dieser Gemeinden erst erzeugt worden war." See *Der Weg Jesu*. Berlin: Alfred Töpelmann, 1966, p. 23. Historical criticism employs knowledge of the religious environments of first-century Judaism and Hellenism. For more information on the types of New Testament criticism see George E. Ladd, op. cit.

[34] Jeremias responded to the following eleven objections to the last supper as a Passover meal: 1) Mk.14:22 used the common term for bread (Artos) instead of `unleavened bread' (Azuma) that one would have expected for the Jewish feast. Jeremias found examples in the Jewish scriptures, Philo and Josephus where Artos was used for unleavened bread. 2) Some have rejected the Passover as the time of the Last Supper in the gospels because it was celebrated only once a year instead of a daily practice. To this Jeremias replied that the early church repeated the daily table fellowship meals of Jesus and only gradually did the church align these fellowship meals with the Last Supper. 3) Further objections stemmed from the fact that Mk. 14:22-25 does not contain any explicit references to the Passover ritual, especially with regard to the paschal lamb and the famous bitter herbs. Jeremias down-played the lack of a Passover description in view of the text's "cultic formula." 4) Next Jeremias dealt with the fact that the description of the Last Supper deviated from the customary Passover ritual. 5) Mk.14:2 recorded that

the Sanhedrin did not want to arrest Jesus during the feast in order not to stir up the people. Jeremias felt that this did not annul the synoptic chronology because the phrase mâ en tâ heortâ (lit. "not in or during the feast") did not refer to time but rather should be understood as "among the festal crowd." 6) *Mishnah* tractate *Pesahim* 8:6 seems to follow the Johannine chronology because of the agreement of the custom to give amnesty to a prisoner in time to celebrate the Passover. But Jeremias passed this objection off simply by not accepting the *Mishnah* text as relevant for dating Passover events. 7) In response to the argument that in I Cor.5:7b ("For Christ, our paschal lamb, has been sacrificed") Paul made the death of Jesus correspond to the slaying of the Passover lambs before the Passover meal Jeremias retorted that this reference to Christ grew out of the sayings of Jesus at the Last Supper and not from the actual time of the sacrifice of the lambs. 8) Similarly, I Cor. 15:20 ("Christ the first-fruits") has been used to designate the date of Nisan 16 as Easter Sunday and then Nisan 14 Good Friday. To this charge Jeremias abruptly said that this phrase should only be taken figuratively and not for chronological deciphering. 9) The many events of Mk.14:17-15:47 fell on Nisan 15, a holy day in the scheme of Judaism, and thus make these accounts in Mk. irreconcilable with keeping solemn days or the halakah. But Jeremias painstakingly placed each of the narrative's events of that day within the accepted realm of Jewish laws. 10) Jeremias felt that the main objection came from the report of the fourth gospel. John 18:28 only implied that Jesus died before the Passover evening. Jeremias covered each of the difficult texts in John's gospel where the apparent date of a crucifixion twenty-four hours earlier really amounted to a case of mistaken "typology" and not chronology. 11) The final objection that Jeremias refuted dealt with the supposed evidence of the Quartodecimanians that would have put the date of the crucifixion at Nisan 14. Jeremias produced evidence that showed the Quartodecimanians celebrated the Passover in accordance with the synoptic tradition. Although Jeremias' responses to these objections come across somewhat "cavalier" (cf. Geoffrey Wainwright, op. cit., p. 158, fn. 51) he nonetheless has spanned the field of scholarly inquiry concerning the Passover controversy.

[35] A. J. B. Higgins has reproduced much of Jeremias' line of defense on the Last Supper as a Passover in a succinct form, see *The Lord's Supper in the New Testament*. London: SCM Press LTD, pp. 13 ff. Josef A. Jungmann's statement, "It is an almost universal belief that the Last Supper was a paschal meal," does not represent the academic community. Cf. *The Early Liturgy to the Time of Gregory the Great*, trans. by Francis A. Brunner. Indiana: University of Notre Dame Press, 1959, p. 31. Some supporters of the Passover theory of late are, E. Gaugler, *Das Abendmahl im Neuen Testament*, 1943; Marcus Barth, *Das Abendmahl : Passamahl, Bundesmahl, und Messiasmahl*, 1945; F. J. Leenhardt, *Le sacrement de la sainte céne*, 1948; I. Howard Marshall, *Last Supper and Lord's Supper*. Grand Rapids: William B. Eerdmans Publishing Company, 1980; C. S. Mann op. cit., p. 574. The list is long for those who oppose the identification of the Last Supper with a Passover meal. To mention a few: Cf. E. Schweizer, op. cit., pp. 18-19; Lietzmann, op.cit., p. 212; E. Lohmeyer, op. cit.; E. Haenchen, op. cit., p. 484; Günther Bornkamm, *Jesus of Nazareth*, trans. by Irene and Fraser McLuskey with James M. Robinson, New York, 1960, cf. p. 161; Herbert Braun, *Jesus of Nazareth: The Man and His Time*. Philadelphia: Fortress Press, 1979, pp. 34, 39, 56-57, 113. More recently the opinion seems to be shifting to the position that we simply cannot determine from the present evidence if the Last Supper was a Passover celebration, cf. Joseph A. Fitzmyer, *The Gospel According to Luke*, in *The Anchor Bible*, ed. by William F. Albright. Garden City: Doubleday & Company, Inc., Vol. 2, 1985, p. 1382.

[36] Notably the Eastern Orthodox Church has adopted the chronology of the Fourth Gospel and consequently does not use unleavened bread in their eucharistic services.

[37] I. H. Marshall concludes that, "Jesus held a Passover meal earlier than the official Jewish date, and that he was able to do so as the result of calendar differences among the Jews," op. cit., p. 75.

[38] J. Delorme gives a survey of these theories cf. op. cit., pp. 60 f. Billerbeck suggested that the synoptics followed the Pharisees' calendar

and the Fourth Gospel adhered to the Sadducees', *Kommentar zum Neuen Testament aus Talmud und Midrasch*, II, 1924, pp. 847-853.

[39] Cf. Anne Jaubert, *La Date de la Céne*. Paris: Librairie Lecoffre, 1957. See also Jaubert in NTS, 7, 1960, I, pp. 1-30.

[40] Cf. William S. LaSor, *The Dead Sea Scrolls and the New Testament*. Grand Rapids: William B. Eerdmans Publishing Company, 1972, pp. 59 ff; also see *The Manual of Discipline* (1QS) 9:6.

[41] W. D. Davies said, "Passages such as CD (Damascus Document) III, 13-16; 1QS 1:14; X, 1-9, point to a calendar different from that of official Judaism, a solar one." *The Scrolls and the New Testament*, ed. by Krister Stendahl. New York, Harper & Brothers Publishers, 1957, p. 167. The solar calendar was divided into four equal parts of ninety-one days each so that the Passover would have fallen on Wednesday each year and the Passover meal was eaten on the Tuesday night before. The Samaritans also observed the solar calendar, cf. Gillian Feeley-Harnik, *The Lord's Table Eucharist and Passover in Early Christianity*. Philadelphia, University of Pennsylvania Press, 1981, p. 119.

[42] Also see supra fn. 56, and H. Braun, op. cit.

[43] Cf. Delorme, op. cit., p. 58.

[44] Cf. supra fn. 54, point # 5; see also Higgins, op. cit., p. 17, item 4. See also W. H. Cadman, *The Christian Pascha and the Day of the Crucifixion - Nisan 14 or 15 ?* In Studia Patristica, ed. by F. L. Cross. Berlin, Akademie - Verlag, Vol. V, 1962, pp. 8- 16. C. S. Mann, (op. cit., pp. 563-4, note 12), has commented on Mark's identification of Passover with the feast of Unleavened Bread. Mann admitted that "Unleavened Bread" may have been a generic term used to cover both feasts. But the problem of too little time to prepare for the Passover sacrifice remains. G. Dalman said of the Marcan verse, "No instructed Jew could possibly have called the eve of the Feast 'the first day of the Feast'; only a Gentile could possibly have thought of the day of the

offering of the Passover lamb and the night of the Passover meal as the first day of the Feast." Fitzmyer, op. cit., p. 1382.

[45] Raymond Brown says the Passover characteristics in John's Gospel are "undeniable." Brown thinks that the Gospel of John preserved the correct date of the Last Supper, Thursday evening, the fourteenth of Nisan, the day before Passover according to the official Jerusalem calendar. The synoptics were so enthusiastic, according to Brown, to implement their theological ramifications from the Passover that they assumed the Last Supper actually occurred on the Passover. For John Brown adds: "If the fourth evangelist does not identify the day itself as Passover, he still has Jesus condemned to death at noon on Passover Eve (xix 14), the very hour at which the priests began to slaughter the paschal lambs in the temple area." See, *The Gospel According to John*, (*The Anchor Bible*, general ed. William F. Albright). New York, Doubleday & Company, Inc., (xiii-xxi), 1979, pp. 556, 584-557. Recent scholarship recognizes John's Gospel contains much more historical information than was thought just over a decade ago.

[46] Cf. op. cit., pp. 58-59.

[47] C. S. Mann has proposed several strong objections to the Last Supper as a "quasi-religious" meal and argues in the spirit and scholarly style of Jeremias. Mann (p. 570) thinks that the religious meals cannot adequately explain the Passover theme. Mann finds it noteworthy that unlike the announcement of treachery at the Last Supper the words of interpretation over the bread and wine cause no surprise among the disciples. Mann explained this lack of incredulity by indicating that those present at a Passover would have expected an interpretive word over the elements as in Exodus 12: 26-27, and the slaughter of lambs in the Temple courts of Jerusalem would have further fit the symbolic words of Jesus at the Passover meal. Interpretations were always expected by the head of the gathering, but no one fixed or standard interpretation. Cf. op. cit., pp. 574 ff. James Dunn offered two possible explanations. Either Jesus considered the supper as a special Passover meal or that intentionally gave exceptional significance to what was

otherwise an ordinary meal, James D. G. Dunn, *Unity and Diversity in the New Testament*. Philadelphia: The Westminster Press, 1977, p. 163.

[48] Jeremias, op. cit., p. 66.

[49] Ibid., p. 66.

[50] Op. cit., pp. 26-36.

[51] Ibid., p. 27. Jeremias cites several others for proof that the Kiddish lacked any sacrificial significance, cf. his notes, p. 27.

[52] Kiddish means "sanctification" in Hebrew, from kadush, "holy," see Jeremias, op. cit., p. 26; Brown Briggs Driver. The fact that Kiddish meant "sanctification" would certainly make it a likely candidate for sacrificial connotations.

[53] Ibid., p. 26. The Kiddish rite, though not a sacrifice, forms part of a protective barrier with the Habdalah around feast days where some form of sacrifice is performed. The profane remains outside of the sacrificial realm set apart for communion between man and God in the ritual meal. This parenthetical ritual act is reminiscent of the Vedic rite of Ishti preparation rites. Cf. supra, chapter three, p. 10.

[54] Supra pp. 11-14. Also Dix, op. cit., pp. 50-51.

[55] The Hebrew Berakah can easily be understood by Greek terms Eulogia and Eucharistia, "blessing" or "thanksgiving." The Habûrah also used a hand-washing ceremony at both the beginning and the end. We should note that the Jews considered the blessing over the cup was considered more important than that over the bread.

[56] He also mentions that our sources are entirely rabbinic, see op. cit., p. 25.

[57] See K. G. Kuhn, as discussed at length by Jeremias, cf. op. cit., pp. 31-36. See also Delorme, op. cit., pp. 65-67.

[58] Op. cit., p. 1382. Paul Neuenzeit said, "Ob sich die Ordnung des jüdischen Festmahles bei den frühen christlichen Eucharistiefeiern erhalten hat, ist nicht definitiv auszumachen," cf. *Das Herrenmahl, Studien Zum Alten Und Neuen Testament,* ed. Vinzenz Hamp and Josef Schmid. München, Kösel-Verlag, 1960, p. 71.

[59] Gamber does not accept the Passover identity for the Last Supper opting rather for the Habûrah, op. cit., p. 11. Jungmann has promoted the theory that the Apostles did not attempt merely to repeat the Last Supper as a paschal meal, but rather modeled the first Eucharists after the Habûrah, *The Early Liturgy,* p. 31.

[60] See "Les structures fondamentales de l'eucharistie," in *Questions Liturgiques,* ed. E. Moeller. Louvain: Abbaye du Mont Cesar, vol. 1, 1971, p. 7. However, Verheul did say, "Il est donc important pour nous de connaître ces rites, car leur structure fondamentale déterminera celles rites eucharistiques," p. 8.

[61] Feeley-Harnik, *The Lord's Table : Eucharist and Passover in Early Christianity.* Philadelphia, University of Pennsylvania Press, 1981, p. 116. Feeley-Harnik suggests the last suppers in the texts were really "new passover haggadahs," cf. p. 116.

[62] Ibid., p. 116.

[63] Op. cit., pp. 162-165.

[64] K. Gamber said that the house fellowship meals (Acts 2: 42, 46) were held in the fashion of the Jewish ritual meals, just as a Habûrah would have been. In fact, he said that the Koinonia of Acts 2:42 and 46 was the equivalent to the Hebrew term Habûrah. Thus Gamber (p. 13) argued that the "breaking of bread" in Acts was also accompanied with a cup of blessing at the conclusion of the ceremonial meal even though it was not mentioned. Higgins (p. 59) also noted that wine most likely accompanied the "breaking of bread" in the earliest celebrations even though wine was not mentioned. Eduard Schweizer (p. 17) understands the Last Supper as Jesus' last table-fellowship in which Jesus' service

gave bodily expression to the promise of God's grace and covenant fulfillment.

[65] Dunn (p. 163) compared this practice to the "Ebionites whose beliefs closely paralleled those of the primitive Jerusalem community."

[66] This third suggestion resulted from assuming I Cor. 10: 16 may have inspired it (with the shorter Lukan text, e.g., minus Luke 22: 19d-20), ibid., p. 165. He did not discuss why the Annual Passover type may have inspired I Cor. 11: 25, "after supper," without Paul noticing the different order in his own text.

[67] Eduard Schweizer, *Neotestamentica*. Stuttgart: Zwingli Verlag, 1963, p. 345. This theory follows Lietzmann's with regard to the lack of wine used in the eschatological table fellowship type as in the case of the book of Acts. But Mark's eschatological statement comes clearly attached to the cup. Bultmann felt that it was very doubtful whether "the breaking of bread" (Acts 2:42) or "to break bread" (Acts 2:46; 20:7, 11) was ever a technical designation of the Lord's Supper," cf. *Theology of the New Testament*, translated by Kendrick Grobel. New York: Charles Scribner's Sons, vol. 1, p. 144.

[68] This raises the question of why Passover typology was "added" so early to the traditions of the Eucharist. Already in the writings of Paul (I Cor. around 55 A.D.) the Passover motif surfaces in relation to the Lord' Supper as a contrast to pagan sacrifices (10: 16-22). Paul related the "cup" in regard to the "blood of Christ" to partnership with Christ. Paul obviously connected these ideas to the "new covenant" (11:25) established by the blood of Christ. Many have considered Paul's associations here as having the Passover in the background. See William F. Orr and James A. Walther, *I Corinthians*, (*The Anchor Bible*, ed. by William F. Albright). Garden City:Doubleday & Company, Inc., 1976, pp. 250-252. "The term "body" was applicable to Passover societies that were formed for the festival; the group joining in the meal believed all of the persons were members of each other (an idea which Paul develops in 12: 12-26)," Orr, p. 272. Also see C. S. Mann, op. cit., p. 571, point 6.

[69] Supra, p. 20.

[70] One would think that the association with Passover, Yahweh's deliverance of the Jews out of Egypt that was celebrated in a memorial meal of thanksgiving, would have hardly escaped notice in the context of the early Christian's Kerygma. Their messages were preached originally to a Jewish audience with the aid of Jewish scriptures (Acts 2:5) concerning the death and resurrection of Jesus Christ and the forgiveness of sins, and accompanied by cultic union with Christ in baptism (Acts 2: 14-36, 38). The above finds support from the fact that the passion narratives were probably the earliest part of the gospel traditions to have a fixed form (first orally), and the most coherent form that exists within the Passion narratives is the Kerygma. Cf. Mann, op. cit., p. 553; see also, Ruldof Bultmann, *History of the Synoptic Tradition*, trans. by John Marsh. New York: Harper & Row, Publishers,1976, pp. 275 ff. Bultmann said "We have to reckon this Kerygma as the earliest connected tradition of the Passion and Death of Jesus," p. 275. C. S. Mann noted "Whatever the origins of the Passover, by the time of Jesus sacrificial ideas had taken firm hold of the festival, partly due to the centralization of the cult in Jerusalem, and partly also due to the exclusive part played by the temple clergy in the slaughter of the lambs," cf. op. cit. p. 570. We shall return to this sacrificial aspect later as well as the significance of the early Christian rites.

[71] Jeremias, op. cit., p. 96.

[72] Supra p. 17 and note 57.

[73] Cf. ibid., pp. 173 ff. Jeremias used Eulogâsas, "having blessed," as one of his examples of a semitism in Mark's account (14:22). He understood this aorist participial form of the Greek infinitive Eulogeîn to be the equivalent of the Hebrew Berak or the Aramaic Barek, cf. 175.

[74] Cf. I Cor. 11:23. The question of whether Paul received this tradition of the "Lord's Supper" from the risen Lord Himself or from an earlier oral tradition has been widely debated, cf. Orr and Walther op. cit., pp. 270 ff; also see Higgins op. cit., pp. 27-28.

[75] Jeremias op. cit., p. 188. Here he also sees contact between the Lukan and Johannine Hellenistic traditions and Paul's. Fitzmyer recently wrote "the Lucan formula over the bread and the wine is closer to the Pauline and is often judged today as an echo of an Antiochene liturgy, which both would reflect independently. The Marcan formula may reflect a Jerusalem liturgy, which Matthew has redacted on his own." Op. cit., p. 1393.

[76] Luke also has the same aorist infinitive temporal expression with the preposition meta; meta to deipnâsai translates, "after dining." Deipnon referred to the main meal and was also used to express a cultic meal, seeWalter Bauer, *A Greek-English Lexicon of the New Testament and Other Early Christian Literature.* Translated by William F. Arndt. Second edition with F. Wilbur Gingrich and Frederick W. Danker, Chicago: The University of Chicago Press, 1979.

[77] Dix (p. 20) and Gamber (pp. 77-78) have indicated that the meal Habûrah was completely separated from the Eucharist by the end of the second-century. Dix also said that the Agape or Lord's Supper became a different entity from the Eucharist. The whole process of separation begun in the first century perhaps with Paul's congregations because of the trouble in the Corinthian congregation. The bringing together of the two sayings over the bread and the cup has also incurred discussion concerning the different nature of these two sayings. Scholars have taken stock of the diverse use of the term "body" (Soma) and "blood" instead of the more parallel flesh (Sarks) and blood. E. Schweizer thinks that if these two were originally separated by a meal then they would not have been understood as parallel terms, and body and blood would not have been hard to see if they wereoriginally independent, cf. op. cit., p. 13, 14. Haenchen proposed that Mark/Matthew adapted the cup word to the form of the bread word because it would not be reasonable to imagine that an original unity was later destroyed. Op. cit., p. 480.

[78] Jeremias cited the omission of the copula in 22:20 as evidence of this semitism , op. cit., p. 185.

[79] Ibid., p. 185.

[80] "Andererseits hat Schürmann wahrscheinlich gemacht, daß Mk 14,25 aus der volleren Lk-Fassung stammt und nicht etwa umgekehrt." Cf. E. Schweizer, RGG, op. cit.,p. 15. Jeremias commented on H. Schürmann's theory that Luke presents the earliest text of the words of interpretation. Jeremias could not accept this hypothesis in its totality but did recognize its particular contribution to the textual dispute about Lk. 19:19b-20. Op. cit., pp. 189 ff. Fitzmyer too thinks that Luke used a special source of his own. Op. cit., p. 1386. According to Jeremias Luke 22:14 ff. are from a non-markan "Urlukas" source.

[81] The Lucan account (22:17-20) has two principal witnesses, a shorter, or Western text that omits verses 19b and 20, resulting in a cup-bread order; and a longer text evidenced by all Greek manuscripts with the exception of "D" and most ancient versions and the Church Fathers whose sequence runs cup-bread-cup. See, Bruce M. Metzger, *A Textual Commentary on the Greek New Testament*. London, United Bible Societies, third ed., 1971, pp. 173-177. Also see Nestle-Aland, *Novum Testamentum Graece*. Stuttgart, Deuche Bibelstiftung, twenty-sixth ed., 1979, p. 233 and textual apparatus. As it stands today most textual critics accept the longer text. In Luke the 'Western' text usually omitted or changed longer original readings. So Jeremias, among others, who accepted the longer reading of the Lucan eucharistic, text correspondingly rejected the shorter reading as a "Western omission." For an argument against the longer text see Rudolf Otto in, *The Kingdom of God and the Son of Man*, translated by Floyd V. Filson and Bertram Lee-Woolf. Boston: Star King Press, 1957, pp. 266 ff; and R. D. Richardson who also specifically opposes Jeremias' view, op. cit., pp. 225 ff.

[82] Higgins raised the possibility that Luke 22:19-20 may have been an independent source that went back to the same tradition as the one Paul used. Here the command to repeat came after the bread but not after the cup. Cf. op. cit., p. 44. Jeremias agreed with Dibelius that the longer version of Luke represented a "third variant" of the eucharistic formula and therefore was independent from Mark and Paul, op. cit., p. 152 and note 4. Fitzmyer thought that both Mark and Luke had been influenced by a liturgical tradition. (Although one need not subscribe to Bultmann's

"cult legend," op. cit., p. 1387.) Jeremias also considered Paul's introduction, "the Lord Jesus on the night he was betrayed," to be a "liturgical stylizing," op. cit., p. 192.

[83] See op. cit., pp. 1393-1395. Fitzmyer's experiment involved putting Mark's and Luke's interpretive words over the bread and cup back into Aramaic "with almost equal ease and problems," p. 1394.

[84] See F. J. Leenhardt, *Le Sacrement de la sainte Céne*, Paris, Neuchâtel, 1948, pp. 51 ff.

[85] Cf. op. cit., pp. 480-481. E. Schweizer felt that Paul had preserved the more pure form "im ganzen" even though both Mark and Paul went back to an older form, RGG, op. cit., p. 14. Mann pointed out that the Markan and Matthean version of "this is my blood of the Covenant" are impossible in Aramaic, op. cit., p. 579. E. Schweitzer said the Pauline formula, "my body for you," is impossible in Aramaic, cf. RGG, op. cit., p. 13. Haenchen thought that the oldest tradition of the Last Supper would have only had the single interpretive saying over the bread e.g., "this is my body." He further indicated that the Aramaic term for body (Uph) was used. This original term simply meant "form" or "person," in other words "my body" in Aramaic means `nichts anderes als "ich"´, op. cit., p. 482.

[86] Haenchen op. cit., p. 481.

[87] Jeremias changed his mind with regard to Mark's text as representing the oldest, cf. his preface.

[88] However, Jeremias did not think that these traditions went back to a common Greek source, ibid. p. 186.

[89] Cf. ibid., pp. 186-190. Jeremias thought the Fourth Gospel's discourse on the bread of life (6:53-58) may have been an independent source for Jesus' word of interpretation concerning the bread, p. 107. Raymond Brown also thinks that John's gospel may preserve the words

of the institution because of their liturgical form, cf. op. cit., vol. 1, pp. 284-285.

[90] Matthew had merely reworked the text of Mark. Higgins said Matthew's narrative was "an expanded and more liturgical form of Mark's account," op. cit., p. 24. See also Mann, op. cit., p. 572. P. Benoit said of the Markan and Pauline/Lukan traditions that "between these two there is no immediate literary dependence of either one on the other. They are parallel traditions with common characteristics explained by the common source from which they come." See *The Eucharist in the New Testament*, translated by E. M. Stewart. Baltimore, Helicon Press, 1964, p. 72.

[91] Paul's eschatological account differed from the gospels by excluding the abstention saying and merely stating that by eating of the bread and by drinking of the cup "you proclaim the Lord's death until he comes" (I Cor. 11:27). Haenchen said the eschatological saying originally formed an unity in itself and that the evangelistcombined it in a distinctive way to the actual words of the Last Supper, op. cit., p. 479.

[92] Ibid., p. 161. E. Schweizer asked how could two self-contained eschatological reports have arisen from the Last Supper if both were combined at the beginning. Cf. RGG, op. cit., p. 15.

[93] Dunn, op. cit., p. 166.

[94] Dunn held that the Markan text, "My blood of the covenant," rendered a form incompatible with the Aramaic, cf. ibid., p. 166.

[95] For example, the labors of New Testament scholars on the Eucharist have yielded important information for those non-specialists interested in different aspects of the Eucharist. I refer to the name already mentioned above of G. Feeley-Harnik who sought to study the Eucharist from sociological and anthropological bases in addition to the historical. Although C. G. Jung did not rely heavily on the findings of New Testament historical research he did deal extensively with the Eucharist

in his *Gesammelte Werke*, vol. 11. We shall return to Jung's work on the Eucharist later.

[96] For liturgical developments in the texts cf. supra pp. 14, 27 (with fn. 104), 29. Redaction criticism also explains certain differences in the texts.

[97] Another point of agreement that came to light through a simple comparison of the texts centered on the sequence of four verbs used to describe Jesus' action at the Last Supper e.g., Jesus took bread, gave thanks, broke bread and gave the bread and cup to the disciples. Scholars have also noticed that John 8:1-10 used the same verbs in the account of the multiplication of the loaves.

[98] See chapter five.

[99] Dunn, op. cit., p. 167.

[100] Ibid., p. 168.

[101] Ibid., p. 168.

[102] Ibid., p. 168. Dunn seems to infer that these developments not only deviated from the original meals but also from the true meaning of the first meals.

[103] Jeremias, op. cit., p. 97. One must keep in mind that virtually no material exists on what happened in the first-century liturgies outside of the New Testament texts themselves. No ritual handbooks existed for the Eucharist in the first century.

[104] Jeremias (p. 187) spoke of the harmonizing tendency over the bread and wine words. For example, the "blood poured out for many" later became "for you" in order to facilitate distribution during the rite.

[105] For instance he thought the introductory Kai, "and" was pre-liturgical and followed a literary tradition that went back to the historical accounts in the Old Testament, ibid. pp. 191 ff.

[106] Ibid., pp. 125-126.

[107] New members were sworn to keep certain teachings, names of angels and writings secret as well as holding secret meals, ibid., p. 126. Jeremias used the term "Essene" for the Qumranians while others have differentiated between the two, cf. W. La Sor, op. cit., pp. 136-139. After the discovery of the *Temple Scroll* these two terms are no longer differentiated.

[108] Ibid., pp. 126-136. Here Jeremias gave other examples of protection against "profanation."

[109] Ibid., p. 126.

[110] The Gnostics would later (second-century) understand the eucharistic words to hold magical powers, cf. H. Graß, "Abendmahl," " II. Dogmengeschichtlich," RGG, third edition, p. 22. S. Angus has pointed out that the Mysteries used allegory so that the archaic part of the ritual that had lost its original meaning could still be preserved. The same was true for the repulsive aspects of their ancient rites. In other words, the ritual acts were not simply discarded even when they were felt to be offensive. On the contrary, the acts received a new interpretation and remained in consort with their accompanying words. See, *The Mystery-Religions and Christianity*. New York: Charles Scribner's Sons, 1928, p. 49.

[111] G. Dix op. cit., pp. 12 ff. After the fourth-century the situation started to reverse with the rite becoming primarily something said rather than done. Also see infra chapter five.

[112] Ibid., p. 11.

[113] I do not mean to imply here that a distinct Hellenistic influence was operative for Gentile Christiansas in the case of Bultmann's "cult legend of the Hellenistic circles," cf. *History of the Synoptic Tradition*, p. 265.

[114] Norman Perrin, *Rediscovering the Teaching of Jesus*. New York, Harper & Row, 1967, p. 104.

[115] See Jeremias, op. cit., pp. 237 ff.

[116] See C. S. Mann, op. cit., p. 575.

[117] Mann relates the Greek pronoun Touto (this) to the broken loaf, while attaching "to soma mou" (my body) to the coming death of Jesus, op. cit., p. 577.

[118] Bultmann thought that the words, "of the covenant," interpreted Jesus' death "as the sacrifice of the (new) covenant," see *Theology of the New Testament*, p. 146.

[119] Fitzmyer, op. cit., p. 1391.

[120] C. S. Mann, p. 575.

[121] Bultmann, *Theology of the New Testament*, pp. 84, 149. Bultmann said the words, "poured out," interpreted Jesus' death "as an expiatory sacrifice for sins," p. 146.

[122] Ibid., p. 575.

[123] Otto, *The Kingdom of God and the Son of Man*, pp. 290 ff.

[124] The Jews responsible for first century Judaism should be distinguished from the ancient Hebrews and the Israelites of the Northern Kingdom. Judaism began its own particular historical identity with the exiled Judahites after the destruction of the kingdom of Judah in 587 B.C. Samuel Terrien said, "The Jews transmitted the Hebrew Scriptures and produced the manuscripts, but their sacred library reflects

Mosaic and prophetic Yahwism far more than it reflects the ritual cultus of the Second Temple." Cf. *The Elusive Presence*, San Francisco, Harper & Row, 1978, p. 7. We should note that by the time of the first century, Judaism consisted of a variety of different political and religious factions. Some scholars have thought it more accurate to use the plural "Judaisms" when referring to the Jewish religious environment of this period in Palestine. This same type of religious diversity characterized the early Christian church. From its inception, Christianity included both Greek speaking and Aramaic speaking members, cf. Acts 6,1. Early in this century the history of the earliest Christian traditions (Traditionsgeschichte) drew attention to the contrasts between Palestinian Jewish Christian congregations and later Hellenistic-Jewish-Christian congregations. This school with the likes of S. Schulz, M. Dibelius, and R. Bultmann based these distinctions on their form-critical analysis of particular types of sayings of Jesus in the Synoptic Gospels. Bultmann, for example, concluded that the synoptic tradition took its shape from Jesus' original teachings which were Jewish. These earliest Christian communities Bultmann labeled as Palestinian and he maintained that the characteristic Christian features of their message were the proclamation of the risen Lord and the coming of the Son of Man, while the characteristic Jewish element of these communities rested upon their use of first-century Judaism's language and mythology. Bultmann traced the development of Christianity further through the synoptic tradition by citing a later Hellenistic Christian group that had moved out of Palestine and held a radically different view of the Jewish Law that resulted in a different cult. Cf. *History of the Synoptic Tradition*, E.T. by John Marsh. London: Harper & Row, 1963. Today such clear cut lines of differentiation between Palestinian and Hellenistic Christianity fail to appear. This is especially true in light of the work done by Martin Hengel. Hengel showed that the influence of Hellenism upon Palestinian Judaism was deeply rooted by the first-century B.C.E. Cf. *Judaism and Hellenism*, E.T. by John Bowden, Philadelphia: Fortress Press, 1974, esp. chapter 3. Also refer to James Dunn, op. cit., Chapter I. See also Günther Bornkamm, *Jesus of Nazareth*, translated by Irene and Fraster McLuskey with James Robinson. New York: Harper & Row, Publishers, 1960, pp. 39 ff.

¹²⁵ I am adopting the vocabulary of and the basic premises of the Documentary Hypothesis Theory that understood the Pentateuch, or Hexateuch in the Case of Wellhausen, as the product of at least four different traditions, viz., the Yahwist, the Elowist (eight-century B.C.E.), the Deuteronomist (seventh-century) and again the Priestly Code. Wellhausen followed the influence of religious historians of his day by viewing Israel's religion in specific evolutionary terms. The particular scheme that he adopted came from the English anthropologist E. B. Tylor who postulated that all religions began with animism and evolved from this "lower form" to monotheism. For a treatment of the problems with Tylor's theory and other evolutionistic theories of the nineteenth-century see Kees Bolle's article in *The Encyclopedia of Religion*, Mircea Eliade, editor in chief, New York: MacMillan Publishing Company, vol. 1, 1987. Although J. Wellhausen and the early proponents of this theory thought that these four traditions were written, today most feel that these four represent different oral traditions, cf. John Bright, "Modern Study of Old Testament Literature," *The Bible and Ancient Near East*, ed. by G. E. Wright, Garden City, New York, 1961, pp. 13-31.

¹²⁶ Jesus himself did not espouse the removal of sacrifice or the Law of Moses, cf. E. P. Sanders, *Jesus and Judaism*, London: SCM Press Ltd., 1985, chapters one and nine.

¹²⁷ See Genesis 14:18-22, 16:13, 17:01, 31:13, and Terrien, op. cit., p. 68.

¹²⁸ See Eliade, *Patterns in Comparative Religion*, translated by Rosemary Sheed. New York, Merdian, 1958, pp. 72, 93-96. Yahweh has been characterized as a "storm god."

¹²⁹ Ibid., p. 69.

¹³⁰ Scholars gave the name "Yahwist" to the southern tradition (usually indicated by the letter J from the German word Jahwist) that compiled its material around the ninth-century B.C.E. in Judah, and "Elowist" to the northern tradition (E) in the eighth-century B.C.E. Terrien

characterized the Yahwist as concerned more with the distinction between the laity and the priests and accordingly gave the priests (Levities) more status through their seeing the glory of Yahweh in the epiphanies. In the Yahwist scheme of things Moses represented a type of eternal priesthood. This particular emphasis in J Terrien traced to the establishment of the center of the cult in Jerusalem and through the Exile to the Second Temple. The editors of the Pentateuch in the Second Temple period gave an authoritative slant to the whole system of the laws surrounding the Temple cult. According to Rich, this gave more power to the inherited priesthood of the Aaronides while limiting the prophets and subordinating Israel to the authority of the High Priests, see John Rich, *Jesus and the Transformation of Judaism*. New York: Seabury Press, 1982, p. 67. The same authoritative structure and emphasis on cultic purity and sacrifice held power in Jesus time under the Hasmoneans who gained power after the Maccabean revolt and sustained their rule as friends of Caesar. However, the Elowist placed no glorified distinction between the laity and priestly cast when it came to the appearances of Yahweh. Terrien referred to their representation of Yahweh's presence among the people as a "theologomenon of the name" rather than the "glory" of Yahweh. See op. cit., especially chapters 1-4.

[131] Ibid., p. 93.

[132] Exodus 3:5; RSV.

[133] Exodus 19:10-11, 15.

[134] Exodus 19:12-13. The prohibition against touching the profane shows that the Hebrews thought that defilements or impurities could be transferred through physical contact as in Vedic religion. This whole matter of consecration and concern for purity divulges the ritual environment of these divine epiphanies.

[135] Exodus 19:18, 22.

[136] Exodus 19:5-6.

[137] Exodus 19:24.

[138] Exodus 19:21-22.

[139] The word originally is thought to come from the image of a thundercloud that brought both destructive powers in the lightening and blessings of life in the rain, cf. Terrien, op. cit., p. 128. Such an origin for this term and its use in Near Eastern mythology to designate storm gods does not mean that we have come across an argument for the birth of religion in the veneration of natural phenomena such as thunder and lightening. See de Vries on Nature Mythologists, op. cit., pp. 80-90.

[140] Exodus 19: 22.

[141] See Terrien op. cit., p. 128.

[142] Friedrich Lang, "Fire," in the *Theological Dictionary of the New Testament*, edited by Gerhard Friedrich, translated by Geoffrey W. Bromiley. Grand Rapids: Wm. B. Eerdmans Publishing Company, 1968, vol. VI, p. 935. Lang also said that fire meant ritual purification in the cult and that fire could be used at times to remove what had been sanctified in order to protect it from profanation, (Exodus 12:10, 29:34; Leviticus 4:12), p. 935.

[143] For R. E. Clements "divine presence is the basic presupposition of the cult." Clements spoke of the expectation of God himself coming to Israel to bless them. The progressive spiritualization of the sacrificial cult resulted in an even more transcendent nature for God, according to Clements, and also "weakened the assertions of his direct presence," cf. *Eucharist Theology Then and Now*, p. 5.

[144] Exodus 19:24-26.

[145] Ancient Hebrew does not have a word for either transcendence or immanence. The Hebrew adjective that means "near" (Karov) occurs seventy-five times referring to cultic nearness (Ez. 42:13, Ps. 148:14) and salvific nearness (Ps. 85:10, Deut. 4:7). The Hebrew word for

"distance" (Rahok) appears one hundred-sixty-two times in the Hebrew Bible with regard to the consequences of sin (Jer. 2:5), the absence of God (Ps. 10:1), divine transcendence (Ps. 139:2), and God's distance from Sinai (Isa. 30:27). Cf. Brown, Driver, Briggs, op. cit., pp. 897-99, and 934-35 respectively. An interesting conflict shows up over the tension involving God's transcendence and immanence between the Hebrew and Greek texts of Jeremiah 23:23-24. The Hebrew text reads, "Am I a God who is near, says the Lord, and not a distant God?" While the Greek (LXX) reads, "I am a God who is near (Engizon), says the Lord, and not a distant God." In keeping with the whole of Hebrew thought God is certainly both, near and far. The Greek translators seem to have been trying to stay within a particular theological statement of God's nearness versus an uncaring Deus Otiosus. The Hebrew scribes, on the other hand, appear to have preserved the original meaning from the theological context of Jeremiah. See, Werner E. Lemke, "The Near and the Distant God" *Journal of Biblical Literature*. Chico: Society of Biblical Literature, 1981, vol. 100, no. 4, pp. 541 ff.

[146] For a list and description of sacrifices in the Old Testament see T. H. Gaster, "Sacrifices and Offerings, OT," in *The Interpreter's Dictionary of the Bible*, edited by George A. Buttrick et. al. New York: Abingdon Press, 1962, vol. 4, pp. 147-158. Also refer to Gary A. Anderson, "Sacrifice and Sacrificial Offerings (OT)," in *The Anchor Bible Dictionary*, editor by David Noel Freedman et. al. New York: Doubleday, 1992, vol. 5, pp. 870-886.

[147] The victim could be either male of female unlike the Holocaust sacrifice that required a male victim only, cf. Lev. chapter three and 7:11-38. The blood and fat were said to belong to Yahweh and one must not eat these parts, see Lev. 3:16-17; 7:23-25.

[148] The breast and right thigh were prescribed for the priests, cf. Lev. 7:28-34 while the sacrificer received the remainder of the flesh that he could in turn share with his family and guests, providing that these people were ritually pure, cf. Lev. 3:31; Exodus 29:31.

[149] Cf. Leviticus 22:18-20.

[150] See Roland de Vaux, *Les Sacrifices de L'Ancient Testament*. Paris, J. Gabalda, 1964, p. 28. In the Hollocaust rite the sacrificer himself presents the victim after placing his hand upon its head as in the "scape-goat" rite. But here the victim remained pure whereas the scape goat received the sins of the people and was driven into the wilderness (Leviticus 16:21). De Vaux thinks that this can not be a magical practice or a symbol of substitution, p. 29. I accept De Vaux's reasoning that it was a symbolic act of substitution where the victim perished in place of the sacrificer.

[151] See Leviticus 1:5,6,9.

[152] The word in Leviticus 1:9 is 'Isseh, thought to be related to 'ês, supra, fn. 165. Cf. de Vaux, op. cit., pp. 30-31.

[153] This altar was called the "table of Yahweh," while the sacrificial offerings became known as "Yahweh's food." Cf. Ezekiel 44:7, 16; Malachi 1:7, 12; Leviticus 21:6,8. The Communion and Holocaust sacrifices seem to go back to a pre-Semitic civilization from which the Canaanites borrowed both of the above sacrifices prior to the settlement of the Israelites in Palestine, as evidenced by the texts of Ras Shamra. Cf. de Vaux op. cit., p. 46. However the blood rites were not a part of the Canaanite or Greek sacrifices that were otherwise quite similar to Israel's sacrifices, cf. de Vaux, p. 48.

[154] Leviticus 17:11. We are reminded of the text in the New Testament that said in reference to Christ's sacrifice that, "...without the shedding of blood there is no forgiveness of sins" (Hebrews 9:22). R. Hentschke said, "Mit dem Sünd-Opfer (Hâtta't) sind besondere mit dem Blut zu vollziehende Riten verbunden (Lev 4)," cf. "Opfer II. Im AT," RGG, Vol. IV, p. 1645. Blood was dashed on the sides of the altar to expiate for sin in the 'Olâ (Leviticus 1:4), Minhâ (Leviticus 14:20), and 'âsâm (Leviticus 5:16, 18) sacrifices.

[155] Semitic cognates from the Akkadian word for "wipe" and the Arabic word for "cover" substantiate both meanings. However, the debate as to the preference of one meaning over the other continues among some, see

J. Milgrom, "Atonement in the OT," in *The Interpreters Dictionary of the Bible*, Supplementary Vol., 1976, p. 78, who prefers both meanings.

[156] Scholars now think that early Israel did not know of forgiveness of sin but only a repentance of sin to avoid evil. The concept of forgiveness of sin can only be verified in postexilic texts, cf. Milgrom, ibid., p. 83. Even the abstract idea of "expiate" took some time to develop in the cult from the action of rubbing off impurities to expiation in a more general sense, see ibid., p. 80.

[157] Frances M. Young said with regard to Kippêr, "In the Old Testament it is construed with the priests or Jahweh as the subject, and the Temple, altar or iniquity as the object," *The Use of Sacrificial Ideas in Greek Christian Writers From the New Testament to John Chrysostom.* Cambridge: The Philadelphia Patristic Foundation, 1979, p. 42. Kippêr developed from its strictly ritual application to a more theological usage in the prophets. The prophets used God as the subject of Kippêr and sin as the direct object. Kippêr bore the meaning of "forgiveness" in these cases, (e.g., Jeremiah 18:23; Ezekiel 16:63). Kippêr was also used to consecrate the land (e.g., Leviticus 18:25, Deuteronomy 21:23).

[158] This word comes from the Hebrew word for "sin" (Hatah) that carries the notion of "missing the mark" or of "falling short." The rite of Hattâ'th was used to cleanse or purge whatever it touched and to regenerate the person(s) for whom it was applied, cf., T. H. Gaster, op. cit., pp. 151-152. Kippêr was used independently of Hattâ'th in some instances, see Leviticus 16:19, 21-22; Exodus 30:16; Numbers 25:1-15. For Milgrom: "Whenever a sacrifice concludes the purification ritual for physical impurity, it is always a Hattâ'th, and its purpose is to Kippêr or purge the contaminated sanctuary," op. cit., p. 80.

[159] Numbers 20:9-10. The formula, "whatever touches them will become holy" (Exodus 30:29), refers to everything made ritually holy or pure in the sanctuary for sacrifice. The ashes remained in a state of intense purity from their contact with the holy realm of the sacrifice by virtue of Yahweh's contact through the sacred fire.

[160] Numbers 20:9. This water was used for the "removal of sin."

[161] The design of the sanctuary complex symbolized a graded degree of holiness in conjunction with the ritual as it moved inward toward the Holy of holies. The outer court was accessible to the laity because it was less holy than the tabernacle or inner sanctuary. Only the priests who were consecrated for contact with the inner parts could go beyond the outer court. The Holy of holies inhibited the presence of everyone except the priest with special consecration and only during special sacrificial occasions. In the following chapter we shall see how this ritual model influenced the sanctuaries and eucharistic liturgies.

[162] Hanck pointed out the fact that the Greek verbal adjective, Hagios ("holy"), originally signified "that which awakens religious awe." Etymologically, Hagios has a link with the Sanskrit word Yaj ("to sacrifice" or "to reverence"), but not to the Latin Sacer, cf., "Holy," TDNT, vol. I, p. 122.

[163] Cf. Milgrom op. cit., pp. 77-78. The Ancient Near East gave a great deal of attention to expiatory rites that cleansed their temples. The Babylonian New Year's festival of Akîtu required cleansing of the temple Nabu in a ritual called Kuppuru. A beheaded sheep's carcass was rubbed on the walls. The ritual remains of this sheep were then tossed into the river after which those who performed this rite of preparation went out of the city until the end of the festival, see Gaster, op. cit., p. 153. However de Vaux said, "La Mésopotamie n'a pas connu l'équivalent du sacrifice pour le péché," op. cit., p. 96.

[164] Cf. Leviticus 16:16.

[165] Cf. Leviticus 4:1-5, 13. R. Abba wrote: "In its general sense of "making atonement" it (Kippêr) signified an action which is directed toward sin or ceremonial uncleanness," "Expiation," *The Interpreter's Dictionary of the Bible*, vol. 3, p. 200. The concept of sin in Judaism was determined by the Law (Torah). Transgressing against the Law was the same thing as violating the revelation of God's will. Judaism also stressed the individual's responsibility with regard to the consequences

of disobeying the Law, see Stählin and Grundmann, "sin," TDNT, vol. I, PP. 289-293. E. P. Sanders said that an impure person was not necessarily a sinner. Although Sanders did say that regardless of the cause of impurity, purification was "necessary before entering the temple or otherwise contacting something holy," op. cit., p. 183. Sanders described the religious environment during first century Judaism. Ancient Israel did not make as much distinction as to what caused the impurity when it came to participation in the cult.

[166] In many cases sin (Hatt'ât) denoted a particular form of sacrifice, cf. Leviticus 4:1-5. See Bertram, "Sin in the OT," TDNT, vol. I, pp. 267-289. Again, when expiation had as the object the sanctuary or some other material thing the sense of cleansing and purifying were understood for Kippêr, cf. Exodus 29:37; 30:10. The LXX used Katharizein. Procksch said that "cultic qualification is inconceivable without purity," and "Yahweh's holiness demands the holiness of His people as a condition of intercourse," cf. "Holy," TDNT, vol. I, p. 92.

[167] The distinction was made between the sanctuary and the "Holy of holies" by their physical separation, cf., Exodus 26:34; Numbers 18:10. "Mercy seat" came from the feminine abstract noun form of Kippêr and can be translated as "that which expiates," see Milgrom op. cit., p. 80. The Ark was linked to "holiness" because Yahweh dwelt there, e.g. Exodus 25: 10 ff. The Ark represented such holiness that if anyone were to look into it, let alone touch it, they would die immediately, e.g., I Samuel 6:20. Anderson said "If the impurity is allowed to accumulate, the deity will be forced to leave the sanctuary." Op. cit., p. 880.

[168] "Most closely related materially to Qadosh or holiness is the term Tohar ("purity")," Procksh, "Holy," TDNT, vol. I, p. 89. Qadosh most likely came from a Canaanite root (Qd) that mean "to divide." The underlying idea would have been to separate or mark off from the secular, p. 80. So the most basic notion of "holy" began in Israel from the differentiation between everyday life (profane or common ) and cultic life. Procksch (p. 89) also observed: "Anything related to the cultus, whether God, man, things, space or time, can be brought under the term Qadosh."

[169] Leviticus 10:10-11. The Hebrew word, Bâdal, translated "to distinguish" in the RSV, is in the causative (Hiph`îl), infinitive verb form, Lehavdîl. The literal meaning of this verb form "to divide," "separate" or "set apart" seems to depict more accurately the ritual action of the priest during the sacrifice. See Brown, Briggs, Driver, op. cit., p. 95.

[170] Procksch (p. 91) wrote that "the concept of holiness merges into that of divinity, so that Yahweh's holy name contrasts with everything creaturely," op. cit., p. 91.

[171] See Stanislas Lyonnet, *Sin, Redemption, and Sacrifice*. Rome, Biblical Institute Press, 1970, p. 17, where he said that sin "did away with God's transcendence." The name of R. Otto surfaces again in this discussion, see above chapter II, p. 52. After quoting Otto, Bertram concluded: "Sin is thus a spontaneous human reaction to the holy and divine." Op. cit., p. 274.

[172] Leviticus 16:2.

[173] Leviticus 16:1. In 10:1 ff. the text explained that the sons of Aaron had offered "unholy fire before Yahweh, "and as a result of this ritual mistake fire came forth from Yahweh and consumed them.

[174] Leviticus 16:3

[175] Leviticus 16:4,5.

[176] In all likelihood Yahweh was thought to manifest himself in the altar fire. See George B. Gray, *Sacrifice in the Old Testament*. Prolegomenon by Baruch A. Levine, New York: KTAV Publishing House, Inc., 1971, p. XXXIII.

[177] Leviticus 16:12-15.

[178] Leviticus 16:16.

[179] Leviticus 16:23.

[180] Before Israel built one temple in Solomon's reign several temples and altars were used, see G. A. Barrois, "Temples," *The Interpreters Dictionary of the Bible*, vol. 4, pp. 534-568.

[181] See M. Eliade, *Myth and Reality*, translated by William R. Trask. New York: Harper & Row, Publishers, 1975, pp. 47-50. The Scandinavian and British Myth-and-Ritual scholars have over-emphasized the importance of the nature myths in Israel's worship and failed to discern clearly the weaving of Israel's feasts into historical events in comparison to her Egyptian and Semitic neighbors, see Terrien, op. cit., pp. 14-17. Terrien (p. 20) said of Israel's cultus, "From the start, nature was demyththologized by a theology of transcendence over the natural elements." His use of "demythologize" may lead to confusion if one were to imagine that Israel simply replaced her neighbor's mythology with her own theology. We may think of Israel's developing theology of Yahweh's transcendence as being integrated into her own mythology. But Israel's myths clearly show syncretistic features. See E.O. James, *Myth and Ritual in the Ancient Near East*. London: Thames and Hudson, 1958, pp. 60-67.

[182] This did become a concern after the destruction of the Temple and the exile in 587 B.C. The prophets and poets response to the whole question of the temple cult and Yahweh's presence resulted in a theology that now emphasized God's hiddenness in a new way as well as his presence in spiritual worship. See Terrien, op. cit., pp. 287 ff.

[183] Even when human kings began to rule in Israel the king was only a representative of Yahweh. Israel maintained the distinction between the monarchy and the rule of Yahweh through the king. Eliade said it this way:"the unique position of Yahweh makes the "divinization" of the king impossible, the latter is preeminently the "servant" of Yahweh (the word is applied to David sixty times." See *A History of Religious Ideas*, vol. 1, p. 334.

[184] Eliade (p. 235) commenting on the Jerusalem Temple cult said, "In the last analysis, the liturgical practice renews the structure of the world." See Psalm 72.

[185] Azazel type rites were frequent and ubiquitous in the Ancient Near East. The purpose of these rites was to remove the influential powers of evil (demons) through an animal that carried the impurities away, see Milgrom, op. cit. p. 83. Also p. 80, for a comment on this practice in Mesopotamia.

[186] Leviticus 16:20-22.

[187] The Seleucids had originally been a part of Alexander's tremendous military forces. Seleucus II finally gained freedom from the Ptolemies around 229 BC and Antiochus III began his campaign to regain Seleucid possessions in 219 BC, see N Turner, "Selucia in Syria," IDB, vol. 4, pp. 264-266.

[188] This fact provides yet another reason why we cannot make a sharp distinction between "Hellenistic" and "Palestinian Judaism." Additionally, a great deal of contact with Diaspora Jews and Jerusalem came about through travel and trade, see M. Hengel, op. cit., vol. 1, p. 170. Werner Jaeger said that the Jews in Palestine itself had been Hellenized "to a considerable extent" by the time of Paul. See his *Early Christianity and Greek Paideia.* New York: Oxford University Press, 1961, p. 6.

[189] See Riches, op. cit., p. 64.

[190] Hengel, op. cit., p. 24. Hengel also noted that while the Seleucids gave their "temple states" a good deal of freedom, the Ptolemies watched over the financial proceeding very closely.

[191] The Gerousia made up of the heads of influential families also helped limit the high priest's powers in the political and economic affairs of Judea, see Hengel, op. cit. pp. 25 ff.

[192] Hengel, ibid., pp. 58 ff. Note: Attic Koinê made the first appearance in Palestine. The Hellenizers had little interest outside of the cities to implant their transforming agenda.

[193] Ibid., p. 58.

[194] This Greek translation come at the hands of the Jews themselves. The translations of the Jewish prophets, etc. continued for at least another eighty years.

[195] Riches, op. cit., p. 64.

[196] Ibid., p. 65.

[197] See Hengel, op. cit., pp. 175 ff. D. S. Russel called the Hasidim the predecessors to the Pharisees, see *Between the Testaments*. Philadelphia: Fortress Press, 1960, p. 27.

[198] Riches (p. 66), following Hengel, pointed to the association that the Pharisees had during this time with the synagogues. The Pharisees helped instruct the people in matters of Jewish religion and especially in observance of the Law.

[199] The rich, prophetic eschatology and apocalyptic literature that came out of this struggle helped liberate the Jews in the sense meant by K. Bolle who spoke of myth's ability to set man "free from all forces which impair his human possibilities." *The Freedom of Man in Myth*, p. 72. For detailed information on the influence of Hellenism on Jewish literature see Hengel, op. cit., chapter three. See also Paul Hanson, *The Dawn of Apocalyptic*. Philadelphia: Fortress Press, 1979, pp. 8-31. Hanson has shown that Israel's apocalyptic writers "return to their ancient myths" in order to construct their new visions of God's salvation and the defeat of the Israel's enemies. The symbolism of Jewish apocalyptic portrays heavenly forces against evil demonic forces. Qumran also produced writing in the apocalyptic genre with its dualistic features, e.g., "sons of light" verses the "sons of darkness." See John G.

Gager, for early Christianity as a millennial movement, *Kingdom and Community*. Englewood Cliffs: Prentice-Hall, Inc., 1975, pp. 37-57.

[200] See R. E. Clements, op. cit., p. 3.

[201] Their efforts seemed to have focused primarily on the maintenance of a pure table, and they ate only with those who had prepared themselves, the food and the table settings according to their laws for such. See Sanders, op. cit., pp. 186-211. According to Gerd Theissen, the term `Am Ha-Aretz came from Nehemiah 10:28 and referred to Gentiles who were living in Palestine, cf., *Sociology of Early Palestinian Christianity*, translated by John Bowden. Philadelphia: Fortress Press, 1978, p. 85.

[202] Robin Scroggs, "The Earliest Christian Communities as Sectarian Movement," p. 10.

[203] Sanders makes this point to suggest that Jesus' table fellowship with "sinners' would have been with those who were in a state of impurity but not necessarily sin. If purity laws were considered trivial, Sanders maintained, then Jesus "opposed Jewish trivialization of religion," op. cit., p. 210.

[204] IQS 5:13-14; quoted from LaSor, op. cit., p. 70.

[205] See ibid., p. 71. The IQS has several references to "common purity" (Tohorat Ha-Rabbîm) that could not be touched by outsiders, and the term "purity" referred to "ritually purearticles, especially food." The Rabbinic term Tohorotappliedto food and other ritually prepared utensils used in the Levitical sacrificial code. See Joseph M. Baumgarten, "Sacrifice and Worship Among the Jewish Sectarians of the Dead Sea (Qumran) Scrolls," in *Harvard Theological Review*. Cambridge: Harvard University Press, Vol. XLV, 1952, p. 148.

[206] See ibid., pp. 150-151.

[207] This word translated "community" came from the root Whd that means to unify and separate at the same time, cf. Riches, op. cit., p. 120.

[208] Ibid., p. 124.

[209] See Riches, pp. 121-122. Riches (p. 132): "The Law as understood in Qumran is a means of union with a God of holiness."

[210] IQS 12:7-9, quoted from Baumgarten, op. cit., p. 142.

[211] "Cario Fragments of a Damascene Covenant" (CDC) 11:18 21, quoted from ibid., p. 145.

[212] Clements op. cit., p. 13. Even after the literal sacrifices ceased in Judaism after the destruction of the Temple in 70 C.E., sacrifice continued to be a central part of Judaism. Material sacrifices on the altar were replaced with spiritual sacrifices of praise to Yahweh. The study of the Torah was one such example of spiritual sacrifice, just as the study of the Vedas eventually came to be thought of as the true sacrifice in India during the period of the Upanishads.

[213] Philo Judeus explained their name as a variation of Hosiotês (holiness). Most scholars today view Qumran as a sect of the Essenes, see O. Betz, "Essenes," *The Interpreter's Bible of the Bible, Supplementary Vol.*, pp. 277 ff.; and especially Y. Yadin, *The Temple Scroll*, who makes a positive identification.

[214] Baumgarten op. cit., p. 155.

[215] Ibid., p. 157.

[216] Ibid., p. 157.

[217] The Zealots represent yet another group within first century Judaism concerned with foreign interference and Temple corruption. Their response to the situation centered on the sword as a means to oust the Romans. The Zealots also had strict purity requirements involving a

ritual bath and rigid observances of the Sabbath. They demanded circumcision even of the heathen. But now R. Horsley who shows that the "Zealots" as such did not exist until 67 C.E. See *Bandits, Prophets, and Messiahs*, Berkley: Harvest Press, 1988.

[218] See Joachim Becker, *Messianic Expectation in the Old Testament*, translated by David E. Green. Philadelphia: Fortress Press, 1980, pp. 83-94.

[219] See Baumgarten, op. cit., p. 157.

[220] See Terrien, op. cit., p. 398.

[221] In this episode Jesus drove those who were selling sacrificial animals, money-changers, and the animals themselves out of the Temple, cf. John 2:13-22; Matthew 21:12ff; Luke 19:45ff; Mark 11:15ff. The synoptics have Jesus saying after his attack, "It is written, 'My house shall be called a house of prayer; but you make it a den of robbers." John has, "Take these things away; you shall not make my Father's house a house of trade," with the addition of "Destroy this temple, and in three days I will raise it up," 2:16,19. See R. Horsley, *Jesus and the Spiral of Violence*, New York: Harper & Row, 1987. See Also Bruce Chilton, *The Temple of Jesus*, University Park: Penn State Press, 1992, chapter 6.

[222] Riches, op. cit., p. 142. Sanders proposed that the Temple episode was a symbolic action that Jesus used to threaten (or predict) the destruction of the Temple and "he acted to demonstrate it." He further suggested that Jesus did not think that the Temple was impure and in need of cleansing because the early apostles continued to gather at the Temple (Acts 2:46; 3:1,21, 26), op. cit., p. 76.

[223] Ibid., p. 142.

[224] Ibid., pp. 142, 168, 169.

[225] Riches based much of his thesis that Jesus rejected cultic purity as a means for human relationships on Mark 7:15 ff.: "there is nothing outside of a man that by having come into him is able to defile (Koinosai) him; but the things that come out of a man are the things that defile a man... do you not understand that all that comes into a man from the outside can not defile him, because it does not enter his heart but his stomach, and so passes on?" Part of Riches' interpretation of this "authentic saying" of Jesus went as follows (p. 138): "Jesus in accepting the sentence 'Nothing which enters a man from the outside can pollute a man' is also by implication rejecting a whole range of other sentences. He is, first, rejecting Levitical and Pharisaical purity regulations which regulate the Jews' conduct to one another and to those outside by means of ritually reinforced barriers."

[226] See both Bartchy's articles, "Table Fellowship With Jesus and the "Lord's Meal" at Corinth" in, *Increase in Learning: Essays in Honor of James G. Van Buren*, Owens and Hamm, editors, Manhattan, Kansas: Manhattan Christian College, 1979, pp. 54-61; and "Table Fellowship," in *Dictionary of Jesus and the Gospels*, edited by Joel B. Green et. al., Downers Grove: InterVarsity Press, 1992, pp. 796 ff.

[227] See Norman Perrin, *Jesus and the Language of the Kingdom*. Philadelphia: Fortress Press, 1976, pp. 38-55. On page 38 Perrin said: "kingdom of God is a symbol with deep roots in the Jew's consciousness of themselves as the people of God. It functions within the context of the myth of God active in history on behalf of his people; indeed by the time of Jesus it had come to represent particularly the expectation of a final eschatological act of God on behalf of his people."

[228] Crossan, *The Historical Jesus*, San Francisco, Haper San Francisco, 1991, p. 345.

[229] Ibid., p. 360.

[230] Perrin, *Rediscovering the Teaching of Jesus*, pp. 104-105.

[231] See Perrin, pp. 106-107.

[232] Cf. I Corinthians 11:17-22. Cf. Theissen, "The Social Setting of Pauline Christianity," originally in *Novum Testamentum*, translated by J. H. Schütz. Philadelphia: Fortress Press, 1982, pp. 145-172.

[233] See S. Scott Bartchy's article, op. cit., pp. 45-61.

[234] Ibid., p. 50.

[235] Ibid., p. 56.

[236] See Bartchy, op. cit., pp. 54-58.

[237] M. J. Cook, "Hellenistic Judaism," in IDB, Supplementary Volume, p. 506. Cook also pointed out that the Hellenistic Jews represented Judaism as if it were "in essence and as a totality law and nothing but law," p. 506.

[238] Ibid. p. 507.

[239] See Hosea 14:3; and Young op. cit., pp. 102-106.

[240] Cf. Karl Suso Frank, *Das Opfer Jesu Christi und seine Gegenwart in der Kirche*, ed. by K. Lehmann and E. Schlink. Göttingen, Herder Freiburg im Breisgau, 1983, p. 45.

[241] Behm, "Thusia," TDNT, vol. III, p. 189.

[242] See Eliade, *A History of Religious Ideas*, vol. 2, p. 187. The most profound lesson of the Greeks' primordial sacrifice (Thusia) comes from the distance that must be maintained between man and the gods, especially Zeus. See also Eliade, op. cit., vol. 1, pp. 256-259.

[243] Young (op. cit., pp. 11 ff.) lists the following
types of sacrifices: "Votive offerings," in which the sacrificer made promises to sacrifice to the gods if they in turn meet certain requests: "do ut des." This "business transaction" with the gods was popular in Homeric literature as, for example, Chryses' prayer reminded Apollo,

"Hear me, Lord of the silver bow,...if ever I have roofed over a temple pleasing to thee, or if ever I have burnt in thy honor fat thighs of bulls or of goats, then accomplish this my prayer." Iliad I:37-41, Clifford H. Moore, *The Religious Thought of the Greeks*. Cambridge: Harvard University Press, 1916, p. 22. "The Great Festival" sacrifices (Thusiai) offered thanksgiving for the gods' protection over the city. The city ate with the gods who were thought to be present on the altar during these great sacrificial events. The gods were thought to be present to feed on the sacrifices (Iliad I:423-24; 548-552). "Holocaust" sacrifices brought together two essential yet opposite aspects of Greek religion and sacrifice symbolized by the Olympian (Ouranian) and chthonian deities. In this case "service" rites (Therapeia) and "aversion" rites (Apotropâ) were performed for the Olympians and chthonians respectively. Each part of the sacrificial symbolism for the Olympians and chthonians conflicted. The method for killing the animals differed for each with the Olympian execution placing the victim's throat upwards while the chthonian positioned the throat downward. The Olympian rite required a high altar for sacrifice whereas the chthonian altar was either low to the ground or in a trench. The selection of victims also differed from one another, e.g. white for Olympians and black for chthonians. The temple for the Olympians was the classical type while the chthonian shrine consisted in a cave. Olympian sacrifice occurred during the morning and chthonian sacrifice was performed in the dark of night. (See W. K. C. Guthrie, *The Greeks and Their Gods*. Boston, Beacon Press, 1955, pp. 221 ff.) Most associate the chthonian "aversion" rites with the ancient scapegoat rituals for the removal of sins and impurities. As in the case of Greek religion and sacrifices in general, the Greek Holocaust sacrifices required many purification rites and the contrasting aspects of Olympian and chthonian symbolism. "Placatory" sacrifices simply averted the anger of the gods through a sacrificial payment. In "communion" sacrifices the sacrificer partook in the nature of the deity itself, as in the Dionysus cult.

[244] Republic, II: 364, quoted from Francis MacDonald Cornford's translation of, *The Republic of Plato*. New York, Oxford University Press, 1945, pp. 49-50.

[245] The taurobolium sacrifice was "so costly that sometimes the expense was borne by the whole brotherhood." Angus, p. 94.

[246] See Young, op. cit., p. 18. Young said this argument continued into the fourth century A.D., see also his fn. #18 on p. 18.

[247] This brought the charge of atheism against the Epicureans, see ibid., p. 20, fn. 21.

[248] See S. Angus, *The Mystery-Religions and Christianity*. New York: Charles Scribner's Sons, 1925, pp. 47 ff.

[249] Young mentions Marcus Aurelius, see op. cit., pp. 19-20, fn. 20.

[250] Ibid., p. 21.

[251] Ibid., p. 22.

[252] Ibid., pp. 22-23.

[253] De Abstinentia II 34 ff. See Karl Suso Frank, op. cit., p. 45.

[254] Ibid., p. 41.

[255] Young, op. cit., pp. 24-34.

[256] Ibid., p. 29. Porphyry and Iamblicus disagreed with regard to the purpose of sacrifice. Porphyry thought that sacrifice could only be gratitude to the gods.

[257] I accept Richard Reitzenstein's characterization of the Hellenistic religions. He said, "Ich bezeichne dabei mit dem Worte `hellenistisch' Religionsformen, in denen orientalische und griechische Elemente sich mischen, mag das Griechentum auch nur darin bestehen, daß ihm die Sprache und Begriffe oder die philosophische Deutung und Rechtfertigung entnommen sind, und mögen andrerseits auch Vorstellungen und Stimmungen, die jetzt aus dem Orient

herüberdringen, sich in einer weit zurückliegenden Epoche des Griechentums schon nachweisen lassen, ja mag in manchen Fällen der Orient nur den Anstoß zu einer Wiederbelebung dessen gegeben haben, was in der Frühzeit aus ihm hierher gedrungen war." *Die Hellenistischen Mysterienreligionen.* Stuttgart: B. G. Teubner Verlagsgesellschaft, 1956, pp. 2-3. Reitzenstein must be read today with caution.

[258] Reflecting on P.-L. Couchoud's thesis that Jesus was an invention of history A. Benoit said, "Il faut faire ici une remarque: la thèse radicale qui considère le christianisme comme un mystère analogue aux autres est liée indissolublement à l'idée que Jésus n'a pas existé et qu'il n'est pas un personnage de l'historie. Cette conception qui nie l'historicité de Jésus relève d'une lecture et d'une interprétation particulière du Nouveau Testament." In *Mystères et Syncrétismes.* Paris: Librairie Orientaliste Paul Geuthner, 1975, p. 82. It is not the purpose or intention of the present study to attribute a totally unique status to the figure of Jesus Christ. However, the striking similarities between Jesus Christ and the cultic deities of the mystery religions should not be used to discount the historical differences between each. Syncretism does not necessarily preclude original or distinctive elements that survive their assimilation into the new syncretistic form through the language and symbols of another tradition. Part of this confusion arises from the difficult hermeneutical problems that surround religious symbolism. Too often scholars attempt to reduce religious phenomena to scientific categories that enable them to explain the mysterious elements away. The problem goes beyond whether Jesus Christ was the invention of history as the mere product of cultural and historical forces expressed in concert with the collective unconscious in response to particular circumstances. Part of the task requires the patience (Epoché) to collect scientifically and examine the historical documents, knowing that the mysterious elements are not the result of a lack of data or refined scientific method but rather simply beyond the scope of this type of empirical investigations.

[259] See ibid., p. 76.

[260] For example G. Bornkamm (*Jesus of Nazareth*, p. 29) said of Judaism around the time of Jesus:

> In this history, full of changes, small Israel was, however, in no way a mere plaything without a will of its own. It still possessed something which was completely its own among the oriental nations. Its God was different from gods of the world around it, and the faith in this God was the vital nerve centre and the sustaining power of this nation. Through the power of this faith, not only ancient Israel but no less post-exilic Judaism did its best to hold aloof from the changing foreign powers, although the land lay in the magnetic field of their aspirations.

[261] Hans Conzelmann (p. 71) said concerning the double influence of the "new Greek-oriental" religions and Judaism on Christianity:

> Christianity is not exclusive by virtue of its introducing religious ideas which had not existed earlier. Indeed, according to primitive Christian interpretation, historically new is precisely what the basic Christian ideas are not. The church knows itself to be the true Israel; its book of religion is the Jewish Holy Scripture. There the outline of the idea of redemption is prefigured, the idea of the covenant and its renewal, of atoning and vicarious sacrifice, and so on. What is new is God's saving act itself. The message of this saving act applies to the Jew as Jew, and to the Gentile as Gentile. Here and there existing ideas are appropriated in order to expound this saving act:

See *History of Primitive Christianity*, translated by John E. Steely. Nashville: Abingdon, 1973, p. 71. Geoffrey Wainwright (*The Study of the Liturgy*, op. cit. p. 35) wrote:

> Jungmann has shown how the early Church took into its worship many features of pagan religion and filled them with Christian significance: the language and style of prayers; the symbols used in catacomb painting and sculpture; the kissing of holy objects; the bridal crown; the funeral meal and the refrigerium; the dates of processions and festivals....It was in this way that the liturgy, with increasing effect from the fourth century, played its part in the "transformation of pagan society."

[262] Ibid., pp. 84-92. According to Benoit, Christians avoided "le risque de confusion et d'assimilation abusive" by not using the language of the mysteries up until the latter's extinction, p. 92.

[263] See Angus, op. cit., pp. 271 ff. Most historians mark the destruction of the Alexandrian Serapis temples in 389 as the final victory of Christianity over the Mystery cults.

[264] Benoit (p. 78) wrote the following:
En ce qui concerne son origine et son expansion, le christianisme participe à la dynamique généale des religions à mystères. Comme les cultes à mystères il a son origine en Palestine, c'est à dire en Orient, et il naît à peu près à la même époque. Sa diffusion extrêmement rapide va de l'Orient vers l'Occident, comme celle des religions similaries. Et tout comme certains empereurs sont fait initier aux mystères, l'empereur finira au quartrième siécle par devenir chrétien et recevoir l'initiation chrétienne.

[265] "With the exception of Dionysianism, all of the Mysteries are of Oriental origin: Phrygian (Cybele and Attis), Egyptian (Isis and Osiris), Phoenician (Adonis), Iranian (Mithra)." M. Eliade, *A History of Religious Ideas*, vol. 2, p. 279.

[266] According to Apuleius, Tyché no longer had any power over those who gave honor to the goddess Isis (Metamorphoses 11:15). The Gnostics escaped Fatum through the special saving knowledge (Gnosis) that enabled their spirit (Nous) to master Destiny, (Lactantius, *Institutions* 2: 16, from ibid., p. 279, fn. 5). Salvation was regarded as a spiritual re-birth in the mysteries. The neophyte was regarded as experiencing a new birth after undergoing a mystical death in the Mysteries of Isis, Cybele, Phryga and Mithra, and the initiant's symbolic descent to the underworld and ascent to "divinization," as in the Isis Mysteries, illustrates victory over the decaying world of man, see ibid., p. 280.

[267] "A Mystery-Religion was a religion of Redemption which professed to remove estrangement between man and God, to procure forgiveness

of sins, to furnish mediation. Means of purification and formulae of access to God, and acclamations of confidence and victory were part of the apparatus of every Mystery." Angus, p. 50. Angus named three stages of initiation into a Mystery Religion, " (1) Preparation and Probation, Katharsis; (2) Initiation and Communion, Muesis; (3) Blessedness and Salvation, Epopteia," p. 72. Also see Geuthner, op. cit., p. 78.

[268] Angus, op. cit., p. 78. The notion of pure and impure also played an important role in the mysteries. The notion and practice of secrecy itself figured as a means of protecting the holy, transcendent mysteries.

[269] Eliade, op. cit., p. 283, referring specifically to the Dionysus rite.

[270] "The Mysteries" in, *The Study of the Liturgy*, ed. by Cheslyn Jones et al. London, SPCK, 1978, p. 54. "By taking part in prescribed rites the worshipper became united with God, was enabled in this life to enjoy mystical communion with him, and further was assured of immortality beyond death," C. K. Barrett, *The New Testament Background: Selected Documents*. New York: Harper & Row, Publishers, 1961, p. 91. See also Reitzenstein, op. cit., pp. 245 ff. Other related notions and themes derived from this central cultic structure, i. e. cleansing, redemption, rebirth, immortality, etc.

[271] Cf. supra, fn. 278. According to Eliade, "if we consider the fact that, before the invasion by the Mycenaeans influences from Egypt and Asia Minor had resulted in an Asianic-Mediterranean synthesis, we can gauge the antiquity and complexity of the Greek cultural phenomenon. Hellenism sends its roots into Egypt and Asia; but it is the contribution of the Mycenaean conquerors that will produce the `Greek miracle'" . He went on to say that "despite symbiosis with the countless pre-Hellenic traditions, the Aryan-speaking conquerors succeeded in imposing their pantheon and in maintaining their specific religious style." *A History of Religious Ideas*, vol. 1, pp. 136 and 138 respectively.

[272] Ibid., pp. 133-134.

[273] Ibid., p. 135.

[274] Some refer to this as the Dorian invasions.

[275] See R. Pettazonni, supra chapter one fn. 2.

[276] See Angus, op. cit., pp. 83-84.

[277] Bultmann, *Theology of the New Testament*, p. 149.

[278] Cf. Romans 7:4, 10:4; Acts 1:16, 3:18; Luke 22:37.

[279] Romans 10:4.

[280] I Corinthians 5:7b.

[281] Hebrews 9:23-26, RSV. The writer of Hebrews was much more interested in philosophical categories than Paul.

[282] Both Soter and son of God are familiar terms in the Hellenistic period, taken over from old eastern mythologies, according to Bultmann, cf. op. cit., p. 130.

# CHAPTER FIVE

# TRANSCENDENCE AND THE IMMANENCE IN THE EUCHARIST

## 5:1 Sacrificial Developments in the First Four Centuries

This chapter continues to examine the problem of transcendence and immanence in the context of ritual. However, the investigation now centers on the Eucharist[1] as it took the form of a ritual that temporarily linked the sacred and the profane while maintaining the distinctive character of each.[2] As a religious ritual, the Eucharist used a variety of symbols to communicate transcendent realities to the profane world. The Eucharist's sacred materials, acts, and words symbolized, first and foremost, the mysterious union attained between the participants and Jesus Christ. The provisions and consequences of this fundamental encounter created a discernible pattern or structure in the Eucharist that has weathered many centuries of changing liturgies and doctrines.[3] This chapter also pays particular attention to the task of recognizing and evaluating the Eucharist's symbolic structure from its historical background and development.

Many ancient religious themes continued to flourish in the cultic union experienced by human beings and God in the Eucharist through the mediation of Jesus Christ. Yet none was more prominent than the sacrificial theme. The Eucharist, although certainly not always understood as an actual sacrifice in the first few centuries, received its basic symbolism from the mythology[4] of Jesus Christ as the perfect sacrifice for sin.[5]

Early Christian writers clearly believed that the blood of Christ brought about purification from sin.[6] The New Testament documents also interpreted the sacrifice of Christ as an expiation for sins in much the same way that the Hebrew Bible characterized its expiation sacrifices.[7] However, the New Testament does not seem to know of a sacrificial ritual for Christians.[8] As Frances Young said, "The Christian spiritualization of sacrifice was radical. In general it meant that only prayer, charity, a life of Christian virtue, and self-offering in martyrdom were reckoned to be suitable sacrifices for the one true God who was in need of nothing but loyalty and devotion of his creatures."[9]

On the other hand, as we observed in the previous chapter, literary criticism has established that the New Testament eucharistic texts display a liturgical (oral) form behind these very texts to which the gospels added sacrificial language. We found sacrificial ideas connected to the death of Jesus Christ developing in the Eucharist even in the New Testament. The Last Supper associated with the Jewish Passover, the death of Jesus Christ aligned symbolically with the eucharistic elements, the combined use of the bread and cup words together, and the apostle Paul's comparison with pagan rites (I Cor. 10:4 ff) all give evidence of the Eucharist's growing sacrificial symbolism in the first century.

New Testament scholars continue to steer clear from labeling the Eucharist as a sacrifice as it appears in the gospels, and rightly so. For example, Ferdinand Hahn said that "das ursprüngliche Herrenmahl war alles andere als ein Opfermahl, vielmehr eine Form gottesdienstlicher Gemeinschaft, die sehr bewußt abseits des offiziellen Kultes im Tempel wie in der Synagoge stattfand."[10] Hahn went on to recognize that the Herrenmahl developed a certain sacrificial conception in the New Testament, having cited the bread and cup words as well as its passover identification. Hahn claimed that these sacrificial concepts resulted only under specific theological conditions. He maintained that the New Testament did not employ the use of sacrificial terminology concerning the Lord's Supper and avoided cultic-ritual sacrifices because of a dominant christology that corresponded to the "independent proclamation of the early Christians." In other words, the early Christians' message about Jesus precluded a simple identity to the popular sacrificial cults of the first century. According to Hahn, this cautious Christological use of sacrificial concepts in the New Testament faltered in later times and "unspecified sacrificial concepts" were accepted under premises other than those that operated in the New Testament.[11]

Although Hahn's general observations concerning the New Testament Eucharist and the ensuing liturgies remain true, he never bothered to explain why this deviation might have occurred, especially given his characterization of the New Testament's aversion to sacrifice. What so quickly induced the sacrificial nature of the early liturgies if their predecessors used such care to practically avoid any sacrificial associations in the earliest traditions? How did the eucharistic elements themselves become so important that the Apostle Paul reprimanded the Corinthian Church for placing too much spiritual value in the liturgical act of partaking of the "bread" and "cup" at the expense of neglecting the poorer members in the Agape meal that preceded?[12] What caused the shift from Paul's notion of Christ's presence in the body of belivers gathered together to worship (I Cor. 11-12) to the practice of Christ's presence in the consecrated elements? Were all these changes due to a christological development or liturgical change, both or neither? And what motivated these developments? Were the changes meant to combat heresies, or heresies themselves? Could all of this simply have been a part of the normal evolution of religious ideas? Hahn, like so many others, set out to persuade his readers that the New Testament Eucharist was not a sacrifice and lacked any real sacrificial qualities. But this attempt to minimize or remove altogether the Eucharist's dependence on sacrifice and its resemblance to cultic ritual has virtually relinquished the sacrificial symbolism[13] that so quickly developed in the New Testament eucharistic texts themselves.[14]

The Eucharist took on an increasing resemblance to sacrificial rites in the writings of the early church fathers as the initial covenant fellowship meals of the first century began to change. As R. D. Richardson stated, "The typical sacrifice of Christians had at first been considered to be a prayer, or the spirit of prayer; but with the destruction of the Jewish Temple, and the infiltration of ideas from contemporary pagan mysteries, the Christian Supper rite began to be interpreted as the pure sacrifice."[15] The ancient liturgical texts from the third and fourth centuries onwards leave no doubt as to the importance of the concept of sacrifice in the Eucharist.

These later eucharistic liturgies and prayers reveal concerns for preparatory consecration and the removal of sin, the notion of the transformation of reality during the ritual, and theological as well as liturgical efforts to reaffirm the distinctiveness between humans and God. Consequently Hubert and Mauss' threefold scheme can also be applied to the Eucharist in much the same way as we did for Vedic fire sacrifice when contemplating its sacrificial structure. Yet even in view of the glaring historical differences between the Eucharist and Vedic sacrifice the problem of bringing sinful humans and a holy God together in the ritual act remained. I hope to show that the notion of transcendence and immanence in ritual context has played a determining role in both the liturgical and theological structure of the Eucharist, a structure that also appeared in sacrificial rituals of Vedic religion.

The second century disclosed an expanded emphasis on the sacramental elements and their consecration along with the necessity of having qualified persons to administer them.[16] Now during those decades the Eucharist began to look more like a re-presentation of Christ's sacrifice rather than the initial covenant fellowship meals enjoyed by the first century communities. By the middle of the second century the metaphorical sense of sacrifice in the Eucharist had, in some cases, already changed into a specific sacrificial act. John Reumann said, "To "give thanks" (Eucharistein) was more and more coming to mean "consecrate" and was eventually to mean "offer sacrifice".[17]

*Didache* chapter 14 (early second century) used the term "sacrifice" more than once when referring to the Eucharist. For example, the Didache used the following quote from Malachi as Jesus' own reference to the Eucharist, "Always and everywhere offer me a pure sacrifice, for I am a great King, says the Lord, and my name is marveled at by the nations."[18] No doubt such references to sacrifice here belonged to the eucharistic prayers said before the actual Eucharist as a type of sacrifice of thanksgiving contrasted to the Jewish or pagan bloody rites. But the offering of the special eucharistic prayer contained the idea of sacrifice in conjunction with the bread and wine, which were believed to be the body and blood of Christ, and this combination functioned together with the same results as a literal sacrifice in the Eucharist.[19] In fact the Eucharist was thought to have replaced Jewish sacrifices.[20] The Didache insisted on a preliminary confession of sins "so that your sacrifice may be pure", and also demanded the avoidance of a defiled sacrifice through reconciliation with ones neighbor.[21]

At the end of the second century the term "priest" (Greek Hierus, Latin Sacerdos) could be used for the bishop who offered the sacrifice known as the Eucharist.[22] Dix informs us that:

> The Israelite might not offer prayer without ablution, as the priest in the Temple might not approach the altar to 'liturgise' without it (Ex. 30:20). The Berakah in a sense offered the preceding meal to God, and so might not be offered by one who was uncleansed. All these customary ablutions reappeared in the early christian practice,

> cannot say. Thus the bishop approached his own 'liturgy' at the altar with the same symbolism as the jewish priest, and the christian layman washed his hands before even private prayers.[23]

In the first part of the second century Ignatius, the earliest christian Syrian author, referred to the eucharistic assembly as Thusiasterian, "the place of sacrifice."[24] Little doubt remains why Ignatius labeled the eucharistic assembly as a Thusiasterian once we realize his understanding of the nature of the sacraments. In Ignatius' attack on the Docetists we find the following sacrificial identity of the eucharistic elements and the flesh of Jesus Christ:

> They abstain from the eucharist and from prayer, because they confess not the Eucharist to be the flesh of our Saviour Jesus Christ, which suffered for our sins, and which the Father, of His goodness, raised up again. Those, therefore, who speak against this gift of God, incur death...[25]

Around the year 177 C.E. Irenaeus also identified the eucharistic elements with the physical body and blood of Jesus Christ. Irenaeus' purpose for this identification appears quite obvious in light of his dispute with the "heretics" (Gnostics) who rejected the Incarnation with along with the notion that God would have saved the world with the material sacrifice of Christ, and hence placed no significance on the sacraments. Irenaeus responded in part by saying of the Eucharist that:

> ...when the mixed cup and the bread that has been prepared receive the Word of God, and become the Eucharist, the body and blood of Christ, and by these our flesh grows and is confirmed, how can they say that flesh cannot receive the free gift of God, which is eternal life, since it is nourished by the body and blood of the Lord, and made a member of him?[26]

This mysterious link between Christ and the sacraments attached new meaning to the presence of Christ at the eucharistic celebrations.[27] The understanding of Christ's presence at the Eucharist resulted in demonstrable attempts to insure a pure ritual environment with special emphasis on purity and the removal of sin. The worthiness of those who participated was now stressed to the point that only those who had been "baptized into Christ" for the "remission of sins" were permitted to celebrate the Eucharist. Writing around the year 150 C.E. Justin said,

"This food we call Eucharist, of which no one is allowed to partake except one who believes that the things we teach are true, and has received the washing for forgiveness of sins and for rebirth, and who lives as Christ handed down to us."[28] The *Didache* also warned, "But let none eat or drink of your Eucharist except those who have been baptized in the Lord's name. For concerning this also did the Lord say, "Give not that which is holy to the dogs".'[29] We see comprehensive restrictions on eucharistic participation began to appear at the end of the apostolic era.[30] According to Origen (185-254 C.E.), Christians scrutinized everyone before allowing entrance to their assemblies as a "hearer."[31] If the one desiring entrance proved to be of sincere intentions, then access was granted to hear the "Service of the Word." But after attending the hymns, lections, sermon, and prayers of this assembly, the authorized visitors along with the catechumens had to leave. The reason for their dismissal was the belief that during the celebration of the Eucharist the elements "become a certain holy body which sanctifies those who partake of it with a pure intention", to use Origen's words.[32] This type of ritual protection went back to at least the middle of the second century. The liturgical books VII and VIII of the *Apostolic Constitutions* (first half of the third century) describe the dismissal from the Eucharist and tell how the deacons and subdeacons guarded the doors during the liturgy of the sacrifice.[33] Werner Elert correctly summed up the purpose for this exclusion by saying, "The formative influence was not the keeping of secrecy but the keeping of unholy people from what is holy in accordance with the Old Testament understanding of holiness."[34]

It is not surprising then to come upon Cyprian's words from the third century that identified Christ's sacrifice on Calvary with his sacrifice in the Eucharist. His famous line reads, "The Lord's passion is the sacrifice we offer."[35] Lietzmann said:

> Within the first three centuries the eucharist was conceived as a sacrifice in a threefold sense: first the prayers, secondly the bread and wine laid on the altar by the congregation or by individual members of it, and thirdly the sacred action at the altar itself as an analogue of the sacrificial death of Christ.[36]

The early church fathers never understood the Eucharist as an expiatory sacrifice apart from Jesus' death on the cross. The atoning sacrifice of Jesus Christ figured heavily in the writing of the early church fathers and their understanding of the Eucharist. Origen, inspired by Levitical depiction of the priests who ate the sin-offering, commented that "Christ, who is priest as well as victim, eats the sins of the people. God is a consuming fire. The God of fire consumes human sins; he assumes them, devours them and purges them. Christ thus took upon himself our sins, and like a fire, he ate and assumed them himself."[37] Origen taught that because Christ was a pure and unblemished sacrifice anyone who "touches the flesh of this sacrifice is sanctified."[38] Origen's understanding of the eucharistic bread and wine as the body and blood of Christ easily made the application of the sacrificial death of Christ to the Eucharist.

This application resulted in the combination of both realism and spiritualism in regard to the eucharistic elements. For example, Origen warned that nothing must fall to the ground when receiving the "body of the Lord."[39] Yet on the other hand, Origen offset this type of crass realism by saying that the true food was the Word of God and the elements were only symbols of this food.[40]

By the fourth century a clear notion of expiatory sacrifice for sins had emerged in the Eucharist.[41] The fourth century's growing tendency to speak of the consecration of the eucharistic elements in conversionist language stopped short of an actual reproduction of the sacrifice on Calvary. G. W. H. Lampe shows how far sacrificial language had gone during this period when he said:

> With the clearer assertion of the fourth century writers that the eucharistic body is actually identical with the body born of Mary and crucified, belief in the incorporation of the faithful into Christ's body through the Eucharist, and their divinization through participation in the flesh of the Logos, made eucharistic belief a central underlying factor in the Christological controversies.[42]

Cyril of Jerusalem (348 C.E.) was the first to call the Eucharist an "unbloody sacrifice."[43] But this did not prevent him from describing the Eucharist in poignant sacrificial language. He wrote: "when the holy and most awful sacrifice is set forth."[44] A few years later Chrysostom (387 C.E.), who understood the Eucharist as a commemoration, still resorted to sacrificial realism when referring to the Eucharist: "You are approaching an awful and holy sacrifice; Christ is set before you slain."[45] According to K. Gamber, it was during the fourth and into the fifth centuries that the prayers of thanksgiving at the Eucharist were becoming sacrificial prayers.[46] Lietzmann also found evidence from the fourth century that incense had been incorporated into eucharistic liturgies as a symbolic gesture that the sacrifice had ascended to the heavenly altar by an angel's hands.[47] The eucharistic sacrifice became more realistically described as time passed, and with these developments came a heightened sense of danger for the unworthy to participate in the Eucharist.

This sacrificial intensity of the early eucharist continued without resistance. However, some of the church fathers from the middle of the second century to around the first quarter of the third did speak of the Christian's spiritual worship as opposed to offering a victim or any visible thing. For example, about the year 200 C.E. Clement of Alexandria wrote that ,"The offering of the Church consists in a prayer in which all our thoughts, given over to God, are wrapped up along with the offering."[48] Justin instructed Christians that by helping the poor and singing songs of praise the church honored God.[49]

But such statements from this period should not be taken out of context and interpreted as the ante-nicene fathers' rejection of an eucharistic sacrifice.[50] The occasions for these statements accented the differences between paganism and Christianity. For example, in another place Justin explained that the pagan Mithra initiation rite was similar to the Eucharist only because the "wicked demons" had imitated it.[51] Justin was certainly not trying to repudiate the idea of sacrifice in the Eucharist. On the contrary, he taught that the bread and cup of the Eucharist were the incarnate flesh and blood of Jesus Christ offered to worthy believers[52], and identifief this bread and cup as their sacrificial gift.[53]

Similarly, the name of Tertullian (150-220 C.E.) has also appeared as evidence for an offering of thanksgiving rather than a sacrificial offering. Tertullian did say that, "Christians have no altars."[54] But the purpose of this statement was clearly to contrast the way that the pagans sacrificed and not to spurn sacrifice for Christians. In this particular case the Christian apologist Tertullian saw his sacrifice, the Eucharist, as the true form of worship and hence opposed to the pagan rites. Victor Saxter said concerning Tertullian's sacrificial concept of the Eucharist:

> To begin with, the eucharist is a genuine sacrifice that fits into the general framework of the sacrifices of old: it is a "prayer of sacrifice," it is celebrated at an altar, it binds (obligat) man to God, and communion is a "participation in the sacrifice." Above all, however, it is the true sacrifice, "the new sacrifice" which was prefigured by the Old Testament sacrifices, and the priest of which is Christ.[55]

So even in the ante-nicene fathers the Eucharist had developed an unmistakable sacrificial character that continued to influence the shape of eucharistic liturgies and doctrines for centuries to come.[56]

The early Christian writers had been influenced by spiritualizing trends in both Judaism and Greek philosophy concerning sacrifice, but they still allowed the Eucharist to approach such graphic sacrificial descriptions. Young interpreted Clement of Alexandria as having turned the Greek ascetic ideal of Apatheia into the Christian's "offering of oneself purified from sin, honoring God by prayer" as "the only sacrifices worthy of God who needs nothing."[57] Martyrdom likewise came to be regarded as an acceptable sacrifice for the Christians who were accused of being atheists because they seemed to lack any cult.

Platonism, advocating that only "pure thoughts" could ascend to God, had inadvertently reinforced the Jewish-Christian concept of transcendence and cultic purity. Thus Athanasius felt that humanity ascended to heaven in Christ who served as the perfect platonic form (idea) of mankind. Athanasius believed that mankind could be transformed by Christ into a perfect human (Andra Teleion). Accordingly, God could accept such a person as a purified and perfect creation.[58] Origin thought that it was through Christ that "spiritual sacrifices could reach the throne of God who transcends all that man could offer."[59] But all these philosophical views of transcendence took on a much more concrete nature in the ritual performance of the Eucharist. Jungmann said, "We are therefore certain from the very start that in the Eucharist not only do prayers of thanksgiving rise from the congregation to god, but that at the same time a gift is offered up to God."[60]

All in all, the Eucharist appears to have been quite flexible and yet remarkably similar in all important aspects of its liturgy "between the last quarter of the first century and the first quarter of the third."[61] In the fourth century, when Christianity became the official religion of the empire, the church began efforts to protect the Eucharist from a new threat of defilement.[62] Those who were baptized in the fourth century constituted a different kind of church member than those in previous times that had gained access to the Eucharist. The fundamental response of the church to this situation involved placing even more control of the Eucharist into the hands of the clergy. The end result meant that a much more rigid eucharistic form developed as the liturgical texts began to take on a fixed shape.

For the most part, the Eucharist had already acquired its basic structure as a result of sacrificial concepts that the early Christians associated with Jesus Christ's death as an expiation for sin. The rapid conversion of the initial fellowship meals into separate Agape fellowships and liturgical Lord's Suppers hinged on the latter's development of the mystical presence of Christ in the eucharistic elements as a representation of Christ's sacrifice on the cross. Early eucharistic prayers, such as the one from Hippolytus (215 C.E.), show the desire of the participants to be made worthy to partake of the holy supper that was considered a sacrifice. These early eucharistic prayers petitioned God to purify the partakers and remove their sins so that they could offer an acceptable sacrifice to God on the altar before taking communion. After this consecration the gifts went to heaven and the participants communed with God. Shortly after Hippolytus, Cyprian carried the Eucharist's transformation a step further by identifying the eucharistic sacrifice in terms of a propitiatory sacrifice.[63] Thus the Eucharists in the fourth century witnesses reveal stringent concerns for proper preparation for sinful human beings to participate with a holy God in the eucharistic sacrifice.

In this early period church leaders also made provisions that no part of the left-over eucharistic elements were subject to profane contact. Hippolytus wrote: But let everyone take heed that no unbeliever partake of the eucharist, nor any mouse or other animal, and that nothing of it fall, or be lost, for the body of Christ is to be eaten by the faithful and not despised. For blessing it indeed in the name of God thou hast taken the chalice as the antitype of the blood of Christ. Wherefore be careful not to spill it, lest a strange spirit lick it up, as though thou despises it: thou wilt be guilty of the blood as one who scorns the price by which he was redeemed.[64]

Cyril also insisted upon precaution with the leftover elements[65], as did Origen[66], Athanasius and others.[67] This concern for the eucharistic elements extended to include the eucharistic vessels. During the Middle Ages detailed procedures had been implemented to cleanse the eucharistic vessels. Priests used water, wine and the combination of both to purify vessels used in the Eucharist.[68] The development of the Ablutions had became so rigorous that even a wornout altar or any other item that had come into contact with the consecrated elements had to be burned, and then the ashes were thrown into the baptistery or a place where the holy ashes could not be defiled by anyone.[69]

The Eucharist extended its ritual control beyond the consecration and sacrifice to make sure that the profane did not come into contact with the sacred remains. This was no mere magic but rather the continued influence of the divine mystery that took place during the ritual act. The Eucharist had left its effects on the participants; but the divine was still not easily accessible to them, nor did the sacred and profane merge together so as to make the two indistinguishable. God remained in heaven with Christ at his right hand after the ceremony, and the need to commune with him again in the Eucharist for the forgiveness of sins and eternal life persisted.

## 5:2 The Eucharistic Link Between East and West

Scholars have identified two main types of eucharistic liturgies as found in eastern and western traditions. The eastern centers were located in Antioch and Alexandria, while the western types owed their form to the tradition found in Rome.[70] Dix and others have been able to trace verbal borrowings in the eucharistic prayers in which Egypt and Syria shared with each other. A strong possibility exists that Rome borrowed from both Antioch and Alexandria. However, evidence also reveals at least one case of the reverse.[71] The two major liturgical traditions in the East and West developed from these early centers. Dix stated that:

> The present main Eastern type has developed from the fourth century rite of the Eastern 'holy city.'Jerusalem, as remodelled and expanded in the Eastern political centre, Constantinople. The present main Western type has developed from the fourth century rite of the Western 'holy city," Rome, as remodelled and expanded in the

Western political centre, the nucleus of Charlemagne's empire in Gaul and the Rhineland.[72]

The fourth century exhibited no great differences between these two main types. However, the break up of political unity in the Roman empire fostered a tendency in the fifth century for eastern and western liturgies to lose their external uniformity, that is to say, their liturgical homogeneity. The West particularly demonstrated many new instances of local varieties up to the ninth century when the Carolingian empire provided less than a hundred years of political unity and consequentially the resurgence of liturgical uniformity. The East, on the other hand, continued to experience political unity in the Byzantine empire that understandably helped to promote liturgical consistency.[73]

But in spite of the many differences that developed after the fourth century the East and West continued to share a common underlying structure up to the present that surpassed their varying external forms. All eucharistic rites in the eastern and western traditions, then and now, contain four actions, the Offertory, the Consecration Prayer, the Fraction and the Communion. These four actions came from the ancient liturgies' four actions, (1) taking the bread and wine together; (2) blessing them; (3) breaking the bread; (4) the distribution of both. This format was in turn based on the seven fold action in the New Testament's Last Supper.[74] Beneath this pattern lies still a deeper, more basic structure determined by the notion of transcendence and immanence in the Eucharist. As a result we find the basic religious symbolism of sacrifice, consecration and presence.

Dix advocated that the close similarities between the eastern and western eucharistic prayers from the second and third centuries suggests that both went back to a general type in the first century.[75] In addition to this I would like to postulate that the perpetual notion of Christ's presence at the eucharistic sacrifice continued to give the East and West a basis for structural similarity between their respective Eucharists. For this reason we will consider those aspects in the development of the East's and West's Eucharists that maintained their similar structure while surviving the more apparent outward differences in the particular liturgies.

Customarily, the differences between the eastern and western eucharistic liturgies have been based on the rites themselves and not on particular doctrines. This resulted from the fact that the clearest distinction between the liturgies remained in the rites and not the eucharistic doctrines. The earliest eucharistic prayers in the second and third centuries show us that the East and West both continued to place the same emphases on sacrifice, consecration and presence. The external differences have come about by the manner in which the Eucharist portrayed these three constant aspects of the ritual act. For example, the West from the third century on considered the Eucharist as a sacrifice that had the power to remove the participant's sins during the Offertory.[76] The East also understood the Eucharist as a sacrifice offered for the remission of sins.[77] But the forgiveness of sins in the East came through the reception of the Communion after the Epiclesis (the calling down of the Holy Spirit from heaven).

Another example of the structural similarity between the West and East having been worked out differently in their rites has to do with consecration. Both deemed consecration as essential. Yet for the West consecration resulted from the recital of the institutional words concerning the bread. Wainwright observed that "the Latin church, beginning perhaps at the time of Ambrose, placed more and more stress on the recital of the institution narrative, and especially on the Lord's own words spoken by the priest in persona Christi..."[78] On the other hand, the East effected their consecration through the invocation of the Holy Spirit (Epiclesis). In the middle of the fourth century Cyril of Jerusalem said, "We beseech the merciful God to send forth (Eksaposteîlai) the Holy Spirit upon the elements, that he may make the bread the body of Christ and the wine the blood of Christ; for whatever the Holy Spirit has touched is sanctified and changed."[79] Clearly, the notion of Christ's presence made consecration a necessity in both East and West.

A subtle but important ritual distinction between the West and East pivoted on the treatment of the participant's offerings as they brought the eucharistic elements to be presented on the altar. Members of western congregations brought their own bread and wine before the altar where the deacons took charge of them for the actual Offertory.[80] Eastern church members delivered the elements to be used at the altar to the deacons before the liturgical worship began.[81] The development of this practice lead to an elaborate rite in the East by the fifth century called the "Great Entrance" (Prothesis). The symbolism behind the

Great Entrance amounted to a detailed preparation rite that dramatized the full scope of Christ's saving work through his incarnation, sacrifice and resurrection. The symbolic movement in the Great Entrance portrayed the downward act of God in the incarnation and the upward return to heaven in Jesus Christ's resurrection and ascension.[82] The East summoned the Holy Spirit in order to consecrate and make the presence of the Son of God real in the elements. This act gave significant force to the role of the Holy Spirit in the East and shrouded the entire eucharistic ritual with an aura of divine presence.[83] But here again, both East and West considered Christ to be mystically present in the consecrated elements.

The use of the Veil and Screen in the East marked yet another example of the different ritual actions between the East and West. This particular liturgical difference started when the East prohibited its people from seeing much of the eucharistic rite while the West did not conceal its liturgies from the faithful. This basic difference eventually led to the more profound liturgical differences experienced today between the East and West. Wainwright noted that:

> The Roman high mass, between the early middle ages and the modern liturgical movement, was a propitiatory sacrifice performed by a priest at a distant altar, the congregation's high-point being its glimpse of the consecrated wafer at the elevation. The Orthodox liturgy is still, particularly in the Russian tradition, a mysterious celebration mostly hidden away behind the icon-screen.[84]

Still the two traditions show similarities along with their differences. The liturgies gradually became the responsibility of the priesthood as the people watched passively from a safe distance.

The East's prohibition against seeing the actual eucharistic ritual reveals another development in the Eucharist. A veil was first used near the end of the fourth century in the eastern liturgies to hide the sanctuary from the people. In the sixth century a solid screen was employed at Constantinople for the same purposes. In general, the practice of separating the people from the consecrated elements accompanied the feeling of awe and fear in the East with regard to the sacraments.[85] Cyril used the word Phrikodestatos (most dread, literally, what makes one's hair stand on end) in reference to the consecrated elements.[86] As we have seen, the fear of the unworthy partaking of the eucharistic elements held a crucial place in several early church father's writings. But Cyril's use of fear and terrifying in reference to the consecrated elements signaled a new type of awareness experienced in the Syrian churches with regard to the eucharistic ritual.[87] Dix said "perhaps it found a specially congenial soil in Syria, where since time immemorial the holy had also meant in some way the dangerous.[88] In any event, the stage was now set for a host of similar expressions of fear and dread regarding the consecrated elements. Accordingly, Theodore of Mopsuestia did not hesitate to say that the "faithful should be afraid to draw nigh unto the sacrament without a mediator and this is the priest who with his hand gives you the sacrament."[89]

The problem of bringing the sacred and profane together in the East's Eucharists not only created the sensation of fear but also engendered more graphic ritual precautions. The presence of the consecrated elements had taken on a numinous aspect akin to the presence of Yahweh's holiness in ancient Israel's sacrifices. The problematic presence of the "unworthy" or "unbaptized" began to include the people (Laos) assembled to worship.[90]

Justin, among others, used the term Laos (the "people") to distinguish the assembled congregation from its leaders.[91] Here the word later translated layman still designated one of the people of God with full privileges and liturgical duties up to the fourth century in the East. But by the middle of the fifth century the term for laymen "had almost come to mean profane as opposed to sacred."[92] This new inimical connotation of Laos developed in direct relationship to the eucharistic liturgy.

The liturgy was rapidly becoming more and more the duty of the clergy alone as a safeguard, along with the veil and screen, to protect against illegitimate contact with the sacred in their presence. Now more than ever before the Eucharist established its boundaries between the sacred and profane. The ritual had begun to exclude any possibility of the blending together of the two realms. The use of veils, screens, priests, the elaborate liturgies, and the proper disposal of the ritual leftovers all helped to maintain the altogether profound difference between humans and the God in the ritual act.[93]

Chrysostom around the year 390 C.E. reminded the congregation at Antioch of the transcendent realities that confronted humans in the Eucharist. He said "When the sacrifice is borne forth (for the communion) and Christ the Victim and the Lord the Lamb, when thou hearest (the deacon proclaim) 'let us entreat together...', when you see the veil drawn aside-then bethink you that heaven is rent asunder from above and the angels are descending."[94]

Another development in the East that also led to the association of fear with the Eucharist comes to light from the church's struggle with Arianism. Arianism held that Jesus Christ, the Son of God, was a creature made by God and thus did not always exist. In other words, Arianism denied Christ's complete divinity.[95] We find in the writings of Basil the Great (d. 379 C.E.) the typical new wording in the eucharistic prayers. Instead of giving praise to the Father "through the Son in the Holy Ghost", Basil and others began to word their prayers of praise to the Father "with the Son, at one with the Holy Ghost."[96] The divinity and transcendence of Christ started to eclipse the expression of his humanity in the liturgy. This trend magnified the growing awareness of sin and unworthiness in the eastern liturgies where the sense of divine presence in the Eucharist had already established itself preeminently among liturgical concerns. The prospect of coming into the presence of the transcendent Christ who was one in nature with God aroused ambivalent feelings of praise and anxiety. Basil entitled a chapter in one of his works, "With what fear...we ought to receive the Body and Blood of Christ."[97] Chrysostom also used morose expressions for the Eucharist such as, "shuddering hour" and "the terrible and awful table."[98]

The West had likewise developed considerable precautions to respect the presence of Christ in the eucharistic elements.[99] The most visible sign of this evolution in the West came in the form of the declining role of the lay persons in the liturgies. Here again, both East and West experienced this common phenomenon. Before the fourth century the churches placed more emphasis on performing the Eucharist or "performing the mysteries", and "doing the oblation" , as the early fathers used to say.[100] With the intervention of the clergy in the Latin West the Eucharist had been transformed into something more said than done by the Middle Ages.[101] Besides this distinction, the West also conceived the Eucharist as a private and not corporate affair. An assembly of individuals heard the Eucharist in the Latin West churches from Middle Ages to the present.

The West did continue its special interest concerning sin and grace in connection with the Eucharist. This helped to perpetuate the

Eucharist as a repetition of the sacrifice on the cross offered for sinners.[102] In short, western eucharistic theology in the early Middle Ages reveals an increasing emphasis on the " `Ambrosian' or corporeal understanding of the Eucharist over against an `Augustinian' or more spiritual understanding."[103] Thus we find Paschasius Radbertus on the corporeal side of the controversy who made statements such as the following: "We continually reproduce the memory of his most holy death by daily offering the sacrifice of his most sacred body and blood on the altar."[104]

The mystical text of the Byzantine theologian Nicolas Cabasilas (d.1363 C.E.) shows that the East continued to stress the entire redemptive work of Christ in their eucharistic liturgies during the Middle Ages. Cabasilas likewise continued to emphasize the "Great Entry" and the "Epiclesis." Cabasilas' *Divinae Liturgiae Interpretatio* portrayed the redemptive work and revelation of Christ as gradually unveiled in the liturgy. The liturgy dramatized a paradoxical reality for Cabasilas. Heaven gradually descended to earth transforming its human participants and raising them up to heaven. The power of this symbolic union attained through the eucharistic sacrifice between earth and heaven evoked Cabasilas to speak of the priest's gradual return from his union with God through "proper prayer."[105] In Cabasilas' writings we also find that the East remained committed to the notion of "real presence" through the transformation of the bread and wine into the body and blood of Christ. Similarly, Cabasilas and the East in general continued to view the Eucharist as a sacrifice through the transformed elements on the altar.[106]

## 5:3 The Church Fathers

Neoplatonic thought influenced both the Greek and Latin church fathers' teaching on the sacraments of baptism and the Eucharist[107], but not always in the same way.[108] Part of the West's sacramental theology begins with their rejection of some eastern concepts of the sacraments.[109] However, the differences again do not outweigh the more profound similarities based on both the East's and West's mutual understanding of the Eucharist as the mysterious result of a corresponding act in heaven. The Greek term Mustêrion" that had figured so eminently into the hellenistic mystery religions became another term for baptism and the Eucharist by the fourth century.[110]

Eusebius of Caesarea (260-340 C.E.) wrote: "The Lord and Saviour Himself, and the priests who go out from Him... present in veiled form in the bread and wine: the mysteries of His body and saving blood."[111]

The greatest aspect of the eucharistic mystery converged on Christ's presence in the consecrated bread and wine. In similar fashion to the hellenistic mysteries the church fathers understood its Mustêrion as a cultic act performed by the community, in the presence of Christ from which they received salvation as a result of their mysterious communion with God.[112] The use of Mustêrion also helped to explain the sacrifice of Christ in the Eucharist. For example, Augustine (354-430 C.E.) taught that the Eucharist contained the reality of Christ's sacrifice presented by the church to God "symbolically represented in the sacramental action."[113] Therefore, Augustine could speak of the mysterious role of Christ in the Eucharist as "both the Sacrificer and the Sacrifice."[114]

The Latin West began to translate mustêrion as Sacramentum.[115] But the meaning of the two remained synonymous[116] until the rationalism of the Scholastics in the Middle Ages deviated from former understandings.[117] Sacramentum, like Mustêrion, signified a consecrating act that lifted a person or object up into the region of the Sacrum or "divinity."[118] The West attempted to understand better the Sacramentum of the Eucharist with its theory of substance change or as it was later named Transubstantiation.[119] The East used the Greek term Metousiosis and an older word Metabolê for its theory on substance change.[120] Both theories were practically identical, and both seriously considered the "real presence" of Christ in the sacraments through the notion of Mustêrion-Sacramentum.

The basis for understanding the subtle differences between the East and West on the consecrated elements goes back to the platonic conception of "image" (Eikon) and "original form" (Idéa) that also continued in neoplatonism. "Image" served as the earthly representation of the transcendent "original form." The image owed its existence to the original form in platonic thought. The Greek and Latin fathers thought of Christ's presence in the sacraments along these same philosophical lines. The East used the relationship between image and form to interpret Christ's presence in the consecrated elements. Eastern theologians spoke of the presence and absence of Christ in the sacraments in order to affirm the fact that Christ remained hidden within the revelation of his sacramental presence.[121] In any case, the Greek and Latin fathers understood the Mustêrion in the eucharistic sacraments as the divine operation that could lead one from earthly image to heavenly original form.

Augustine epitomizes the West's neoplatonic expression of the sacraments and the difference between the East and West up to the Scholastic period. Augustine, like most of his contemporaries, thought in neoplatonic categories. But Augustine did not understand the Greek father's conception of "original form" in the same manner. Consequently, Augustine began to distance himself from the eastern conception of Mustêrion by seeing in "image" (Imago) only a similarity to the "original form" and not an identity (Homoioma).[122] The West could not accept the Greek understanding that the original form was present in the image, if only in a hidden form. By maintaining that only a similarity existed in the image with the original form, the West interpreted Imago differently than the East understood Eikon.[123]

In good neoplatonic fashion, Augustine placed emphasis on visible signs. Since God had revealed himself in history through visible signs to humans, the sacraments could also be considered signs that dealt with divine things, according to Augustine. Augustine, in agreement with neoplatonic thought, connected visible signs to the invisible reality. Applying this to the Eucharist meant that something becomes visible in the sacraments of the bread and wine but something else is understood by it. The Eucharist could represent the divine for Augustine but could never become identical with it.[124] Therefore, Augustine claimed that Christ remained undivided in heaven and could not be distributed in pieces during communion.[125]

One must not conclude that the eucharistic symbols were empty signs for Augustine. On the contrary, these symbols bore the divine action by which God administered his grace to the faithful. Nor should we assume that Augustine's teaching on the symbolic nature of the consecrated elements lessened the notion of "real presence" in the Eucharist. Here too, the reality of Christ's presence stood unabated through the Latin definition of sacrament as both "corporeal" and "spiritual."

The next pivotal separation between the East's and the West's doctrine on the eucharist resulted from the introduction of aristotelian thought to the scholastics in the West. The West accepted much of

Aristotle's philosophical forms while the East debated and ultimately disputed Aristotelian ideas. Aristotle's works came into the church in the West through the Dominican order after the twelfth century scholastics eventually appropriated Latin translations.[126] The aristotelian concept of "material" and "form" eventually led to a new grasp of the sacraments in the West.

Clearly the most influential scholastic thinker that helped solidify the shift to aristotelian concepts concerning the Eucharist was Thomas Aquinas (1225-1274 C.E.). Aquinas can not be considered a pure adherent of Aristotelian thought because of his synthesizing efforts between aristotelian and platonic thought with regard to the perception of God. Hotz said, "Der Aquinate sucht in seinen Erörterung über das Wesen Gottes einen Mittelweg zwischen einer vermenschlichten Gottesvorstellung und der neuplatonischen Auffassung von der völligen Jenseitigkeit und Tranzendenz Gottes."[127] Aquinas understood the first perception of God in "being" rather than the neoplatonic notion that one first realizes God in the "soul" and gradually perfects this recognition through the stream of forms that lead to the original form. The perception of God could come to light through the material thing, or through one's sense perception of creation, since the material thing possessed an actual pre-existence in God. On this point Aquinas followed platonism.[128] The only major distinction between neoplatonism and aristotelianism for Aquinas centered on how one perceived God.

Aquinas' aristotelian influence eventually came to bear upon his doctrine on the Eucharist. For Aquinas the "more perfect" belonged to the "words" rather than the "thing."[129] Both words and the material things together remained necessary in the Eucharist in order to form a type of unity. But Aquinas qualified this relationship between the words and things by giving more prominence to the spoken words than to the visible elements. Thus the "Word" completed the liturgical act in such a way that the visible sacraments did not bear God's grace alone. Even an "unworthy" priest could administer a valid sacrament because the sacraments were independent of the giver and receiver Ex Opere Operato.[130] Therefore Aquinas and his school taught that the actual moment of change and consecration came when the priest spoke the institutional words over the elements while others (Franciscans) maintained that only a direct act of God alone determined this transformation of reality.[131]

The church fathers had applied neoplatonism to the Eucharist in order to understand the powerful mystery that took place in the consecration of the elements. Neoplatonism's transcendent conception of the divine served to bolster the problematic presence of a holy God in the ritual. The fathers could discuss the mystery of Christ's presence in the eucharistic elements in platonic language without threatening the notion of God's transcendence. The platonic notions of "image" and "original form" not only provided an intellectually acceptable means to articulate the Mustêrion but more importantly insured a theologically appropriate format to speak of the unfathomable.

The emergence of the West's aristotelian thought in connection with the eucharistic doctrine resulted in two importance divergences from the neoplatonic dogmas in the East. In the first place the notion of transcendence in the Eucharist declined with Aquinas' compromising understanding that God was not altogether transcendent. Secondly, the more rationalistic approach to the sacraments in aristotelian categories made the Eucharist both more abstract and at the same time less mysterious. Beginning with the ability to conceive of the changed substances through one's sense perception Aquinas had opened the door to give the "Word" ultimate victory over the irrational act in the Eucharist. Aquinas had begun to transform the Eucharist from primarily a mysterious deed to more of a rational doctrine for which the church found several purposes. Ironically, this rationalistic trend would also give the Reformation fuel to refute Rome's transubstantiation doctrine.

## 5:4 The Protestant Reformers and "Real Presence"

The Protestant Reformation in the sixteenth century insisted upon understanding the Eucharist as a commemoration of Calvary in contrast to the Roman Catholics who argued that it was a repetition of Calvary.[132] But the Protestants did not abolish the sacrificial character of the Eucharist altogether because they too accepted Calvary as a sacrifice. The Eucharist continued to be practiced when the prevailing attitude among many Reformers concerning the rite's true nature was that of only a memorial.[133] Not even Zwingli, the most ardent opponent of Roman sacramentalism with its claims of salvific effects for the partakers, de-emphasized the importance of the Eucharist. The Roman

Catholic doctrine of the Eucharist represented a real challenge for the Reformers because it threatened their doctrine of justification by faith alone through God's grace. Nonetheless, the Protestants continued to celebrate the Eucharist under the careful scrutiny of "correct doctrine."

The sixteenth century controversy extended the eucharistic debates of the Middle Ages. The Reformers rejected "real presence" in the sense of the Roman doctrine of transubstantiation articulated at the Fourth Lateran Council (1215 C.E.). This doctrine perpetuated the idea that the sacrifice of the altar actually comprised Christ's body and blood by means of the God's own transforming power in the consecrated bread and wine. The battle centered on the mode of Christ's presence and included the relationships between the sacraments and the theological topics of grace, faith and salvation. The whole meaning of an eucharistic sacrifice centered on the doctrine of the "real objective presence of Christ in the consecrated elements."[134]

The Roman Catholic Church specifically attacked several of the Reformation's "errors" concerning the Eucharist during the Council of Trent. On January 17, 1546 the Council set forth several such Church canons of the Mass directed against the Reformers.[135] For example, canon number four established anew the necessity of the sacraments for salvation, because faith alone was not sufficient (contra Reformers). Canon five refuted Luther's doctrine of "justification by faith" since it denied the sacraments' power to awaken faith. Canon six claimed that the sacraments were more than mere "signs", but also contained God's saving grace. Canon eight employed the phrase that the Reformers found so nocuous, Ex Opere Operato. In others words, the sacraments effectively issued grace in a manner that the Reformers deemed as mechanical and magical.[136]

Luther's particular doctrines on the Eucharist must be seen in the polemical context of his debate with the Roman Catholic Church. Even before his excommunication (1521), Luther had accepted the scholastic position that the sacraments entailed faith as the bond between "signs" and "objects."[137] The sacraments meant nothing without faith to Luther. Only when received in faith could the sacraments work for one's salvation, because faith released the effects of the sacraments. Luther taught that the proclaimed Word had to accompany the sacraments in order for faith to activate the sacraments.[138] Luther fervently stressed that the preaching of the Word of God brought the same effect as the sacraments in bestowing forgiveness of sins and eternal life. However, he distinguished between the Word and the sacraments in his *Sermon von dem Sakrament des Leibes und Blutes Christi* (1526): "He (Christ) is truly present there in the Word, yet not in the same sense as in the sacrament, because he has attached his body and blood to the Word and in bread and wine is bodily to be received."[139]

Luther's notion of "real presence" deviated from both the Roman Church as well as some of the other Reformers. Unabashed by Zwingli's "figurative" sense of eucharistic presence, Luther continued to contend for Christ's "real presence" on the altar.[140] But Luther refused the Roman Catholic doctrine of transubstantiation and began to speak of the ubiquity of Christ's presence. Christ could indeed be both sacramentally present at every Eucharist and in heaven at the same time.[141]

Luther's rejection of transubstantiation did not include the abolishment of the "elevation" in the Eucharist as it had for other Reformers. Luther spoke out about what he thought were the dangers of this practice.[142] In *The Misuse of the Mass* he claimed that the elevation caused his opponents to call the Mass a sacrifice.[143] Luther regarded the Eucharist as a memorial or commemoration of Christ's sacrifice on Calvary. He did not go so far as to equate the Eucharist with a repetition or representation of Calvary. On the contrary, Luther wrote, "In truth your re-sacrificing is a most impious re-crucifying,"[144] to the papists who held that Christ was immolated repeatedly at every Eucharist.

Zwingli and Calvin both subordinated the sacraments to the Word and, like Luther, they understood the Eucharist as a memorial of the sacrifice on Calvary in opposition to the Roman position. But whereas Zwingli removed almost all of the mystical aspects from the Eucharist, Calvin did not.[145] John Nevin paraphrased part of Calvin's thinking on the mystical union realized in the Eucharist between Christ and the believer:

> The body of Christ is in heaven, the believer on earth; but by the power of the Holy Spirit, nevertheless, the obstacle of such vast local distance is fully overcome, so that in the sacramental act-while the outward symbols are received in an outward way-the very body and blood of Christ are at the same time inwardly and spiritually communicated to the worthily receiver...[146]

Calvin could affirm that the true believer received Christ with the sacramental "signs", and therefore the bread and wine imparted grace. For Calvin grace in the sacramental signs enabled the participant to "realize the sacrifice of Christ on the cross."[147] The believer received the body and blood of Christ through the work of the Holy Spirit, but only by that individual believer's faith.[148] The believer's mystical union with the constantly present Christ constituted the most significance teaching on the Eucharist for Calvin.[149] Calvin wrote, "We communicate in the Lord's Supper not with the divine promise merely, not with the thought of Christ only, not with the recollection simply of what he has done and suffered for us, not with the lively present sense alone of his all sufficient, all - glorious salvation; but with the living Savior himself, in the fullness of his glorified person, made present to us for the purpose by the power of the Holy Spirit."[150]

The Reformer's struggle with the Roman Catholic eucharistic doctrines not only defended "justification by faith alone" but also produced an anti-sacramentalism for all of Portestanism. Although most of the Reformers still expressed the mystical union between the believer and the Risen Christ in the Eucharist doctrinally, the Protestant celebrations of the Eucharist themselves became quite incapable of symbolizing the mysteries found in the prayers and liturgies of the early church fathers. Rationalism had eroded much of the ritual's once fertile symbolism in the guise of spiritual interpretation. Those who advocated that the Eucharist represented only a "memorial" impoverished the symbolism of the act itself and subsequently reduced it to a mere doctrine incapable of rationally deciphering the mystery of Christ presence.

Since the early eucharistic texts established the central themes for the later liturgies in the centuries that followed we shall now briefly examine one of these early prayers in comparison to two later eucharistic texts.[151] I have translated following the eucharistic prayer from the *Apostolic Tradition of Hippolytus* (215 C.E.) because it provides a good basis for comparing other eucharistic texts with the structure of this nascent tradition at Rome.[152] This prayer begins after the "kiss of peace" while the deacons are bringing the oblation (sacrifice)[153] to the "worthy" (consecrated) bishop who begins the prayer with the presbytery.[154]

### 5:5 Prayer of Hippolytus

The Lord [be] with you. And with your spirit. Lift up [your] hearts.[155] We have to the Lord. Let us give thanks to the Lord. [It is] worthy and just.

We thank you[156], God, through your beloved servant Jesus Christ, whom in latter times you sent to us as saviour and redeemer and messenger of your will. [He is] the Word from you, through whom you have made all things, whom you were well pleased to send from heaven into a womb of a virgin. And being conceived he became flesh and your son was manifested by the Holy Spirit having been born of a virgin. He, having fulfilled your will and having prepared for you a holy people, extended his hands while suffering in order that he might release suffering for those who have believed in you.
Who, when they handed [him] over he suffered willingly, in order that he might abolish death and tear the bonds of the devil and trample [down] hell and enlighten the righteous and fix a way, and manifest [his] resurrection[157]; having received the bread he gave thanks [and] said:

Take, eat, this is my body, the one broken for you. And likewise the cup saying: This is my blood poured out for you. As often as you do this, do in my memory.

Remembering, therefore, his death and resurrection we present[158] to you the bread and the cup while giving thanks to you, because you have considered us worthy[159] to stand in your presence and serve as your priests.[160]

And we honor you so that you might send down your Holy Spirit upon this sacrifice[161] of the holy church, which you may grant unity to all holy ones who partake; that they might be filled with [the] Holy Spirit so that [their] faith might be confirmed in truth; in order that we might sing hymns to you and glorify [you] through your servant Jesus Christ, through whom glory and honor to you Father and [the] Son with the Holy Spirit in your holy church now and always and for ever. Amen.

Hippolytus made it clear that the bishop had to undergo proper preparation and consecration in order to be deemed "worthy" to perform the Eucharist.[162] As we have already seen, preparation by means of baptism for the remission of sins, prayers confessing sins, petitioning God to be made worthy to partake and prayers for a "pure" or "acceptable sacrifice" represent ubiquitous features in the early eucharistic writings. The liturgical importance of consecration and the worthiness to participate in the Eucharist developed in conjunction with growing theological expressions of God's transcendent holiness and human creaturely sinfulness. The combination of ritual consecration and God's transcendent holiness in the eucharistic liturgies resulted in symbolism analogous to that of the jewish priests who performed sacrifices before the "face of Yahweh."[163]

The Egyptian tradition represented by Sarapion in the middle of the fourth century discloses no drastic break with the prayer of Hippolytus. The more wordy prayer of Sarapion not only described God in loftier transcendent language but also Jesus Christ in response to the fourth century Arian controversy.[164] Here are a few lines from Sarapion's text:

### 5:6 Prayer of Sarapion

> It is worthy and just to praise thee, to celebrate thee, to glorify thee eternal Father of the only-begotten Son, Jesus Christ.
>
> We praise thee, eternal God, inscrutable, indescribable, incomprehensible to every created nature.
>
> Thou art attended by thousands upon thousands and myriads upon myriads of Angels and Archangels,
>
> With theirs, accept also our acclamations of thy holiness:
>
> Holy, holy, holy is the Lord Sabaoth! For this reason, we too, celebrating the memorial of his death, have offered this bread and pray: through this sacrifice, reconcile us to thyself, be favorable to us, O God of truth.[165]

The Syrian Liturgy of James[166] (early fifth century) also portrays the development of an increasing tendency to emphasize God's transcendent holiness in contrast to the participants unworthiness and therefore, the need to make them worthy. This liturgy also took on the tone of a sacrifice performed by priest before a holy God. This text also conjures up the more typical eastern expressions of fear in approaching God's presence at the sacrifice. The following excerpts from the Liturgy of James illustrate the early East's particular expression of this sacrificial structure in the Eucharist.

## 5:7 Prayer of James

Sovereign Lord our God, condemn me not, defiled with a multitude of sins: for, behold, I have come to this Thy divine and heavenly mystery, not as being worthy; but looking only to thy goodness, I direct my voice to Thee: God be merciful to me, a sinner; I have sinned against Heaven, and before Thee, and am unworthy to come into the presence of this Thy holy and spiritual table, upon which Thy only-begotten Son, and our Lord Jesus Christ, is mystically set forth as a sacrifice for me, a sinner, and stained with every spot.

Sovereign Lord Jesus Christ, O Word of God, who didst freely offer Thyself a blameless sacrifice upon the cross to God even the Father, the coal of double nature, that didst touch the lips of the prophet with the tongs, and didst take away his sins, touch also the hearts of us sinners, and purify us from every stain, and present us holy beside Thy holy altar, that we may offer Thee a sacrifice of praise: and accept from us, Thy unprofitable servants, this incense as an odor of a sweet smell, and make fragrant the evil odor of our soul and body, and purify us with the sanctifying power of Thy all-holy Spirit: for Thou alone art holy; who sanctifiest...

O beneficent King eternal, and Creator of the universe, receive Thy church, coming unto Thee through Thy Christ: fulfil to each what is profitable; lead all to perfection, and make us perfectly worthy of the grace of Thy sanctification...

God, who didst accept the gifts of Abel, the sacrifice of Noah and of Abram, the incense of Aaron and of Zacharias, accept also from the hand of us sinners this incense for an odor of a sweet smell, and for the remission of our sins...

Our Lord and God, Jesus Christ, who through exceeding goodness and love not to be restrained wast crucified,...who didst provide this mysterious and awful service as an everlasting memorial for us perpetually...

God Almighty, Lord great in glory, who hast given to us an entrance into the Holy of Holies...we supplicate and invoke Thy goodness, since we are fearful and trembling when about to stand at Thy holy altar; send forth upon us, O God, Thy good grace, and sanctify our souls, and our bodies, and spirits...

For the remission of our sins, and forgiveness of our transgressions, and for our deliverance from all tribulation, wrath, danger, and distress, and from the uprising of our enemies, let us beseech the Lord.

O Sovereign, that we may become servants of Thy new testament, ministers of Thy holy altar, according to the greatness of Thy mercy, that we may become worthy of offering to Thee gifts and sacrifices for our transgressions and for those of the people; grant to us, O Lord, with all fear and a pure conscience to offer to Thee this spiritual and bloodless sacrifice, and graciously receiving it unto Thy holy and spiritual altar above the skies...

We therefore, being counted worthy to enter into the place of the tabernacle of Thy glory, and to be within the veil, and to behold the Holy of Holies, cast ourselves down before Thy goodness: Lord, have mercy on us: since we are full of fear and trembling, when about to stand at Thy holy altar, and to offer this dread and bloodless sacrifice for our own sins and for the errors of the people...

And, uncovering the robes that darkly invest in symbol this sacred ceremonial, do Thou reveal it clearly to us: fill our intellectual vision with absolute light, and having purified our poverty from every pollution of the flesh and spirit, make it worthy of this dread and awful approach...

Having taken the bread in His holy and pure and blameless and immortal hands, lifting up His eyes to heaven, and showing it to Thee, His God and Father, He gave thanks, and Hallowed, and broke, and gave it to us, His disciples and apostles, saying; For the remission of sins and life everlasting.[167]

These few example from early liturgical texts show the Eucharist had a great deal of flexibility and variety within the first four centuries. However, these texts also reveal that both eastern and western traditions concentrated on the theological problem bringing a holy and transcendent God into the presence of sinful humans for the purpose of the eucharistic sacrifice.

The theological question of whether or not the Eucharist can be considered a sacrifice or only a memorial continues to be elusive and controversial. This is primarily due to the symbolic and mysterious nature of the Eucharist itself. No literal sacrifice occurred apart from the symbolic words and acts of the varied rites themselves.[168] But early practices of the Eucharist continued to indicate that an actual sacrifice did occur or at least the same results occurred when the consecrated elements had been offered to God. Some liturgies made it clear that not only was a sacrifice taking place in the Eucharist but a repetition of Christ's sacrifice on Calvary.

Hellenistic Judaism made spiritual sacrifice attractive to the early Christians who began to look beyond the Jewish law and temple for their own worship of God in Jesus Christ. However, the Eucharist quickly utilized more and more sacrificial symbolism as Christianity developed its own theology and worship. Platonism had already set the stage for the eastern fathers to confirm the reality of God's presence in the ritual's symbols. The West's predilection for the Word over the mysterious act did not ultimately repudiate Christ's mysterious presence nor the sacrificial nature of the Eucharist. The mystery of the resurrected Christ some how being present as the sinner participated and actually consumed the consecrated elements magnified the liturgical experience of God's holiness. This experience exceeded the boundaries of East and West, Roman Catholics and Protestants. Even the Reformation's war of words ultimately acknowledged the mystery of Christ's presence and union with the participant. But in the final analysis, the sacrificial question concerning the Eucharist needs to be compared with the problem of a transcendent holy God uniting mystically with sinful people in the ritual act. In the historical development of the Eucharist we found that a variety of different rites arose in different traditions. The diversity of the different traditions never discarded the Eucharist's basic structure as a ritual that brought God and humans together. The history of eucharistic symbolism lucidly reveals preparation rites in the form of different consecrations for the participants and materials, elaborate symbols for the moment of encounter between humans and God in the consecrated elements, and examples of exit rites that served to separate the sacred from the profane and reestablish God's transcendence. So each celebration of the Eucharist initiated the need to continue performing the Eucharist. From the first century Christians also have understood their responsibility to "do this in remembrance of me." Human beings' compulsory participation in the Eucharist forms a partnership with God who operates behind the visible liturgy, either in the sacraments or the "sacrament of the Word", to administer his grace. Thus, the Christian not only continues to require communion with Christ but also continues to look forward to the eschatological hope of the final banquet with God in heaven.

## ENDNOTES TO CHAPTER FIVE

[1] I have chosen to use the term "Eucharist" to broach the total scope of this rite from its origins throughout its development. Eucharist comes from the Greek word Eucharistein which means "to give thanks", the noun, Eucharistia. In the second century this word had become a technical term for the Christian rite of celebrating "the Lord's Supper", a term which Paul used in First Corinthians based on the tradition of the "last supper" Jesus had with his disciples before his death.

[2] G. Wainwright said: It is not unimportant that the weight of the Bible's usage, in both Old and New Testaments, of the imagery of the feeding and of the meal should fall in favor of God as the transcendent giver who 'feeds' His people, and of a fellowship between man and God in which the distinction between them is clearly maintained (as when Israel eats 'before the Lord' and when Jesus eats with men both in His earthly ministry and, according to the sayings opening up the eschatological prospect at the Last Supper, in the final kingdom). *Eucharist and Eschatology*, p. 107.

[3] "It is true that by careful analysis there is to be found underlying most of these varying rites and all of the older ones a single normal or standard structure of the rite as a whole." See Gregory Dix, *The Shape of the Liturgy*, Westminster, Dacre Press, 1945, p. XI. What I propose as a discernable structure in the Eucharist differs from the "structure" Dix recognized. Dix cited a basic fourfold action that developed from an earlier seven fold pattern based on the institutional words in the synoptic gospels and I Corinthians 10. Dix mentions the "offertory", "prayer", "fraction", and "Communion", see p. 78. These form the basic structure Dix speaks of in the eucharistic liturgies. The structure I intend to chart out in the Eucharist follows a pattern of sacrificial symbolism in which case a holy God and humans are brought together in the ritual act. This structure follows the basic scheme of Hubert and Mauss mentioned in chapter two of this study. We should also note that the structure Dix spoke of can be found in other ancient meals.

[4] By mythology I mean the traditions that the early church held to be the truth about Jesus Christ passed on first in oral form and then in written

documents. This use of the term myth also must be distinguished from Rudolf Bultmann's hermeneutical device that he termed "demythologizing." Bultmann attempted to separate the message in the Gospels from their time bound (geschichtliche) point of reference (first-century mythology) in order to bring the timeless message (Historie) of faith to modern man. Cf. Bultmann et al., *Kerygma and Myth: A Theological Debate*, edited by Hans Werner Bartsch, New York, Harper & Row Publishers, 1961. Cf. *The New Testament and Criticism* pp. 47 ff. Bultmann wanted to interpret the mythological statements in the New Testament, not eliminate them. In this manner he intended to uncover the "deeper meaning" beneath the mythology of Jesus Christ, cf. Bultmann, *Jesus Christ and Mythology*, New York, Charles Scribner's Sons, 1958. But as W. Baird ("Myth In The N.T.", IDB, Sup. Vol., p. 612) has pointed out, "...his use of existentialism as a method of interpreting the meaning of myth has led to the claim that Bultmann has exchanged the old myth for a new philosophical and scientific one."

[5] I Cor. 15:3, "...Christ died for our sins according to the scriptures"; I Peter 1:18 f., "Knowing that you were redeemed from your futile ways inherited from your fathers not by perishable things, such as silver or gold, but by the precious blood of Christ like a lamb without blemish or spot"; Ephesians 5:2, "And walk in love just as Christ loved us and for our sakes delivered himself as a fragrant offering and sacrifice to God"; John 1:29, "...the lamb of God that takes away the sins of the world"; I Cor. 5:7, "Christ our passover lamb has been sacrificed"; Hebrews 9:26b, "Now he has appeared at the end of the age for the removal of sins through his sacrifice." Cf. also to, Hebrews 7:27, 10:12; Philippians 2:17, 4:18.

[6] See I John 1:7b, "...the blood of Jesus his son cleanses us from all sin." Also see I Clement 7:4; Ignatius, *Smyrn.* I:1. F. Young said that, "...it was generally accepted that he died to save from sin and that his blood was the purifying agent which dealt with man's sins", *The Use of Sacrificial Ideas in the Greek Christian Writers From the New Testament to John Chrysostom*, p. 160. Origen also claimed that Christ's blood shed at Calvary not only cleansed mankind on earth but this same

blood on the heavenly altar also purified the heavenly beings from their sin, cf., Hom. Lev. I.3.

[7] See Büchsel, "hilaskomai--hilasmos", *Theological Dictionary of the New Testament*, Vol. III, pp. 314-318. Büchsel reminds us that Hilasesthai was primarily a cultic term for Jews, pagans and Christians. But Christians did not limit this term to the death of Jesus Christ. They also applied it to the totality of Jesus' person and work. Young noted that Hilaskesthai in the New Testament carried the notion of expiation as in the Old Testament, that is, God provided the means of expiation, op. cit., p. 162.

[8] See Klaus Gamber, *Sacrificium Laudis*, Studia Patristica et Liturgica, Regensburg, Friedrich Pustet, Fasc. 5, 1973, p. 53. Gamber cites Paul's letter to the Romans 12:1:"I therefore encourage you, Brethren, through the mercies of God, to present your bodies as a living, holy sacrifice, acceptable to God as your spiritual worship (Latreîn)." I translated, Tân Logikân Latreîn, as an adverbial accusative.

Ernst Käsemann said concerning the context of this verse that, "What was previously cultic is now extended to the secularity of our earthly life as a whole. Basically this means the replacement of any cultic thinking ...Naturally this does not mean any disparagement of worship and the sacraments. Nevertheless, these events are no longer, as in cultic thinking, fundamentally separated from everyday Christian life in such a way as to mean something other that the promise for this and the summons to it"; see his, *Commentary on Romans*, trans. by Geoffrey W. Bromiley, Grand Rapids, Eerdmans Publishing Company, 1980, p. 327. Käsemann's observation captures the prevailing attitude of New Testament writers and especially Paul with regard to ritual, and especially in regard to the Jewish rite of circumcision. Christians devotion to God extended into their everyday relationships with one another and with those outside the community. See also Ferdinand Hahn, "Das Verständnis des Opfers im Neuen Testament", in *Das Opfer Jesu Christi und seine Gegenwart in der Kirche*, edited by Karl Lehmann and Edmund Schlink,Göttingen, Herder, 1983. On pp. 84-85 Hahn summarized the relationship between the Eucharist and sacrifice in the New Testament in the following way:

> Vier Sachverhalte sind vorweg festzuhalten: Zunächst ist unbestreitbar, daß im Neuen Testament an keiner Stelle Opferbegriffe auf das Herrenmahl angewandt werden. Daneben ist aber zu beobachten, daß sich implizit gewisse Berührungen mit Opfervorstellungen erkennen lassen, deren Tragweite genauer bestimmt werden muß. Hinzu kommt, daß zumindest im hellenistischen Bereich die Analogie zu heidnischen Opfermahlen durchaus empfunden worden ist, wie 1 Kor 10, 18-22 zeigt. Schließlich ist zu beachten, daß das Herrenmahl kein Kultmahl im eigenlichen Sinn gewesen ist, sondern daß eine gewöhnliche Mahlzeit, bei der sich Christen in Häusern versammelten, einen kultischen Rahmen erhielt, wobei die Zusammenkünfte insgesamt durchaus die Funktion eines Gottesdienstes hatten, bei denen aber gerade der Alltag bewußt einbezogen worden ist.

[9] Young, op. cit., p. 98.

[10] See Ferdinand Hahn, op. cit., p. 85.

[11] Ibid, cf. pp. 85-91.

[12] Scott Bartchy said "it was not that the Corinthians had "too low a view" of the elements of the bread and wine but rather "too high a view" in which these elements were believed to bond each believer to the resurrected Lord in a very individualistic manner." See *Increase in Learning*, p. 49.

[13] Gerhard Schneider as a "kultkritik" opposed Hahn's premise that the growing migration towards a sacrificial concept of the Eucharist was to be understood as moving away from Jesus' own intentions. On the contrary, Schneider felt that the New Testament texts followed Jesus' intentions understanding his sacrificial blood to have special power. See ibid, pp. 92-95.

[14] G. Wainwright (*Eucharist and Eschatology*, p. 91) also gives evidence of the growing sacrificial developments for the Eucharist in the West. Notice his comments:

> Two particularly unfortunate developments took place in the later Western history. First, an ever-increasing emphasis was placed on

the offering of the sacrifice as that which availed for the remission of sins, and there was a corresponding recession in the importance of communion as the means of receiving the benefits which Christ Himself gives. And second: though warning against unworthy communion has always been a universal feature of theology, the West developed such a stress on preparatory purification through the sacrament of penance that even the great Saint Thomas was mildly embarrassed by the fact that remission of sins was ascribed to communion itself by the liturgical texts...

[15] Richardson, "Eastern and Western Liturgies: The Primitive Basis of Their Later Differences", *Harvard Theological Review*. Vol. XLII. 1949, p. 144. Note that we have no clear evidence that the "destruction of the Jewish Temple" in 70 A.D. had any influence on the developing Christian liturgies.

[16] Already in the writings of Ignatius of Antioch, who died around the year 117, the prerequisite for church life to be lived under the auspices the bishop clearly stands out. Ignatius wrote in his letter to the *Smyrneans* 8, 1, "Let that be considered a valid Eucharist which is celebrated by the bishop, or by one whom he appoints." Quoted from, Kirsopp Lake, translator, *The Loeb Classical Library: The Apostolic Fathers* Vol. I. Edited by T. E. Page et al. Cambridge, Harvard University Press, 1959,p. 261. Tertullian also concerned himself with the proper liturgical administration of the sacraments. He wrote, "The sacrament of the Eucharist, which was instituted by the Lord at a mealtime and enjoined upon all, we take in assemblies before day-break, and only from the hands of the presidents." *Documents of the Christian Church*, second edition, edited by Henry Bettenson. London, Oxford University Press, 1963, p. 76.

[17] Reumann, op. cit. p. 57.

[18] Ibid., p. 178.

[19] Willy Rordorf wished to deemphasize the role of sacrifice in the Didache. He said, "Le "sacrifice" signifie ici plutot le sacrifice d'action de grâce dont parlent les textes chrétiens les plus anciens, et qui

s'opposent précisément aux sacrifices sanglants tant juifs que païens." See *Le Point Théologique: L'Eucharistie des Premiers Cheétiens*, 17, Paris, Éditions Beauchesne, 1976, p. 26. But E. Kirber thinks that the notion of sacrifice in the eucharistic prayer in the Didache shows the developmet of the idea that the Eucharist (Abendmahl) was a repetition of the sacrifice of Christ on the cross. Cf. "Opfer", in, *Die Religion in Geschichte und Gegenwart*, ed. Hans v. Campenhausen et al., Tübingen, J. C. B. Mohr, 1960, Third Edition, Vol. IV, p. 1652.

[20] Cf. Klaus Gamber, *Sacrificium Vespertinum: Studia Patristica et Liturgica*. Regensburg, Friedrich Pustet, 1983, Fasc. 12, p. 10. Here he comments on Clement's First Letter, chapter 40.

[21] Didache 14:1, quoted from, *Early Christian Fathers*, p. 178. Kirsopp Lake translated Thusîa in Didache 14:1 as "offering." See *The Apostolic Fathers*, Cambridge, Harvard University Press, 1959, vol. I, p. 331.

[22] Cf., John Reumann, *The Supper of the Lord*, Philadelphia, Fortress Press, 1985. Reumann writes, "As ministry thus developed, the Eucharist became more and more that sacrifice offered by the presiding clergyman (male), functioning in Christ's stead, imitating what Christ did. Paul's words, "Do this in memory of me" could "to pagan ears mean 'this do ye sacrifice'" (Conybeare, *Encyclopaedia Britannica*, p. 872). ", pp. 57 ff.

[23] Dix, op. cit., p. 124.

[24] Ignatius, *Eph.* 5:2.

[25] *Smyrn.* 7:1,2 quoted from Alexander Roberts and James Donaldson, editors, *The Ante-Nicene Fathers: The Writings of the Fathers down to A.D. 395*, Vol. I, revised with notes by A. Clevend Coxe, Grand Rapids, Wm. B. Eerdmans Publishing Company, 1985, p. 89. H. Graß, ("Abendmahl", RGG, p. 22), said that Ignatius "bezeichnet das zu brechende Brot als Heilmittel der Unsterblichkeit (Phârmakon Athanasîas), als Gegengift (Antîdoton) gegen das Sterben (IgnEph 20:2)."

[26] Irenaeus, (*Adv. Haer.* 5:3), quoted from *Early Christian Fathers*, p. 388. Irenaeus also felt that the Jews could no longer offer the true sacrifice to God since they rejected the "Word through whom men offer sacrifice to God", cf. *Adv. Haer.* 4: 18,4 as edited by Adalbert Hamman, *The Eucharist of the Early Christians*, p. 89.

[27] "Real presence" in the ante-nicene period expressed both the thought that the bread and wine were symbols or figures of the Body and Blood and the identification of the bread and wine as the Body and Blood. The Post-Nicene period increased the emphasis on the latter identification.

[28] First Apology of Justin 66, quoted from *Early Christian Fathers*, p. 286.

[29] See *Didache* 9:5 in *The Apostolic Fathers*, vol. I, p. 323.

[30] Ibid., p. 75. Some have suggested that already in I Corinthians 16:20-24 we find part of a eucharistic liturgy because Paul knew that the Eucharist would follow the reading of his letter. The purpose of the "anathema" was to exclude the unworthy from the Eucharist at the beginning of the ceremony.

[31] See Werner Elert, *Eucharist and Church Fellowship in the First Four Centuries*, Translated by N. E. Nagel. Saint Louis, Concordia Publishing House, 1966, p. 75.

[32] Quoted from Lampe, *SPCK*, p. 43. See Origen Hom. 13:3,4.

[33] See Marcel Metzger, *The Eucharist of the Early Christians*, p. 203, and Werner, op. cit., p. 75.

[34] Werner, op. cit., p. 77. By "secrecy" Werner refers to the mysteries where the initiants vowed to keep the practices of their rites secret. Werner used Tertullian's defence to show that the Christians were not trying to conceal secrets of their eucharistic rites, pp. 76-77.

[35] 62, 17, 1, see *The Ante-Nicene Fathers*, vol. V, p. 363. E. Kinber said, "Vom 3 Jh. an finden sich genauere Definitionen des Opfercharakters der Eucharistie", Op. cit., p. 1652. Some want to remove any notion of a literal reproduction of the sacrifice of Calvary in Cyprian's words (cf. G. W. H. Lampe in, *Eucharistic Theology Then and Now*, London, S.P.C.K., 1968, p. 37) by citing the immediate context of this saying. Here Cyprian argued against those who only used water and no wine in the rite. But such a suggestion also simply ignores the full context of Cyprian's teaching and language on the Eucharist. Cyprian held the that sacrifice (Sacrificium) enabled Christians to realize the promise of drinking the fruit of the wine in the Kingdom of God with Christ, (cf. 63, 9, 2-3.) This reality that the sacrifice on Calvary made possible was the same reality now available through the commemorative (Commemoratio) sacrifice of the Eucharist. While we can not know exactly how Cyprian thought of the connection between Calvary and the Eucharist we need not ignore the obvious symbolism of his language. Sixteenth century writers would later try to figure out the exact nature of this connection in Cyprian's statement for its own theological battles.

[36] Lietzmann, *Mass and Lord's Supper*, p. 82.

[37] Origen, *Hom. Lev.* 5:3; quoted from Young op. cit., p. 180. The Acts of Thomas (latter part of the second century, written originally in Syriac then in Greek ) also connected the Eucharist to the forgiveness of sins;

> And after they had been baptized and were come up, he brought bread and the mingled cup; and spake a blessing over it and said: "Thy holy Body, which was crucified for our sake, we eat, and Thy life-giving Blood, which was shed for our sake, we drink. Let Thy Body be to us for life, and Thy blood for the remission of sins, c. 158.

Quoted from A. F. J. Klijn, *The Acts of Thomas*, (Supplements to *Novum Testamentum*, vol. V).Leiden, E. J. Brill, 1962, p. 149.

[38] Origen, *Hom. Lev.* 4:7,8; quoted from Young p. 180. According to Young (p. 210) Gregory Nazianzen also spoke of Christ "as priest who sacrifices himself, as victim, for us, so cleansing the world."

[39] See Graß, op. cit., p. 23.

[40] Ibid., p. 23.

[41] "...so that all who partake might grow in devotion, obtain the forgiveness of their sins, be freed from the devil and his deceit, and, be filled with the Holy Ghost, might be made worthy of Thy Christ and partake of everlasting life...", The Apostolic Constitutions 39, quoted in Joseph A. Jungmann in, *The Mass of the Roman Rite: Its Origins and Development*, Trans. by Francis Brunner, Westminster, Christian Classics, 1986, Vol. 1, p. 37. *The Apostolic Constitutions* sounds very much like the Apostolic Tradition of Hippolytus that was written around the year 215. Lietzmann (p. 86) said of the Epiclesis of Basil the Great, "It is clear that the original place for the entreaty that the partaking of the eucharist may be for the blotting out of sin and not for condemnation..."

[42] Lampe, "The Eucharist in the Thought of the Early Church", *S.P.C.K.*, p. 47.

[43] See Dix, op. cit., p. 166.

[44] Cyril *Catech.* 23:8,9, See Lampe op. cit., p. 43.

[45] Ibid., p. 44.

[46] "Zu beachten ist auch, daß diese späteren Texte nicht mehr, wie in der Didache, Dankgebet, sondern Opfergebet (Anaphora) genannt werden", K. Gamber, op. cit., p. 66. Also see Gamber on the archeological evidence on house churches in fourth and fifth centuries. Here the bishop separated himself from the people by his station at the altar in order to present the sacrifice, ibid, p. 23.

[47] Lietzmann, op. cit., cf., pp. 71, 86.

[48] *Stromata*, 7, 7 (Migne, Patrologia Graeca XI, 444 C). Quoted from, Joseph A. Jungmann, op. cit., vol. I, p. 24.

[49] *Apology.* I, 13 (Migne, Patrologia Graeca VI, 345). See ibid., p. 25,

[50] An argument runs that before Irenaeusthe church recognized no offering except thanksgiving. Cf. J. A. Jungmann, op. cit., for one who opposes this view, p. 24, and fn. 10.

[51] *First Apology* 66, in *Early Christian Fathers*, pp. 286-7.

[52] Ibid., p. 286.

[53] *Dial.* XLI, 3, *The Ante-Nicene Fathers*, vol. 1, p. 215.

[54] *De Spec.* 13, Quoted from Victor Saxer in, *The Eucharist of the Early Christians*, p. 149.

[55] Ibid., p. 148.

[56] J. G. Davies said the early centuries witnessed three main topics in the development of the Eucharist: "sacrifice, consecration and presence"; and continued with,"Christians in the period before Nicaea were quite emphatic that the Eucharist was a sacrifice", see, "Christianity: The Early Church", in, *The Concise Encyclopedia of Living Faiths*, edited by R. C. Zaehner. Boston, Beacon Press, 1959, p. 82.

[57] See Young p. 155 and Clement, *Strom.* 7:14, *The Ante-Nicene Fathers*, vol. II, pp. 547-549.

[58] See Young's treatment of Athanasius, op. cit., pp. 214 ff. Athanasius also taught that, "We offer up not a material lamb but the true Lamb that was already offered, the Lord Jesus Christ", (Ep. heort., 2,9; quoted from Jungmann, *The Mass of the Roman Rite*, vol. I, p. 180, fn. 11.

[59] Young, op. cit., p. 289.

⁶⁰ Jungmann, op. cit., vol. I, p. 25. I also offer an extended quote by Jungmann here to reflect a modern Roman view of the present and ancient liturgies:

> There is actually a definite contrast between this language of the liturgy and the language we are used to nowadays in sermons, catechisms, and other religious writings. We prefer to insist on the fact that on our altars Christ renews His Passion and death in an unbloody manner. We talk about the renewal of the sacrifice of the Cross, about an oblation in which Christ gives Himself to His heavenly Father. But it is only in very general terms that we mention the sacrifice of the Church, and for this reason even our theological textbooks in discussing the ensuing problem as to precisely where Christ consummates His sacrifice, refer without much reflection to His presence in the sacred Host.
>
> If, by way of contrast, we skim through the pertinent writings of the Fathers even casually, we are surprised to note that they use similar terms in reference to Christ's oblation in the Eucharist and in reference to our own. They emphasize with equal stress the fact that we (or the Church or the priest) offer up the Passion of the Lord, indeed that we offer up Christ Himself. This is likewise true of the pre-Scholastic Middle Ages. Seldom, it is true, do they use words of their own to express the traditional teaching, but when they do they are especially clear in pointing out that it is the priest at the altar, who, in place of Christ, offers up our Lord's Body, that in so doing he is the Coadjutor Redemptionis and Vicarius Eius. And at the same time they declare that the Church offers up the sacrifice through the ministry of the priest.

Vol. I, pp. 180-181.

⁶¹ G. Dix, op. cit., p. 112.

⁶² See The Council of Hippo (399) and its measures to protect the eucharistic prayer.

⁶³ G. Wainwright observes, "From Cyprian onwards the typical Western theology was that the eucharist was above all a (commemorative) sacrifice which brought to the penitent and faithful communicant

remission of sins, communion serving also to ensure his continuing dwelling in Christ through His ecclesial body", op. cit., p. 91.

[64] Quoted from, W. Lockton, *The Treatment of the Remains at the Eucharist After Holy Communion and the Time of the Ablutions*. Cambridge, Cambridge University Press, 1920, pp. 2,3.

[65] Cyril taught that nothing of the elements should be left discarded. See Pius Parsch, *The Liturgy of the Mass*, translated by Frederic Eckoff. St. Louis, B. Herder Book Co., 1945, p. 319.

[66] See supra, p. 9.

[67] See Lockton, op. cit., pp. 15ff.

[68] See Parsch, op. cit., pp. 320-321.

[69] See Lockton, op. cit., p. 118.

[70] According to Dix, the local liturgies were assimilated to those "patriarchal ones." Op. cit., p. 8.

[71] Ibid., p. 8,9. For more information on the influence and borrowing of one tradition from another see Allan Bouley, *From Freedom to Formula: The Evolution of the Eucharistic Prayer from Oral Improvisation to Written Texts*. Washington, D. C., The Catholic University of America Press, 1981, pp. 245-253.

[72] Ibid., pp. 10-11. Lietzmann recognized four main types of existing rites, a "Syro-Byzantine, Egyptian, Roman and Gallican." Op. cit. pp. XII ff.

[73] It must be pointed out that the efforts by the Churchin Constantinople to enforce its liturgical uniformity in the East failed. The Byzantine rite followed the Antioch-Syrian tradition as a basis for its developments to the seventh century. Some eastern rites took on several Antioch-

Jerusalem characteristics. Before the seventh century the East had undergone several liturgical changes, see Dix. op. cit., pp. 546 ff.

[74] The reduction from seven to four came about as the result of the removal of the meal from the Eucharist which in turn became the Agape or Love Feast. The original seven actions from the New Testament are as follows: 1. taking the bread; 2 blessing it; 3 breaking it; 4 distributing it, (followed by the meal and its conclusion); 5 taking the cup; 6 blessing it; 7 distributing it. See Luke 22:14-20.

[75] Ibid., p. 11.

[76] Wainwright pointed out that "...the typical movement of thought (West) is from a present and continuing purification of sin (Purificatio, Mundatio, Purgatio, Absolutio) to a future enjoyment of the full blessings of heaven...", ibid., p. 88.

[77] Eis àphesin hamartion kai eis zoân aionion.

[78] See Wainwright (op. cit., p. 95). Also see Graß, op. cit. p. 24, who said, "Doch galten die Einsetzungsworte erst seit dem 12. Jh. allgemein als das Konsekrationsmoment."

[79] Copied from Wainwright, op. cit., p. 95. For more on the Epiclesis and the Eucharist in the Jerusalem churches see André Tarby, *La Prière Eucharistique de L'Église de Jérusalem*. Paris, Beauchesne, 1972, pp. 65-68; 155-159.

[80] Some evidence suggests that the East practiced this particular act in the third century see Syrian *Didascalia* (250 C.E.), while the western witnesses first appeared in the fifth century, see also Dix, op. cit., pp. 121-122.

[81] I would place this action within the protective realm of the ritual as part of the entrance rites. In other words, the ritual guidelines had already been established prior to the actual start of the worship. The

same would be true for the West. The deacons served as a type of ritual police screening out the unworthy.

[82] The East pondered the cosmic effects of the Eucharist through this reenactment that dramatized the total aspect of the work of Christ, cf. Graß, op. cit., p. 24.

[83] Dix said "many Greek and Syrian authors, particularly from the later fourth century onwards, assign a prominent role in the eucharist to the Holy Spirit", op. cit., p. 101.

[84] Wainwright, op. cit., p. 18.

[85] Dix thinks that the origin of "the language of fear" came from the church of Anastasis at Jerusalem. Although Jerusalem did not appear to use a veil, this origin would give a much earlier origin to the apperception of fear. Cf. ibid., p. 481. Nonetheless, both East and West had solemn appreciations for the mysterious presence of Christ at the Eucharist which would account for the fear of coming into the presence of the numinous powers at work in this rite.

[86] See Dix, op. cit., p. 200.

[87] After Cyril this perception became common place in Syria, see Chrysostom's sermons.

[88] Ibid., p. 480. Certainly this axiom need not be limited to Syrian soil.

[89] Theodore, *Catecheses*, 4., see Dix p. 480.

[90] Part of the problem arose from the indiscriminate baptisms of the fourth century that included children. But this fact alone does not account for the feeling of awe and dread in the eucharistic liturgies.

[91] See Justine Ap., I,67,5; and Strathmann, Laos, TDNT, vol. IV, p. 57.

[92] Dix, op. cit., p. 480. Dix also cites here the French phrase Lois Laïques, "anti-christian", as a development of the church's use of Loas.

[93] Dix said that the "real liturgical action" was thought to be taking place behind the screen in the sixth century's eastern rites where two simultaneous services occurred, one outside the screen for the people. Ibid., p. 481.

The great architectural designs of the basilicas evidence not only the inspiration of transcendence in their structures but also show the intent of symbolically separating the people from the altar, cf., Alfred Stange, *Das Frühchristliche Kirchengebaüde als Bild des Himmels*. Köln, Comel, 1950. Stange mentions that the church architecture in the Middle Ages was based in part on the "heavenly Jerusalem", after the imagery in the last chapter of the Book of Revelation in the New Testament. He also found in the architectural relationship between heaven and earth an emphasis on design for the cult and sacraments, with the special emphasis on the Elevation in the Mass, on walls to shut out the world and on consideration for purification with water, see, pp. 8, 9, 12, 19, 21.

[94] Ibid., pp. 480-481.

[95] This doctrine came from Arius around 319 C.E. in Alexandria. The Council of Nicaea in 325 C.E. condemned Arius' doctrine and responded with the statement that the Son was "begotten not made" and also stipulated that Jesus Christ was "of one substance with the Father." The West also entered into this attack against Arianism. The East and West were in essential agreement with the doctrine "of one substance with the Father." See Davies, op. cit., pp. 70-72.

[96] Basil, *De Spiritu Sancto*, I,3; cited by Jungmann, *The Mass of the Roman Rite*, vol. I, p. 39, cf. fn. 15.

[97] Basil, *Shorter Rule*, quoted from Jungmann, ibid., p. 39.

[98] Ibid., p. 39.

⁹⁹ It was not until the ninth and eleventh centuries' that actual controversies arose over the nature of Christ's presence in the Eucharist. But in these cases the sacrificial nature of the rite was never rejected.

¹⁰⁰ Ibid., p. 12. See also the Liturgy of Saint James.

¹⁰¹ This was never quite the same for the eastern liturgies even where western influences clearly implanted themselves in the East.

¹⁰² See Graß, op. cit., p. 26.

¹⁰³ Gary Macy, *The Theologies of the Eucharist in the Early Scholastic Period.* Oxford, Clarendon Press, 1984, p. 5.

¹⁰⁴ Quoted from C. W. Dugmore, *Eucharistic Theology Then and Now.* London, S.P.C.K., 1968, p. 60. Dogmore also cited Radbertus' line that reads, "...because we daily fall, Christ is daily immolated for us mystically", p. 60.

¹⁰⁵ See Constantine N. Tsirpanlis, *The Liturgical and Mystical Theology of Nicolas Cabasilas.* New York, 1979, p. 27. "The Great Entry" and Cabasilas' writings indicate a similar pattern of preparation, union with divinity, and exit or return to the profane.

¹⁰⁶ Ibid., cf., pp. 53, 82.

¹⁰⁷ The East only recognizes these two sacraments while the Latin West has seven including Baptism and the Eucharist.

¹⁰⁸ Christianity also had a lasting impact on Neoplatonism. Many of the church fathers thought that Plato was the closest philosopher to Christianity. Justin assumed that the Greek philosophers must have gone to school with the Hebrews and the former created their truth from the teachings of Moses and the Prophets. See Robert Hotz, *Sakramente - im Wechselspiel zwischen Ost und West.* Köln, Benziger, 1979, p. 31. The East has relied on Platonism more so than the West, and one can not fully appreciate the eastern Christian tradition apart from its use of

Platonism for theological expression. Plato's "form" and "image" played key roles in the East's teaching on Baptism and the Eucharist. Note also that in post-nicene literature, after 360 C.E., the Christian Platonism of the Cappadocian Fathers gave form to Greek theology, e.g., Basil of Caesarea, Gregory of Nyssa and Gregory of Nazianzus  Edward R. Hardy, "Fathers of the Church", in *Encyclopaedia Britannica*. Chicago, William Benton, 1967, vol. IX, p. 111.

[109] See Robert Hotz, op. cit., p. 32.

[110] As alluded to previously, the context of this identification arose in contradistinction to the pagan mysteries. See Justin. In the New Testament Mustêrion referred to the apocalyptic time table (see I cor. 15:51), and the hidden plan of God in Christ (Ephesians 1:9).

[111] *Dem.Ev.*, V, 3, 19; quoted from Bornkamm, "Mustêrion", TDNT, vol. IV, p. 826.

[112] See Hotz, op. cit., pp. 27-28. Hotz also said, "Taufe und Eucharistie sind, wie übrigens auch die andern kirchlichen Heilsriten, `heilige Handlungen', eine Art Brücke zwischen Gott und Menschen. Man könnte sagen, diese heiligen Handlungen `bringen' den Menschen Gott bereits in geheimnisvoller und verhüllter Weise und `fuhren'gleichzeitig die Menschen hin zu Gott", p. 37.

[113] Bornkamm, "Mustêrion", p. 827. The consecrated elements were not empty signs for Augustine but images filled with reality. However, they represent only a lower visible reality that itself points to a higher invisible one. Here we see Augustine's Neoplatonism utilized to discuss the sacraments, see Graß, op. cit., p. 25, and Hotz, op. cit., p. 58.

[114] Augustine *Civ.D.*, 10,20, (quoted from Bornkamm, op. cit., p. 827.)

[115] Originally Sacramentum was used for a soldier's oath, meaning that there was no place for the unworthy in this noble devotion. See Bornkamm, op. cit., p. 827.

[116] The Scholastics in the Medieval West departed from the East with their interpretation of Sacramentum, ibid., p. 827.

[117] See Hotz, op. cit., p. 73. Bolle said that "the desire for concreteness and precision pushed the sacrament into a direction of magic", *Secrecy in Religions*, edited by Kees W. Bolle. Leiden, E. J. Brill, 1987, p. 11.

[118] See Hotz, op. cit., p. 57.

[119] It became a official dogma in 1215 C.E. at the Fourth Lateran Council.

[120] The Council of Jerusalem officially accepted Metabolê in 1672 C.E.

[121] See Hotz, op. cit, pp. 41-42.

[122] See Hotz, op. cit., p. 50.

[123] According to the Greek fathers Eikon meant "antitype" or a sameness, see ibid., p. 50.

[124] Ibid., pp. 58 ff.

[125] See Graß, op. cit., p. 26.

[126] Up to the twelfth century Aristotle's works had not been available in Latin in the West. The scholastics first got hold of Aristotle through the Arab philosopher Averroes (1198 C.E.) and Moses Maimonides (1204 C.E.).

[127] Ibid., p. 82. Aquinas said the perception of God was three fold: (1) The work of God in nature, (2) the similarities between Creator and the creature, and (3) the percecption of God by putting this information together piece by piece. According to Aquinas, revelation only teaches us that God is the Creator.

[128] Platonic thought rejects the possibility that consideration of the "thing's" outer form leads to the perception of the "thing." The "thing" stands in relationship to the "soul" through its unchanging spiritual nature and can therefore only be perceived through this inner contact that has been created with the soul.

[129] Ibid., p. 83.

[130] See pp. 83-86.

[131] The Franciscans meant that the institutional words were merely incidental to the determination of God to effect the change at that point in the ritual. The Dominicans agreed with the later concerning the change of the bread substance into the substance of Christ body but argued that Christ's body also remained in heaven simultaneously. See Graß, op. cit., pp. 27-28.

[132] This repetition was not a literal one for the Roman Catholics. Max Thurian noticed "The Protestants of the sixteenth century considered that the doctrine of the sacrifice of the mass impaired the uniqueness of the sacrifice of the cross for the remission of sins, and they opposed a popular heresy to the effect that Christ died for original sin while the mass is offered for present sins." *The Eucharistic Memorial*, translated by J. G. Davies. Richmond, John Knox Press, 1963, p. 85.

Dix said the notion of a "fresh sacrifice of Christ" and "His immolation again at every eucharist" was forced on the church in the late medieval period because the alternative to this "objective reality outside of the mind" was "purely mentally remembering or imagining", op. cit., p. 623.

[133] Thurian made the concession that "it is possible to speak of the Eucharist as a sacrifice within the context of the biblical conception of the memorial", ibid., p. 76.

[134] Dugmore, op. cit., p. 63.

[135] See Hubert Jedin, *Geschichte des Konzils von Trient*. Freiburg, Herder, Band II, 1970.

[136] See Hotz, op. cit., pp. 103-104. Hotz (p.107) addressing the effects of the Council of Trent on the Roman Catholic practice of the Eucharist commented:

> Die eucharistische Frömmigkeit konzentrierte sich vor allem auf die Anbetung des im Tabernakel gegenwärtigen Herrn und vernachläßigte dafür den Eucharistieempfang. Bei der hl. Messe wurde der Opfercharakter so sehr in den Vordergrund gestellt, daß dabei die kirchliche Mahlgemeinschaft nicht mehr richtig gesehen wurde. Es erfolgte sogar eine eigentliche Trennung von hl. Messe und hl. Kommunion. Und anstelle des ekklesialen Aspekts der Heilsvermittlung rückte der personale eines individualistischen Heilsemphangs völlig in den Vordergrund.

[137] See Hotz, ibid., p. 87. According to C. W. Dugmore, (op. cit., p. 65), most scholastic philosophers believed that "quantity" was a reality distinct from "substance" and "quality." The Scholastics went on to conclude that Christ was present in the Eucharist by virtue of "his quantity." The Scholastics continued to discuss questions related to the sacrificial nature of the Mass, cf. Graß, op. cit., p. 29.

[138] 1520 *Sermon on the Mass*, see ibid., p. 91.

[139] Cited by Dugmore, (op. cit., p. 66), from Roland Bainton, *Here I Stand*, New York, 1950, p. 224.

[140] Luther and Zwingli had their famous disagreement at the Colloquy of Marburg in 1529. Luther accepted Biel's position that Christ did if fact become present on the altar at the moment of consecration.

[141] Luther restricted the doctrine of sacramental presence to the administration of the sacrament, see Dugmore, op. cit., p. 67.

[142] The "elevation" had become the "high point" of the Eucharist in the Middle Ages. Luther felt this practice had continued from the Hebrew

rite's lifting up what was received with thanksgiving to God. He believed that this rite would best be left as a part of the Eucharist, otherwise its removal might harm those who had become so accustomed to its use in the liturgy. See Byran Spinks, *Luther's Liturgical Criteria And His Reform of the Canon of the Mass*. Cambridge, Grove Books, 1982, pp. 34-35.

[143] Ibid., p. 35.

[144] Cited by Dugmore, op. cit., p. 62.

[145] For a comparison between Calvin and Luther on the Lord's Supper see Alexander Barclay, *The Protestant Doctrine of the Lord's Supper*. Glasgow, Jackson, Wylie & Co., 1927, see pp. 232 ff. The problem of Calvin's disagreement with Luther sparked several letters exchanged between many leading Reformers. In the end, Calvin affirmed he was not far from Luther on his basic eucharistic doctrines.

[146] John W. Nevin, *The Mystical Presence and Other Writings on the Eucharist*. Edited by Bard Thompson and George H. Bricker (Lancaster Series on the Mercersburg Theology, vol. IV, Philadelphia, United Church Press, 1966, p. 39.

[147] See Reinhold Seeberg, *The History of Doctrines*, translated by Charles E. Hay. Grands Rapids, Baker Book House, vol. II, 1978, p. 418. Calvin argued against Peter Lombard who saw a work or material cause of salvation in the sacraments, cf. Hotz, op. cit., p. 100.

[148] Ibid., p. 418. Calvin emphasized the Holy Spirit as the link between the church and Christ in the Eucharist.

[149] See Calvin, "Short Treatise on the Holy Supper of our Lord and only Saviour Jesus Christ", in Calvin: *Theological Treatises*, edited by J. K. S. Reid (Library of Christian Classics, XXII), London, 1954, p. 166.

[150] Ibid., p. 34.

[151] I am not in any way here opting for the traditionalist school of thought on the eucharistic prayers that has sought to establish one standard outline or framework for the prayers in order to suggest or recover the lost text from which all the other prayers developed. Nor am I inclined to accept the radical dualism that the critical school applied to the origin and development of the ancient eucharistic prayers such as Lietzmann's theory of two types, e.g., as seen in the western Hippolytus (Rome) type and the eastern Sarapion (Egypt) type. See supra chapter four, "The History of New Testament Interpretation." Within the great variety of the first three centuries the eucharistic prayers show no great deviation from the major eucharistic themes. See the conclusion to this chapter.

[152] Dix thinks that this prayer goes back to the "days of the Jewish apostles at Rome." Op. cit., p. 160. The extant text of Hippoloytus-Roman prayer is a Greek reconstruction, cf. Lietzmann, op. cit., p. 142. For textual evidence cf. Burton Scott Easton, *The Apostolic Tradition of Hippolytus*. Cambridge, The University Press, 1934, pp. 28-34. The fullest text is the Ethiopian. Dix, op. cit., p. 157, said that Hippolytus' document "contains the only pre-Nicene text of a eucharistic prayer that has reached us without undergoing extensive later revisions." I am translating from the Greek text exclusively and quite literally. Brackets mean that the word has been omitted in the Greek text.

[153] We remember that Oblatio, (Greek - Prosphora), "is the `sacrifice' which the church lays on the Lord's table", see Lietzmann, op. cit., p. 147.

[154] The president of the Eucharist or the bishop/clergy said the prayers and often added his own variation to the general anaphoras. The liturgical responses and duties of the participants/laity remained largely the same in the first several centuries until their roles were limited. Hippolytus did not attempt to create a standard prayer here. Nonetheless, the basis themes are extant in all early Eucharists with different theological emphasis. For example, Hippolytus' expressed his theology of the Trinity while the eucharistic prayer of Sarapion (Egypt 340 C.E.) reveals the Logos theology of the third century. In the fourth century an

anti-Arian nomenclature began to appear in some eucharistic prayers, see Dix, op. cit., pp. 7 ff., and p. 159.

[155] Some have divided the liturgies into two parts. The first part called the "proanaphoral part" comes before the phrases referring to "lifting up our hearts." The part that follows this phrase has been called the Anaphora.

[156] Jungmann, op. cit., p. 19, fn. 60, thinks this phrase, Eucharistoumen Soi, came from the Jewish Berachah.

[157] Lucien Deiss concludes that these formulas followed the influence of Irenaeus. See, *Early Sources of the Liturgy*, translated by Benet Weatherhead. New York, Alba House, 1967, p. 39, fn. 1.

[158] Prospherein ("to present") is the Greek verb connected to the idea of sacrificing in the early liturgies. See Lietzmann, op. cit., p. 148.

[159] Katâksiosas renders the meaning of a special favor of God that allowed one to perform the sacred office of a priest while at the same time stressing the priest's own unworthiness. See Lietzmann, op. cit., p. 42.

[160] Hierateuein is a Greek term that means, "to perform the service of a priest", cf. Luke 1:8. See Schrenk, Hierateuo, TDNT, vol. III, pp. 248-251.

[161] The Greek text uses the word Thusian here, a feminine singular noun in the accusative case, "sacrifice." However, Easton's (op. cit., p. 36) translation reads, "offerings", thus obscuring the sacrificial identity of the liturgical act with Christ's own sacrifice. The two consecrated elements have become the one sacrifice of Christ. Hippolytus' prayer reveals the greatness of this mystery already in the early third century. (Dix thinks that textual evidence may place the phrase, "so that you might send down your Holy Spirit upon the sacrifice of your holy church", in the fourth century. Op. cit., p. 158. But the sacrificial theme was certainly not new to fourth century liturgies, or to the second

century for that matter. Dix also said that there is nothing in this prayer of Hippolytus that Justin sixty years earlier would have repudiated, p. 160.) Easton's deemphasis of the original sacrificial tone amounts to a deviation from the mystical nature of the rite. Ironically, Easton claimed to give a translation that followed "no text precisely" in order to represent what he felt was the "most likely original form", p. 35, fn. 1. The epiclesis appeared in all the eastern liturgies and in many in the West. It has now disappeared from the Roman rite.

[162] "When he has been consecrated bishop, let all give him the kiss of peace and acclaim him with the words: "He has become worthy"', Deiss, op. cit., p. 37.

[163] See supra, fn. 157 and 158.

[164] See supra, pp. 22-23.

[165] Quoted from Deiss, op. cit., pp. 113 ff.

[166] Scholars do not think that this was the ancient local rite used in Antioch. The liturgy of James became closely associated with the fourth century of Jerusalem and therefore shared from a tradition outside of Antioch. In any case, by the sixth century this liturgy had become the standard for the West Syrian tradition. See Dix, op. cit., pp. 176-177. The text derived from both a Greek and Syriac version.

[167] Quoted from the translation of William Macdonald, *Liturgies and Other Documents of the Ante-Nicene Period*, edited by Alexander Roberts and James Donaldson, (Ante-Nicene Christian Library: Translations of the Writings of the Fathers), Edinburgh, T. & T. Clark, 1872, see pp. 11 ff.

[168] We have evidence that some western liturgies in the ninth century did offer a lamb upon an altar together with the eucharistic elements as an elaboration of the practice of eating a lamb during the Sunday of the Pascha. Both East and West practiced eating the lamb sometime after communion on these Pascal Sundays and the sacrifice of the lamb with

the eucharistic sacrifice developed as the lamb meal was brought in closer conjunction with the Eucharist itself. See R. D. Richardson, "Eastern and Western Liturgies: The Primitive Basis of Their Latter Differences", in *The Harvard Theological Review*, Cambridge, Harvard University Press, Vol. XLII, 1949, p. 134 and fn. 20.

# EPILOGUE

Vedic fire sacrifice and the Christian Eucharist belong to a universal religious structure. The ancient symbolism that dealt with the concept of God's transcendence and immanence in the ritual gave this structure its form. If viewed independently apart from their rituals the multitude of historical and theological differences between these two religious traditions might otherwise obscure their structural similarity. For example, the mythological mediator between humans and the Indian gods, Agni, scarcely fits the redemptive scenario of Jesus Christ's mediatorship. The former functioned exclusively within the sacrificial system of Vedic religion and enabled the sacrifice to continue despite the great differences between the humans and gods. Vedic religion never made "faith" contingent upon the outcome of the sacrifice, let alone faith in Agni Prâjapati. One must perform the sacrifice in Vedic religion. Agni helped both humans and the gods overcome the numerous obstacles for a successful sacrifice. The cooperation between humans and the gods in Vedic sacrifice resulted in a re-creation of the entire cosmos, a virtual re-presentation of the first sacrifice by the gods.

Jesus Christ's sacrifice on the cross certainly engendered christological and theological ramifications of his death for the cosmos. But Christian theology never claimed that Jesus' historical death re-created the cosmos in the Vedic sense. Jesus Christ's sacrificial death and resurrection signaled the advent of God's redemption and hence renewal of his creation, clearly a spiritual re-creation.[1] The on going role of Jesus Christ extended beyond the Eucharist in the economy of God's salvation in Christian theology and focused at the same time on the future consummation of the age. According to this eschatological scheme the Eucharist will have become obsolete or rather fulfilled in heaven. Unlike later Hinduism, Vedic religion had no such future apocalyptic drama based on divine intervention that would have renewed the world outside of the sacrifice.[2]

The concept of sin also differed significantly between Vedic religion and Christianity. According to the former, sin was more specifically connected to the improper performance of the sacrifice, while Christianity saw sin primarily as a theological and inter personal problem and only secondarily as a liturgical dilemma. God's forgiveness of sins through Christ's sacrifice restored fellowship with the sinner. In Christianity, sin separates humans from a holy God who seeks fellowship with "fallen" huamnity; and in similar fashion to Vedic sacrifice, God did not compromise his transcendent holiness in restoring this relationship. Christ's sacrifice purified, cleansed, removed and forgave sin; and thus consecrated, sanctified and saved human beings for eternal fellowship with God. Christian theology fashioned this as part of the eternal plan of God in creation.

The forgiveness or removal of sin in Vedic religion always has participation in the sacrifice and a successful sacrifice as its principal goal. Beyond doubt, one performed the sacrifice in the first place because the gods' primordial sacrifice served as the paradigm for subsequent sacrifices to maintain "universal order." But one also sacrificed because along with a successful sacrifice came amenities like the protection from "evil" mishaps, birth of a healthy son, productive livestock and a fruitful harvest. Cleansing sin represented more of an actual removal of impurities rather than moral improprieties. Purification also enabled transformation of the profane so that one could come into contact with the transcendent realm to sacrifice. As we have seen, the ultimate sin in Vedic religion was simply not to sacrifice.

Outside of the sacrifice the idea of sin destroying personal fellowship with God would have been a very odd thing for the Vedic worshipper. Vedic religion understood sin primarily as the inimical forces working against the sacrifice that must be subdued through prescribed ritual action. Fellowship with God apart from faith in Jesus Christ and sacrifice not directly connected to the notion of restoring fellowship with God would be equally strange to the Christian.

Despite all the differences and distinctions between Vedic religion and Christianity we can make some correlations based on the common religious symbolization they share. This book has focused on ritual with the specific purpose of examining how each tradition handled the problem of transcendence and immanence in the context of the ritual act. Both traditions understood the ritual as bringing the two worlds together. Both made the deity's presence a central aspect of this encounter that mystically united humans and God. The Indian text advocated, "...he who offers the horse sacrifice and who thus knows it obtains intimate union with all these deities..."[3] The Christians participating in the Eucharist pondered such statements as "I am the living bread that has come down from heaven. If anyone eats of this bread he shall live forever and the bread that I shall give for the life of the world is my flesh...The one eating my flesh and drinking my blood abides in me and I in him."[4]

Sacrifice provided the basis for human beings' union with God in both cases. Without going into the mechanical distinctions between Vedic fire sacrifice and the Eucharist again, we noted that the ritual's symbolism had common features in each. Both expressed the distance or distinction between the profane world and the sacred as part of the absolute difference between human sinfulness and God's holiness. Sacrifice illustrated this contrast between sin and holiness by three basic successive actions in the ritual; namely, preparation or consecration of the profane, transformation of the profane during the actual encounter between mortals and God thus attaining the ritual's highest point of sanctity, and the exit or return to the profane. Both traditions symbolically depicted the movement between the altar on earth and in heaven. The act of descending to earth and ascending to heaven or gestures of raising the eyes, sacrificial elements and voices towards heaven, likewise symbolized the convergence and temporary union between both worlds. The use of mediators that functioned symbolically as both the sacrificial victim and the sacrificer or host represented the difficulty of bringing the two worlds together. The symbolic architecture of the sacrificial complex and basilica also played a part in portraying the separation and sacrificial link between the two realms.

But for all the effort exerted in the ritual to bring the two worlds together, neither tradition forfeited God's transcendent holiness. By solving the problem of God's transcendence the sacrifice created the additional problem of God's presence in the profane realm. Theologically this meant the problem of nondifferentiation between human beings and God, the threat of blending the profane and sacred together, and the end of sacrifice. The sacrifice symbolized the problem of God's immanence by the laborious preparatory rites the sacrificer had to perform as one encountered the ritual's sacred boundaries. Before each step in the "ascent" to the altar the ritual demanded a proper act correlated to the cosmic directions and sacrificial code. The Eucharist also required ritual scrutiny as the participants approached the high point in the Mass, the presence or consecration of the elements. This symbolic movement upwards or inward to the most holy places represented a growing danger for the sacrificer or communicant.

The ritual could overcome the problems of bringing sinful humans and a holy God together as each tradition required, but not without casting an ambivalent shadow over the entire proceedings. The danger of drawing near to the "altogether other" served to demonstrate the continuing difference between the two in the ritual act. This distinction continued after the actual high point of the ceremony when the ritual extended its protective control over the profane realm. That which had come into contact with the sacred had to be returned to the profane and this act thereby re-established God's transcendent holiness and the perpetual need to sacrifice.

Our comparison has shown that sacrifice always involved bringing the two worlds together and the consecration or transformation of the profane. Otherwise no such union would be possible. This union was always temporary in the full sense of humans and God coming into contact through a victim or offering that had been consecrated. Thomas Aquinas' definition of sacrifice fits this scheme well. He said "A true sacrifice is any act that is done in order that we may cleave in an holy union to God."[5]

Again, the dichotomy between transcendence and immanence in the ritual is not the only nor best way to examine sacrifice. I have attempted to include religious symbolism as one of the central aspects of Vedic sacrifice and the Eucharist. This approach has been similar to Joachim Wach's suggestion that we can identify "universals in religion" when sifting through the masses of materials deposited by "geography, anthropology, sociology, archaeology, philology, history, and the history of religions."[6] Wach specifically addressed "religious experiences" that help us identify universals in religion. He listed the following four categories of religious experiences. According to Wach: "1. Religious experience is a response to what is experienced as ultimate reality." "2. Religious experience is a total response of the total being to what is apprehended as ultimate reality." "3. Religious experience is the most intense experience of which man is capable." "4. Religious experience is practical, that is to say it involves an imperative, a commitment which impels man to act."[7]

All four of Wach's categorizations of religious experience relate to Vedic religion and Christianity. But his fourth best applies to our investigation of the Indian and Christian rituals. In other words, the simple fact that the emphasis remains on the symbolic act. Yet too often serious consideration of the ritual act itself in both Vedic sacrifice and the Eucharist has been avoided by labeling it as magical, or by psychological explanations that reduce ritual to some type of puerilism. Under the guise of a more scientific and objective methodology this very thing continues today.

But how far should our quest for "objectivity" lead us? For example, what should be done with critics, such as the deconstructionalist Jean François Lyotard, who now advocate that narrative no longer facilitates valid information and epistemology. Lyotard argues for the scientific experiment as the legitimate, non-abstract paradigm of logic that does not create its own rules out of "self legitimization." Lyotard says that narrative's self legitimization serves only to heap up more language "metanarrative."[8]

If we were to submit to Lyotard's new method of epistemology, then religious ritual might easily be viewed as a type of scientific experiment. Both Vedic fire sacrifice and the Eucharist could stand apart from traditional narrative with a full range of controlled procedures for our observation. Eventually we would have to come back to the humble realization that religious ritual also participates in the irrational by virtue of the perceived "transcendent." Therefore religious ritual will always leave something outside of the realm of objective epistemology and deeply imbedded in the experience of transcendent mysteries. Because of this irrational factor, Wach's types of religious experiences remain valid if not saving for part of the descriptive task.

The transcendence and immanence paradigm for Vedic fire sacrifice and the Eucharist also relates in part to C. G. Jung's work on the psychology of religions in the East and West, which dealt specifically with the Eucharist (Messe).[9] Jung saw the Eucharist as both a symbol of one's perception of the transcendent, otherworldly and a legitimate object for psychological and analytical research.[10] The psychological connection or the collective aspect of the unconscious allowed Jung to launch the Eucharist in his universal sea of religious symbols. Jung found the human psyche expressing itself symbolically in dreams, rituals and writings from both eastern and western religions.[11] According to Jung, a symbol could not be fully known in human terms because the mysteries it contains surpass one's intellect.[12] Thus he designated the Eucharist as a ritual that conformed to this type of symbolic paradigm.

Jung's universal symbolic characterization of the Eucharist in psychological terms did not prevent him from recognizing this rite's specific historical and theological aspects. For example, Jung recognized from his historical research the importance of consecration in the Eucharist and the notion of God's presence. He even constructed a structure of the Eucharist that included a before and after "mass" with the "oblation," "consecration," and "communion" respectively in between the two.[13] Jung suggested that the eucharistic sacrifice was continually offered because of God's transcendence.[14] Christ functioned as both the "sacrifice" and "sacrificer" in the Eucharist, according to Jung,[15] a ritual that had both a human and divine side. Jung went on to specify that even the human side was in actuality a mere "outer shell" in which no human but only a divine act occurred.[16] In this way Jung acknowledged the protective symbolism built into the ritual that covered both sides of the act.

No doubt Jung owed many of his basic insights on religious symbolism to Rudolf Otto, Eliade, and William James, not to mention his indebtedness to the early church fathers for much of his material on the Eucharist. But Jung's application of the universal connection between the Eucharist and other forms of religious symbolization, especially ritual, adds credence to the discernible structure he was able to discover from a predominately psychological perspective. Additionally, Jung's approach did not suffer from a reticence to include the concept of transcendence as germane to the Eucharist's symbolization. Transcendence existed in the mind for Jung so it neither posed a scientific embarrassment nor a hermeneutical problem for his work. He could simply discuss the concept of transcendence as a reality of the mind's symbolism in much the same way that the historian of religions begins with the given symbolization of religious texts, acts, places and artifacts.

Beyond the descriptive and hermeneutical task of this comparison between Vedic sacrifice and the Eucharist lies yet another model for the "christian West." In their reverence for the sacrifice's "universal order," the ancient Indians instilled a poignant lesson on the necessity of cosmic responsibility and cooperation for the sustenance and maintenance of all life. At the same time we have seen that sacrifice expressed the mystery and wonder of God's transcendence and the religious desire to be linked to the "wholly other" in a way that equals any theological expression of transcendence in the West. Ritual did not diminish the concept of God's transcendence nor preclude soaring philosophical speculations in India. In fact ritual had the opposite effect in the far East. Sacrifice in ancient India preserved the mystical, irrational experience of the altogether different realm.

The differences between Roman Catholics, Eastern Orthodox, and Protestants concerning the Eucharist should be expected and welcomed in some respects. The dissimilarities have arisen in the mist of a greater symbolic structure based on God's transcendent holiness and the sinner's need to commune with God. Each expresses certain aspects of the Eucharist that together represent a more complete symbolism of the many dimensions of this ritual. The Eastern Orthodox continues to emphasize the mysterious presence of Christ through the Holy Spirit and the strict boundaries between this world and the transcendent reality on the altar. The Protestants have opted to avoid any danger of "misappropriating" God's grace through receiving the eucharistic sacraments by emphasizing the "sacrament of the Word." The immediate and lasting result of Protestantism's more rational approach to the Eucharist has removed many of its symbolic acts and sacrificial symbolism, because the New Testament did not corroborate much of what the Roman Catholics had retained from the eucharistic traditions as far back as Hippolytus. The Protestants have preserved a more biblical characterization of Paul's teaching on the grace of God through faith in Christ, while the Roman and Eastern Orthodox Churches' have better preserved the mystery of Christ's presence and the communicants mystical union with God in the ritual act. By relinquishing the mystery of the ritual act Protestants have also lost something of God's transcendence and immanence experienced in the eucharistic sacraments. C. Traets stated it this way:

> Not only the evocative but also the demanding character of the sacramental event involves us with our entire personality and our entire world in the mystery that embraces us, the mystery from which we live and toward which we are directed, the mystery we call God. But this God, who reveals Himself in His nearness in and through our human world, is not reduced to this revelation. He remains - also in His approach to us -the totally Other. God lets Himself be known

> in and through the symbol, but not in an unmediated manner. This implies, as far as our sacramental experience is concerned, that we can never get a grip on God, not even through the specific words and gestures that we call sacraments.[17]

As long as symbols of Christ's presence and sacrifice remain in the context of the ritual act, the Eucharist shall continue to provide access to the church's greatest mystery for all Christians. Outside of the ritual the eucharistic sacraments have become the objects of theological speculation for a few doctors of the faith.

The lack of the mysterious element in Protestant worship has not been the only symptom of a culture disinclined toward the value of ritual. Part of western, modern secular society's spiritual poverty surfaced in the religious dreams of Jung's "non-religious" patients. But the general disdain for religious ritual in the West as "irrational" or "primitive" also has something to do with our own inability to seek to understand those cultures that continue to practice religious rituals. Buddhist monks who set themselves on fire and religious "extremists" who use violence in the name of God not only represent a particular religious understanding of the world but also reveal a greater emphasis on the religious act as a necessity that makes a "real" difference in this world. It has little to do with what corresponds with acceptable social behavior or morality and everything to do with acting in accordance with the transcendent paradigm. Thus, its a matter of ultimate reality and truth, a religious matter that human beings will never have access to unless we begin to understand the religious symbolism behind the rest of the world.

## ENDNOTES TO EPILOGUE

[1] *II Corinthians* 5:17 reads, "hoste ei tis en christo, kainâ ktisis. ta archaîa parâlthen, idou gegonen kaina," (If anyone is in Christ he is a new creation. The old has passed away, the new has come into being). Also according to Paul in Romans 8:19 "all of creation eagerly awaits for the revelation of the sons of God." But this eschatological hope for creation itself does not find fulfillment in the completion of a successful performance of the Eucharist.

[2] Later the *Mahâbhârata* described the end of the world and the emergence of a new one after the great battle between the Devas and Asuras. Indo-European eschatological wars that preceded Hinduism have been well documented by G. Dumézil and others. We find no Vedic myth that corresponds to the Christian return of Christ at the end of time.

[3] TB 3.9.20.

[4] John 6:51, 56. I am in agreement with Raymond Brown, (See *The Gospel According to John*. The Anchor Bible, Garden City, Doubleday & Company, Inc., vol. 29A, 1978, pp. 272 ff) who takes verses 35-58 in the discourse on "the bread of life" to refer both to revelation and the eucharistic flesh of Jesus Christ.

[5] See Augstine, *The City of God*, X, 6.

[6] Joachim Wach, *Types of Religious Experience Christian and Non-Christian*. Chicago, University of Chicago Press, 1951, see chapter two.

[7] Ibid., pp. 32-33.

[8] See Jean-François Lyotard, *The Postmodern Condition*, translated by Fredric Jameson. Minneapolis, The University of Minnesota Press, 1984.

[9] See C. G. Jung, *Zur Psychologie westlicher und Östlicher Religion*, in *Gesammelte Werke*. ZÜrich, Rascher Verlag, vol. 11, 1963.

[10] Ibid., p. 225.

[11] See Jung's examples, the dream of the consecrated house, pp. 37 ff. ; the Aztec's sacrifice, pp. 244 ff; and the third century gnostic alchemist Zosimos of Panopolis, pp. 246 ff.

[12] Ibid., pp. 225 ff. Jung also understood the limitations of scientific research when it came to irrational religious matters as well as the difference between myth and science, cf. pp. 37 ff. ,pp. 328 ff. However, he did not ultimately differentiate between a religious symbol and the symbolic function of the human psyche. Thus a religious symbol originated as the extension or "individuation" of the unconscious and consequently became one of the elements of the dreams, even of non-religious moderns. For Jung, religious expressions represented an immediate experience of the numinous, a type of "living mythologem," see p. 328. Natural science could not discern this with its empirical basis of investigation. But Jung's psycho-analysis continues to push religious phenomena so far back into the unconscious that one wonders how the conscious mind rationally organized its religious experiences in the empirical world. This same type of problem haunted R. Otto's "altogether different" concept of the holy. I have suggested that this paradigm works best within the context of the ritual act and should be used with caution in the study of religious phenomena in everyday life where the two often blend together.

[13] Ibid., pp. 222 ff.

[14] Ibid., p. 224.

[15] Ibid., p. 225.

[16] Ibid., p. 271.

[17] C. Traets, "Abide With Me, God's Nearness and Activity in and Through the Sacraments," in *Questions Liturgiques*, 1978, vol. 1 - 2, pp. 6,7.

# BIBLIOGRAPHY

Abba, R. "Expiation." *The Interpreter's Dictionary of the Bible*. 4 vols. Edited by George Arthur Buttrick. New York: Abingdon Press, 1962.

Aguilar, H. *The Sacrifice in the Rgveda*. Delhi: Bhartiya Vidya Prakashan, 1976.

Anderson, Gary A. "Sacrifice and Sacrificial Offerings (OT)." David Noel Freedman, editor in chief, *The Anchor Bible Dictionary*, vol. 5, New York, Doubleday,1992.

Angus. S. *The Mystery-Religions and Christianity*. New York: Charles Scribners Sons, 1928.

Augustine of Hippo. *The City of God*. Library of Christian Classics. Edited by J.Baillie, et al., 1953.

Aurobindo, Sri. *On the Veda*, vol. 5. Pondicherry: Ashram, 1956.

Bainton, Roland. *Here I Stand*. New York: Abingdon Press, 1950.

Baird, W. "Myth in the New Testament." *I.D.B.* Supplemental volume, 1976.

Barclay, Alexander. *The Protestant Doctrine of the Lord's Supper*. Glasgow: Jackson, Wylie and Company, 1927.

Barrett, C. K. *The New Testament Background: Selected Documents*. New York:Harper and Row, Publishers, 1961.

Barrios, G. A. "Temples." *I.D.B.* Vol. 4, 1962.

Bartchy, S. Scott. "Table Fellowship with Jesus and the Lord's Meal at Corinth." *Increase in Learning: Essays in Honor of James G.*

Van Buren. Edited by Owens, and Hamm. Manhattan Christian College, Manhattan, Kansas, 1979.

Bartchy, S.S. "Table Fellowship." *Dictionary of Jesus and the Gospels.* Editors: Joel Green et. al.. InterVarsity Press, Downers Grove, Illinois, 1992.

Barth, Karl. *Church Dogmatics.* Vol. 3. Part 2. Translated by Harold Knight, et al. Edited by G. W. Bromiley. Edinburgh: T & T Clark, 1975.

Barth, Marcus. *Rediscovering the Lord's Supper.* Richmond: John Knox Press, 1987.

Basham, A. L. "Hinduism." *The Concise Encyclopedia of Living Faiths.* Edited by R. C. Zaehner. Boston: Beacon Press, 1959.

Bauer, Walter. *A Greek-English Lexicon of the New Testament and Other Early Christian Literature.* 2nd. ed. Translated by William F. Arndt and F. Wilbur Gingrich. Edited by F. Wilbur Gingrich and Fredrich Danker. Chicago: The University of Chicago Press, 1979.

Baumgarten, Joseph M. "Sacrifice and Worship Among the Jewish Sectarians of the Dead Sea (Qumran) Scrolls." *Harvard Theological Review* 45(1952):148.

Becker, Joachim. *Messianic Expectations in the Old Testament.* Translated by David E. Green. Philadelphia: Fortress Press, 1980.

Behm, Johannes. "Thusia." *Theological Dictionary of the New Testament.* Vol. 3. Edited by Gerhard Kittel. Translated by Geoffrey W. Bromiley. Grand Rapids: William B. Eerdmans Publishing Company, 1976.

Bell, Catherine. *Ritual Theory Ritual Practice.* New York, Oxford University Press, 1992.

Benoit, A. "Les mystères païens et le Christianisme." *Mystères et Syncrétismes*. Paris: Librairie Orientaliste Paul Geuthner, 1975.

Bergaigne, Able. *Vedic Religion*. Translated by V. G. Paranjpe. Delhi: Motilar Banarsidass, 1978.

Bertram, George. "Sin in the Old Testament." *T.D.N.T.* Vol. 1, 1976.

Bettenson, Henry, ed. *Documents of the Christian Church*. London:Oxford University Press, 1963.

Betz, O. "Essenes." *I.D.B.* Supplementary volume, 1976.

Biardeau, Madelaine, and Malamoud, Charles. *Le Sacrifice dans L'Inde Ancienne*. Paris: Presses Universitaires de France, 1976.

Bodewitz, H. W. *Jaiminiya Brâhmana*. Leiden: E. J. Brill, 1973. *The Daily Evening and Morning Offering (Agnihotra) According to the Brâhmanas*. Leiden: E. J. Brill, 1976.

Bolle, Kees W. "A World of Sacrifice." *History of Religions* 23(1983):37-63.

_____. "Animism." *The Encyclopedia of Religion*. vol. 1. Edited by Mircea Eliada. New York: Macmillan Publishing Company, 1987.

_____. *The Bhagavadgîtâ: A New Translation*. Berkely: The University of California Press, 1979.

_____. *The Freedom of Man in Myth*. Nashville: Vanderbuilt University Press, 1993.

_____."Imagining Ritual", Review Article in the *History of Religions*, Nov. 90, Vol.30,Number 2, p. 204-212.

_____. "Myth." *The Encyclopedia of Religion*. vol. 10. Edited by Mircea Eliada. New York: Macmillan Publishing Company, 1987.

Bolle, K. "Wendy Doniger In Retrospect." *Religious Studies Review*, no. 10 (1984), pp. 23 ff.

Bornkamm, Gunther. *Jesus of Nazareth*. Translated by Irene and Fraser McLuskey with James M. Robinson. New York: Harper and Row Publishers, 1960.

*Eucharistic Prayer from Oral Improvisation to Written Texts.*

Bouley, Allan. *From Freedom to Formula: The Evolution of the* Washington D.C.: The Catholic University of America Press, 1981.

Braun, Herbert. *Jesus of Nazareth: The Man and His Time.* Philadelphia: Fortress Press, 1979.

Bright, John. "Modern Study of Old Testament Literature." *The Bible and Ancient Near East*. Edited by G. E. Wright. Garden City, New York: Doubleday and Company, Inc., 1961.

Brown, Raymond. *The Gospel According to John*. The Anchor Bible. Edited by Willian F. Albright. New York: Doubleday and Company, Inc., 1979.

Buchsel, Hermann. "Hilaskomai-hilasmos." *T.D.N.T.* Vol. 3, 1976.

Bultmann, Rudolf. *Jesus Christ and Mythology*. New York: Charles Scribners Sons, 1958.

_____. *History of the Synoptic Tradition*. Translated by John Marsh. New York: Harper and Row, Publishers, 1976.

_____. *Theology of the New Testament*. vol. 1. Translated by Kendrick Grobel. New York: Charles Scribners Sons, 1955.

Burkert, Walter. *Homo Necans: Interpretationen altgriechischer Opferriten und Mythen,* Berlin, 1972.

_____. "The Problem of Ritual Killing." *Violent Origins*, edited by Robert G. Hamerton-Kelly. Stnaford, Stanford University Press, 1987.

Cadmann, W. H. *The Christian Pascha and the Day of the Crucifixion Nisan 14 or 15 ?* In Studia Patristica. Vol. 5. Edited by F. L. Cross. Berlin: Akademie-Verlag, 1962.

Calvin, John. "Short Treatise on the Holy Supper of our Lord and only Saviour Jesus Christ." *Calvin: Theological Treatise.* vol. 22. Edited by J. K. S. Reid. London: Library of Christian Classics.

Clements, R. E. et al. *Eucharistic Theology Then and Now.* no. 9. London: S. P. C. K. 1968.

Conzelmann, Hans. *History of Primitive Christianity.* Translated by John E. Steely. Nashville: Abingdon Press, 1973.

Cook, M. J. "Hellenistic Judaism." *I.D.B.* Supplementary volume, 1976.

Cornford, Francis MacDonald, trans. *The Republic of Plato.* New York: Oxford University Press, 1945.

Crossan, John Dominic. *The Historical Jesus.* San Francisco, Harper San Francisco, 1991.

Cullmann, Oscar, and Leenhardt, F. J. *Essays on the Lord's Supper.* Richmond: John Knox Press, 1958.

Davies, J. G. "Christianity: The Early Church." *The Concise Encyclopedia of the Living Faiths.* Edited by R. C. Zaehner. Boston: Beacon Press, 1959.

Davies, W. D. *The Scrolls and the New Testament.* Edited by Krister Stendahl. New York: Harper and Brothers Publishers, 1957.

Deiss, Lucien. *Early Sources of the Liturgy.* Translated by Benet Weatherhead. New York: Alba House, 1967.

Delorme, J., et al. *The Eucharist in the New Testament: A Symposium.* Translated by E. M. Stewart. Baltimore: Helicon Press, 1964.Dix, Gregory. *The Shape of the Liturgy.* Westminster: Dacre Press, 1945.

Dodd, C. H. *The Old Testament in the New.* Facet Books Biblical Series, no. 3. Edited by John Reumann. Philadelphia: Fortress Press, 1963.

Douglas, Mary. "Deciphering a Meal." *Myth, Symbol, and Culture.* Edited by C. Geertz. New York: Norton, 1972.

_____. *Purity and Danger: An Analysis of Concepts of Pollution and Taboo.* London: Routledge and Kegan Paul, 1966.

Drury, Naama. *The Sacrificial Ritual in the Shatapatha Brâhmana.* Delhi: Shri Jainendra Press, 1981.

Dugmore, C. W. *Eucharistic Theology Then and Now.* London: S. P. C. K., 1968.

Dumézil, Georges. *Rituals indo-européens a Rome.* Paris: Libraire C. Klinksieck, 1954.

Dumont, P. E. *L'Asvamedha: Description du sacrifice sonennel du dans le culte védique.* Paris: Paul Geuthner, 1927.

_____. "The Horse-Sacrifice in the *Taittirîya-Brâhmana,*" *Proceedings of the American Philosophical Society,* vol. 92, pp. 447-503.

Easton, Burton Scott. *The Apostolic Tradition of* Hippolytus. Cambridge: The University Press, 1934.

Eggeling, Julius, trans. *Shatapatha Brâhmana* in the *Sacred Books of the East*. Vol. 44. Edited by F. Max MÜller. Oxford: Clarendon Press, 1894.

Elert, Werner. *Eucharist and Church Fellowship in the First Four Centuries*. Translated by N. E. Nagel. Saint Louis: Concordia Publishing House, 1966.

Eliade, Mircea. "History of Religions and a New Humanism." *History of Religions*, 1(1961):6.

_____. *History of Religious Ideas*. Vol. 1. Translated by Willard R. Trask. Chicago: The University of Chicago Press, 1978.

_____. *Patterns in Comparative Religion*. Translated by Rosemary Sheed. New York: Meridian, 1958.

_____. *The Sacred and the Profane*. Translated by Willard R. Trask. New York: Harper and Row Publishers.

Feeley-Harnik, Gillian. *The Lord's Table: Eucharist and Passover in Early Christianity*. Philadelphia: University of Pennsylvania Press, 1981.

Fitzmyer, Joseph A. *The Gospel According to Luke* in The Anchor Bible. vol. 2. Edited by William F. Albright. Garden City: Doubleday and Company, Inc., 1985.

Frank, Karl Suso. *Das Opfer Jesu christi und seine Gegenwart in der Kirche*. Edited by K. Lehmann and E. Schlink. Gottingen: Herder Freiburg im Breisgau, 1983.

Frazer, Sir James G. *The Golden Bough*. New York: The Macmillan Company, 1922.

Gager, John G. *Kingdom and Community*. Englewood Cliffs: Prentice Hall, Inc., 1975.

Gamber, Klaus. *Sacrificium Laudis*: *Studia Patristica et Liturgica*. Fasc. 5. Regensburg: Friedrich Pustet, 1973.

_____. *Sacrificium Vespertinum*: *Studia Patristica et Liturgica*. Fasc. 12. Regensburg: Friedrich Pustet, 1973.

Gaster, Theodor H. "Sacrifices and Offerings, OT." *I.D.B.* vol. 4, 1962.

_____. trans. *The Dead Sea Scriptures*. Garden City, New York: Doubleday and Company, Inc., 1956.

Girard, Rene. *Violence and the Sacred*. Translated by Patrick Gregory. Baltimore, The John Hopkins University Press, 1972.

Gonda, Jan. *A History of Indian Literature*. 2 vols. Leiden: E. J. Brill, 1975.

_____. *Change and Continuity in Indian Religion*. London: Mouton and Company, 1965.

_____. *Die Religionen Indiens*. Vol. 1. Stuttgart: W. Kohlhammer, 1960.

_____. *Hymns of the Rgveda not Employed in the Solemn Ritual*. Amstredam: North-Holland Publishing Company, 1978.

_____. "The Sacred Character of Ancient Kingship." *La Regalita Sacra: Contributions to the Central Theme of the VIIth International Congress for the History of Religions*. Leiden: E. J. Brill, 1969.

_____. *The Haviryajñâh Somâh*. Amsterdam: North-Holland Publishing Company, 1980.

_____. *Vedic Literature*. 2 vols. Wiesbaden: Otto Harrassowitz, 1975.

Gonda. *Vedic Ritual: The Non-Solomn Rites*. Leiden: E. J. Brill, 1980.

Gosha, Ramachandra. *A Brief Survey of Ancient Sanskrit Literature.* New Delhi: Classical Publications, 1977.

Graß, H. "Abendmahl." *RGG.* Vol. 1. 3rd ed. Tubingen: J. C. B. Mohr, 1960.

Gray, George B. *Sacrifice in the Old Testament.* Prolegomenon by Baruch A. Levine. New York: KTAV Publishing House,Inc., 1971.

Guthrie, W. K. C. *The Greeks and Their Gods.* Boston: Beacon Press, 1955.

Haenchen, Ernst. *Der Weg Jesu.* Berlin: Alfred Topelmann, 1966.

Hahn, Ferdinand. "Das Verständnis des Opfers im Neuen Testament." *Das Opfer Jesu Christi und seine Gegenwart in der Kirche.* Edited by Karl Lehmann and Edmund Schlink. Göttingen: Herder, 1983.

Hanson, Paul. *The Dawn of the Apocalyptic.* Philadelphia: Fortress Press, 1979.

Hardy, Edward R. "Fathers of the Church." *Encyclopedia Britannica.* vol. 9. Chicago: William Benton, 1967.

Hawkes, Terence. *Structuralism and Semiotics.* Berkley and Los Angeles: The University of California Press, 1977.

Hecht, Richard David. "Sacrifice, Comparative Study and Interpretation." Ph.D. dissertation, University of California, Los Angeles, 1976.

Heesterman, J. C. *The Inner Conflict of Tradition.* Chicago: The University of Chicago Press, 1985.

Heesterman. *The Broken World of Sacrifice.* Chicago, University of Chicago Press, 1993.

Hengel, Martin. *Judaism and Hellenism*. Translated by John Bowden. Philadelphia: Fortress Press, 1974.

Henninger, Joseph. "Sacrifice." *The Encyclopedia of Religion*. vol. 12. Editor in chief, Mircea Eliade. Translated from German by Matthew J. O'Connell. New York: Macmillan and Company, 1987.

Higgens, A. J. B. *The Lord's Supper in the New Testament*. London: SCM Press, Limited, 1972.

Hillebrant, Alfred. "Ritual-Literatur Vedishe Opfer und Zauber." *Grundiss der Indo-Arischen Philogie und Altertumskunde*, vol.3, no. 2. Edited by G. Bühler. Strassburg: Verlag von Karl J. Trübner, 1897.

_____. *Vedic Mythology*. 2 vols. Translated by Sreeramula Rajeswara Sarma. Delhi: Motilal Banarsidass, 1981.

Hopkins, T. *The Hindu Religious Tradition*. Belmont: Wadsworth Publishing Company, 1971.

Horsely, R. *Bandits, Prophets and Messiahs*. Berkley: Harvest Press, 1988.

_____. *Jesus and the Spiral of Violence*. New York: Harper and Row Publishers, 1987.

Hubert, Henri and Mauss, Marcel. *Sacrifice: Its Nature and Function*. Translated by W. D. Hollis. Chicago: University of Chicago Press, 1964.

Jaeger, Werner. *Early Christianity and Greek Paideia*. New York: Oxford University Press, 1961.

James, E. O. *Myth and Ritual in the Ancient Near East*. London: Thames and Hudson, 1958.

Jaubert, Anne. *La Date De La Cene*. Paris: Librairie Lecoffre, 1957.

_____. "The Date of the Passover." *New Testament Studies* 1 (1960):1-30.

Jedin, Hubert. *Geschichte des Konzils von Trient*. vol. 2. Freisburg: Herder, 1970.

Jeremias, Joachim. *The Eucharistic Words of Jesus*. Philadelphia: Fortress Press, 1966.

Johanny, Raymond. *The Eucharist of the Early Christians*. Translated by Matthew J. O'Connell. New York: Pueblo Publishing Company, 1978.

Johansson, J. F. "Dhisanâ." *Äber die altindische Götten Dhesanâ und Verwandtes*. Uppsala, 1919.

Jung, C. G. *Zur Psychologie westlicher und östlicher Religion* in *Gesammelte Werke*. Vol. 11. Zürich: Rascher Verlag, 1963.

Jungmann, Joseph A. *The Early Liturgy to the Time of Gregory the Great*. Translated by Francis A. Brunner. Indiana: University of Notre Dame Press, 1959.

_____. *The Mass of the Roman Rite: Its Origins and Development*. 2 vols. Translated by Francis A. Brunner. Westminster, Maryland: Christian Classics, Inc., 1986.

Kähler, Martin. *The So-called Historical Jesus and the Historic Biblical Christ*. Translated by Carl E. Brasten. Philadelphia: Fortress Press, 1964.

Käsemann, Ernst. *Commentary on Romans*. Translated by Geoffrey W. Bromiley. Grand Rapids: Eerdmans Publishing Company, 1980.

Keith, A. B. *The Religion and Philosophy of the Veda and Upanishads*, vol. 31 in the *Havard Oriental Series*. Edited by Charles Rockwell Lanman. Cambridge: Harvard University Press, 1925.

_____. *The Veda of the Black Yajus School*, vol. 18 in the *Harvard Oriental Series*. Edited by Charles Rockwell Lanman. Cambridge: Harvard university Press, 1914.

Kirber, E. "Opfer." *Die Religion in Geschichte und Gegenwart*. 3rd ed. vol. 4. Edited by Hans von Campenhausen. Tübingen: J. C. B. Mohr, 1960.

Kitagawa, Joseph M., ed. "Cultural Fashions and the History of Religions." *The History of Religions: Essays on the Problem of* Understanding. Collaberation of Mircea Eliade and Charles H. Long. Chicago: University of Chicago Press, 1967.

Klijn, A. F. J. *The Acts of Thomas*. Supplements to *Novum Testamentum*. vol. 5. Leiden: E. J. Brill, 1962.

Krick, Herta. *Das Ritual der Feuergründung*, vol. 399, no. 16. Edited by G. Oberhammer. Wien Verlag: Der Österreichischen Akademie der Wissenshaften, 1982.

Ladd, George. *The New Testament and Criticism*. Grand Rapids: William B. Eerdmans Publishing Company, 1978.

Lake, Kirsopp, trans. *The Apostolic Fathers*. The Loeb Classical Library. 2 vols. Cambridge: Harvard University Press, 1959.

Lampe, G. W. H. *Eucharistic Theology Then and Now*. London: S.P.C.K., 1968.

Lampe, G. "The Eucharist in the Thought of the Early Church." London: S.P.C.K., 1968.

Lang, Friedrich. "Fire." *T.D.N.T.* Vol. 6. Edited by Gerhard Kittel and Gerhard Friedrich. Translated by Geoffrey W. Bromiley. Grand Rapids: William B. Eerdmans Company, 1976.

La Sor, William S. *The Dead Sea Scrolls and the New Testament.* Grand Rapids: William B. Eerdmans Publishing company,1972.

Leenhart, F. J. *Le Sacrement de la sainte Cene.* Paris: Neuchâtel, 1948.

Leeuw, Gerardus van der. *Der Mench und Die Religion.* Basel: Haus zum Falken, 1941.

_____. *Religion in Essence and Manifestation.* 2 vols. Translated by J. E. Turner. Gloucester, Massachusettes: Peter Smith, 1967.

Lefever, H. *The Vedic Idea of Sin.* Nagercoil: London Missionary Press, 1935.

Lemke, Werner E. "The Near and the Distant God." *Journal of Biblical Literature* 100(1981):541.

Léon-Dufour, Xavier. *Le partage du pain eucharistique selon le Nouveau Testament.* Paris: Editions du Seuil, 1982.

Lévi-Strauss, Claude. *Structural Anthropology.* Garden City, New York: Doubleday and Company, 1963.

Lévi, Sylvain. *La Doctrine du Sacrifice dans le Brâhmanas.* Edited by Ernest Leroux. Paris: Bibliotheque de L'Ecole des Hautes Etudies - Sciences Relieuses, 1898.

Levy-Bruhl, Lucien. *Primitive Mentality.* Translated by Lilian A. Clare. New York: Macmillan and Company, 1923.

Lietzmann, Hans. *Mass and Lord's Supper* in 10 Fascicles. Translated by Dorthea H. Reeve. Introduction and Supplementary Essay by Robert D. Richardson. Leiden: E. J. Brill, 1976.

Littleton, C. Scott. *The New Comparative Mythology: An Anthropological Assessment of the Theories of Georges Dumézil*. Berkley and Los Angeles: University of California Press, 1966.

Lockton, W. *The Treatment of the Remains at the Eucharist After Holy Communion and the Time of the Abolutions*. Cambridge: Cambridge University Press, 1920.

Lohmeyer, Ernst. "Vom urchristlichen Abendmahl." *Theological Rundschau* 9(1937).

———. "Vom urchristlichen Abendmahl." *Theological Rundschau* 10(1938).

Löwith, Karl. *Meaning in History*. Chicago: The University of Chicago Press, 1949.

Lyonnet, Stanaslas. *Sin, Redemption, and Sacrifice*. Rome: Biblical Institute Press, 1970.

Lyotard, Jean-François. *The Postmodern Condition*. Translated by Frederic Jameson. Minneapolis: The University of Minnesota Press, 1984.

Macdonnell, A. A. *A Practical Sanskrit Dictionary*. Oxford: Oxford University Press, reprinted 1979.

Macy, Gary. *The Theologies of the Eucharist in the Early Scholastic Period*. Oxford: Oxford University Press, 1984.

Mann, C. S. *Mask* in the Anchor Bible. vol. 27. Edited by William F. Albright. Garden City: Doubleday and Company, Inc. 1986.

Marshall, Howard. *Last Supper and Lord's Supper*. Grand Rapids: William B. Eerdmans Publishing Company, 1980.

Meier, John P. *A Marginal Jew*, vol. I. New York, Doubleday, 1991.

Metzger, Bruce M. *A Textual Commentary on the Greek New Testament*. 3rd ed. London: United Bible Societies, 1971.

_____. *The Text of the New Testament*. New York: Oxford University Press, 1968.

_____. *The Greek New Testament*, ed. by Bruce Metzger et al., third edition. Münster: United Bible Societies, 1975.

Metzger, Marcel. *The Eucharist of the Early Christians*. translated by Matthew J. O'Connell. New York: Pueblo Publishing Company, 1976.

Meyer, J. J. "Trilogie." *Trilogie altindischer Mächte und Feste der Vegitation*. Zurich: Leipzig, 1937.

Milgrom, J. "Atonement in the OT." *I.D.B.* Supplementary volume, 1976.

Miller, Jeanine. *The Vision Cosmic Order in the Vedas*. London: Routledge and Kegan Paul, 1985.

Moeller, E. *Questions Liturgiques*. vol. 1. Lorwain: Abbaye du Mont Cesar, 1971.

Moore, Clifford H. *The Religious Thought of the Greeks*. Cambridge: Harvard University Press, 1916.

Mowinckel, Sigmundo. "Kultus." *Die Religion in Geschichte und Gegenwart*. 3rd ed. vol. 4. Tübingen: J. C. B. Mohr, 1960.

Nestle-Aland. *Novum Testamentum Graece*. 26th ed. Stuttgart: Deutsche Bibelstiftung, 1979.

Neuenzeit, Paul. "Das Herrenmahl." *Studien Zum Alten und Neuen Testament*. Edited by Vinzenz Hamp. München: Kösel-Verlag, 1960.

Nevin, John W. *The Mystical Presence and Other Writings on the Eucharist*. Lancaster series on the Mercersburg Theology. vol. 4. Edited by Bard Thompson and George H. Bricker. Philadelphia: United Church Press, 1966.

O'Connell, Matthew J., trans. *The Eucharist of the Early Christians*. New York: Pueblo Pulishing Company, 1978.

O'Flaherty, Wendy. *The Rig Veda*. New York: Penguin Books, 1981.

Oldenberg, Hermann. *Ancient India Its Language and Religions*. Calcutta: Punthi Pustak, 1962.

_____. *Die Religion des Veda*. Berlin: Wilhelm Hertz, 1894.

_____. *The Sacred Books of the East*. vol. 46. *Vedic Hymns*. Edited by Max Müller. Oxford: Clarendon Press, 1897.

Orr, William F. and Walther, James A. *I Corinthians* in The Anchor Bible. Edited by William F. Albright. Garden City: Doubleday and Company, Inc. 1976.

Otto, Rudolf. *The Idea of the Holy*. Translated by John W. Harvey. London: Oxford University Press, 1981.

_____. *The Kingdom of God and the Son of Man*. Translated by Floyd V. Filson and Bertram Lei-Woolf. Boston: Starr King Press, 1957.

Pace, David. "An Exercise in Structural History: An Analysis of the Social Criticism of Claude Lévi-Strauss." *Structuralism An Interdisciplinary Study*. Edited by Susan Wittig. Pittsburg: The Pickwick Press, 1978.

Panikkar, Raimundo. *The Vedic Experience*. London: Darton, Longman and Todd, 1977.

Parsch, Pius. *The Liturgy of the Mass*. Translated by Frederic Eckoff. Saint Louis: B. Herder Book Company, 1945.

Patte, Daniel, ed. *Semiology and Parables*. Pittsburgh: The Pickwick Press, 1976.

Paul, Judith. "Scrifice in India." *Epochê, Journal of the History of Religions at U.C.L.A.*, 10(1982):55-60.

Penner, Hans H. "Language Ritual, and Meaning." *Numen*. International Journal of the History of Religions vol. 32, 1985.

Perrin, Norman. *Jesus and the Language of the Kingdom*. Philadelphia: Fortress Press, 1976.

_____. *Rediscovering the Teaching of Jesus*. New York and Evanston: Harper and Row Publishers, 1967.

Pettazzoni, Raffaela. *La Religion dans la Grèce antique*. Translated by Jean Gouillard. Paris: Payot, 1953.

Philips, Gary; The Entrevernes Group; et al., trans. *Signs and Parables Semiotics Gospel Texts*. Pittsburgh: The Pickwick Press, 1978.

Potdar, S. *Sacrifice in the Rgveda*. Bombay: Bharatiya Vidya Bhavan, 1953.

Preston, James. "Purification." *The Encyclopedia of Religion*. vol. 12. New York; Macmillan Publishing Company, 1985.Procksh, Otto. "Holy." *T.D.N.T.* Vol. 1., 1976.

Puhvel, Jaan. "Vedic *Ashvamedha* and Gaulish *IIPOMIIDVOS*," *Language*, vol. 31(1955):353-354.

Ranade, H. G., trans. *Katyâyana Srauta Sûtra*. Poona: *SMS Letter Press*, 1978.

Reitzenstein, Richard. *Die Hellenistischen Mysterienreligionen.* Stuttgart: B. G. Teubner Verlagsgesellschaft, 1956.

Renou, Louis. *Hinduism.* New York: George Braziller. 1961.

\_\_\_, and Filliozat, Jean. *L'Inde Classique.* 2 vols. Paris: Payot, 1947.

Reumann, John. *The Supper of the Lord.* Philadelphia: Fortress Press, 1985.

Richardson, Cyril C., ed. and trans. *Early Christian Fathers.* New York: Macmillan Publishng Company, Inc., 1979.

Richardson, R. D. "Eastern and Western Liturgies: The Primitive Basis of Their Later Differences." *Harvard Theological Review* 42(1949):125-149.

Riches, John. *Jesus and the Transformation of Judaism.* New York: Seabury Press, 1982.

Roberts, Alexander and Donaldson, James, editors. *The Ante-Nicene Fathers: Translations of the Writings of the Fathers down to A.D. 325.* vol. 4. Revised by A. Cleveland Coxe. American Reprint of the Edinburgh Edition. Grand Rapids: William B. Eerdmans Publishing Company, 1982.

Rordorf, Willy. *Le Point Théologique,17,L'Eucharistie des Premiers Chrétiens.* Paris: Éditions Beaichesne, 1976.

Russell, D. S. *Between the Testaments.* Philadelphia: Fortress Press, 1960.

Sanders, E. P. *Jesus and Judaism.* London: SCM Press Limited, 1985.

Schimmel, A. "Opfer." *Die Religion in Geschichte und Gegenwart.* 3rd ed. vol. 4. Edited by Hans von Campenhausen Tübingen: J. C. B. Mohr, 1960.

Schrenk, Gottlob. "Hierateuo." *T.D.N.T.* Vol. 3, 1976.

Schwager, Raymund. *Must There Be Scapegoats?* Translated by Maria L. Assad. San Francisco: Harper & Row, 1987.

Schweitzer, Albert. "The Lord's Supper in Relationship to the Life of Jesus and the History of the Early Church." *The Problem of the Lord's Supper According to the Scholarly Research of the Nineteenth Century and the Historical Accounts.* vol. 1. Translated and edited by A. J. Mattil with an introduction by John Reumann. Macon: Mercer University Press, 1982.

Schweizer, Eduard. "Abendahl Im NT." *RGG.* vol. 1. 3rd ed. Tübingen: J. C. B. Mohr, 1960.

___. *Neotestamentica.* Stuttgart: Zwingli-Verlag, 1963.

Scroggs, Robin. "The Earliest Christian Communities as Sectarian Movement." *Harvard Theological Review.*

Seeburg, Reinhold. *The History of Doctrines.* vol. 2. translated by Charles E. Hay. Grand Rapids: Baker Book House, 1978.

Shires, H. *Finding the Old Testament in the New.* Philadelphia: the Westminster Press, 1974.

Smith, Brian. "Gods and Men In Vedic Ritualism: Toward a Hierarchy of Resembalance." *History of Religions* 24(1985):293-295.

___. *Classifying The Universe.* New York, Oxford University Press, 1994.

___. *Reflections on Resemblance, Ritual, and Religion.* New York, Oxford University Press, 1989.

Smith, Johnathan Z. Smith, *To Take Place.* Chicago, University of Chicago Press, 1987.

Smith, William Robertson. *Lectures on the Religion of the Semites*. London: Adam and Charles Black, 1914.

Spinks, Byran. *Luther's Liturgical Criteria and His Reform of the Canon of the Mass*. Cambridge: Grove Books, 1982.

Staal, Fritz. "The Meaninglessness of Ritual." *Numen: International Review for the History of Religions*. Edited by M. heerme van Voss. Leiden: E. J. Brill, 1979.

_____. *Rules Without Meaning*. New York: Peter Lang, 1989.

Stählin, Gustav, and Grundmann, Walter. "Sin." *T.D.N.T.* Vol. 1, 1976.

Stange, Alfred. *Das Frühchristliche Kirchengebaüde als Bild des Himmels*. Köln: Comel, 1950.

Stone, Darwell. *A History of the Doctrine of the Holy Eucharist*. 2 vols. London: Longmans, Green, and Company, 1909.

(Strack, H. L.)- Billerback, P. *Komentar zum Neuen Testament aus Talmud und Midrasch*. vol. 2. München, 1924.

Strathmann, Hermann. "Labs." *T.D.N.T.* Vol. 4, 1976.Strauss, David F. *The Christ of Faith and the Jesus of History*. Translated by Leander E. Keck. Philadelphia: Fortress Press, 1977.

Tarby, André. *La Prière eucharistique de L'Église de Jèrusalem*. Paris: Beauchesne, 1972.

Terrien, Samuel. *The Elusive Presence*. New York: Harper and Row Publishers, 1978.

Theissen, Gerd. *Sociology of Early Palestinian Christianity*. Translated by John Bowden. Philadelphia: Fortress Press, 1978.

Theissen, "The Social Setting of Pauline Christianity." Originally in *Novum Testamentum.* translated by J. H. Schütz. Philadelphia: Fortress Press, 1982.

Thite, G. U. *Sacrifice in the Brâhmana-Texts.* Poona: The University of Poona, 1975.

Thurian, Max. *The Eucharistic Memorial.* Translated by J. G. Davies. Richmond: John Knox Press, 1963.

Traets, C. "Abide With Me, God's Nearness and Activity In and Through the Sacraments." *Questions Liturgiques* 1,2(1978):5-21.

Tripp, D. H. "The Mysteries." *The Study of the Liturgy.* Edited by Cheslyn Jones, et al. London: S.P.C.K., 1978.

Tsirpanlis, Constantine N. *The Liturgical and Mystical Theology of Nicolas Cabasilas.* New York: 1979.

Turner, N. "Selucia in Syria." *I.D.B.* vol. 4, 1962.

Turner, Victor. *The Forest of Symbols*: *Aspects of Ndembu Ritual.* Ithaca and London: Cornell University Press, 1967.

Vaux, Roland de. *Les Sacrifice de L"Ancient Testament.* Paris: J. Gabalda, 1964.

Vries, J. de. *Perspectives in the History of Religion.* Translated with an introduction by Kees W. Bolle. Berkley: University of California Press, 1977.

Wach, Joachim. "The Meaning and Task of the History of Religions (Religions wissenschaft)." *The History of Religions*: *Essays on the Problem of Understanding.* Edited by Joseph M. Kitagawa with collaboration of Mircea Eliade and Charles H. Long. Chicago and London: University of Chicago Press, 1967.

Wach, J. *Types of Religious Experience Christian and Non-Christian.* Chicago: University of Chicago Press, 1951.

Wainwright, Geoffrey. *Eucharist and Eschatology.* New York: Oxford University Press, 1981.

Williams, James G. *The Bible, Violence and the Sacred.* San Francisco: Harper San Francisco, 1991.

Yerkes, Royden K. *Sacrifice in Greek and Roman Religions and Early Judaism.* New York: Charles Scribners Sons, 1952.

Young, Frances M. *The Use of Sacrificial Ideas in Greek Christian Writers from the New Testament to John Chrysostom.* Cambridge: The Philadelphia Patristic Foundation, 1979.

Zuesse, Evan M. "Ritual." *The Encyclopedia of Religion.* vol. 12. New York: Macmillan Publishing Company, 1985.

# INDEX

Agni, 2, 9, 10, 12, 17, 18-19, 21-22, 35 (n.38), 70, 72, 81-83, 86, 105 (n.167), 110, 111, 113, 119-124, 126, 137, 145 (n.24), 146 (n.27), 147 (n.29), 149 (n.53), 154 (n.84), 315

Agnicayana, 35(n.80), 67, 70, 109, 119, 120, 123, 144 (n.17), 153 (n.89)

Agnihotra,12, 29 (n.22), 30 (n.30), 111, 146 (n.25), 146 (n.27)

Agnistoma, 111, 143 (n.11), 146 (n.27), 147 (n.30)

Agnyadhana, 29 (n.22)

Altar, 1, 2, 8, 13, 19, 22, 43-44, 64, 68-70, 81-82, 84, 86-87, 96 (n.71), 108-109, 119-120, 124-125, 137,144 (n.15), 150 (n.61), 151 (n.66), 154 (n.97), 169, 187, 189, 194-195, 200, 205, 238 (n.153),239(n.157), 242 (n.176), 243 (n.180), 257 (n.243), 262-264, 266-269, 271-272, 275, 280-281, 286, 292 (n.6), 304 (n.93), 310 (n.140), 314 (168), 317, 321

Anrita, 18, 74,76, 99 (n.112), 139-140,150

Anthropology, 39, 66-67, 73, 97 (n.87), 229 (n.25), 234 (n.125)

Aquinas, 278-279, 308 (n.127)

Aristotle, 206, 278, 308 (n.126)

Augustine, 276-277,307 (n.113)

Avabhrtha, 85,86

Baptism, 209, 225 (n.70), 275, 284, 304 (n.90),306 (n.107)

Bartchy, 204, 249 (n.226), 250 (n.233, n.236), 293 (n.12)

Barth, K., 2

Bodewitz, 146 (n.27), 162 (n.168)

Biardeau, M., 33 (n.66), 76

Bolle, K., 11, 13-15, 28 (n.19), 30 (n.36), 31 (nn.31-32), 46, 57, 59, 61, 94 (n.58), 132, 234 (n.125), 307 (n.117)

Brahman, 14, 78, 80, 100 (n.115), 105 (n.176), 108, 110, 127, 129, 145 (n.21), 157 (n.129)

Brahmanas, 9-14, 85, 100 (n.115), 110, 129-130, 138, 140, 150 (n.55), 162 (n.164)

Brahmin, 14, 29 (n.22), 55, 67, 72, 77, 80, 86, 110, 112, 122-123, 138, 144

(n.15), 145 (n.24), 146 (n.25), 149 (n.51)
Bread, 168, 170-174, 177-186, 188, 203, 214 (n.14), 215 (n.20), 216 (n.32), 217 (n.34), 219 (n. 36), 220 (n.44), 221 (n.47), 222 (n.55), 223 (n.64), 224 (n.67), 226 (n.75), 227(n.81), 228 (nn.83,89,91), 230 (nn.97,107),260-266, 270-271, 275-277, 280-283, 285, 287, 296 (n.27), 317, 323 (n.4)
Buddhism, 30 (n.28), 88, 146 (n.24), 164 (n.197)
Bultmann, R., 187, 209, 224 (n.67), 225 (n.70),227 (n.82), 232 (nn.113,118,121), 233 (124), 257 (n.282), 291 (n.4)
Burkert, W., 52-54, 92 (n.43)
Butter, 81, 84, 111, 124

Calvin, 168, 281-282, 310 (n.145)
Chariot, 84,113, 121
Chrysostom, 239 (n.157), 265, 273-274, 291 (n.6)
Consecration, 44-48, 50, 60-61, 70, 79-80, 84-86, 91 (n.23), 113-116, 120-121, 125-126, 137-138, 158 (n.138), 168, 188, 190-191, 194,201-202,235 (n.134), 240 (n.161), 261-262, 265, 268-271, 278-279, 284, 288, 299 (n.56), 317-320
Cosmic, 14, 17-18, 21, 63, 76, 95 (n.65), 102 (n.125), 112, 116, 156 (n.112), 303 (n.32), 317, 320
Creator, 140, 286, 308 (n.127)
Criticism; historical, 169, 174, 180, 183-184, 200, 205, 212 (n.6), 213 (n.12), 230 (n.96); literary, 217 (n.33), 260; textual, 216 (n.33)
Crossan, D., 203, 249 (n.228)
Cyril (of Jerusalem), 265,269, 271-273,301 (n.65), 304 (n.97)

Dakshina, 77,109
Death, 41, 55, 60, 73, 76, 91 (n.24), 116, 122, 162 (n.169), 168, 170, 172, 175, 178-179, 187, 190, 196, 204, 206, 209-211, 215 (n.22), 218 (n.34), 232 (nn.117,121), 255 (n.266), 260, 163-265, 275, 283, 285, 290 (n.1), 315
Dharma, 16, 18-20, 32 (n.47), 33 (nn.65,66), 146 (n.24)
Didache, 171, 262, 264, 295 (nn.19,20) 299 (n.46)
Diksha, 48, 84-85; Dikshita, 48, 83

Disorder, 62, 74
Dix, G., 174, 186, 226 (n.77), 262, 269-270, 273, 290 (n.3), 302 (n.70), 303 (nn. 93,95), 312 (n.152), 313 (n.161)
Douglas, M., 61-66, 96 (n.71), 158 (n.138)
Dumezil, G. 131-132, 162 (n.170)
Dumont, P. E., 107, 128-129, 143 (n.9), 144 (n.17)

Eggeling, J., 102 (nn.124,125), 105 (n.160), 112, 127, 138, 143 (n.12), 149 (n.48), 150 (n.55), 153 (n.89), 154 (n.103), 155 (n.110), 156 (n.116), 157 (n.130), 160 (n.146)
Eliade, M., 7, 8, 13, 26 (nn.5,7), 27 (n.10), 30 (n.35), 33 (n.65), 59, 91 (n.23), 95 (n.60), 95 (n.65), 208-209, 243 (n.183), 244 (n.184), 256 (n.271)
Epiclasis, 271, 275, 298 (n.41), 303 (n.79), 313 (n.161)
Expiation, 41-44, 50, 60-61, 110, 187-188, 192, 194-196, 199, 208, 211, 239 (n.156), 240 (n.165), 241 (n.166), 259, 268, 292 (n.7)

Faith, 73, 208, 212 (n.8), 280, 282, 284; faithful, 265, 268, 272-273, 277, 301 (n.63); unfaithful, 99 (n.112), 315-316, 321-322
Fire, 7-10, 12-14, 19, 29 (n.32), 30 (n.30), 35 (n.80), 44, 48, 70, 72, 75, 78-84, 86-87, 105 (n.166), 105 (n.177), 107 ( n.186), 108-110, 113, 115, 117-120, 122, 124, 126, 138, 144 (n.15), 145 (n.24), 146 (n.25,27), 148 (n.39), 152 (n.78), 162 (n.168), 190-192, 194, 215 (n.22), 238 (n.159), 242 (n. 173,176), 261, 265, 315, 317, 319, 322
Freud, S., 40, 53
Frazer, Sir James, 23-24, 36 (n.102), 45, 163 (n.173)

Gift; theory of sacrifice, 39, 40-41, 46, 50, 80, 109, 112, 138-139; Eucharist,262, 266-268, 286
Girard, R., 52-55
Gita, Bhagavad, 58
Gonda, J., 12, 20 (n.1), 27 (n.11), 28 (n.12,14,15,18), 30 (n.28), 77, 84, 132-133, 142(n.3), 144 (n.14), 145(n.19), 148 (n.41), 153 (n.90), 161 (n.164), 163 (n.173)
Gospels, 169,174-175, 180, 182-183, 185, 202, 212

Gospels cont.,(n.4), 217 (n.34),
220 (n.38), 221 (n.45),
225 (n.70), 260, 290
(n.3), 291 (n.4)
Grihya, 108

Harappa, 7
Haburah, 171-172, 176-177,
191, 214 (n.17), 222
(n.55), 223 n.(59,64),
166 (n.77)
Heaven, 8, 12-13, 16-21, 32, 58,
70, 74, 79, 81-82, 84,
87, 109-114, 116, 118-
121, 123-124, 135-140,
145 (n.18), 150 (n.57),
154 (n.104), 156
(n.112), 164 (n.185),
190-191, 202, 210, 266,
269, 271-275, 277, 281
(nn.3,5,7,9), 304 (n.93)
Heesterman, J., 19, 23,34(n.71),
36 (n.99), 52, 55,79
Hebrew, 42, 45-47, 49-50, 62,
64, 181, 187-189, 190-
193, 197, 210, 217
(n.33), 222,(nn.52,55),
232 (n.124), 235
(n.124), 236 (n.145),
339 (n.158), 259, 306
(n.108)
Hellenism, 168, 172, 181, 196-
200, 205-211, 215
(n.22), 217 (n.23), 226
(n.75), 232 (113), 245
(n.192), 252 (n.257)

Hillebrandt, A., 151 (n.68), 152
(nn.76,81,85,86), 160
(n.142)
Hinduism, 2, 14, 17, 20, 26
(n.40, 88, 146 (n.24),
315, 323 (n.2)
Hippolytus; ritual, 171; church
father, 312 (n.125)
Historian, 56, 167, 234 (n125)
Horse, 7, 71, 78, 107, 111, 113-
116, 118-130, 142 (n.2),
147 (nn.29,32), 149
(n.45,48,49), 150
(n.54,59), 151 (n.68),
153 (n.86,87), 155
(n.110), 158 (n.130),
160 (n.146), 164
(n.185),315
Holy,42-44, 51, 56-59, 61, 65,
69, 79, 119, 139-140,
151 (n.66), 157 (n.21),
159 (n.138), 172, 176,
187, 190, 192-195, 210,
218 (n.340, 222 (n.52),
264-265, 268-275, 279,
285-288, 316, 318, 324
(n.12); holiness, 42-47,
49-50, 60, 62-64, 86,
264,273, 284-285, 288;
Holy Spirit, 281-284,
311
Horsley, R., 248 (n.217)
Hubert, H., 44-51, 56, 79, 84

India, 8, 45, 48-49, 55, 78, 80,
82, 86, 107-108, 111-
112, 116, 118, 127-128,
131-135, 138, 141, 159

India cont., (n.136), 321;
    Indian, 9, 16, 18, 20,
    315-316, 319-320
Impure, 48-49, 60-62, 65, 74,
    80-81, 83, 96 (n.67),
    175, 193, 199, 203, 207,
    241 (n.165), 256
    (n.265)
Interpretation, 14-16, 24, 29
    (n.27), 40, 42, 44, 46,
    51, 53, 64-65, 68, 72,
    85, 90 (nn.1,4), 109,
    112, 1260135, 167-168,
    180-185, 187, 203-205,
    213 (nn.7,10), 216
    (n.32), 221 (n.47), 227
    (n.80), 231 (n.110)
Ishti, 111-113, 115-116, 144
    (n.130, 147 (n.28), 158
    (n.133)
Irenaeus, 263, 296 (n.26), 299
    (n.50), 313 (n.157)

Jaimania, 146 (n.27), 162
    (n.168)
Jeremias, J., 171, 174-177, 180-
    186, 216 (n.32), 225
    (n.73), 230 (n.104)
Jews, 96 (n.61),188, 196-199,
    204-206, 210, 222
    (n.55), 225 (n.70), 232
    (n.124), 245
    (nn.194,199), 249
    (n.225), 250 (n.237),
    292 (n.7), 296 (n.26)
Jerusalem, 171-175, 178, 197,
    199-202, 205, 211,
    224 (n.65(, 226

(n.75), 234 (n.130),
    244 nn.(184,188),
    269, 271, 303 (n.85),
    307 (120)
Journey; to heaven, 70, 84, 111,
    115, 121, 135
Jung, C.G., 229 (n.95), 319-
    320,322, 324 (nn.11,12)
Jungmann, J., 267, 300 (n.60),
    312 (n.156)

Karman, 9, 18, 20, 22, 34 (n.68)
Katyayana, 79, 107, 113, 144
    (n.13), 148 (nn.36,37),
    153 (n.89)
Keith, A. B., 85, 111, 127-128,
    143 (n.7), 159(n.136)
Kiddish; meal, 176, 222(nn.51-
    53)
King, 56,-57, 71-72, 75, 80, 87-
    88, 94(n.58), 116-121,
    128-130, 132-138, 140,
    148 (n.37), 150 (n.55),
    152 (n.78), 154 (97),
    157 (n.128),195, 243
    (n.183), 249 (n.227),
    262, 286
Kipper, 192
Kshatriya, 133
Krick, H., 80, 83, 105 (n.163),
    125, 159 (n.140)

Lamb, 176, 210, 217 (n.34), 221
    (n.49), 225 (n.70), 274,
    291 (n.5), 300 (n.58),
    314 (n.168)
Last Suppre, 169-178, 180-184,
    213 (n.7), 216 (n.32),

Last Supper cont.,219 (n.35), 221 (n.47), 260, 270, 290 (n.2)
Leeuw, G.,van der, 24, 66, 80, 89 (n.4), 94 (n.56)
Levi-Strauss, C., 311 (n.151)
Levi, S., 28 (n.20), 66, 98 (n.97)
Lietzmann, H.,171-174, 176, 214 (nn.13,19), 215 (n.26), 219 (n.35), 224 (n.67), 264, 266, 302 (n.72), 311 (n.151)
Liturgy, 23, 173, 176, 185, 187, 226 (n.75), 263-264, 267, 272-275, 285, 289, 296 (n.30), 314 (n.166)
Love feasts, 172, 302 (n.74)
Luther, M., 168, 280-281, 310 (nn.140-142,145),

Magic, 10, 23-34, 36 (n.99), 48-50, 63, 77-78, 83, 85-86, 115, 125-128, 130, 133-134, 136, 138-139, 159 (n.136), 163 (n.173), 163 (n.173), 184-185, 231 (n.110), 269, 280, 307 (n.117), 319
Mantra, 29 (n.25), 107,110, 123, 142 (nn.3,5)143 (nn.6,7)
Malamoud, C., 33 (n.66), 146 (n.26)
Mauss, M., 44-51, 56, 79, 84
Mediator, 315, 317
Meier, J. P., 212 (n.6)

Mind, 20, 24, 40, 50 ,52, 54, 66, 134, 138, 309 (n.132)
Mohejo-Daro, 7
Mystery,51, 58, 65, 80, 108, 167, 269, 276, 279, 282, 285, 289, 313 (n.161), 321-322; religions, 168, 185-187, 207-209, 253 (n.258) 255 (n.263),256 (n.267),275
Myth, 7, 15-18, 20-22, 25, 33 (n.65), 51, 54, 58, 67, 71, 81, 83, 90 (n.20), 94 (n.60), 113, 128, 131-133, 140, 164 (n.194),187-191, 198, 324; mythological, 10,12-13, 15, 51, 59, 62, 64, 66, 75-76, 80, 86, 108-110, 116-118, 125, 128, 131, 257 (n.282), 259, 291 (n.4)

New, 11, 39, 42, 48, 55, 61, 71, 73, 80, 85; birth, 58, 60, 125; body,77; covenant, 172, 177, 180, 187, 259-261, 263, 270, 287, 290 (n.2), 291 (n.7), 293(n.8), 306 (n.110), 321; garment,112; moon, 112-113; reality,81;Testament,16 7, 169, 171-173, 176-177, 180, 182-184, 186; year, 133

Numinous, 56, 76, 95 (n.65),
194, 273, 304 (n.35),
324 (n.12)

Oblation, 21, 21, 75, 77, 78,
119-120, 122, 124, 135-
136, 169, 174, 186, 200,
274, 282, 300 (n.60),
320
Offer, offerings, 8, 42, 46, 49,
53, 55, 68, 75, 78-79,
81-82, 84, 86, 90 (n.18),
102 (n.139), 168-169,
175, 178, 181, 194-195,
200, 202, 204, 206, 210,
242 (n.173), 262, 264-
266, 270, 275, 285-288,
300 (nn.55,60), 314
(n.168), 316, 318, 320
Oldenberg, H. 85, 106 (n.182),
160 (n.141), 163
(n.173)
Otto, R., 56-57, 59, 69, 94
(nn.56,57),95 (n.65), 99
(n.98), 320, 324 (n.12)

Passover, 174-178, 182, 184,
187, 216(n.32), 218
(n.34), 219 (n.37), 220
(n.41), 221 (n.47), 223
(n.59), 224 (nn.66,68),
225 (n.70), 260, 291
(n.5)
Perrrin, N., 203, 249
Plato, 206
Platonic, 267, 276, 288, 308
(N.128); neo-platonism,
207, 275, 277-279, 306
(n.108), 307 (n.113)
Positivism,16
Prajapati, 70, 110, 113, 115-
116, 118-121, 123-133,
136-137, 140, 148
(n.44), 149
(nn.49,53,54), 154
(nn.92,94), 155 (n.102),
157 (N.128), 164
(n.185), 164 (n.194)
Prayer, 19, 22, 85, 200, 202
206, 251 (n.243)
Perparation, 14, 84, 11-114,
119, 122, 137, 140,
175,190,193, 198, 200,
222 (n.53), 240 (n.163),
268, 272, 284, 288, 317
Priest, 8-12, 14, 18, 27, 29
(n.22), 36 (n.99), 108,
110, 112, 124-118, 121-
126, 144 (n.15), 145
(23), 156 (nn.112,117),
262-263, 265, 267, 269,
271-273, 275-276, 278,
283, 285, 298 (n.38),
301 (n.60), 313 (n.159)
Proudfoot, W., 94 (n.57)
Purity, 47, 60-64, 66, 79, 83,
183 (n.139), 191-196,
198-202, 241 (n.166),
246 (nn.203,205), 249
(n.225), 263, 267

Qumran, 175-177, 185, 199-
201, 231 (n.107), 246
(n.199), 247 (n.209)

Queen, 112, 121-123, 129, 136, 156 (n.117), 157 (n.121)

Reality, 25, 34 (n.7), 56-58, 61, 65, 75, 78, 81, 119, 139, 198, 261, 276, 279, 288, 310 (n.137); real presence, 275-277, 279-281, 296 (n.27), 318, 320-322

Renou, L., 11, 23, 26 (nn.3,4), 27 (nn.8,9), 105 (n.176), 108

Resurrection, 168, 204, 225 (n.70), 315

Reumann, J., 174, 262, 295 (n.22)

Revelation, 9, 22, 58, 170, 189, 208, 212 (n.6), 241 (n.165), 275, 277, 308 (n.127), 321, 323 (nn.1,5); Book of, 304 (n.93)

Ritual, 8-15, 21, 23-24, 34 (n.68), 36 (n.99), 40, 42, 44, 46-50, 51-56, 60-80, 107, 176-177, 184-189, 191, 193, 200, 261;behavior, 92 (n.41); chants, 9; formulas, 9; killing, 92(n.41); meals, 223 (n.64); sacrificial, 11, 260

Rig Veda, 8-10, 13-16, 17-18, 20-22, 29 (n.21), 73, 75, 79, 107-108, 117, 125, 137, 142 (n.3), 144 (n.15)

Righteousness, 200, 210, 283

Rishi, 10, 22, 28 (n.14), 78, 136

Rita, 15-24, 32 (n.46), 47, 33 (n.65), 35 (n.81), 41, 73-76, 78-79, 82-83, 88, 99 (nn.102,112), 100 (n.115), 101 (n.125), 103 (n.150), 108, 125, 140, 149 (n.50), 150 (n.56)

Sacrcraments-sacramental, 167,170, 174, 203, 262-263, 272-273, 275-281, 289, 306 (nn.107,113,115), 307 (n.117), 310 (n.141), 321-322; meals, 209

Sama Veda, 9, 11, 29, (n.21)

Samhita, 9, 144 (n.15

Satya, 35 (n.31), 74-76, 78, 80, 100 (n.115), 101 (n.124), 108, 130, 139

Schweitzer, 169-171, 213 (n.10)

Separation, 51, 61-62, 81, 140, 176, 192, 226 (n.77), 241 (n.167), 277, 317

Shatapatha Brahmana, 113, 115, 120, 127, 136-137, 143 (n.9), 144 (n.18), 153 (89)

Sheep, 147 (n.29), 240 (n.163)

Sin, 43, 46, 50, 58, 60-63, 73, 75, 77-79, 85, 99 (n.112), 100

Sin cont., (n.120), 104 (n.163),
    105 (n.173), 125-126,
    138-139, 150 (56), 160
    (n.142), 179, 187-188,
    193, 195-197, 208, 210,
    232 (n.121, 239 (n.156),
    240 (n.165), 242
    (n.171), 259, 261-264,
    269, 271, 275, 281, 284,
    291 (n.6), 298 (n.41),
    301 (n.63), 302 (n.76),
    315-322
Sinai, 187, 190-191, 237
    (n.145)
Smith, B., 30 (n.32), 101
    (n.118), 102 (n.140),
    105 (n.172), 110, 142
    (n.1), 145 (n.20)
Smith, J. Z., 27 (n.7), 92 (n.41),
    93 (n.44)
Smith, Robertson, Wm., 24, 41-
    44, 90 (n.18)
Society, 9, 51, 53-55, 61, 63,
    65-67, 130-131, 159
    (n.138), 197, 201, 245
    (n.261)
Shrauta sacrifices, 14, 67-68,
    70, 79, 108-113
Soul, 192, 205-206, 278, 286,
    308 (n.128)
Structure, sacrificial; 112, 134,
    139, 261; eucharistic,
    259, 270, 285, 288
Staal, F., 67-72, 98 (nn.92,96)
Substitution, 47, 54, 91 (n.24),
    142 (n.1), 238 (n.150)
Symbolism, 7, 8, 11, 21, 38,
    40, 43, 46, 48, 51, 56-
    58, 62, 65-73, 80-83,
    88; of Asvamedha, 112;
    of eucharist, 167-168,
    171, 176, 184, 187, 211;
    words of eucharist, 167,
    186, 221 (n.47); of
    horse, 132-140; of king
    132

Table fellowship, 171-172, 176-
    178, 196, 199-204, 214
    (n.17), 217 (n.34), 246
    (n.203), 249 (n.226)
Tapas, 85, 154 (n.92)
Temple, 64, 175, 189, 191, 197-
    205, 221(n.45), 235
    (130), 240 (n.163), 243
    (n.182), 244 (n.190),
    247 (nn.212,217), 248
    (nn.221,222), 261-262,
    288, 294 (n.15)
Thite G., 85, 129-131, 150
    (n.55), 153 (n.88), 159
    (n.136), 161 (n.161)
    162 (nn.163,165)
Time, 16, 27 (n.9); primordial,
    20, 118, 140; sacred,
    113; passover, 217
    (n.34)
Totemism, 41-44
Transcendent, 8-17, 19, 23, 47,
    51, 55, 57, 60-62, 78-
    80, 83, 88, 95 (n.67),
    101 (n.125), 102
    (n.139), 134, 139, 189-
    193, 204, 210, 236
    (n.145), 243 (n.181),
    262, 267, 270, 274, 279,

Transcendence cont., 289, 304
(n.93), 315-322
Transformation, 26, 261, 268, 279
Truth, 16, 56, 74-75, 88, 114-115, 136, 139, 149 (n.51), 172, 285, 291 (n.4), 322

Upanishads, 9, 12-14, 31 (nn.41,42), 80, 100 (n.120), 105 (n.179), 130-131, 162 (n.164)

Varuna, 10, 21, 73-74, 82, 85, 105 (n.173), 117, 125-126, 136
Vedas, 7, 9-11, 17, 58, 71, 73, 78, 104 (n.166), 105 (n.173), 116, 123, 144 (n.14), 151 (n.66), 164 (n.197)
Victim, 107, 113, 119, 122, 187, 191-192, 194, 237 (n.147), 238 (n.150), 250 (n.243), 265-266, 274, 298 (n.38)
Violence, 52-55, 322

Wach, J. 102 (n.133)
Warrior, 7, 55-56
Water, 80-82, 84-87, 105 (nn.177,179), 111, 113-114, 116-117, 119, 121-122, 126, 128, 133, 136-137, 147 (n.27), 149 (n.52), 152 (n.76), 154 (nn.95,96), 158

(n.132), 192, 195, 199, 240 (n.160), 269, 297 (n.35), 305 (n.97)
Wife, 85, 109, 123
Womb, 17, 61, 87, 283
World, 8-9, 11-14, 16-25, 32 (n.50), 34 (n.69), 46-51, 70, 77-80, 88, 91 (n.31), 109-113, 118-125, 132-140, 196, 198, 206-207, 21o, 263, 298 (n.38), 315-322
Worship, 13, 17, 43, 64, 73, 76, 78, 87, 136, 137, 141, 146 (n.27), 188-189, 191, 197, 199-200, 205, 207, 209, 211, 261, 266, 271, 273, 288, 292 (n.38), 322
Yama, 74
Yajamana, 93 (n.55)
Yajna, 131
Yajur Veda, 9, 11, 29 (nn.21,25), 107-108
Zaehner, R. C., 26 (n.4)
Zwingli, 168, 224 (n.67), 279, 281, 310 (n.140)

www.ingramcontent.com/pod-product-compliance
Lightning Source LLC
Chambersburg PA
CBHW071227230426
43668CB00011B/1330